WHAT CAN BE KNOWN ABOUT GOD IS PLAIN

Re-Envisioning Reformed Dogmatics

SERIES EDITORS:

Myk Habets, W. Ross Hastings, and Jacob Samuel Raju

Re-Envisioning Reformed Dogmatics is a series that explores afresh the rich and diverse dogmatic heritage of the contemporary Reformed tradition. The series will plumb the depths of the riches of the Reformed tradition by engaging in constructive and interdisciplinary study while also challenging assumptions that are sometimes expressed as the Reformed tradition's contemporary consensus. There are, in current discussions, contrary trends at work in Reformed Theology. Some are eager to expand Reformed orthodoxy to include all Protestants while others narrow the definition of what is "Reformed" to what characterizes the teachings of, say, the Dutch Reformed Church or the Church in Scotland. *Re-Envisioning Reformed Dogmatics* is a series that explores the rich and complex plurality of thinking in the wider Reformed tradition. The monographs in this series invite readers to think in fresh ways about various theological loci while exploring constructive developments within this dynamic tradition. They include subject matter that has been hitherto neglected or excluded from conversations about Reformed theology in an effort to recover the intellectual treasures that once made up the full dogmatic deposit of the confessional era. In this way, the *Re-Envisioning Reformed Dogmatics* series is marked by that self-same spirit that once motivated the Reformer's clarion call: *Ad fontes* (to the sources). Now, with five hundred years of theological development since this first call was uttered, the authors in this series renew that clarion call. This time, however, the sources to which the authors in this series turn include those of the Reformers and their theological heirs.

EDITORIAL BOARD:

Gijsbert van den Brink, university research chair for theology & science at the Faculty of Theology (Free University of Amsterdam)

Oliver Crisp, professor of analytic theology and director of the Logos Institute for Analytic and Exegetical Theology (University of St. Andrews)

Christina Larsen, professor of theology (Grand Canyon University)

Paul Nimmo, King's chair of systematic theology (University of Aberdeen)

Carl Trueman, professor of biblical & religious studies (Grove City College)

Adonis Vidu, professor of theology (Gordon Conwell Theological Seminary)

Willem van Vlastuin, professor of theology and spirituality of Reformed Protestantism (Free University of Amsterdam)

What Can Be Known About God Is Plain

A Reformed-Epistemological Response to the Problem of Divine Hiddenness

TYLER M. TABER

Foreword by Gijsbert van den Brink

CASCADE *Books* • Eugene, Oregon

WHAT CAN BE KNOWN ABOUT GOD IS PLAIN
A Reformed-Epistemological Response to the Problem of Divine Hiddenness

Copyright © 2024 Tyler M. Taber. All rights reserved. Except for brief quotations in critical publications or reviews, no part of this book may be reproduced in any manner without prior written permission from the publisher. Write: Permissions, Wipf and Stock Publishers, 199 W. 8th Ave., Suite 3, Eugene, OR 97401.

Cascade Books
An Imprint of Wipf and Stock Publishers
199 W. 8th Ave., Suite 3
Eugene, OR 97401

www.wipfandstock.com

PAPERBACK ISBN: 978-1-6667-1877-5
HARDCOVER ISBN: 978-1-6667-1878-2
EBOOK ISBN: 978-1-6667-1879-9

Cataloguing-in-Publication data:

Name: Taber, Tyler M. [author]. | Brink, Gijsbert van den, 1963– [foreword writer]

Title: What can be known about God is plain : a reformed-epistemological response to the rroblem of divine hiddenness / Tyler M. Taber.

Description: Eugene, OR: Cascade Books, 2024 | Series: Re-envisioning Reformed Dogmatics | Includes bibliographical references.

Identifiers: ISBN 978-1-6667-1877-5 (paperback) | ISBN 978-1-6667-1878-2 (hardcover) | ISBN 978-1-6667-1879-9 (ebook)

Subjects: LCSH: Hidden God | Knowledge, Theory of (Religion) | God—Knowableness | God (Christianity) | Theodicy | Plantinga, Alvin. | Christianity—Philosophy.

Classification: BL200 T33 2024 (paperback) | BL200 (ebook)

12/09/24

Unless otherwise noted, Scripture quotations marked ESV are from the ESV® Bible (The Holy Bible, English Standard Version®), © 2001 by Crossway, a publishing ministry of Good News Publishers. Used by permission. All rights reserved. Any emphases to Scripture quotations have been added.

Chapter two originally published as "Divine Hiddenness and the Problem of Evil," in *Evil and a Selection of its Theological Problems*, Benjamin H. Arbour and John R. Gilhooly, eds. Published with the permission of Cambridge Scholars Publishing.

Contents

Foreword by Gijsbert van den Brink | vii

Abbreviations | ix

Acknowledgments | xi

1. The Problem of Divine Hiddenness: Prolegomena | 1
2. The Problem of Divine Hiddenness in Contemporary Perspective | 42
3. The Problem of Divine Hiddenness and the Aquinas/Calvin Model | 78
4. The Problem of Divine Hiddenness and the Effects of Sin | 121
5. The Problem of Divine Hiddenness and the Extended Aquinas/Calvin Model | 164
6. A Reformed-Epistemological Defense: Products, Problems, and Prospects | 214

Bibliography | 229

Foreword

ONE OF THE CHALLENGES that Christians and other theists have to face is that, to many people, the existence of God is not more obvious than it actually is. For evidently, many of us—especially in the West—are not so sure, to say the least; regularly, repeated polls indicate that the number of agnostics and atheists in the Western world is steadily growing over time. Some people think hard about the existence of God and try to be as conscientious as they can in making up their minds about it. Some of them even start to pray. And yet, they remain inconclusive, due to lingering doubts as a result of a lack of evidence. So if God is almighty and reaches out to us humans, as the Christian gospel holds, wanting us to engage in a personal relationship with him that is characterized by faith and love, why does God not make his existence more unambiguously clear to all of us? Why do so many people—including people who seem to us noble and upright—have to doubt about it, finding insufficient warrant to become convinced of it?

During the past couple of decades, philosophers of religion have become increasingly engaged with this question. Some of them have turned it into an "official" argument against (Christian) theism, next to, for example, the famous problems of suffering and evil. The "argument from divine hiddenness," as it came to be called, was elaborated and substantiated in ever more sophisticated ways. But just so were ingenious rebuttals of it by other philosophers of religion and theologians. So who's right? In the present volume, Dr. Tyler Taber first of all renders us a tremendous service by charting these debates, laying bare their various trajectories as well as their historical, philosophical, and theological ramifications. His superb overview will provide anyone interested in the vexed question of divine hiddenness—either for personal existential reasons or otherwise—a firm grasp of the main issues. Using his analytical skills, Taber also points out which questions, though seemingly related, should not be confused with the problem of divine hiddenness, since they are in fact different. Thus, this book would already be worth its price for only its first chapters, in which Taber shows himself as a reliable guide in helping us to oversee what is going on in this burgeoning field of studies.

On top of that, however, in the next chapters of his book, Taber carves out a new way to address the problem of divine hiddenness, which, he argues, may be the most compelling one—or at any rate should be considered as a serious option. Largely drawing on Alvin Plantinga's modern classic *Warranted Christian Belief*, and in particular on its key notion of warrant, Taber applies this so-called "Reformed epistemology" to the problem of divine hiddenness. In doing so, he reinvigorates the notion of the *sensus divinitatis* as most famously propounded by John Calvin: there is an "antenna" for God built into the human mind through which God reveals God's existence and majesty to all humanity. Indeed, cognitive scientists of religion have recently found some empirical evidence for this thesis, noticing that religion seems to be hardwired in our human brains. Religious belief thus comes to us in a quite natural way. Yet, as a result of human sinfulness, this faculty has become tainted in all of us, leaving us in a state in which our capacity to perceive God is seriously inhibited and God seems hidden to us. It is precisely to free us from this dire situation, however, that God has reached out to all of us, using his "two hands": Jesus Christ and the Holy Spirit. By having faith in this good news, the existence of God can become clear to us—and even gradually clearer over time.

Clearly, Taber does not come up with theological innovations to make his point; what is new, however, is that he shows how, in an important sense, the gospel in fact is a response to the universal human problem of divine hiddenness. No doubt, Taber's challenging thesis will elicit some quite relevant questions and responses, and he is well aware of that. For that reason, he already explicitly addresses a couple of possible objections in passing, thus preempting some of the most obvious rejoinders. But however the reader assesses Taber's proposal, his book fits excellently in a series devoted to the task of re-envisioning Reformed dogmatics. Taber creatively shows how some key insights from the Reformed doctrinal tradition, old-worn as they may sometimes seem to the contemporary observer, can be brought to bear in convincing and helpful ways on one of the most hotly debated issues in contemporary (philosophy of) religion and theology.

Gijsbert van den Brink
Chair of Theology & Science
Faculty of Religion and Theology, VU Amsterdam
Resident Fellow, Henry Center (TEDS), Deerfield, IL

Abbreviations

A/C	Thomas Aquinas and John Calvin
ACCS	Ancient Christian Commentary on Scripture
AOTC	Abingdon Old Testament Commentaries
AsTJ	*Asbury Theological Journal*
BSac	*Bibliotheca Sacra*
CSR	Cognitive science of religion
CTJ	*Calvin Theological Journal*
DHHR	*Divine Hiddenness and Human Reason*. By J. L. Schellenberg. Rev. ed. Cornell Studies in the Philosophy of Religion. Ithaca, NY: Cornell University Press, 2006
DNR	*Dialogues Concerning Natural Religion*. By David Hume. Edited by Richard H. Popkin. 2nd ed. Hackett Classics. Indianapolis: Hackett, 1998
FWD	Free will defense
HALOT	*The Hebrew and Aramaic Lexicon of the Old Testament*. By Ludwig Koehler, Walter Baumgartner, and Johann J. Stamm. Translated and edited under the supervision of Mervyn E. J. Richardson. 4 vols. Leiden: Brill, 1994–1999
HeyJ	*Heythrop Journal*
Int	*Interpretation*
JAAR	*Journal of the American Academy of Religion*
JETS	*Journal of the Evangelical Theological Society*
JR	*Journal of Religion*

KCB	*Knowledge and Christian Belief*. By Alvin Plantinga. Grand Rapids: Eerdmans, 2015
NICNT	New International Commentary on the New Testament
PDH	Problem of divine hiddenness
POE	Problem of evil
PRD	Problem of religious diversity
RCP	Reformed Christian philosophy
RED	Reformed epistemic defense
RelS	*Religious Studies*
SD	*Sensus divinitatis*
SJT	*Scottish Journal of Theology*
SPE	Soteriological problem of evil
TW	If the model is *true*, then theistic belief has *warrant*
VB	"Variability of belief" problem
WTJ	*Westminster Theological Journal*
WCB	*Warranted Christian Belief*. By Alvin Plantinga. New York: Oxford University Press, 2000
WW	*Word and World*
ZST	*Zeitschrift für systematische Theologie*

Acknowledgments

THIS WORK IS ABOUT the hiddenness of God, which means ultimately that it is about *God*, and it takes its cue from the Augustinian tradition of faith seeking understanding whereby one has an "active love of God while seeking a deeper knowledge of God."[1] While this work aims to advance scholarly discussion concerning the problem of divine hiddenness, still it can be said, with St. Anselm, that "I am not trying to scale your heights, Lord; my understanding is in no way equal to that. But I do long to understand your truth in some way, your truth which my heart believes and loves."[2]

Behind every good man, the saying goes, is a better woman. My wife, Abigail, provided enormous support throughout this project; she prayed for me, encouraged me, and read countless drafts. This work, which began its life as a PhD thesis, would not be without her.

I would also like to thank Gijsbert van den Brink and Rik Peels, both of whom were my PhD supervisors at the Free University of Amsterdam and who helped to make this book what it is today. From day one, Gijsbert has been more than kind to me, patiently reading multiple drafts of every chapter, generously answering innumerable emails, and even inviting me into his home during my travels to the Netherlands. Rik Peels has longsufferingly provided invaluable feedback on this book, always prompting me to do the best work that I could. It is not an understatement to say that were it not for Rik's keen supervision, this project would have fallen to utter ruin more than a few times. Thank you, Gijsbert and Rik, for allowing me to sit under your tutelage. A student is not above his teachers, but the student who is fully trained will be like his teachers (cf. Luke 6:40).

Many thanks to Dr. Paul Wolfe for allowing me to teach systematic theology at the Cambridge School of Dallas while I wrote this book; to Drs. Jay Howell and Tyler McNabb for reading the manuscript, and offering helpful feedback; to Dr. Mark Hamilton, a fellow doctoral student at

1. Thomas Williams in Anselm, *Proslogion*, vii.
2. Anselm, *Proslogion*, 6.

the Free University, for friendship and encouragement; and especially to Alvin Plantinga, on whose work this book draws, for modeling Christian scholarship.

1.

The Problem of Divine Hiddenness
Prolegomena

1.1 INTRODUCTION

"ASSUME THERE IS A god," an interviewer quipped to Oxford's Richard Dawkins, "and you were given the chance to ask him one question. What would it be?" Dawkins responds, "I'd ask, 'Sir, why did you go to such great lengths to *hide* yourself?'"[1] Similarly, Friedrich Nietzsche teasingly asks of God in his *Parable of the Madman*, "Did he [God] lose his way like a child? . . . Or *is he hiding*? Is he afraid of us? Has he gone on a voyage?"[2]—jesting elsewhere that God "is a god of goodness notwithstanding and merely could not express himself more clearly! Did he perhaps lack the intelligence to do so? Or the eloquence?"[3] Dawkins's and Nietzsche's comments aside, call this phenomenon "divine hiddenness."

But what, to be more precise, is divine hiddenness? How can it be further analyzed? Perhaps it can be construed as a *problem*: If God exists, then why is his existence not more obvious or apparent or evident? Put very roughly, this is my conception of the problem of divine hiddenness (hereafter PDH); clarification and fine-tuning will be offered later. As shown below, PDH is a significant theme in the history of Western thought. Recently, however, PDH has taken more sophisticated shape from important thinkers such as J. L. Schellenberg, whose original 1993 argument in *Divine Hiddenness and Human Reason* (hereafter *DHHR*) contains premises, from

1. C. Rowe, "Richard Dawkins"; emphasis added.
2. Nietzsche, *Gay Science*, 181; emphasis added.
3. Nietzsche, *Daybreak*, 89–90.

reasonable nonbelief, which lead to an atheistic conclusion (discussed later and in detail in the next chapter). At present PDH, post-1993, is widely debated and examined in the scholarly literature: alongside countless journal articles and several monographs, there are two edited volumes, containing essays from both believers and nonbelievers, devoted to divine hiddenness.[4] And, much like the problem of evil or, say, the traditional arguments from natural theology, or the problem of freedom and foreknowledge, PDH is now considered by many to be its very *own* subsection in analytic philosophy of religion.[5] The subsequent chapter, a formal literature review, provides an in-depth look at divine hiddenness in its contemporary, present-day philosophical (and theological) milieu.

The purpose of this chapter, however, is to investigate *prolegomena* matters surrounding PDH. What exactly is divine hiddenness, and why is it problematic? How are we to think about it? Often one can more clearly and coherently grasp some idea or mystery or puzzle by explaining what it is *not*, and I will apply such reasoning to PDH, by pecking out various attributes traditionally predicated to God (for example, his incorporeality, transcendence, incomprehensibility, and somewhat ironically his omnipresence), as well as by analyzing two important Protestant theologians, Martin Luther and Karl Barth, both of whom examine this theme in their writings; what is the relevance of these listed attributes, and just what do Luther and Barth mean by God's hiddenness? Further, the late Antony Flew in his philosophical work once spoke of the so-called presumption of atheism (defined later); how does this relate to my investigation? I look into these matters below, explaining what PDH is *not*, the goal of which is that it can then be better demonstrated what the concern for this project *is*. This comprises the first portion of my chapter (§1.2).

Second, I offer a more formal definition of what the hiddenness problem *is*, after which I both formulate and state my *research question* and *thesis statement*; these items help to steer my project in forthcoming chapters (§1.3).

This will then enable me, third, to provide a historical overview of the problem by briefly surveying important thinkers in Western thought who have, in some measure, considered it: Blaise Pascal, Joseph Butler, David Hume, Søren Kierkegaard, Alexander Campbell, and (as already mentioned) Friedrich Nietzsche; I justify why these six thinkers are chosen later (§1.4).

---

4. The two edited volumes are Howard-Snyder and Moser, *Divine Hiddenness*; Green and Stump, *Hidden Divinity*. For my review of the latter work, see Taber, "Review of *Hidden Divinity*."

5. See Schellenberg, "Divine Hiddenness." The first edition of Quinn and Taliaferro, *Companion to Philosophy of Religion*, did not contain a chapter on divine hiddenness.

Having a firmer grip on PDH from the previous three exercises, I offer some concluding remarks that will position the project, in my second chapter, to analyze PDH as it is expressed in contemporary scholarship (§1.5).

1.2 WHAT THE PROBLEM OF DIVINE HIDDENNESS IS NOT

The chief purpose of this section is to demonstrate, in seven ways, what the problem of divine hiddenness is *not* so that I may then say subsequently what it *is*. First, many in the Christian tradition maintain that God is *incorporeal*, without body. "God is *spirit*," writes the author of John, "and those who worship him must worship in spirit and truth" (John 4:24; emphasis added). God's incorporeality implies that God is invisible (cf. Col 1:15; 1 Tim 1:17), for he is said to dwell in "unapproachable light, whom no one has ever seen or can see" (1 Tim 6:16). And while there are biblical passages that describe God in bodily terms (e.g., Ps 18:6–10), Christians have traditionally insisted that God is not *physical*, but rather spiritual and invisible.[6] In this sense, therefore, it can in fact be said that God is "hidden" to humanity.

But the *problem* of divine hiddenness (PDH) for which this project is concerned, however, ought to be disconnected from biblical and historical conceptions of God's incorporeality. Thomas V. Morris writes that an attempt to settle the hiddenness problem by appealing to this particular attribute misses the point. From the perspective of divine incorporeality, he explains,

> God's hiddenness consists in the fact that God does not fall within our perceptual purview, and this in turn is to be explained by . . . the fact that God is neither a bodily nor an embodied being, and thus not the sort of being accessible to sense perception. To express dismay over [the problem of] divine hiddenness, on this view, is to evince a basic misunderstanding concerning *the kind of being God is*.[7]

Hence, Morris's implication is that one should not explain why God's existence is not more palpable or more obvious—the *problem*—by appealing to divine incorporeality; this, therefore, is the first way to elucidate what the problem for this project is *not*.

A second way to demonstrate what the problem is not is to examine divine *transcendence*. "Holy, holy, holy," writes the author of Isaiah regarding

---

6. I will not venture into the theological territory on God's incorporeality in light of the incarnation; see Taliaferro, "Incorporeality."

7. T. Morris, *Making Sense*, 90; emphasis added. See also T. Morris, "Hidden God."

God's otherness, "the whole earth is full of his glory" (Isa 6:3), explaining elsewhere that his ways and thoughts are higher than ours (cf. Isa 55:8–9). As Gordon Lewis notes, since God is transcendent, he is uniquely distinct from (and not identical with) his creation—metaphysically, emotionally, and intellectually. "*God is 'hidden' relationally,*" Lewis clarifies, "because [he is] so great in all these other ways."[8] As Stephen D. Boyer and Christopher A. Hall note, "Divine transcendence means that, in a sense, God is always *hidden* from creaturely vision."[9] Further, "belief in divine *transcendence*," as Ian McFarland argues, "raises serious problems for human . . . knowledge of God, because such knowledge is itself a feature of created reality and thus is inherently cut off from a God who *transcends* the creation."[10] Perhaps this is why divine transcendence ought to be analyzed alongside divine *immanence*. For, as Oliver Crisp and Fred Sanders explain, such analysis

> will help us not to end up with an understanding of the creature-creator relationship that privileges *transcendence* over *immanence*, or vice versa. That is, we will be saved from so exalting God (i.e., so emphasizing his transcendence) that we end up with a *hidden* God who cannot be known by us.[11]

Here, as Crisp and Sanders write, the examination of God's transcendence and immanence, however they are to be fleshed out, does in fact lend itself to a discussion of divine hiddenness; but "divine hiddenness" for which this context gives rise is not the same sort of divine hiddenness represented in, say, the following remark from Schellenberg: "Why would God," he asks, "permit his or her own existence to be hidden even from those who are willing to see it," for "wouldn't a loving personal God have good reason to prevent such obscurity?"[12] Clearly this is a different *genre* of divine hiddenness. For as Morris suggests with respect to divine hiddenness and transcendence, the question is not so much "concerning *what God is* [e.g., in his transcendence] as concerning why he acts, or refrains from acting, as he does."[13] Here therefore is a second way in which it can be said what the problem is *not*.[14]

---

8. Lewis, "Attributes of God," 458; emphasis added.
9. Boyer and Hall, *Mystery of God*, 37; emphasis added.
10. McFarland, *Divine Image*, 156; emphasis added.
11. O. Crisp and Sanders, "Introduction," 14; emphasis added.
12. Schellenberg, "Why Am I Nonbeliever," 30.
13. T. Morris, *Making Sense*, 91; emphasis added.
14. For another perspective on the relationship between PDH and divine transcendence, see Rea, "Hiddenness and Transcendence."

Consider a third way. Many in the Christian tradition argue that God is *incomprehensible*, which, according to an Anselmian conception, means that

> the mystery of so sublime a thing [i.e., the unity of the Holy Trinity] seems to transcend every power of human understanding, and for that reason I think one should refrain from attempting to explain how this is true. After all, I think someone investigating an *incomprehensible* thing ought to be satisfied if his reasoning arrives at the knowledge that the thing most certainly exists, even if his understanding cannot fathom how it is so.[15]

Thus when reflecting on God, the finite human mind must at some point yield to mystery, to God's incomprehensibility, and acknowledge that while God can be grasped *truly* he cannot be grasped *exhaustively*. Herman Bavinck explains that because God is incomprehensible, he therefore is "*invisible* in his essence."[16] Similarly, Karl Barth appears to connect this attribute to divine hiddenness, writing that the

> assertion of *God's hiddenness* (which includes God's *invisibility*, *incomprehensibility*, and *ineffability*) tells us that God does not belong to the objects which we can always subjugate to the process of our viewing, conceiving and expressing and therefore our spiritual oversight and control. In contrast to that of all other objects, His nature is not one which in this sense lies in the sphere of our power. God is inapprehensible.[17]

Without pausing here to further analyze his comments, Barth (whose theology I come back to below) ties God's hiddenness to divine incomprehensibility (and invisibility and ineffability); consider, however, Schellenberg's proposal that divine hiddenness can be understood to refer to either:

1. The obscurity of God's existence
2. The *incomprehensibility* of God
3. Our human inability to detect the exact pattern of God's activity in the world

"To the question I am raising," he insists, "only 'hiddenness' in the first sense is relevant."[18] So, according to Anselm, Bavinck, and Barth, God is hidden because of his incomprehensibility; yet I suggest, alongside

---

15. *Monologion* 64 in Anselm, *Saint Anselm: Basic Writings*, 62–63; emphasis added.
16. Bavinck, *God and Creation*, 190; emphasis added.
17. K. Barth, *Doctrine of God* §27.1, 187.
18. *DHHR* 4; emphasis added.

Schellenberg, that (2), while interesting and important, is different from (1). For "all I seek to show," writes Schellenberg with respect to (1), "is that we might expect God's *existence* to be more obvious."[19] Here is another way to say what PDH is *not*.

Fourth, theologians insist that God is omnipresent, filling both heaven and earth (Jer 23:24; cf. Acts 17:27–28). "Where shall I go from your spirit," proclaims the psalmist, "or where shall I flee from your presence?" (Ps 139:7), statements that suggest that God is everywhere present to his creation. Now, incorporeality, transcendence, and incomprehensibility, discussed already, entail God's "hiddenness"; he is hidden because of, or in light of, these attributes (or properties). Can the same be said of omnipresence? How so? I am indebted to Morris yet again; he explains how this *might* go with respect to the *problem* of divine hiddenness. "The solution to our problem," he explains (by way of omnipresence),

> begins by pointing out that for something to be an object of recognition, or perceptual discrimination, it must have a delimited presence, marked off spatially or temporally from some perceptual background. There can be no detection of presence without absence. There must be borders or boundaries to an entity's presence if it is to be discernible. There must be that-where-it-is-not as well as that-where-it-is if it is to be seen at all as present. Since God is omnipresent, pervasive of all reality, and infinite, there are no divine boundaries to make perceptual discrimination possible. *What seems to be a total absence of the divine is only an illusion produced by the reality of his all-encompassing presence.*[20]

As Jeremy Evans writes, "Divine omnipresence . . . provides prima facie reason for one to expect God to be hidden."[21] For God's omnipresence (says Morris) does not stipulate "why it is that he doesn't *act* more decisively and dramatically in the world to disambiguate the world."[22] But again the interest is not in God's attributes but in his actions. "In other words," writes atheist Herman Philipse regarding the hiddenness problem, "if there is any evidence for God's existence at all, the evidence is not very compelling."[23]

---

19. *DHHR* 4; emphasis added.

20. T. Morris, *Making Sense*, 91; emphasis added. Consider also Anselm's comments on God's omnipresence and hiddenness: "You are wholly present everywhere, and yet I do not see you. . . . You are within me and all around me, and yet I do not perceive you" (*Proslogion* 16 in *Saint Anselm: Basic Writings*, 75–98).

21. J. Evans, *Problem of Evil*, 64.

22. T. Morris, *Making Sense*, 91; emphasis added.

23. Philipse, *God in Age of Science*, 303.

His comments, though debatable, at least point us in the right direction toward saying what the problem for this project is *not*.

These four ways (corresponding to four divine attributes) behind us, I now briefly demonstrate two *further* ways—this time analyzing "divine hiddenness" in the thought of two important theologians—to say what the problem is not.

So, fifth, consider Martin Luther's conception of *deus absconditus*.[24] According to Luther (following the scholarly work of B. A. Gerrish), God is hidden *inside* his revelation (Gerrish calls this "Hiddenness I") and God is hidden *outside* his revelation (Gerrish calls this "Hiddenness II").[25] In the former, Luther notes that, at the cross of Christ, the eye of faith sees the hidden God, for it is in the person of Christ that God is revealed. "Faith is the only key," explains Alister McGrath of Luther, "by which the hidden mystery of the cross may be unlocked."[26] In the latter, God is unknown to us; he is mysterious and inscrutable, an all-determining, inaccessible God of predestination.[27] Perhaps Hiddenness II, as Gerrish calls it, is captured by Luther here:

> Wherever God hides Himself, and wills to be unknown to us, there we have no concern. Here that sentiment "what is above us does not concern us," really holds good. . . . God in His own nature and majesty is to be left alone; in this regard, we have nothing to do with Him, nor does He wish us to deal with Him.[28]

Some have called this a dual will within Luther's conception of God.[29] (And there may be a similar theme in John Calvin's work.) Commenting also on

---

24. A classic text on Luther's conception of *Deus absconditus* is Dillenberger, *God Hidden and Revealed*. See also Holmes, "Disclosure without Reservation."

25. Gerrish, "To the Unknown God," 268.

26. McGrath, *Luther's Theology of Cross*, 175. Commenting on the reality of both Christ and Satan in Luther's personal thought, Heiko A. Oberman explains that "the *omnipotent* God is indeed real, but *as such* hidden from us. Faith reaches not for God hidden but for God revealed, who, incarnate in Christ, laid Himself open to the Devil's fury" (*Luther*, 104; emphasis added).

27. McGrath, *Luther's Theology of Cross*, 165–66.

28. Luther, *On Bondage of Will*, 190.

29. Pettit, "Christ Alone," 194. Further, as Louis Berkhof writes: "Luther uses some very strong expressions respecting our inability to know something of the Being or essence of God. On the one hand he distinguishes between the *Deus absconditus* (hidden God) and the *Deus revelatus* (revealed God); but on the other hand he also asserts that in knowing the *Deus revelatus*, we only know Him in his hiddenness. By this he means that even in His revelation God has not manifested Himself entirely *as He is essentially*, but as to His essence still remains shrouded in impenetrable darkness" (*Systematic Theology*, 43; emphasis added; see also 29). There may be a similar theme in Calvin's work.

God's "nature and majesty" in Luther's construal of *deus absconditus*, Boyer and Hall write that this has

> far-reaching implications for Luther as he thinks about how God makes himself accessible—and does *not* make himself accessible—to humanity. If human beings were wise, they would hesitate to approach the transcendent God, lest they find themselves facing their own destruction. But human beings are not particularly wise, and so God himself in mercy takes up their cause. For their own protection, *God hides himself* from sinners.[30]

Now, helpful themes from his notion of divine hiddenness, particularly what Gerrish calls Hiddenness I, can be further examined in Luther's insistence that the one with faith "sees" the hidden God at the cross of Christ (I will return to comparable themes in later chapters). However, it seems that Hiddenness II—an inscrutable, unknown God—is not helpful at identifying the problem pertinent to our study, for it fails to interact with the evidence or experience of God's existence.[31] In short, as Robert McKim notes, Luther's position (though I would limit it to Hiddenness II) does not hold "any promise for contributing to an *explanation* of the hiddenness of God."[32] This brief overview of Luther, as sketchy as it is, yet again helps to clarify what the problem of divine hiddenness for which I am interested is not.

Sixth, consider also Karl Barth, whose *Church Dogmatics* contains an analysis of the "hiddenness" of God.[33] Barth notes that God is knowable only by God:

> In his revelation, in Jesus Christ, the hidden God has indeed made Himself apprehensible. Not directly, but indirectly. Not to sight, but to faith. Not in His being, but in sign. Not, then, by the dissolution of His hiddenness—but apprehensibly.[34]

See Kinlaw, "Determinism and the Hiddenness." Kinlaw writes: "Calvin operates with such a high view of divine agency that he is unwilling to allow even logical limitations on the execution of God's will. This does not mean that God acts arbitrarily or without reasons; however, it does mean that any reasons will often remain hidden, and at any rate, are explicable in terms of God's will itself" (499). Then he writes: "The hidden God of election is beyond our comprehension, a mysterious and frightening abyss" (509). See also Helm, "John Calvin and Hiddenness."

30. Boyer and Hall, *Mystery of God*, 56; emphasis added.
31. See Schellenberg's comments on Luther (*DHHR* 5).
32. McKim, *Religious Ambiguity*, 85; emphasis added. For McKim's fuller critique of Luther, see 85–87. See also H-M. Barth, *Theology of Martin Luther*, 101–34.
33. K. Barth, *Doctrine of God* §27.1, 179–204.
34. K. Barth, *Doctrine of God* §27.1, 199.

"God's hiddenness . . . meets us in Christ," Barth writes elsewhere, "and finally and supremely in the crucified Christ; for where is God so hidden as here, and where is the possibility of offense so great as here?"[35] For Barth, God is both hidden and revealed in Jesus Christ. George Hunsinger clarifies that, according to Barth, there

> is no God apart from, beyond, or behind God as God is in Jesus Christ. In Jesus Christ, God's being is present in its unity and entirety. There is no hidden God beyond the revealed God. The hidden God and the revealed God are essentially one and the same. The hiddenness of God is given in and with God's self-revelation, and God's self-revelation does not exclude but includes God's hiddenness. As revealed in trinitarian self-disclosure, God's identity in and with Jesus Christ is ineffaceably mysterious—concealed in the midst of disclosure and disclosed in the midst of concealment.[36]

Now, Barth's approach, one that takes seriously important biblical and theological themes (themes worth returning to in later chapters), is helpful in fleshing out divine hiddenness but not the *problem* of divine hiddenness. For Michael Rea writes that, for Barth, "divine hiddenness" is (in short) "equivalent to divine incomprehensibility."[37] Moreover, Kevin Diller cautions that there is

> the potential for confusion here in what we mean by God's hiddenness in this discussion [on Barth and divine hiddenness]. Philosophers of religion talk about the experience of divine hiddenness, when God seems silent or without witness. This is often discussed as a problem for belief in God. . . . This is not what Barth means by God's hiddenness in revelation. Revelation means God is *not* silent.[38]

And Schellenberg, having discussed Luther and Barth, says, "We may therefore conclude that the traditional emphasis of theology on the hiddenness of

---

35. Karl Barth, *Göttingen Dogmatics*, as quoted in Migliore, *Faith Seeking Understanding*, 26; see 24–28 for Migliore's comments on Barth and the hiddenness of God.

36. Hunsinger, *How to Read Barth*, 37.

37. Rea, "Hiddenness and Transcendence," 224, which is also what Berkhof takes Barth to mean by divine hiddenness: "When he [Barth] says that even in His revelation God still remains for us the *unknown* God, he really means, *the incomprehensible God*" (Berkhof, *Systematic Theology*, 33; emphasis in original). See also Hunsinger, *How to Read Barth*, 82–84.

38. Diller, *Theology's Epistemological Dilemma*, 55n59; emphasis in original.

God does not imply that the evidence for God's existence must be weak."[39] So, Barth's perspective, like Luther's, does not seem to have in mind the hiddenness problem for which I am concerned.

There is at least one final way—call this the seventh way—to say what the problem is not, stemming from Antony Flew's conception of the presumption of atheism; I describe the presumption and then disconnect it from the hiddenness problem. The presumption of atheism, in short, is the maxim that in the absence of evidence for God's existence one should *presume* that God does not exist, in which case atheism is said to be the neutral (or the default) position regarding belief in God,[40] and that therefore "the onus of proof," as Flew writes, "must lie on the theist." Thus the "atheist becomes: not someone who positively asserts the non-existence of God; but someone who is simply *not* a theist."[41] So, in the absence of evidence for God, one ought therefore to speak of *evidence of absence*.[42] But what is the relationship between this and PDH?

As Peter van Inwagen points out, the hiddenness problem does *not* appeal to the principle of "absence of evidence is evidence of absence," which I believe is, in fact, largely present in the presumption of atheism; they are separate concerns. Van Inwagen argues that "we have no evidence for the existence of an inhabited planet in the galaxy M31, but that fact is not evidence for the *non-existence* of such a planet." He goes on:

> If a proposition is such that, if it were true, we should have evidence for its truth, and if we are aware that it has this property, and if we have no evidence for its truth, then this fact, the fact

---

39. DHHR 5. See Schellenberg's comments on Barth's construal of God's hiddenness (Schellenberg, *Hiddenness Argument*, 125).

40. Scott A. Shalkowski writes that the presumption is a "non-context-relative presumption that warrants what I will call the 'default strategy' for defending atheism" ("Atheological Apologetics," 59).

41. Flew, "Presumption of Atheism," 19–20; emphasis added. See also Theodore M. Drange's similar discussion ("Nonbelief vs. Lack of Evidence"). Flew is reported to have changed his mind, leaving behind his atheism to embrace something like theism. See Habermas and Flew, "My Pilgrimage from Atheism"; Flew and Varghese, *There Is a God*.

42. Moreland and Craig observe: "Other advocates of the presumption of atheism continued to use the word in the standard way and so recognized their need of justification for their claim that atheism is true, but they insisted that it was precisely the absence of evidence for theism that justified their claim that God does not exist. Thus, in the absence of evidence for God, one is justified in the presumption of atheism" (*Philosophical Foundations*, 156).

that we have no evidence for its truth, is (conclusive) evidence for its falsity.[43]

Additionally, as Moreland and Craig argue, since PDH is different from the presumption of atheism, then this could be why, among contemporary philosophers, scholarly analysis has progressed *from* the presumption of atheism *to* talk of the problem of God's hiddenness:

> The debate among contemporary philosophers has therefore moved beyond the facile presumption of atheism to a discussion of the so-called hiddenness of God—in effect, a discussion or expectation that God, if he existed, would leave more evidence of his existence than we have.[44]

This is the seventh way.

In sum, the first four ways for saying what PDH is not included analyzing divine attributes or properties (incorporeality, transcendence, incomprehensibility, and somewhat peculiarly omnipresence); the next two comprised Luther's notion of *deus absconditus* as well as Barth's comments on divine hiddenness (although helpful themes from both Luther and Barth were mentioned); the last found the presumption of atheism disparate. And, in these ways, it has become clear what the problem of divine hiddenness for which this project is concerned is *not*.

1.3 WHAT THE PROBLEM OF DIVINE HIDDENNESS *IS*

1.3.1 Toward a Definition, a Research Question, and a Thesis Statement

Saying what something is *not*, as done above, can often help one get clearer on what something, in fact, *is*, and the fruit from the previous exercise can now be reaped. In this section, I first offer a more formal *definition* of what PDH is, after which I state my *research question* and then my *thesis statement*. This will then aid in the commencement of the historical overview of PDH as defined here, ultimately positioning me to undertake a contemporary literature review of PDH in the next chapter.

---

43. Van Inwagen, *Problem of Evil*, 173n1; emphasis added.

44. Moreland and Craig, *Philosophical Foundations*, 157. I do not comment on this any further since I analyze PDH in its contemporary context in my subsequent chapter. For another theistic response to the presumption of atheism, see A. Plantinga, "Reason and Belief."

Now, as a useful *façon de parler*, it seems at this point that a distinction can be made between *ontological* and *epistemological* mysteries. Ontological mysteries, as William Wainwright explains, are mysteries relevant to the "intrinsic aspect of God's own being," whereas epistemic ones apply to human knowledge of God.[45] Perhaps a similar distinction can be applied to the hiddenness problem. For when it is argued ontologically that "God is hidden," I take it that, used in this sense, the "is" here is an "is" of essential predication (contrasted with the "is" of identity, the "is" of constitution, and so forth). This would mean that the "is" in "God is hidden," taken predicatively, conjoins a name and a predicate symbol.[46] Thus, when the intrinsic *ontological* life of God—the divine essence or nature or substance—is referenced, many do in fact affirm that God is hidden, as I have shown earlier, in that God, as most in the Christian tradition would likely affirm, is not empirically verifiable (i.e., given his transcendence, incomprehensibility, and the like).[47]

But this—to be repetitive—is not what is meant by the problem of divine hiddenness, since by the problem one means the putative anonymity or the obscurity or the elusiveness of God's existence. The intent behind the problem, then, is more *epistemological*. For while some persons claim to have knowledge or belief or experience or awareness of God (or a god), others do *not*. I take it that Wainwright's comments, though applied not to divine hiddenness per se but rather to theological mystery, are helpful ones, and that it is better to speak of the problem of divine hiddenness, at least for which I am concerned here in this project, *not* as ontological but as epistemic. As Sarah Coakley argues, PDH is the effect of an *epistemic* condition, "not an *ontological* state of affairs."[48]

The problem therefore can be defined epistemically. So, "When philosophers talk about divine hiddenness," writes Michael Rea, "they usually have in mind the fact that neither direct and unambiguous experience of

---

45. Wainwright, "Theology and Mystery," 94. Wainwright writes: "Discussions of epistemological mysteries are at home in philosophical theology," whereas the "ontological sense of mystery . . . is perhaps most at home in liturgical worship and the prayer of adoration" (94–95). See also Quash, "Revelation," 325, 327.

46. Kuhn, "Is." For a helpful discussion on predication, see Loux, *Metaphysics*, 25–31.

47. On a similar note, Richard Muller explains (at least for Reformed theologians) that the simple divine essence of God is hidden (*Post-Reformation Reformed Dogmatics*, 3:195–96). See also Michael Horton's comments on the hiddenness of God's essence (*Christian Faith*, 223). The hiddenness of the divine nature, as Oliver Crisp explains, also has Christological ramifications: "The nature of God the Son is divine, and the divine nature is something that we have much less grip on than human natures, since the divine essence or nature is in a number of important respects *mysterious*" ("Desiderata," 41; emphasis added).

48. Coakley, "Divine Hiddenness or Dark Intimacy?," 230; emphasis added.

God nor conclusive evidence of God's existence is widely available."[49] Similarly, Schellenberg notes:

> Contemporary philosophers who employ such expressions [i.e., "divine hiddenness" or "hiddenness of God"] usually have in mind either (1) that the available relevant evidence makes the existence of God uncertain or (2) that many individuals or groups of people *feel* uncertain about the existence of God, or else never mentally engage the idea of God at all.[50]

I take it that these remarks, without trying to parse them out, at least lean toward a definition of divine hiddenness as an *epistemic* problem. But still lacking is a more formal definition of PDH from which I can work. Perhaps one way to get at a more precise definition is to say that "divine hiddenness" is a problem that nonbelievers and believers can both examine. Both wonder why, if there is a God, he is not (more) evident, or at least why he is not evident to more persons.

A nonbeliever may say, "Why would God," if there is a God, to quote Schellenberg (again), "permit his or her own existence to be hidden even from those who are willing to see it," for "wouldn't a loving personal God have good reason to prevent such obscurity?"[51] Perhaps having reflected on the phenomenon of "divine hiddenness" the nonbeliever thinks (like Schellenberg) that, as it turns out, "divine hiddenness" can be used as an *argument* against theism: For "in many places and times, and for many people, God's existence has been rather less than a clear fact, and according to the hiddenness *argument*, this is a reason to suppose that it is not a fact at all."[52] Indeed, Schellenberg's 1993 *Divine Hiddenness and Human Reason* formulates a specific argument, with premises, the conclusion of which says that there just is no God:

1. If there is a God, he is perfectly loving.

2. If a perfectly loving God exists, reasonable nonbelief does not occur.

3. Reasonable nonbelief occurs.

4. No perfectly loving God exists.

5. There is no God.[53]

---

49. Rea, *Evil and the Hiddenness*, vi. See also Rea, "Divine Hiddenness, Divine Silence," 269; Murray and Rea, "Anti-Theistic Arguments."
50. Schellenberg, "Divine Hiddenness," 509.
51. Schellenberg, "Why Am I Nonbeliever," 30.
52. Schellenberg, *Hiddenness Argument*, vii; emphasis added.
53. *DHHR* 83. Reasonable nonbelief occurs "if and only if it is not the result of culpable actions or omissions on the part of the subject" (*DHHR* 3n2).

I do not here analyze this argument (but I will in my next chapter). Still, this is an example of how a nonbeliever may think about divine hiddenness; he or she may reflect on the generic *problem* and wind up constructing a specific *argument*.

But what about (theistic) believers? How can *they* think about the problem that God's existence is not (more) evident? For instance, a theist may characterize PDH in the way that Helen De Cruz does when she writes:

> From a *theistic perspective*, divine hiddenness (or, as it is sometimes called, divine silence) is a puzzling phenomenon in need of explanation. If God exists, why does he not make his presence more unambiguously known?[54]

This way of phrasing the problem is echoed by other (theistic) believers. For example, John Greco says, "The Problem of Divine Hiddenness is to explain why a loving God is not clearly present to all of creation."[55] Peter van Inwagen suggests that theists who engage the epistemic hiddenness problem have the task of "meeting a challenge to belief in the existence of God that has the general form, 'If there were a God, the world would not look the way it does [i.e., devoid of signs and wonders from God].'"[56] Wainwright asks, "If God exists, why isn't his existence more obvious?"[57] Likewise, Robert McKim notes:

> It seems . . . that neither the existence of God nor the nature of God is apparent or obvious. It therefore needs to be ask why, if God exists, it is not entirely clear to everyone that this is so, and why in general the facts about God are not entirely clear to everyone.[58]

Consider the theists just quoted. I define the problem at the intersection of how these aforementioned thinkers do, and here is the definition of PDH from which I will work: *If God exists, then his existence would be more obvious.*

Three comments about the definition are in order. First, the mentioned theists conceive of PDH conditionally or hypothetically: "If there is a God, then his existence would be more apparent or evident or clear," or something along these lines. The hiddenness problem arises for theists because it can be argued that the way the world appears ("The world would not look the way that it does," as Van Inwagen says) is at odds, at least prima

---

54. De Cruz, "Divine Hiddenness," 54; emphasis added.
55. Greco, "No-Fault Atheism," 109.
56. Van Inwagen, "What Is the Problem," 29–30.
57. Wainwright, "Jonathan Edwards and Hiddenness," 98.
58. McKim, *Religious Ambiguity*, 3; emphasis added.

facie, with our presuppositions or pre-theoretical commitments about God. Second, it seems that one can interpret the phrase "more obvious" either *quantitatively* or *qualitatively*. When PDH is considered from a quantitative perspective, perhaps we mean to inquire why God, if he exists, is not "more obvious" to more persons, or why his existence is not more widely known; Greco uses the phrase to "all of creation," and McKim uses the phrase "to everyone." Conversely, when PDH is considered from a qualitative perspective, perhaps we mean to inquire why God's existence is not more deeply impressed upon us or why it is not more strongly perceived; this qualitative aspect of PDH may be what De Cruz and Wainwright have in mind (similarly, Michael Murray appears to be speaking qualitatively when he argues that most do not find God's existence obvious like "when we say that it is *obvious* that the World Trade Center [when it existed] weighs more than a deck of cards or that it is obvious that Van Gogh is a better painter than I").[59] Third, included or entailed in both qualitative and quantitative aspects is a *comparative* sense of "more obvious." Speaking qualitatively, we are asking why God's presence is not more deeply impressed upon us, and we appear to be assuming, from a comparative sense, that it should be clearer than it is if God in fact exists. Speaking quantitatively, we are asking why God's presence is not more widely known to more people, and we seem to be assuming—again from a comparative perspective—that it should be clearer to more persons than it is if there is a God. In light of these comments, my definition of PDH is conditional in nature, and my discussion of the problem will oscillate between quantitative and qualitative aspects (both of which are comparative).

This brings me to my project's *research question*, a question worth raising, having a working definition in hand, to see what light can be thrown on the problem: *Why, if God exists, is his existence not more obvious?*[60] So, how can answering this question be achieved? Now, someone like Schellenberg, himself a nonbeliever, may entertain my definition of PDH as well as my research question only to conclude that there are no satisfactory answers; he or she may reflect on the nature of nonbelief in God—whether it is reasonable or inculpable or nonresistant—and in turn formulate an argument against God's existence, as mentioned above. This is how a nonbeliever may respond to my research question.[61]

---

59. Murray, "*Deus Absconditus*," 62; emphasis in original.

60. Note that stating the research question this way echoes others in the scholarly literature who ask similar questions (Kinghorn, "Why Doesn't God"; Moser, *Why Isn't God*).

61. See also Drange, *Nonbelief and Evil*.

But *my* project, as I understand it, is an exercise in *theistic* philosophy and theology, the theist having the right to think about such problems or puzzles or questions or inquiries from her own perspective. Robert McKim, for instance, writes that he approaches "the issue of the hiddenness of God as an internal problem for *theism*."[62] "How can *theists*," he asks elsewhere, "explain God's hiddenness, and how plausible are their explanations?"[63] I follow this method but specify my perspective from bare *theistic* philosophy and theology to *Christian* theistic philosophy and theology, perhaps even saying that my project on PDH, to steal a thought from St. Anselm, is one of *faith seeking understanding* (which roughly means, as philosopher Thomas Williams writes, "an active love of God seeking a deeper knowledge of God").[64] My aim, then, is to give a distinctly Christian theistic response to the research question.

Now, what options are available to Christian theists in trying to examine PDH? How can they go about answering the research question? Consider PDH's relationship to the problem of evil (hereafter POE). Traditionally, theists have offered two types of responses to POE: defenses and theodicies.[65]

A defense, roughly stated, is a *possible* account explaining why God might allow evil, whereas a theodicy is an *actual* account; there are different sorts of defenses: free will defenses, greater goods defenses, and so forth—the same, too, with theodicies. Some believe methodologically that defenses and theodicies can also apply to PDH. With respect to PDH, a *theodicy* is a theory that attempts to give actual reasons for why God's existence is not (more) obvious, whereas (as Michael Rea writes)

> a *defense* is simply a demonstration of consistency—an effort to show that there is no formal contradiction between the existence of God on the one hand and . . . the phenomenon of divine hiddenness on the other.[66]

---

62. McKim, *Religious Ambiguity*, 92; emphasis added.

63. McKim, "Hiddenness of God," 141; emphasis added.

64. See Williams's introduction in Anselm, "*Proslogion*," vii.

65. I discuss at length the relationship between PDH and POE in the subsequent chapter, explaining similarities and dissimilarities. See Tooley, "Problem of Evil." Alongside defenses and theodicies, an approach called skeptical theism has recently been applied to PDH; skeptical theism is a response to the evidential problem of evil, specifically regarding gratuitous suffering, whereby skeptical theists "express skepticism about our ability to determine whether the evils we encounter really are pointless" (Center for Philosophy of Religion, "Skeptical Theism," para. 2). See Dougherty and McBrayer, *Skeptical Theism*.

66. Rea, *Evil and the Hiddenness*, 2; emphasis added.

Let us zoom in a bit more on the difference between the two. "The difference between a defense and a theodicy," argues Van Inwagen, "lies not in their content but in their purposes."

> A *theodicy* is a story that is told as the real truth of the matter; a *defense* is a story that, according to the teller, may or may not be true, but which, the teller maintains, has some desirable feature that does not entail truth—perhaps (depending on the context) logical consistency or epistemic possibility (truth-for-all-anyone-knows).[67]

Van Inwagen encourages Christian theists to tell "stories," either theodicies or defenses, with respect to PDH.[68]

So, defenses and theodicies are available options for PDH; but which will my project follow? My project will opt for a *defense*, aiming more specifically not to give a mere logically consistent but rather (as Van Inwagen says) an epistemically possible story that is true for all we know; this can be used to answer the research question, which asks why if there is a God his existence is not more apparent. But opting for an epistemically possible defense story is perhaps still a bit unspecific; are there any specific norms or criteria or conditions that my defense can or should meet? Inspired by Justin McBrayer and Philip Swenson (but modifying their comments for my own purposes), I believe there to be some *desiderata* that a defense should aim to satisfy; for instance, it should (in step with how we defined PDH earlier) attempt to:

(i) Develop an account describing why, if God exists, his existence is not more obvious.

(ii) Show that this description is true for all we know.[69]

The first (i) suggests the construction of some sort of an explanation for God's hiddenness, offering an account of why if he exists he is not more obvious, whereas the second (ii) aligns with Van Inwagen's proposal that a defense can be more than simply logically but instead *epistemically* possible: it should be true for all we know (or "truth-for-all-anyone-knows," as Van Inwagen puts its). Now, it was said above that my examination of PDH aims

---

67. Van Inwagen, *Problem of Evil*, 7; emphasis added. W. Paul Franks calls a defense that is only logically consistent a *narrow* defense; he calls a defense that is epistemically possible a *broad* defense ("Original Sin"). For more on defenses and theodicies, see Goetz, "Argument from Evil."

68. Van Inwagen, "What Is the Problem," 30–31.

69. McBrayer and Swenson, "Scepticism," 142. McBrayer and Swenson's (i) is similar, but instead is phrased in terms of reasonable nonbelief.

to be distinctly Christian, Christians having a right to analyze and to examine problems—in this case PDH—from their own perspective; with this in mind, perhaps we can revise (i) to read as follows:

(i*) Develop a *specifically Christian* account describing why, if God exists, his existence is not more obvious.

(ii) Show that this description is true for all we know.

These are the desiderata that my defense will attempt to satisfy. In chapter 2—the literature review—it will be demonstrated what sort of responses present-day theists have provided against PDH (e.g., free will defenses, etc.), and in so doing it will be argued that there is one Christian theistic way of thinking about the problem largely absent from the contemporary discussion: a Reformed epistemological approach following Alvin Plantinga. Reformed epistemology, "a thesis about the rationality of religious belief," is "so called because some of its adherents taught at Calvin College and to some extent looked for inspiration to John Calvin and others in the tradition of Reformed theology."[70] I believe there to be important themes from Plantingean Reformed epistemology applicable as a defense for PDH, answering my research question as well as satisfying conditions (i*) and (ii) above, and here is how.

Very briefly, Plantinga, in an important epistemological work, *Warranted Christian Belief* (hereafter *WCB*), offers two hypothetical theological models—a model being a possible state of affairs—for how Christian theistic belief can have *warrant*, the quality enough of which turns mere true belief into knowledge.[71] Crudely stated, the first model, what he calls the A/C model (after Thomas Aquinas and John Calvin), examines humanity's natural knowledge of God; it explains how bare theistic belief may have warrant. But Plantinga *extends* the generic A/C model—calling this the extended A/C model—in an attempt to show how specifically *Christian* theistic belief may have warrant. In so doing, he analyzes sin's noetic and affective consequences as well as other pertinent Christian themes, all of which are important to his Reformed theological heritage, such as the internal instigation of the Holy Spirit, the inspiration and testimony of Scripture, the work of Jesus Christ, and the like.

These hypothetical models contain much epistemic and theological substance applicable, as I see it, *to* divine hiddenness (sometimes overlooked in the current analytic-philosophical debate, as I will attempt to

---

70. A. Plantinga, "Reformed Epistemology" (1997). See also Wolterstorff, "Reformed Tradition."

71. See also *KCB*.

show in the next chapter's literature review). The models engage distinctively Christian themes, explained just above, thereby meeting criterion (i*), Plantinga having encouraged Christians for many years to analyze philosophical and theological problems from their *own* assumptions and perspectives; he writes, for instance, that Christians have their "own questions to think about" and that Christians have a "perfect right to their own pre-philosophical views."[72] This reasoning applies to my own project on PDH; I think that the A/C and extended A/C models, taken together, can be used as a defense making up a specifically Christian account explaining why if there is a God his existence is not more obvious. Such a Plantingean approach to PDH qualifies as an exercise in Christian theistic philosophy (and theology), as discussed earlier. This is (i*), but what about (ii)? How can my own defense meet this particular criterion? Plantinga says the A/C and extended A/C models for how Christian belief can have warrant are more than "just broadly logically possible"[73] but rather "that these models are *epistemically* possible: they are consistent with what we know,"[74] claiming also of the extended model that it is "*epistemically possible* (i.e., nothing we know commits us to its falsehood)."[75] Dietrich Schönecker writes of the A/C model that "to say that the model is epistemically possible is to say that 'nothing we know commits us to its falsehood.'"[76] James Beilby further explains of the models that

> epistemic possibility is stronger than strict logical possibility or broadly logical possibility. Strict logical possibility is mere freedom from contradiction where broadly logical possibility denotes an actualizable, strictly logically possible state of affairs. . . . Epistemic possibility, on the other hand, is more restrictive than broadly logical possibility. An epistemically possible proposition, according to Plantinga, is "consistent with what we know, where 'what we know' is what all or most of the participants in the discussion can agree on."[77]

Jeroen de Ridder and Mathanja Berger clarify the distinction between logical and epistemic possibility in Plantinga's extended A/C model, saying:

---

72. A. Plantinga, "Advice to Christian Philosophers," 269. See also A. Plantinga, "Christian Life Partly Lived," 78–79, for his comments on Christian philosophy.
73. WCB 168.
74. WCB 168–69; emphasis in original.
75. WCB xii; emphasis in original.
76. Schönecker, "Deliverances," 23; cf. WCB xii.
77. Beilby, *Epistemology as Theology*, 115; quoting WCB 168–69.

Plantinga claims that it is broadly logically possible, i.e., free from contradiction. It is, moreover, also epistemically possible, i.e., consistent with what we know. It thus offers Christians (and others) a way to conceive of the positive epistemic status of Christian beliefs.[78]

Thus, what Plantinga claims of his models—I explain in later chapters what *motivates* his claims—sits well with what Van Inwagen and McBrayer and Swenson suggest above, characterized by (ii); Plantinga says that his models are true for all we know, answering objections to his models in the last part of *WCB*. This is also a reason why my own Plantingean approach to PDH need not be a *theodicy*, since a theodicy aims not at mere possibility but at actuality. Perhaps Christian theists *can* offer actual theodical stories for PDH, but this project will not do so.[79]

Consider now an objection: defenses or theodicies apply not so much to generic problems but rather to specific *arguments*, such as the *argument from evil* (in either its logical [deductive] or evidential [inductive] forms), the conclusion of which says that God does not exist; therefore, in order to reject the conclusion *God does not exist*, a defense or a theodicy must tell a story about God and evil, all while attacking a premise or premises from an argument. So, too, with PDH. An objector could say that my defense (or a theodicy, if I were to give one) must attack not the generic PDH but rather a specific *argument*, such as, say, Schellenberg's 1993 evidential (inductive) argument from divine hiddenness (discussed above, which is technically an argument not from "divine hiddenness" per se but from *reasonable nonbelief*). Thus, by not attacking an argument—or a premise or premises in an argument—my defense is weak or substandard; perhaps I am only attacking a straw man. So, must my defense rebut or refute a specific *argument* in order to be a good one? I am unconvinced that I must attack an argument from divine hiddenness in order to offer a good defense against the problem. Assume POE is similar to PDH in that defenses or theodicies can be offered for either problem. Now, take just POE; Plantinga explains that theists have exhausted a lot of apologetic effort responding to POE, in either its logical or evidential argumentative forms, and rightly so. He says further that

> these responses are useful and important. But in addition to rebutting these *arguments*, Christian philosophers should also

---

78. De Ridder and Berger, "Shipwrecked or Holding Water?," 44.

79. Christian philosopher Paul Moser argues that a theodicy for PDH is unavailable for us ("Cognitive Idolatry," 146–47). For a perspective that argues that theists who engage POE *should* use theodicies and not defenses (which perhaps is applicable also to PDH), see Tierno, "On Defense."

> turn to a different task: that of *understanding* the evil our world displays from a *Christian perspective*. . . . *How should Christians think about evil?*[80]

He then goes on to give a response to POE, but he does not attempt to attack an argument in so doing. The same can be said with respect to my project on PDH. Theists, as the next chapter will show, have in fact provided enormously helpful responses (defenses or theodicies) to formal arguments from divine hiddenness, particularly to Schellenberg's 1993 argument in *DHHR*.[81] But my project, however, is interested in analyzing and understanding the hiddenness of God from a Christian viewpoint: *How should Christians think about divine hiddenness?* Now, I do examine an argument from divine hiddenness in my next chapter (Schellenberg's 1993 argument in *DHHR*), but do not feel obligated to take my project's starting point *from* an argument.

This objection behind me, I now have a definition and a research question (as well as some helpful defense desiderata) for PDH. But what is it that I argue? Put into a statement, my *thesis*, which takes its cue from the research question (which takes *its* starting point from the definition of PDH above), is that *Plantinga's A/C models for how Christian belief may have warrant can be utilized as a defense to explain why, if God exists, his existence is not more obvious*. Chapter 2 will explain, in more detail, *how* my thesis is relevant to the contemporary PDH literature. Chapters 3 through 5 will be an exposition and a defense of my thesis in three parts; chapter 3 applies the bare A/C model to PDH, whereas chapter 4 examines, from a Plantingean perspective, the relationship between sin and PDH. Chapter 5 uses the extended A/C model to analyze divine hiddenness (chapter 2 will explain these mentioned plans in more detail). In chapter 6, concluding remarks will be given. Let me now explain my work's perceived scholarly importance.

1.3.2 The Scholarly Significance of the Thesis

Since J. L. Schellenberg's 1993 *DHHR*, the literature on PDH has exploded. The bibliography in Daniel Howard-Snyder and Adam Green's 2016 *Stanford Encyclopedia of Philosophy* article entitled "Hiddenness of God" lists

---

80. A. Plantinga, "Supralapsarianism," 4–5; emphasis added.

81. As well as to more *recent* arguments advanced by Schellenberg. See Howard-Snyder, "Divine Openness," which responds to a new argument given by Schellenberg in "Divine Hiddenness."

roughly one hundred publications on PDH.[82] Schellenberg's recent article states that since 2010 more than sixty books or papers on PDH have been published.[83] Given such breadth and depth, what possible scholarly significance could my work on PDH have? Here two ways are articulated in which my thesis, if successful, could have scholarly import. First, I am unaware of any scholarly attempts that explicitly analyze PDH from the perspective of Plantinga's Reformed epistemology.[84] Plantingean epistemic scholarship has been utilized and applied (by those other than Plantinga himself) to many notable scholarly avenues, including, for example, the problem of religious diversity,[85] Christian apologetics,[86] theology in general,[87] and (if my thesis succeeds) to the problem of divine hiddenness. Second, the vast majority of scholars who examine PDH do so from almost a purely *philosophical* perspective; I try, without compromising philosophical rigor, to show how *theological* investigation can throw light on a philosophical problem (additionally, my project can be classified under philosophy of religion, systematic theology, or more precisely the recent movement entitled analytic theology).[88] The A/C and extended A/C models, for instance, all contain biblical and theological themes that philosophers do not always utilize in the hiddenness debate but which I think are important to consider; this fits well with what Travis Dumsday says when he explains that "most proponents of the divine hiddenness argument are targeting *generic* theism rather than *specifically* Christian theism."[89] I elaborate more on the importance of my thesis in the next chapter. To get there, however, a historical overview of the hiddenness problem will now be offered.

1.4 HISTORICAL OVERVIEW

The purpose of this section is to provide a historical overview of the problem of divine hiddenness prior to its current conception in contemporary

---

82. Howard-Snyder and Green, "Hiddenness of God."
83. Schellenberg, "Divine Hiddenness: Part 1."
84. Apart from Taber and McNabb, "Problem of Divine Hiddenness."
85. Kim, *Reformed Epistemology*.
86. Mascord, *Alvin Plantinga*.
87. Diller, *Theology's Epistemological Dilemma*; J. Anderson, *Paradox in Christian Theology*; Beilby, *Epistemology as Theology*.
88. Analytic theology, in short, applies the tools of analytic philosophy to theology. See O. Crisp and Rea, *Analytic Theology*; McCall, *Invitation*.
89. Dumsday, "Divine Hiddenness as Deserved," 292; emphasis added.

analytic philosophy of religion. Commenting on this theme, Schellenberg explains that until

> recently there was no developed hiddenness argument in the literature at all. Of course, a certain philosophical notion of Divine hiddenness and its problematic nature *has been with us for a long time*, hovering like a wraith over discussions of the existence of God. Long before any of us [i.e., present-day philosophers and theologians] ever came on the scene, *hints of it could be found in Hume and Nietzsche and other writers*, and there must have been many reflective women and men in times past who have wondered why God's existence is not more evident than it is.[90]

Thus, though the *argument*, with premises and a conclusion, is fairly new, the generic *problem*, broadly conceived, is not, seeds of which can be found in Hume and in Nietzsche. Let us examine Hume's and Nietzsche's analyses of the problem while adding in the analyses of Blaise Pascal, Joseph Butler, Alexander Campbell, and Søren Kierkegaard.

Why these six thinkers? Both Hume and Nietzsche appear to employ the hiddenness of God as a challenge or a problem for theism; I look into what motivates their reasoning. Conversely, as believers, Pascal, Butler, Campbell, and Kierkegaard (although representative of diverse time periods as well as different theological/philosophical persuasions) all seem to feel the hiddenness problem's force and reflect on the problem from their Christian theistic perspectives; what can be learned from their analyses? This exercise, if successful, will not only further elucidate my previous argumentation (what the hiddenness problem is *not* as well as what it *is*), but it will also aid to understand how various past theologians and philosophers, some of whom (I think) anticipate or foreshadow various Plantingean Reformed epistemic themes, have examined this important phenomenon. Methodologically, I draw upon both primary and secondary sources.

1.4.1 Blaise Pascal (1623–1662)

One thinker cognizant of PDH was Blaise Pascal, author of the *Pensées*.[91] "God being therefore hidden," he once famously wrote, "any religion which does not say that God is hidden is not true. And any religion which does not

---

90. Schellenberg, *Wisdom to Doubt*, 307; emphasis added. See also Schellenberg, *Hiddenness Argument*, 24–28, where he discusses other historical precursors to the contemporary hiddenness debate.

91. For a general introduction to Pascal's thought, I am helped by Hammond, *Cambridge Companion to Pascal*; Pascal, *Christianity for Modern Pagans*.

give the reason why does not enlighten. Ours [Christianity] does all this."[92] Pascal notes that Christianity can affirm both God's hiddenness ("That God *wanted* to be hidden"[93]) and it can give good reasons for why God is hidden, one explanation being *human pride*; so long as a person is prideful (toward God), he or she will not "see" God. For if humanity is to find this hidden God, then it must be by the *heart*, for "that is what faith is: God perceived *by the heart*, not by the reason."[94] Hence, if he is sought for the wrong motives, then God will remain hidden:

> Thus wishing to appear openly to those who seek him with all their heart and hidden from those who shun him with all their heart, he has qualified our knowledge of him by giving signs which can be seen by those who seek him and not by those who do not. "There is enough light for those who desire only to see, and enough darkness for those of a contrary disposition."[95]

What of the nature of evidence in Pascal's attitude toward PDH? As Kevin Kinghorn notes, it is not that evidence plays *no part* in one's search for God; it is rather that those who humbly seek him will come to see the truth about him—yet "God has not provided *more* evidence than he has because greater evidence would tend to lead to theistic beliefs among those in whom such beliefs would foster *pride*."[96] The person who merely seeks a sign or a wonder so as to authenticate God's existence—but who is not willing to *submit* to God—is (again) prideful:

> "If I had seen a miracle," they say, "I should be converted." How can they be positive that they would do what they know nothing about? They imagine that such a conversion consists in a worship of God conducted, as they picture it, like some exchange or conversation. True conversion consists in self-annihilation before the universal being whom we have so often vexed and who is perfectly entitled to destroy us at any moment, in recognizing that we can do nothing without him and that we had deserved nothing but his disfavour. It consists in knowing that there is an irreconcilable opposition between God and us, and that without a mediator there can be no exchange.[97]

---

92. Pascal, *Pensées*, 81, frg. 275.

93. Pascal, *Pensées*, 81, frg. 275; emphasis in original. See also frg. 644.

94. Pascal, *Pensées*, 57, frg. 423; emphasis added.

95. Pascal, *Pensées*, 79–80, frg. 149.

96. Kinghorn, *Decision of Faith*, 144; emphasis added. Kinghorn includes a helpful overview of Pascal on PDH (143–46).

97. Pascal, *Pensées*, frg. 378, quoted in Peters, *Logic of the Heart*, 133.

Consider also Pascal's comments on miracles and evidence for God:

> The prophesies, even the miracles and proofs of our religion, are not of such a kind that they can be said to be absolutely convincing, but they are at the same time such that it cannot be said to be unreasonable to believe in them. There is thus evidence and obscurity, to enlighten some and obfuscate others. But the evidence is such as to exceed, or at least equal, the evidence to the contrary, so that it cannot be reason that decides against following it, and can therefore only be concupiscence and wickedness of the heart. Thus, there is enough evidence to condemn and not to convince, so that it should be apparent that those who follow it are prompted to do so by grace and not by reason, and those who evade it are prompted by concupiscence and not by reason.[98]

Thomas Morris writes of Pascal on PDH that those who are "improperly prepared to come to know and love [God], such revelation would be more of a curse than a blessing."[99] Pascal seems to indicate that true humility—the absence of pride—in one's search will yield *enough light* for a relationship with God.

But there is another sense in which PDH is humanity's fault in the fall: "God is partly concealed and partly revealed," writes William Wood of Pascal on PDH, "and so we are culpable for the fact that God appears hidden to us.... According to Pascal, it would be more accurate to say that *we* hide from God, instead of the reverse."[100] Nevertheless, even in humanity's postlapsarian condition, Pascal argues that God is not somehow unavailable. For "what can be seen on earth indicates neither the total absence, nor the manifest presence of divinity, *but the presence of a hidden God*. Everything bears this stamp."[101]

While the evidence for God *is* there, it is subtle and not coercive. Still, the pursuit of the hidden God, according to Pascal, is not a *neutral* endeavor. Morris, on behalf of Pascal, explains that "until we occupy the

---

98. Pascal, *Pensées*, frg. 835, quoted in Peters, *Logic of the Heart*, 134.

99. T. Morris, *Making Sense*, 102.

100. Wood, *Blaise Pascal on Duplicity*, 211; emphasis added. Wood writes, "There can therefore be no innocent unbelief. Such are the cognitive consequences of the Fall, according to Pascal" (211).

101. Pascal, *Pensées*, 170–71, frg. 449; emphasis in original. Commenting on this fragment, Douglas Groothuis writes: "If God were perfectly obvious to everyone, people could not feel their inadequacies and need for grace and redemption. On the other hand, if there were no signs of deity, there could be no reason to hope for grace and redemption" (*On Pascal*, 53).

right ground, the evidence we want is not going to become available."[102] The "right ground"—the condition of one's heart—means that one ought to humbly prepare oneself in one's search for God. Still, Pascal writes:

> Instead of complaining that God has kept himself hidden, you will give him thanks that he has made himself so visible. And you will give him further thanks that he has not revealed himself to the wise people full of pride, unworthy of knowing so holy a God.[103]

In sum, Pascal fastens together many important *theological* themes related to PDH, including pre- and postlapsarian knowledge of God, sin and pride, and the nature of evidence, themes worth returning to in later chapters.[104]

1.4.2 Joseph Butler (1692–1752)

It was the Englishman Joseph Butler who would become an important philosopher of the seventeenth and eighteenth centuries, even formulating a significant apologetic for the Christian faith comparable to, but ultimately distinct from, Pascal's (more on this below).[105] Butler's two main works applicable to PDH are his *Fifteen Sermons Preached at the Rolls Chapel* and his *The Analogy of Religion*.[106] I briefly examine both.

In his fifteenth sermon, "Upon the Ignorance of Man," Butler, drawing from Ecc 8:16–17, sets out to show that there is much human ignorance of God: "The wisest and most knowing cannot comprehend the way and works of God,"[107] even if "it is as certain that God made the world, as it is certain that effects must have a cause."[108] Concerning "the works of God" and "his scheme of government" such things are "above our capacities thoroughly to comprehend."[109] He goes on:

> There possibly may be reasons which originally made it fit *that many things should be concealed from us*, which we have perhaps natural capacities of understanding; many things concerning the designs, methods, and ends of divine providence in the

---

102. T. Morris, *Making Sense*, 108.
103. Pascal, *Pensées*, 7, frg. 13.
104. For further overview of Pascal on PDH, see *DHHR* 132–52.
105. On this point, see Babolin, "*Deus Absconditus*."
106. Both of which are found in J. Butler, *Works of Bishop Butler*.
107. J. Butler, "Upon Ignorance of Man," 140.
108. J. Butler, "Upon Ignorance of Man," 141.
109. J. Butler, "Upon Ignorance of Man," 142.

government of the world. There is no manner of absurdity in supposing a veil on purpose drawn over some scenes of infinite power, wisdom, and goodness, the sight of which might some way or other strike us too strongly; or that better ends are designed and served by their being concealed, than could be by their being exposed to our knowledge.[110]

According to Butler, our natural capacities simply are not cut out for total apprehension of God, and his ways are concealed from us; there is human ignorance (hence the sermon's title). Moreover, God has put us "in a state of discipline and improvement" so that we will submit and resign ourselves "to the divine will."[111] What are we to make of Butler on PDH? Terence Penelhum writes that, in Butler's sermon, "Butler says that God may deliberately *hide* himself from us . . . for purposes that we cannot now grasp, but which relates to our *probationary* state."[112] What of this "probationary state"?

In *The Analogy of Religion*, Butler argues that humanity is on "probation" with God, a trial of sorts, or a state of discipline, which requires humanity to undergo testing in preparation for improvement in this life as well as for the life "which is to follow [presumably heaven]."[113] Through this time of probation, humanity ought to inquire after God; Basil Mitchell writes, "Just as in childhood we have to learn through appropriate discipline to make the sort of decisions that are needed in maturity, so in our present life we are meant to cultivate those virtues which alone will fit us to enjoy life with God in the Communion of the Saints."[114] While on probation, and while there may be obstacles to test one's search for God, Butler insists that ordinary men

> were they as much in earnest about religion, as about their temporal affairs, are capable of being convinced upon real evidence, that there is a God Who governs the world: and they feel themselves to be of a moral nature, and accountable creatures. And as Christianity entirely falls in with this their natural sense of things, so they are capable, not only of being persuaded, but of being made to see, that there is evidence [for God]. . . . But though this proof is real and conclusive, yet it is liable to objections, and may be run up into difficulties. . . . Now if persons

---

110. J. Butler, "Upon Ignorance of Man," 142; emphasis added.

111. J. Butler, "Upon Ignorance of Man," 142.

112. Penelhum, "Butler and Human Ignorance," 137; emphasis added.

113. J. Butler, *Analogy of Religion*, 192. Note the title of this chapter: "Of a State of Probation, as Intended for Moral Discipline and Improvement."

114. Mitchell, "Butler as Christian Apologist," 102.

> who have picked up these objections from others, and take for granted they are of weight . . . will not prepare themselves for such examination . . . or will not give that time and attention to the subject, which, from the nature of it, is necessary for attaining such information: in this case, they must remain in doubtfulness, ignorance, or error.[115]

The evidence for God, according to Butler, is there for those who properly investigate it; contingent upon such inquiry, humanity does have the freedom to become convinced of such evidence (the evidence, for instance, of divine providence as well as moral accountability to a higher power). Babolin notes that, for Butler on God's hiddenness, it is presumptuous for a person not to take the Christian faith seriously.[116]

Consider how Butler's approach to PDH compares to Pascal's; Terence Penelhum writes that Butler's conception of "probation"

> is not the same as the view found in Pascal . . . and others that God hides himself from those who do not sincerely seek him, so that his hiddenness is the divine response to the corruption of their minds. It is rather the theory that those disposed to seek the truth with full seriousness might have to be presented with obstacles to test their moral determination.[117]

Finally, three further insights from Penelhum on Butler on PDH are applicable. First, while true religion must involve some sort of mystery, one can be thankful for the evidence for God that we *do*, in fact, possess. Second, human ignorance on these matters—that we lack full comprehension of God—is a proper response to PDH ("Given that the universe is indeed the work of God, we cannot rule out the possibility that God may have chosen to hide some facts from us that we are quite capable of understanding, but which he thinks it better we should not know. God may hide himself." Thus, "the difficulty of divine hiddenness . . . must have a solution, even if we have to live in ignorance of what it is").[118] Third, one's pursuit of knowledge of

---

115. As quoted in Penelhum, *Butler*, 194.

116. "The hiddenness of God affects . . . the theme of the evidential grounds of a supposed revelation. The *importance* of religion, and particularly of the Christian faith, along with the degree of evidence and probability of its truth, is sufficient to put man under strict obligations" (Babolin, "*Deus Absconditus*," 33; emphasis in original).

117. Penelhum, "Butler and Human Ignorance," 137. Schellenberg asks what we are to make of such probation and evidence scrutiny, writing against Butler that "a loving God would not impose intellectual probation vis-à-vis theistic evidence on anyone" (*DHHR* 180). For Schellenberg's fuller critique of Butler, see *DHHR* 168–80.

118. Penelhum, "Butler and Human Ignorance," 119, 139. This concept sounds close to a contemporary position on the problem of evil, also now applied to PDH, called skeptical theism. See McBrayer and Swenson, "Scepticism."

God should not neglect orthopraxy, or right behavior, since Butler's "arguments are directed always and only towards the removal of barriers to the practice of that mode of life we should be following, and never towards the satisfaction of *mere curiosity*."[119]

1.4.3 David Hume (1711–1776)

Another philosopher whose thought is pertinent to PDH is David Hume. Without entering into the elongated debates on Hume's religious persuasion, my intention is to put forth a possible way of interpreting an embryonic form ("seeds," to use Schellenberg's language) of PDH in Hume's writings.

One could read the entire *Dialogues Concerning Natural Religion* (hereafter *DNR*) as presenting a sort of problem of God's ambiguity.[120] There are three main characters in the book: Cleanthes; Demea; and a skeptic, Philo. The minor characters are Pamphilus and Hermippus. In the prologue, Pamphilus—recounting a past discussion between the three major characters—explains to Hermippus the justification for undertaking a conversation on natural religion.[121] On the one hand, Pamphilus asks, "What truth so obvious, so certain as the *being* of a God, which the most ignorant ages have acknowledged, for which the most refined geniuses have ambitiously striven to produce new proofs and arguments?" On the other hand, however, Pamphilus asks,

> But, in treating of this obvious and important truth, what obscure questions occur concerning the *nature* of that Divine Being; his attributes, his decrees, his plan of providence? These have been always subjected to the disputations of men: Concerning these, human reason has not reached any certain determination.[122]

So there is in the opening pages a distinction between the obviousness of the *being* of God—his existence—and the obscurity of God's *nature* (i.e., his attributes, his decrees, etc.). As Demea says in part 2, "The question is not concerning the *being* but the *nature* of God," since the nature is "altogether incomprehensible and *unknown* to us." Philo agrees and responds, "The

---

119. Penelhum, "Butler and Human Ignorance," 119; emphasis added. For other helpful comments on Butler and PDH, see McKim, *Religious Ambiguity*, 18–19, 39; Penelhum, *Butler*, 93–95, 193–97; Kinghorn, *Decision of Faith*, 141–43.

120. I have been helped on this point by Sloan Lee in conversation; see also his unpublished paper, "David Hume's Theism."

121. O'Connor, *Hume on Religion*, 23–24.

122. *DNR* 2; emphasis added.

former [the being] ... is unquestionable and self-evident," but in our understanding, "we have no experience of divine attributes and operations"—since the divine *nature* is "adorably mysterious and incomprehensible."[123] This discussion continues throughout *DNR*, and it leads Cleanthes, in part 4, to suggest that the

> Deity, I can readily allow, possesses many powers and attributes of which we can have no comprehension. But, if our ideas, so far as they go, be not just and adequate and correspondent to his real nature, I know not what there is in this subject worth insisting on. Is the name, without any meaning, of such mighty importance? Or how do you *mystics*, who maintain the absolute incomprehensibility of the Deity, differ from skeptics or atheists, who assert that the first cause of all is unknown and unintelligible?[124]

While the context here is about the design argument, the discussion seems to presuppose, in some sense, that God has not provided enough evidence of himself with respect to his nature, which appears to irk Cleanthes, for what this distinction actually leads to is either skepticism or atheism. As David O'Connor writes on this point, "As Cleanthes sees it, Demea's distinction leads to skepticism or atheism," ultimately "robbing religion of all content."[125] William Lad Sessions explains that "Demea is not only a 'mystic' with an incomprehensible God, he is also an 'atheist' who denies the existence of any deity whom humans can conceive, discuss, and worship."[126] (Does Demea represent Hume himself more often than thought?[127]) I believe it is fair to interpret this distinction between being and nature as a nascent form of PDH.

Moreover, having discussed the design argument (pts. 4–5), naturalism and skepticism (pts. 6–8), and the problem of evil (pts. 10–11), Hume (through Philo) closes with some final thoughts on the entire project of natural theology in part 12, which throughout the *DNR* has been found wanting. Presumably, if natural theology (including the design argument)

---

123. *DNR* 13–15; emphasis added.
124. *DNR* 28; emphasis in original.
125. O'Connor, *Hume on Religion*, 97.
126. Sessions, *Reading Hume's Dialogues*, 88.
127. Terence Penelhum writes, "The most widely held view of Hume ... has been that he is a deliberate secularizer: that he seeks to persuade us that there are no good reasons to hold religious beliefs" (*Themes in Hume*, 204). See also Reich, *Hume's Religious Naturalism*, 42–43; Yoder, *Hume on God*.

is obscure and "somewhat ambiguous," which is what I take Hume to be proposing, then, as Philo says,

> the most natural sentiment which a well-disposed mind will feel on this occasion is a longing desire and expectation that heaven would be pleased to dissipate, at least alleviate, this profound ignorance by affording some more particular revelation to mankind, and making discoveries of the nature, attributes, and operations of the divine object of our faith. A person, seasoned with a just sense of the imperfections of natural reason, will fly to revealed truth with the greatest avidity.[128]

Here Hume (through Philo) appears to claim that since natural theology is unconvincing,[129] then *revealed* religion, and a little more of it, is needed to alleviate human ignorance of God. It is my estimation, however, that Hume intentionally leaves the question of the viability of revealed religion vague so as to suggest that even it, like natural theology, is lacking. Perhaps we can go a step further. Though Hume is not explicitly endorsing PDH, and while there is debate about his religious persuasion, one possible analysis of part 12 is this: if there were *more* revelation from God, then we would have better grounds for theistic belief. Coupled with the *being/nature* distinction, and perhaps *DNR* as a whole, we have in Hume a problem of divine hiddenness of sorts.

Consider another hint at the presence of PDH in Hume's writings. If *DNR* finds the project of natural theology wanting, then it seems that Hume, in J. C. A. Gaskin's words, leaves his interpreters with this question: "Why does anyone believe in God or gods?"[130] Perhaps an answer is found in Hume's *Natural History of Religion*. "The belief of invisible, intelligent power," writes Hume,

> has been very generally diffused over the human race, in all places and in all ages; but it has never perhaps been so universal as to admit of no exception, nor has it been, in any degree, uniform in the ideas, which it has suggested. *Some nations have been discovered, who entertained no sentiments of Religion,* if travellers and historians may be credited; and no two nations, and scare any two men, have ever agreed precisely in the same sentiments. . . . It would appear, therefore, that this

---

128. *DNR* 89; emphasis added.
129. Penelhum, "Hume's Criticisms."
130. Gaskin, "Hume on Religion," 318–19. Gaskin asks in light of Hume's critique of natural theology: "Why is it that religious belief persists, even among well-informed people?" (336).

> preconception springs not from an original instinct or primary impression of nature, such as gives rise to self-love, affection between the sexes, love of progeny, gratitude, resentment; since every instinct of this kind has been found absolutely universal in all nations and ages, and has always a precise determinate object, which it inflexibly pursues.[131]

Commenting on this passage, Terence Penelhum writes:

> The causes that actually generate religion in human beings, then, are *environmental* rather than *inborn*, and with luck we may escape them by living in a society where the influences on us are exclusively secular ones.[132]

And just as John Calvin argued that God has implanted in all persons a *sensus divinitatis*—implying widespread, universal (and inborn) belief in God—one may take Hume to be denying such a claim.[133] As Gaskin notes, the evidence for natural religious belief, according to Hume, is problematic and indefinite.[134] "Despite the failure to identify belief in the Divine as a genuine natural belief," Gaskin goes on, "modern philosophical theology is marked with attempts to employ some notion of natural belief for *apologetic purposes*."[135] One of the "apologetic purposes" is what Gaskin calls "the American school of 'Basic Belief Apologists,' associated with Alvin Plantinga."[136] In the next two chapters, I revisit Plantinga's construal of basic theistic belief.

1.4.4 Alexander Campbell (1788–1866)

A skilled theologian, debater, and rhetorician, Alexander Campbell was an important figure in America's restorationist movement.[137] Seeking to

---

131. Hume, *Natural History of Religion*, 21; emphasis in original.

132. Penelhum, *David Hume*, 188; emphasis added. See also Gaskin, "Hume on Religion," 316–19. For a different perspective, see Reich, *Hume's Religious Naturalism*.

133. For an argument that Hume was, in fact, indirectly challenging something like Calvin's conception of the *sensus divinitatis*, see Penelhum, who writes that Hume "is trying to answer Calvin, who was the primary source of the Scottish religious upbringing from which he had extricated himself" ("Hume and Religion," 139).

134. Gaskin, "Hume on Religion," 336. See also David Fate Norton, who writes, "The widespread but not universal belief in invisible and intelligent power can be traced to derivative and easily perverted principles of our nature" ("Hume, David," 403).

135. Gaskin, "Hume on Religion," 340; emphasis in original.

136. Gaskin, "Hume on Religion," 339–40.

137. Noll, "Foreword"; Cherok, *Debating for God*.

restore Christianity to its New Testament roots, Campbell was confident in his ability to discern the simple message of Scripture. Though perhaps not as important a figure as his European counterparts, what follows is a brief exposition of Campbell's insights into PDH.[138]

Unconvinced by various arguments for atheism, Campbell claims that he has never "seen or heard a rational, philosophic, or logical argument in favor of any form of skepticism or infidelity."[139] He explains that all of humanity has "an idea of God," and that this idea is

> of a Creator, a being who has produced in the whole material universe by the bare exhibition of physical creative power. This *idea*, we contend, can have no archetype in nature, because we have never seen anything produced out of nothing. But we have the *idea* of the existence of this creative power.

Moreover, "if we appeal to traditionary or historic evidence," writes Campbell, "we shall find that all nations had originally some ideas of the existence of a Great First Cause."[140] The implication of this, then, is that

> to form ideas concerning spiritual things, imagination has to travel out of her province. To form the very idea of a God, she must transcend the visible material world. . . . I therefore conceive that it develops [or depends] upon [the opposition to Christianity] . . . to show that we possess those powers which can enable us to reason from sensible material objects up to spiritual, immaterial existences. *It behooves him* [the opposition to Christianity] *to show that ignorant men, or men in the rudest ages of the world, were competent to invent and establish religion.*[141]

If the opposition cannot shoulder this burden, then what follows, Campbell thinks, is this:

> If it be so that man is destitute of power to create something out of nothing, or to originate the fundamental ideas and terms found in all religions—if he cannot clear up this matter, how

---

138. For specific content on Campbell and PDH, I depend mostly on a leading Campbell scholar, Clanton, *Philosophy of Religion*, chapter 4, which is an entire chapter on the problems of evil and divine hiddenness. See also Wiebe, "Letters to a Skeptic."

139. W. A. Morris, *Writings of Alexander Campbell*, 167.

140. W. A. Morris, *Writings of Alexander Campbell*, 48; emphasis in original.

141. W. A. Morris, *Writings of Alexander Campbell*, 48; emphasis in original.

can he affirm that all religion is founded upon the ignorance of man?[142]

Campbell suggests that there is within humanity an idea of God, particularly of God as the cause of the universe.[143] The nonbeliever, Campbell suggests, owes an account of the *origin* of such an idea of God, an account that unfortunately she cannot, in fact, properly explain; thus what follows, Campbell thinks, is that such an idea must have come from *God* himself and that, hence, God must exist. J. Caleb Clanton, a recent Campbell commentator, maintains, however, that this is not a traditional natural theological argument but is rather best conceived as a "revealed-idea argument" for God's existence. "In short," Clanton explains,

> Campbell argues that we have an *idea* of God, the original acquisition of which we cannot explain except by an appeal to revelation from God himself. In Campbell's view, the original idea of God is not innate, nor do we receive it from sensation or reflection, nor could we have invented it, given the limits of our imagination. By elimination, then, the only possible cause of the original idea is divine revelation. Thus, God exists.[144]

As Clanton notes above, humanity's idea of God has its origin in divine revelation; consequently, it must have been given by the Creator.

Why is it then, according to Campbell, that God's existence is hidden? Or, to quote Campbell, why does God not "speak in all the languages of the world in the same instant of time, and inform all nations, *viva voce*, that the contents of the New Testament were worthy of universal acceptance"?[145] One answer, Campbell suggests, is because

> all excellency in faith would have been destroyed. . . . While a small proportion of the evidence [that we actually have] is sufficient for some, it is all necessary for others; and those who do not believe upon the whole of it and have one objection remaining the whole is heard and examined, that which would remove this one objection would destroy every virtue and excellency properly belonging to faith. *Faith built upon evidence greater*

---

142. Robert Owen and Alexander Campbell, *Evidences of Christianity*, quoted in Clanton, "Alexander Campbell's Revealed-Idea Argument," 106–7.

143. Eames, *Philosophy of Alexander Campbell*, 34.

144. Clanton, *Philosophy of Religion*, 38; emphasis added. "Campbell's revealed-idea argument is similar to Calvin's conception of the *sensus divinitatis*; but this revealed-idea is not given *by* a *sensus divinitatis*" (J. Caleb Clanton, email to author, c. early 2015).

145. As quoted in Clanton, "Alexander Campbell," 192.

THE PROBLEM OF DIVINE HIDDENNESS 35

than the whole amount divinely vouchsafed, would have nothing moral about it; it would be as *unavoidable* as the motions of the mill wheel under a powerful head of water, or as the waving tops of pines beneath a whirlwind.[146]

Campbell here appears to presuppose that, on the one hand, humanity already has enough evidence of God's existence, but that, on the other hand, God will not provide *more* than what is given (that which is "divinely vouchsafed"), since the human race would be overpowered and the decision to choose God would be "unavoidable." The concept of "unavoidable" evidence, Clanton explains, is what might be called "superevidence"—a *greater* amount of evidence for God's existence than the *sufficient* evidence which is already provided. He notes that, on Campbell's view, God "would actually want to withhold a certain amount of evidence of his existence—the difference between superevidence and the amount of evidence we actually have—in order to preserve the moral significance of believing in God's existence."[147]

But if the current evidence provided *is* enough (yet given in such a way that respects humanity's moral sensibilities), then why, in Campbell's thinking, is there nonbelief in God? I am once more indebted to Clanton's insights, wherein he argues that (according to Campbell) although there are, in fact, well-informed and honest nonbelievers, still a person can blind or prejudice *herself* to the available evidence for God;[148] what drives one's appraisal of evidence in general, and for God in particular, is one's *epistemic orientation*; if one's epistemic orientation is faulty, then one may evaluate the evidence for God only to find it deficient. "But, in Campbell's view," explains Clanton,

> the problem is wrapped up in how her *will* affects her epistemic orientation and how that orientation, in turn, affects her assessment of the evidence; the problem is not that the *evidence* is lacking.[149]

Although somewhat underdeveloped, Campbell's theology makes room for how *sin* and its effects can distort one's cognitive faculties; in this vein, "Campbell's view," Clanton argues, "is somewhat similar to the view developed most thoroughly by *reformed epistemologists such as Alvin*

---

146. As quoted in Clanton, *Philosophy of Religion*, 108; emphasis added.
147. Clanton, *Philosophy of Religion*, 109.
148. Clanton, *Philosophy of Religion*, 110.
149. Clanton, *Philosophy of Religion*, 112–13; emphasis added.

Plantinga,"[150] sin being an important theological locus to which I return in later chapters.

Last, Campbell explains that, in order to "hear" or to "perceive" the evidence for God rightly, a person must not only withdraw "from the pride, covetousness, and false ambition from the love of the world," but also must come

> within the circle, the circumference of which is unfeigned humility, and the center of which is God himself—*the voice of God is distinctly heard and clearly understood*. All within the circle are taught of God; all without it are under the influence of the wicked one. "God resisteth the proud, but he giveth grace to the humble."[151]

If one is to be "within the circle"—where, presumably, the voice of God is clearly heard and understood—then one must nurture one's own epistemic and moral sensibilities. For, as Clanton says, "there are some free and morally significant choices involved in orienting oneself to the evidence of God's existence."[152]

1.4.5 Søren Kierkegaard (1813–1855)

Though at times difficult to interpret, the Danish philosopher Søren Kierkegaard has important contributions to PDH.[153] "How can I demonstrate God's existence," he writes, "from such an arrangement of things? Even if I began, I would never finish."[154] Kierkegaard's statement concerning the "arrangement of things" means the entirety of human experience. "In short," he goes on,

> to demonstrate the existence of someone who already exists is the most shameless assault. It is an attempt to make him ludicrous. The trouble is that one does not even suspect this, that in dead seriousness one even regards it as a godly undertaking. How could it occur to anyone to demonstrate that God exists unless one has already allowed himself to ignore him?

---

150. Clanton, "Alexander Campbell," 201; emphasis in original.

151. Campbell, "Letters to Humphrey Marshal," 514; emphasis added.

152. Clanton, "Alexander Campbell," 202. I thank J. Caleb Clanton of Lipscomb University for commenting on an earlier draft covering Campbell.

153. For general content on Kierkegaard, I am helped by C. S. Evans, *Kierkegaard*.

154. C. S. Evans, *Kierkegaard*, 75.

On the one hand, when Kierkegaard explains that God "already exists," perhaps the implication, in some sense, is that God's existence is already as clear as it could be; but on the other hand a

> king's existence is demonstrated by way of *subjection* and submissiveness. Do you want to try and demonstrate that the king exists? Will you do so by offering a string of proofs, a series of arguments? No. If you are serious, you will demonstrate the king's existence by your *submission*, by the way you live. And so it is with demonstrating God's existence. It is accomplished not by proofs but *by worship*.[155]

Knowledge of God is intimately interwoven with submission and subjection to God. Commenting on this passage, C. Stephen Evans suggests that a possible interpretation of Kierkegaard here is to say that God "is or can be evident to human beings but not to anyone and everyone; to become aware of God a person must have or acquire a certain kind of spiritual sensitivity," what Kierkegaard calls "inwardness" or "subjectivity."[156] And this requires risk. As Kierkegaard says:

> Without risk there is no faith. Faith is precisely the contradiction between the infinite passion of the individual's inwardness and the objective uncertainty. If I am capable of grasping God objectively, I do not believe, but precisely because I cannot do this I must believe. If I wish to preserve myself in faith I must constantly be intent upon holding fast the objective uncertainty, so as to remain out upon the deep, over seventy thousand fathoms of water, still preserving my faith.[157]

Faith in God, according to Kierkegaard, is subjective—that is, faith ought "to be the result of a *subjective* decision to believe."[158] Couple this with Kierkegaard's further advice that since God himself is of infinite value then one ought in turn to seek, or to strive, for God with an infinite passion. An *objective* search for God, say through natural theology, scientific inquiry, or by the gathering of other evidence, is dispassionate; the person of *passionate*

---

155. "Folly of Trying to Prove God's Existence," in Kierkegaard, *Provocations*, 75–76; emphasis added.

156. C. S. Evans, "Can God Be Hidden," 243.

157. Kierkegaard, *Concluding Unscientific Postscript*, as quoted in Cahn, *Classics of Western Philosophy*, 1114. Robert McKim expounds upon this excerpt (*Religious Ambiguity*, 17–18).

158. Kinghorn, *Decision of Faith*, 76; emphasis added.

conviction, conversely, will seek God subjectively and is willing, as M. Jamie Ferreira puts it, to risk everything.[159]

Suppose we could put the question "Why does God not give us *objective* revelation of himself?" to Kierkegaard. What would he say? According to Ferreira, it is not that an "objective revelation of God by God would be misleading—the problem is that it would not be God revealing *Godself*."[160] To know God, explained above, requires an appropriate spiritual sensitivity: "inwardness" or "subjectivity." Similarly, one reason why God does not merely write in the sky "Here I am; repent and believe" (to follow Evans's thinking on Kierkegaard) is because such divine behavior may be tantamount to deception, and a person would not come to know God "*as* God really is."[161] Evans elaborates, with respect to Kierkegaard and PDH, by saying that "subjectivity" does not mean that "God literally comes into existence when a person is subjectively developed," but rather that Kierkegaard is "speaking phenomenologically." For "when a human being is not spiritually attuned, God is not experienced as real, and in a sense God is not real for that person."[162] Finally, Evans has recently argued that a modern-day thinker whose ideas are comparable to Kierkegaard on subjectivity can be found in Alvin Plantinga's conception of properly basic belief in God.[163]

1.4.6 Friedrich Nietzsche (1844–1900)

Previously quoted in this chapter's introduction, the German philosopher Friedrich Nietzsche seems to have sowed seeds, as Schellenberg indicates, concerning PDH.[164] "A god who is all-knowing and all-powerful," Nietzsche insists,

> and who does not even make sure his creatures understand his intention—could that be a god of goodness? Who allows creatures' doubts and uncertainties to persist, for thousands of years, as though the salvation of mankind were unaffected by them, or

---

159. See Ferreira, "Kierkegaardian View," 176.

160. Ferreira, "Kierkegaardian View," 177; emphasis in original.

161. C. S. Evans, "Can God Be Hidden," 244; emphasis in original. See also C. S. Evans, "Relevance of Historical Evidence." For another perspective on Kierkegaard and divine hiddenness, see Kline, "Absolute Action."

162. C. S. Evans, "Can God Be Hidden," 244.

163. See chapters 10–11 in C. S. Evans, *Kierkegaard on Faith*. I make use of these chapters in my fifth chapter.

164. For general content on Nietzsche, I am helped by Gemes and Richardson, "Introduction."

who, on the other hand, holds the prospect of frightful consequences if any mistake is made as to the nature of truth? Would he not be a cruel god if he possessed the truth and could behold mankind miserably tormenting itself over that truth? But perhaps he is a god of goodness notwithstanding and merely could not express himself more clearly! Did he perhaps lack the intelligence to do so? Or the eloquence? So much the worse, for then he was perhaps also in error as to that which he calls the "truth," and is himself not so very far from being the "poor deluded devil."[165]

First, Nietzsche seems to explain that God, if he exists, goes to great lengths to make himself unavailable—so much for an all-knowing, all-powerful God. Second, he announces, although somewhat satirically, that perhaps God—the "poor deluded devil"—is not *able* to express himself more clearly (recall from above his "Parable of the Madman," where Nietzsche jests, "Did he [God] lose his way like a child? . . . *Or is he hiding*? Is he afraid of us? Has he gone on a voyage?"). Further, the problem of divine hiddenness, for some persons, can even be intensified and exacerbated, since many, Nietzsche argues, "search for God with apparent sincerity but come away feeling unfilled."[166] Whereas Pascal claims that a genuine search, devoid of pride, can yield a relationship with God, Nietzsche here suggests otherwise. For "on the 'hidden God,'" Nietzsche writes of Pascal,

> and on the reasons for keeping himself thus hidden and never emerging more than half-way in to the light of speech, no one has been more eloquent than Pascal—a sign that he was never able to calm his mind on this matter: but his voice rings confidently as if he had at one time sat behind the curtain with this hidden god. He sensed a piece of immortality in the "*deus absconditus*" and was very fearful and ashamed of admitting it to himself: and thus, like one who is afraid, he talked as loudly as he could.[167]

Pascal's comments on how pride, and therefore sin, can obscure one to God's presence would not likely satisfy Nietzsche's frustration, since "Christianity," Nietzsche claims,

> has sided with everything weak, low, and botched; it has made an ideal out of antagonism towards all the self-preservative instincts of a strong life: it has corrupted even the reason of

165. Nietzsche, *Daybreak*, 89–90.
166. Nietzsche, *Daybreak*, 90.
167. Nietzsche, *Daybreak*, 91.

the strongest intellects, by teaching that the highest values of intellectuality are *sinful*, misleading and full of temptations. The most lamentable example of this was the corruption of Pascal, who believed in the *perversion of his reason* through *original sin*, whereas it had only been perverted by his Christianity.[168]

I leave it to Nietzsche's interpreters to decide if he misrepresented Pascal on PDH.[169] Nevertheless, Nietzsche, like Hume, seems attentive to the hiddenness problem, a problem that he appears to think can provide reasons for thinking that there is no God.

1.4.7 Historical Overview Conclusion

The above historical background is now complete, and while other figures could have been discussed, such as Jonathan Edwards or St. John of the Cross,[170] my sample serves to confirm Schellenberg's earlier comment that PDH is an aged problem (particularly in Hume's and Nietzsche's writings), although I believe that my survey above brings to light at least two unique perspectives. First, while each of the Christian thinkers—Pascal, Butler, Campbell, and Kierkegaard—comes to their own distinctive conclusions, it may be said that they all share common ground in that, for them, PDH is not a problem purely or solely about the evidence for or against God's existence; there may be more to one's awareness or experience or knowledge of God than the simple weighing or combing of evidence (e.g., the traditional arguments from natural theology, etc.). Perhaps it is fair to generalize that the theists agree that one's "will" can color how one perceives, or fails to perceive, God (Butler may be the exception); it can also be summarized further that their evaluations of PDH are not only philosophical but are *theological* in nature (e.g., in terms of the doctrine of sin, etc.). This is an important point to which I return in my second chapter.

Second, the overview bolsters the definition of PDH offered earlier, which is epistemic in nature, and it also validates the importance of my proposed research question. For I explained above, in the exposition of Campbell and Kierkegaard (and, somewhat ironically, in Hume), the relevance of Plantinga's Reformed epistemology—a Christian theistic perspective—to the problem, and this will permit me in the subsequent chapter to show

---

168. Nietzsche, *Antichrist*, 6; emphasis added.
169. See Williams, *Shadow of the Antichrist*, 137–42.
170. For instance, Wainwright, "Jonathan Edwards and Hiddenness"; Garcia, "St. John of the Cross"; Coakley, "Divine Hiddenness or Dark Intimacy?" For a perspective on Thomas Aquinas and divine hiddenness, see Di Ceglio, "Christian Belief."

how a Plantingean approach to PDH is applicable to, and significant for, the contemporary discussion of divine hiddenness.

1.5 CONCLUSION

This chapter has considered prolegomena issues concerning PDH. I first explained what PDH is not by analyzing various divine attributes as well as by examining Luther and Barth's conception of divine hiddenness; I also discussed the presumption of atheism (described by Antony Flew) and its putative relationship to PDH. Next, PDH was defined to be an epistemic problem: *If God exists, then his existence would be more obvious*, out of which came the research question (the main question to be answered in this project): *Why, if God exists, is his existence not more obvious?* It was then said that I will offer a defense for PDH, which will attempt to meet two desiderata or conditions:

(i*) Develop a specifically Christian account describing why, if God exists, his existence is not more obvious.

(ii) Show that this description is true for all we know.

This in turn led me to formulate my thesis statement that Plantinga's A/C models for how Christian belief may have warrant can be utilized as a defense to explain why, if God exists, his existence is not more obvious. Reasons were listed for how my thesis, if successful, could have scholarly impact. In all of this, however, my claim has been to examine PDH as an exercise in Christian philosophy and theology.

Third, a historical overview of PDH was provided; major figures in Western thought were surveyed, including Pascal, Butler, Hume, Kierkegaard, Campbell, and Nietzsche, all of whom have contemplated, even if in some embryonic form, the hiddenness problem. I emphasized those thinkers whose contribution is germane to my research question and thesis, seeking to draw upon the overview's relevant epistemic and theological themes in later chapters.

What light can be thrown on the present-day conversation regarding the hiddenness problem? What, if anything, can be said afresh? Among other things, I get clear on these sorts of questions in chapter 2, to which I shall now turn.

2.

The Problem of Divine Hiddenness in Contemporary Perspective

2.1 INTRODUCTION

CHAPTER 1 WAS CONCERNED with prolegomena matters regarding the problem of divine hiddenness (PDH); I clarified what the problem is *not*, as well as what it *is*, offering also a historical overview. PDH was defined, in short, to be an epistemic problem: *If God exists, then his existence would be more obvious*. This in turn sparked the research question that this project will attempt to answer: *Why, if God exists, is his existence not more obvious?* I followed Peter van Inwagen when he explains that theists, with respect to PDH, can tell "stories" that can take the form of either a defense or a theodicy. I chose the former mode, saying further that my defense, which aims not at mere logical but rather at *epistemic* possibility, will attempt to satisfy two desiderata; namely, that I will

(i*) Develop a specifically Christian account describing why, if God exists, his existence is not more obvious.

(ii) Show that this description is true for all we know.

It was then argued that Christians have available a Reformed epistemic story, taken from *Warranted Christian Belief* (*WCB*), which can both answer the research question and meet the mentioned desiderata. I then drafted my thesis statement that *Plantinga's Aquinas/Calvin (A/C) models for how*

Christian belief may have warrant can be utilized as a defense to explain why, if God exists, his existence is not more obvious.[1]

This chapter seeks to build upon the first chapter's foundation, thereby demonstrating how PDH has taken shape in light of (approximately) two decades of analytic-philosophical attention. In doing so, I provide a *contemporary* literature review of PDH consisting of two parts, the overarching purpose of which is to validate my defense's perceived place in current scholarship. First, in part 1, I explain how PDH has been used as a formal argument against God's existence. To do this, I exposit J. L. Schellenberg's original yet still much-discussed five-premised atheistic argument from reasonable nonbelief given in *Divine Hiddenness and Human Reason* (first published in 1993). Next, I allow the argument's two most important premises to act as a guide through the relevant literature, intentionally highlighting notable theistic responses. Finally, having emphasized these notable theistic responses, I explain in part 1's conclusion that a Plantingean Reformed epistemic approach to PDH is largely absent from the present-day literature, saying how it can be included.

Second, in part 2, I continue the literature review by examining PDH's relationship to the problem of evil (hereafter POE). Many contemporary philosophers and theologians—perhaps most—suggest that there is a tight relationship between POE and PDH. I spell out *similarity* as well as *dissimilarity* between the two, arguing in part 2's conclusion that my Reformed epistemic defense has the resources to address some of the perceived dissimilarity.

Third, having reviewed the literature and having noted how my defense is applicable to the current analytic-philosophical PDH debate, I then *combine* part 1 and part 2's conclusions, which will position me to describe how I will exposit and defend my thesis statement in chapters 3 through 5. Finally, concluding remarks will be made.

2.2 LITERATURE REVIEW PART 1: SCHELLENBERG'S 1993 ARGUMENT: EXPOSITION, THEISTIC OBJECTIONS, AND THE RELEVANCE OF MY THESIS

While others in the contemporary literature have used PDH to justify nonbelief,[2] it is Schellenberg's work that is the most detailed and compre-

---

1. For more on the definition, research question, defense desiderata, and thesis statement, see chapter 1.

2. Examples include Drange, *Nonbelief and Evil*; "Nonbelief vs. Lack of Evidence"; Maitzen, "Divine Hiddenness and Demographics"; see Schellenberg, "Divine Hiddenness," where he includes a helpful bibliography.

hensive, all of which began with his 1993 publication *DHHR*. There he developed his highly influential and much discussed five-premised argument for atheism. Daniel Howard-Snyder explains—in a recent symposium dedicated to various themes from Schellenberg—that *DHHR*

> set the agenda for the next two decades on the so-called "problem of divine hiddenness," or "the problem of inculpable nonbelief" as it is called by some, and it continues to do so today, with hundreds of pages published in the journals and elsewhere in response to it.[3]

Although Schellenberg's own work has matured since 1993,[4] the initial argument for atheism presented in *DHHR* is still extensively discussed in the contemporary literature, showing little signs of cessation.[5] The argument is as follows:

1. If there is a God, he is perfectly loving. [prem.; def.]
2. If a perfectly loving God exists, reasonable nonbelief does not occur. [prem.]
3. Reasonable nonbelief occurs. [prem.]
4. No perfectly loving God exists. [from (2), (3); *modus tollens*]
5. There is no God. [from (1), (4)][6]

Let me (briefly) explore each premise. Schellenberg explains, in the introduction to *DHHR*, that premise (1) is uncontroversial; traditional theists will not wish to deny it. The more sensitive premises, he notes, are (2) and (3). Premise (2) states that if the loving God of traditional theism exists,

---

3. Howard-Snyder, "Introduction." Schellenberg, "My Stance"; "Replies to My Colleagues."

4. Books, or contributions to books, include (but are not limited to): Schellenberg, "What Hiddenness of God Reveals"; "Divine Hiddenness Justifies Atheism"; "Reply to Moser"; *Prolegomena*; *Wisdom to Doubt*; *Will to Imagine*. Journal articles include (but are not limited to): "Response to Howard-Snyder"; "Hiddenness Argument Revisited (I)"; "Hiddenness Argument Revisited (II)"; "Hiddenness Problem"; "Divine Hiddenness: Part 1."

5. To take just a sample, consider the following articles, all of which analyze the 1993 argument: Lovering, "Divine Hiddenness"; Poston and Dougherty, "Divine Hiddenness"; McBrayer and Swenson, "Scepticism"; Azadegan, "Divine Hiddenness"; Brown, "Incarnation and Divine Hiddenness"; Rea, "Hiddenness and Transcendence."

6. *DHHR* 83. Schellenberg notes that this is "the first full-dress presentation of a hiddenness argument for atheism" (vii). A different form of the argument appears in his *Wisdom to Doubt*, 204–6, which Terence Cuneo has recently critically examined ("Another Look").

then he would not allow reasonable nonbelief, which occurs "if and only if it is not the result of culpable actions or omissions on the part of the subject."[7]

For presumably, if God is perfectly loving, one then has good reasons to think, so the argument goes, that God would do whatever it takes, whenever possible, to be in a relationship with those persons who desire to reciprocate. Schellenberg argues that there are grounds to suppose that a loving God would "put his existence beyond reasonable nonbelief," since "it is possible for God to prevent it [reasonable nonbelief]."[8] To clear up misunderstandings of premise (2), Schellenberg, in the 2006 preface to the original 1993 argument, writes

> that readers should beware of . . . conflating what my argument claims—that if God exists, reasonable nonbelief does not occur [premise (2)]—with "If God exists, reasonable nonbelievers receive evidence sufficient for belief." What the former claim says is that if God exists, there is *never* a time when someone inculpably fails to believe (belief is made available as soon as there is a capacity for relationship with God). In other words, if there is a God, *there are no reasonable nonbelievers about who may be treated in the imagined fashion.*[9]

However, premise (3) maintains that (given divine hiddenness) reasonable nonbelief *does*, in fact, occur. Schellenberg argues further:

> The claim that reasonable nonbelief occurs is therefore the claim that the nonbelief of at any rate some nonbelievers is not the consequence of their culpable actions or omissions—that it arises through no fault of their own and so they are not in any sense to blame for it.[10]

Thus, premise (2)'s consequent, that reasonable nonbelief does not occur, is false. Therefore, by *modus tollens*, from (2) and (3), there is no perfectly loving God (4). And, from (1) and (4), there is thus no God at all (5). As he explains, the entire argument hinges on (2), for "if it is true," then the argument is "sound."[11] Moreover, it is important to note that Schellenberg's argument here is not, technically speaking, an argument from *divine*

---

7. *DHHR* 3n2.
8. *DHHR* 3.
9. *DHHR* ix; emphasis in original.
10. *DHHR* 59. Schellenberg writes further that "S has a rational belief that p if and only if his evidence, inductive standards, and belief to p's probability on the evidence have been, in his own view, at the time, adequately investigated" (61).
11. *DHHR* 84.

hiddenness; it is rather, as he notes in a more recent work, an argument from *reasonable nonbelief*.[12] Nonetheless, "all I seek to show," he writes, "is that we might expect God's *existence* to be more obvious."[13] Now, the conclusion does follow from the premises; but are the premises (specifically [2] and [3]) *true*? I describe various theistic attempts to show otherwise below.

Let me briefly comment on the *current* status of Schellenberg's scholarship. After twenty years (or so) of refinement, he explains that his "stance in philosophy of religion has evolved considerably." He is now an "atheist but not a metaphysical naturalist." Neither is he an agnostic but rather an advocate of ultimism, the view "which invites no more than doubt."[14] In a newer essay, he describes ultimism as that "which says only that there is a metaphysically, axiologically, and soteriologically ultimate reality of *some* kind"—either personal or impersonal; he argues for the latter.[15] Supportive of "non-doxastic imaginative faith," he still stands by his argument for atheism in *DHHR* but he has now created a "new way of being religious," entitled "sceptical religion."[16] He explains:

> Uncertainty is central in all of this [i.e., sceptical religion] (perhaps because it is central in me). One might say I have sought to exploit its creative potential. Just as the uncertainty about theism we call the hiddenness of God is only the starting point for a new proof of atheism, so the more general uncertainty of religious scepticism is only the starting point for a path leading back to religion—though a somewhat different brand of religion than any extant! Utilizing the idea of non-doxastic faith and an understanding of the propositional heart of religion broader than most, reason propels us through a novel forward-looking version of religious scepticism to a form of religion that can exist only on the other side: sceptical religion.[17]

---

12. Schellenberg, *Hiddenness Argument*. Schellenberg writes there that he had trouble finding a name for *DHHR* but that "'hiddenness' kept cropping up and I kept reminding my editor that a problem of divine hiddenness could really literally exist only for people who believed in God." He goes on to explain that it was only when he phoned his undergraduate mentor Terence Penelhum that the title for *DHHR* came to be. Indeed, "human reason would here *test* the notion that a God would be hidden in such a way as to make nonbelief inculpable" (15; emphasis in original).

13. *DHHR* 4; emphasis in original. See also 5–6.

14. Schellenberg, "My Stance," 144.

15. Schellenberg, "Divine Hiddenness and Human Philosophy," 32.

16. Schellenberg, "My Stance," 143.

17. Schellenberg, "My Stance," 143–44. See also his *Evolutionary Religion* where he further discusses "sceptical religion."

Still, philosophers and theologians continue to grapple with the enduring importance of the 1993 argument.[18] Therefore, it is to my advantage, while not ignoring Schellenberg's work since 1993, to limit the literature review here, in part 1, to the argument presented in *DHHR*.[19] Thus I use *DHHR*'s two most controversial premises ([2] and [3]) as an outline for analyzing PDH in the contemporary literature, demonstrating (in part 1's conclusion) my thesis's relevance to the scholarly discussion in general as well as to already-established theistic responses in particular. There have been two main theistic objections to the 1993 argument: efforts to challenge premise (2) and efforts to challenge premise (3), referred to hereafter as "type-2 objections" and "type-3 objections" respectively.[20]

2.2.1 Type-2 Objections

Premise (2): *If a perfectly loving God exists, reasonable nonbelief does not occur.* Assume that accepting premise (1) is necessary for theists. Attempts have been made, however, to object to premise (2)—hence "type-2 objections." Most of these, roughly stated, describe a state of affairs in which God's existence is in some sense hidden *and* in which God may have sufficient reasons for permitting at least some reasonable (or inculpable) nonbelief.[21] Type-2 objections can be divided, so I think, into four subcategories: a free

---

18. I thank J. L. Schellenberg for reading an earlier version of this short overview concerning his work.

19. I mention this because, in personal correspondence, Schellenberg states that should one desire to engage the most representative Schellenbergian work, then one would need to go beyond what is found in *DHHR*, including for instance his recent trilogy (*Prolegomena*; *Wisdom to Doubt*; *Will to Imagine*) as well as "Divine Hiddenness and Human Philosophy" (email to author, Feb. 5, 2015). However, my justification for not directly engaging these sources in part 1 of my literature review is twofold: (1) this is not a book *about* Schellenberg; (2) the 1993 argument from *DHHR* is, again, still *widely* discussed among philosophers.

20. A caveat: not every author described below is *directly* challenging Schellenberg's 1993 argument; this is the reason why the more generic label "type-2" or "type-3 objector" was chosen instead of "premise-2" or "premise-3 objectors." Nonetheless, the authors chosen who do not directly challenge the 1993 argument are included because they either foreshadow or mimic the respective objection.

21. Note, for instance, the theist Chad Meister's comments, which capture my definition when Meister writes that "divine elusiveness *should be expected given Christian theism*. God is not a human person, so we should not expect to experience him in that way" ("Evil and the Hiddenness," 149; emphasis added). Then, regarding inculpable nonbelief, he writes, "I think there are also (many?) cases of reasonable and morally nonculpable nonbelief" ("Evil and the Hiddenness," 142).

will/coercion objection, the (closely related) improper response objection, a filial objection, and (finally) doxastic responses.

First, there is a free will/coercion objection. Consider Michael Murray's suggestion that God's hiddenness may be essential to preserve human freedom. For if God were more obvious, then he might coerce humans into believing in him. God, however, is unlike a moral patrolman. "For if we knew that God was there," explains Murray,

> watching over us continuously, [then] all incentives to choose evil would be lost along with our ability to choose between good and evil actions. Our moral free choice would have been eliminated. Some have argued that this need to prevent pervasive coercion is one reason why God must remain hidden, at least to the extent that his existence is not as obvious as a patrol car following us on the highway.[22]

Understanding PDH as a part of the larger POE (discussed more below), Murray's response explains why God is not evident to all persons, for divine hiddenness, he notes, is "the only way to go if God hopes to preserve the ability of free creatures to engage in soul-making."[23] Elsewhere Murray proposes that God simply may be unable to make himself more evident. How evident must God's existence be, one might ask, such that it is accessible but not coercive? "For all we know," Murray writes, "the answer is: *just as accessible as it is*."[24]

A similar but slightly different free will/coercion objection is James Keller's; examining PDH and its relationship to evil, he writes:

> God's relation to the world is such that God cannot *manipulate* its details in such a way as to make the information about Godself any more clear. All communication with human beings that would make these matters more clear would require manipulating details of the world: writing in the sky, "whispering" in people's ears, performing dramatic miracles, or causing each person's conscience to be a direct indication of what God wants done in the situation being considered. *If God's relation to the world is not such that God can perform these manipulations, then the hiddenness of God is what we would expect.*[25]

---

22. Taylor and Murray, "Hiddenness," 374.

23. Murray, "*Deus Absconditus*," 80. Murray explains that his approach challenges premise (2) (66); see also his "Coercion and Hiddenness"; "Why Doesn't God."

24. Murray, "Heaven and Hell," 313–14; emphasis added.

25. Keller, "Hiddenness of God," 22; emphasis added.

Richard Swinburne's approach is comparable. For "if God's existence and intentions," he explains, "became items of evident common knowledge, then our freedom to choose between good and evil would be vastly curtailed."[26] He elaborates with an analogy:

> We will be in the situation of the child in the nursery who knows that mother is looking in at the door, and for whom, in view of the child's desire for mother's approval, the temptation to wrongdoing is simply overborne. We need "epistemic distance" from God in order to have a free choice between good and evil.[27]

The late John Hick also seems to have favored a similar approach; though not replying to Schellenberg's 1993 argument, Hick proposes that God must have epistemic distance from humanity, which in turn preserves one's cognitive and moral freedom: "In order, then, to give them the freedom to come to Him, God creates them at a distance—not a special but an *epistemic distance*."[28] Perhaps John O'Leary-Hawthorn captures this response most succinctly when he explains that, for many Christian traditions, it is essential to God's plan that Christian beliefs are chosen freely:

> While the spectacles of faith may render God's existence manifest, it is important to God's plans for free creatures and the love and devotion he desires that one's vision be less than perfect *prior to* putting those spectacles on.[29]

The free will/coercion objection, as mentioned, argues that God is hidden, at least to some extent, and that God has sufficient reasons for permitting inculpable nonbelief.[30]

The second type-2 objection, closely related to the first, is entitled an "improper response objection," which suggests, as Justin McBrayer and

---

26. Swinburne, *Existence of God*, 293.

27. Swinburne, *Existence of God*, 269. See also his *Revelation*, 95–106. Kevin Kinghorn, commenting on Swinburne's suggestion that abundant theistic evidence would preclude one's proper moral choice, appears to agree with my interpretation of Swinburne in that God has good reasons for withholding overwhelming confirmation of his existence from various persons ("Why Doesn't God," esp. 194–96).

28. Hick, *Evil and the God*, 372,–73; emphasis added. For an interpretation of Hick on PDH, see Trakakis, "Epistemically Distant God?"

29. O'Leary-Hawthorn, "Arguments for Atheism," 130–31. Additionally, Daniel Howard-Snyder notes that perhaps God has prima facie reason to permit or to allow inculpable nonbelief *for a time* ("Argument from Divine Hiddenness," esp. 434–35).

30. For others in the literature who seem to utilize something like a free will/coercion response for PDH, see Dumsday, "Divine Hiddenness, Free-Will"; "Divine Hiddenness as Divine Mercy"; McKim, "Hiddenness of God"; *Religious Ambiguity*.

Philip Swenson write, that "not only is there a *good* that might require God's hiddenness, there might be an *evil* that can only be prevented by his hiddenness."[31] Though not endorsing this objection, the authors argue that it *may* go as follows:

> God wants all persons to be in a certain type of relationship with him, and believing in God [i.e., believing that God exists] is a necessary condition for being in that relationship. However, belief in God is not *sufficient* for being in that type of relationship. Those who believe must take the further step of freely entering into the relationship. Now there are some people who (even if they did believe in God) would not enter into the desired relationship, in fact, their believing that God exists might make the situation worse because they would respond badly if they acquired this belief. Thus, God does not have a reason to ensure that these people learn that he exists, and he may in fact have a reason to refrain from informing them of his existence.[32]

God remains ambiguous since there may be persons who, through no fault of their own, would come to love or to know him *improperly*, resulting in a defective relationship not chosen freely. Perhaps Peter van Inwagen captures the improper response objection most forcefully when he explains that if God were to make himself more apparent, then this could impede his redemptive purposes, for it could *cause* some persons to believe for the wrong, or improper, reasons: "If that is so," notes Van Inwagen, "then the vast array of miracles would not only be useless from God's point of view, *but positively harmful*, a barrier to putting his plan of reconciliation into effect."[33]

Additionally, the Molinist's strategy could also be included under the umbrella of the improper response objection,[34] since God in his middle knowledge, which is his knowledge of counterfactual truths,[35] is said to know how free persons *would* respond had they heard God's plan of redemption, the implication of which is that those who do not respond are just those persons who would not have believed even *if* they had heard.[36]

---

31. McBrayer and Swenson, "Scepticism," 135; emphasis added.
32. McBrayer and Swenson, "Scepticism," 135; emphasis in original.
33. Van Inwagen, *Problem of Evil*, 149; emphasis added.
34. I owe this point to McBrayer and Swenson, "Scepticism," 138.
35. See, for instance, Tucker, "Divine Hiddenness," 269–87. Tucker proposes that PDH *cannot* be solved by way of counterfactuals. For his response to Tucker, see Schellenberg, "Response to Tucker."
36. See, for example, Thune, "Molinist-Style Response."

Hence, God through his middle knowledge just knows who would (or who would not) respond *properly* to his revelation.[37]

The third type-2 objection is what I call a "filial objection," having most commonly come from the work of Paul Moser.[38] Leery of natural theology (particularly in the context of divine hiddenness),[39] Moser explains that there is both *propositional* and *filial* knowledge of God; the former is simply de facto knowledge of God, whereas the latter, however,

> includes our being reconciled to God (at least to some degree) through *volitional* submission to God as Lord and Father, on the basis of conclusive purposively available authoritative evidence. It requires our entrusting ourselves as obedient children to God in grateful love, on the basis of undefeated evidence, thereby becoming transformed in who we are and in how we exist and act, not just in what we believe. We may think of this as *filial attunement* to God.[40]

Mere propositional knowledge is not enough, according to Moser, since perceiving the hidden God must come from one's own volition, a filial response whereby one expresses a willingness to undergo moral transformation, lest she be a spectator guilty of "cognitive idolatry."[41]

Epistemically, Moser is an evidentialist and, for him, God has in fact provided evidence of himself, such as the inner witness of the Holy Spirit, to those who heed his internal instigation (a theme to which I return in my fifth chapter).[42] Yet God will not provide evidence—for instance, extravagant

---

37. Stephen Maitzen, whose work I discuss in chapter 3, argues that the uneven distribution of theistic belief around the world is better explained by naturalism than by theism ("Divine Hiddenness and Demographics"). For a Molinistic response to Maitzen, see Marsh, "Do the Demographics."

38. Moser, "Divine Hiding"; "God Who Hides and Seeks"; *Elusive God*; *Evidence for God*; *Severity of God*. Other relevant works by Moser include: "Gethsemane Epistemology"; "Natural Theology and Evidence." For a critique of Moser on natural theology (applicable to PDH), see Cervantez and Coffman, "Hiddenness, Evidence, and Idolatry."

39. See Moser, "Religious Epistemology Personified."

40. Moser, *Elusive God*, 126; emphasis added.

41. See Moser, "Cognitive Idolatry." See also Michael J. Murray and Michael C. Rea's remarks on Moser on PDH (*Introduction to Philosophy of Religion*, 187–88).

42. See Geivett and Moser, *Testimony of the Spirit*. Moser has his own unique contribution to "evidence" and "evidentialism." He writes that evidence for God's reality "becomes salient to inquirers as they themselves responsively and willingly become evidence of God's reality in receiving and reflecting God's moral character for others," something he calls "personifying evidence for God." This "requires the evidence to be personified in an intentional agent, such as a purposive human, and thereby to be evidence inherently of an intentional agent" (*Evidence for God*, ix). He then applies this theme to divine hiddenness.

miracles or grandiose signs—for the hard of heart.[43] Answering the question "Why isn't God more obvious?," Moser, as a type-2 objector, suggests that the

> question suffers from a misplaced emphasis. It should be redirected. Why do *we* fail to apprehend God's loving reality and presence? Recall . . . [Bertrand] Russell's reply to God: "God, you gave us insufficient evidence." In God's presence, we do well to question *ourselves* rather than blame God. Russell overlooked this lesson, as we do at times. In our willful pride, we often overlook God's supreme ways of humble love. If our hearts are *willingly attuned* to God's self-giving transformative love, God will be obvious enough.[44]

Moser's response affirms the necessity of God's hiddenness, which draws on certain biblical passages in forging its case (e.g., Matt 11:25; Luke 10:21; John 12:37–50; cf. the title of his notable book, *The Elusive God*), and his position suggests that not only can one fail to be aware of God but that some simply are not *prepared* to receive evidence of this hidden God's reality.[45] The implication is that God will not provide evidence of himself until the needed filial preparation is in place (e.g., attuning one's heart toward God).

The fourth type-2 objection contests premise (2) by arguing that disclosure of God may not require a person to be aware of God *doxastically*. Three examples in the literature will suffice.

Trent Dougherty and Ted Poston insist that Schellenberg's construal of nonbelief is overly rigid since it assumes too strong a view of belief *de dicto*. Thus, Dougherty and Poston—in asking the question, "What kind of belief is required for a personal relationship with God?"—distinguish between belief *de dicto* (belief *that*; or "of the proposition") and belief *de re* (belief *of*; or "of the thing"). The authors give an example:

---

43. Moser, "Christianity and Miracles."

44. Moser, *Why Isn't God*, 58; emphasis added. See Imran Aijaz and Markus Weidler's comments on Moser ("Some Critical Reflections," 18–20). See also Schellenberg and Moser's point-counterpoint discussion on atheism and divine hiddenness: Schellenberg, "Divine Hiddenness Justifies Atheism"; "Reply to Moser"; Moser, "Divine Hiddenness Does Not Justify Atheism"; Moser, "Reply to Schellenberg."

45. Moser states that he rejects premise (2), explaining that "some people are not ready to receive evidence of God's reality" (email to author, Apr. 24, 2014, with permission to quote). Similarly he writes elsewhere that "God is elusive and hides his existence from some people at some times. God does not offer his existence as ever transparent, in part because some people are not ready to face his reality" ("Confirmation Model," 199). Unfortunately, McBrayer and Swenson wrongly place Moser as what I call a type-3 objector ("Scepticism," 138). Further, Moser's position may be close to Lehe, who argues that God has good reasons for remaining hidden from some people, and that this does not impugn the goodness of God ("Response").

For instance, we believe *de dicto* that Mark Twain is a great author. But even if we did not realize that Mark Twain is Samuel Clemens, we would also believe *of* Sam Clemens that he is a great author. So we have the *de re* belief *Sam Clemens is a great author*.[46]

The authors propose that a person can lack strong *de dicto* belief in God but not belief *de re*, for the latter is less strict and "could be the basis for some *further* kind of belief still short of *de dicto* belief."[47] If a person has only *de re* belief but lacks what is traditionally taken to be full-blown doxastic disclosure of God, then it may be the case that God is justified in remaining hidden from that person *for a time*, since "one should not expect God to bring about *full doxastic disclosure for everyone now*."[48] There may be, for instance, either relational goods (e.g., a person having the right affections for God) or personal goods (e.g., character formation) that one must acquire before God's existence is more evident. Fortunately, as there could be circumstances when a person *lacks* highly confident belief in God, Christianity, argue Dougherty and Poston, "attests that God will accept far less: He will 'meet us where we are.'"[49] By distinguishing belief *de dicto* and *de re*, the authors claim to have undercut premise (2), since Schellenberg's 1993 argument is framed with only full-blown *doxastic* disclosure (and not necessarily belief *de re*) in mind.[50]

C. Stephen Evans's Kierkegaardian approach to PDH (cf. my chapter 1, which discusses Kierkegaard on PDH) could also be seen as doxastic in nature. Evans explains that God is not hidden except to those who blind *themselves* to him; this does not, however, make all atheists culpable for their nonbelief, Evans notes, since there could be atheists who lack propositional knowledge but who nevertheless may be "aware of God's reality *without realizing* that they are aware of that reality."[51] One could, in other words, without propositional belief still theoretically be aware of God without being aware of him "as God." Evans uses an analogy. Suppose a person in a dark room comes in contact with a furry animal; lacking propositional

---

46. Poston and Dougherty, "Divine Hiddenness," 185. See also LePore, "De Dicto."
47. Poston and Dougherty, "Divine Hiddenness," 192; emphasis added.
48. Poston and Dougherty, "Divine Hiddenness," 196; emphasis added.
49. Poston and Dougherty, "Divine Hiddenness," 196.
50. For Schellenberg's response to Poston and Dougherty, see his "On Not Unnecessarily Darkening." For even more work on this theme, see Cordry, "Divine Hiddenness and Belief"; Howard-Snyder, "Schellenberg on Propositional Faith."
51. C. S. Evans, "Can God Be Hidden," 250; emphasis added. See also C. S. Evans, *Natural Signs and Knowledge*, 149–90; C. S. Evans and Manis, *Philosophy of Religion*, 180–82. For another perspective on Kierkegaard and divine hiddenness, see Kline, "Absolute Action."

knowledge as to what type of animal it is or where it came from, the person has some sort of "knowledge" of the animal through the sense of touch. As it turns out, however,

> the animal is in fact *my* dog, and thus I am aware of my dog through the sense of touch. However, it is clearly possible that I might not recognize my dog *as my dog*, or even as a dog. I might mistakenly think he is some other dog or even think he is some other kind of animal. It is true that I am aware of my dog, and also that this awareness is sufficient for me to gain some true information that could be useful in guiding my conduct. However, if I am aware of my dog *as* my dog, then I may learn much more from this perceptual awareness and what I learn may bear on the relationship I have to my dog.[52]

Theists can hope that the needed propositional knowledge, explains Evans, will *become* more evident to those who attune themselves to God.

Similarly, Imran Aijaz and Marcus Weidler, in their allusion to Matt 25:37–40 (where Jesus says, "Truly, I say to you, as you did it to one of the least of these my brothers, you did it to me"), propose that even a nonbeliever can participate in God's kingdom since "it appears coherent to suppose that one can engage in both an explicit and reciprocal relationship with God without *believing* that God exists."[53] For insofar as one exhibits some sort of positive *attitude* about God's existence (which again need not be doxastic), then the authors claim to have undercut Schellenberg's argument. In sum, type-2 objectors respond to premise (2) by trying to show why God may have reasons for allowing reasonable nonbelief.

---

52. C. S. Evans, "Can God Be Hidden," 249–50; emphasis added. Evans more explicitly answers the question as to why God is hidden later in the article: "My answer to this question is a simple one: I do not know why God does not make his reality so obvious that everyone who wishes to know him has full, explicit propositional knowledge about God. So far as I can see my ignorance on this point is only troubling if the following proposition is true: 'If God has a good reason for being partially hidden, then Evans would know that reason.' I see no reason at all to think the above proposition is true, and therefore it seems rash to infer from my ignorance about God's reasons for arranging the world as he is done that God has no good reasons for the arrangement" (251).

53. Aijaz and Weidler, "Some Critical Reflections," 19; emphasis added. For Schellenberg's reply, see his "Reply to Aijaz and Weidler"; see also Chignell, "Prolegomena."

2.2.2 Type-3 Objections

Recall premise (3): *Reasonable nonbelief occurs*, which is to say, put roughly, that nonbelief arises through no fault of the nonbeliever.[54] Challenges to this premise, which are far less frequent,[55] attempt to show, in some way, that reasonable nonbelief does not obtain and that nonbelief may, in fact, be culpable. I explain two main variations of type-3 objections.[56]

First, Douglas Henry argues that there has been considerably less attention on premise (3) and, in quoting Rom 1:20–21, suggests that theists can be skeptical of inculpable (or reasonable) nonbelief: "If what may be known about God is plain," as Paul in Romans appears to explain, Henry says, then "how could nonbelief be reasonable?"[57] Should Henry be right, then the sort of nonbelief that Schellenberg needs for his (1993) argument to succeed, at least on biblical grounds, is unlikely to obtain. Now, one counter response to Henry's argument is to note that there *are* persons who claim to have adequately investigated spiritual matters (i.e., the reality of God) but who have not succeeded;[58] hence, there may be at least some cases of reasonable nonbelief.

Yet Henry has doubts. For "how do we judge the adequacy of a given person's investigation?" he asks: "After all, we can certainly deceive others about whether we have fulfilled our epistemic responsibilities properly, and worse yet, we can deceive ourselves through rationalizations, qualifications, and excuses."[59] Robert Lehe's position is similar to Henry's, when Lehe argues that Christians, for instance, may have good reason to challenge premise 3, since the psychology of religious belief, contra Schellenberg, is quite complicated:

> Whether or not to convert to Christianity is a momentous decision, and there may be ambivalence in a person's attitude toward it. Even people who honestly profess a strong desire to

---

54. *DHHR* 59.

55. Michael Rea writes that premise (3) "has been the subject of much dispute" but I do not think that that is quite right, at least not in *comparison* to the attention that premise (2) has received. See Rea, "Hiddenness and Transcendence," 211.

56. As mentioned, not all of the authors here are responding directly to the 1993 argument; such contributions are included because they can be categorized, generically speaking, under the heading of "type-3 objections."

57. Henry, "Does Reasonable Nonbelief Exist?," 77.

58. See for instance *DHHR* 64n13, where Schellenberg writes, quoting Swinburne (*Existence of God*), "that (in the absence of special considerations) the experiences of others are (probably) as they report them."

59. Henry, "Does Reasonable Nonbelief Exist?," 80.

believe may also have fears and apprehensions about submitting to the rigors of a religious life [e.g., church involvement, prayer, etc.]. . . . With the possibility of bias and self-deception ever present, especially when religious beliefs are under consideration, it is very difficult for anyone to be justified in asserting her own epistemic inculpability.[60]

Schellenberg responds to Henry and Lehe;[61] Henry offers a counter reply.[62] I will not rehearse these finely tuned exchanges here but rather surface Henry's and Lehe's articles because, in my assessment of the literature, they are two of the *few* who challenge premise (3), a discussion to which I return below.

The second variation of the type-3 objection, closely related to the former, is what I have termed "human defectiveness challenges."[63] These objections, stated roughly, attempt to explain PDH by appealing to various shortcomings in *humanity*, which, in the Christian tradition, certainly include the doctrine of sin. Two philosophers deserve attention here: Mark Talbot and William Wainwright. While Talbot's particular work (i.e., "Is It Natural to Believe in God?") predates Schellenberg's 1993 argument, his comments are relevant and may anticipate a challenge to premise (3). Taking a Calvinistic position, Talbot argues that human persons have a *sensus divinitatis*, a sense of the divine, such that, when undamaged by sin, humanity *would* naturally believe in God in much the same way that one innately believes in the existence of the past or in minds other than one's own.[64] If one's epistemic sets are reliable, says Talbot, then such sets "enable us to believe that the world is more or less as it actually is." And, when functioning rightly:

> To sense God's glory in his handiwork and to feel his majesty within us is, by this account, a matter of possessing reliable epistemic sets. Since . . . we naturally possess these sets, anyone's not possessing them signals, according to Calvin, his having worked to dismantle or lose them.[65]

---

60. Lehe, "Response," 170–71.

61. See Schellenberg, "On Reasonable Nonbelief."

62. Henry, "Reasonable Doubts." I am not aware of a counter reply by Lehe to Schellenberg, and I refer the reader to *DHHR* 58–69 for the bare context regarding the exchanges between Schellenberg, Henry, and Lehe.

63. McKim, *Religious Ambiguity*, 17–18. I have borrowed this terminology from McKim because it captures the essence of this response; his terminology is not describing responses to Schellenberg's argument; nor would I take McKim himself to be a type-3 objector.

64. See also A. Plantinga, *God and Other Minds*, 187–271, where Plantinga argues that belief in God may be comparable to belief in other minds.

65. Talbot, "Is It Natural," 164–65.

Talbot argues that it is, in fact, both natural and instinctive to believe in God.[66] However, when such belief does not obtain, then "Christians can be justified in asserting that everybody would believe, *if it weren't for sin*," which implies, then, that a sinner's judgment about spiritual matters is, as Talbot argues, "unreliable."[67] There has been epistemic damage to humanity's *sensus divinitatis*, the author writes, and it is the nonbeliever who, in not forming belief in God, is at fault. Talbot's approach is similar to Alvin Plantinga's, in his own Reformed approach, when Plantinga explains, for example, that "this is the natural human condition; it is because of our presently unnatural sinful condition that many of us find belief in God difficult or absurd."[68] So, too, Nicholas Wolterstorff, who writes that "one of the characteristic effects of sin is that we do resist [belief in God]."[69] Not surprisingly, Schellenberg rejects this type of response, proposing that

> honest inquirers have very good reason indeed to accept that not *all* failures to believe are due to the sin of the nonbeliever, and in particular, that inculpable doubt occurs. There is, for example, good reason to suppose that some who claim they have no private experiences apparently of God or that such experiences as they do have are ambiguous, and who have carefully examined the relevant arguments, finding them indecisive, have no wish to be in doubt.... Why, we may ask, should this be the case if all doubt is due to a sinful rejection of belief?[70]

Consider also William Wainwright, a Reformed Christian in the vein of Jonathan Edwards, who claims that Edwards would likely reject Schellenberg's premise (3).[71] In Wainwright's interpretation of Edwards, critics like Schellenberg "paint a distorted picture of our actual situation when they imply that God is largely hidden," for God has, in fact, provided humanity with adequate, objective evidence of his existence;[72] he contends that the corrupt and faulty dispositions of humanity can cause a person to be

---

66. For further examination on this topic, see Schloss and Murray, *Believing Primate*.
67. Talbot, "Is It Natural," 167; emphasis added.
68. A. Plantinga, "Reason and Belief," 66.
69. Wolterstorff, "Is Reason Enough?," 145.
70. *DHHR* 82; emphasis added. Schellenberg's fuller critique of Talbot can be found on 75–82. See also Schellenberg, "Breaking down the Walls," where he discusses Calvinistic/Reformed understandings of sin and nonbelief.
71. I have been helped by Taylor and Murray ("Hiddenness," 369–70) in their overview of Wainwright.
72. Wainwright, "Jonathan Edwards and Hiddenness," 107.

blinded to God's reality, and that, because in Adam all have sinned (cf. e.g., Rom 5:12), humans are *responsible* for their own corruption:

> Insofar as our own guilty choices contribute to the perpetuation of sinful social structures, we are responsible for the blindness [toward God] they partially cause. In this view, then, we are not only (partially) responsible for our own noetic failure. We are also (partially) responsible for that of others. Noetic blindness *can* be traced back to sinful human choices, but the choices aren't only ours but those of countless others. Human freedom includes the ability to cause significant epistemic harm to others as well as to ourselves.[73]

Seeds of this theme appear in Wainwright's earlier work, where he explains that every person is in possession of a passional nature, which, briefly stated, is the totality of one's desires, yearnings, or dispositions that motivate the appraisal of evidence.[74] One's passional nature, or one's *heart*, plays an important role in one's belief formation, including belief for or against God, and a person can situate herself in epistemic circumstances that in turn lead to nonbelief in God. For insofar as one is responsible *for placing oneself* in various epistemic circumstances then one can be held accountable for nonbelief in God. And even *social* sin, Wainwright explains, can cause epistemic failure.[75] Indeed, Wainwright, writing on behalf of Edwards, ascribes nonbelief to a failure of the heart, since "one's own sinful proclivities infect and distort one's thinking about God."[76] Kevin Kinghorn, though not commenting on Schellenberg's premise (3), argues for something similar. "Motivated by a desire," he writes,

> that the content of the message be false, she may engage in intentional actions that she believes to be wrong and that contribute to a self-deceptive process the result of which is that she fails to believe what she otherwise would have believed: Namely, that the message under consideration does in fact come from God and does accurately identify where her moral obligations lie. In such a scenario, a person can rightly be described as culpably "blinding herself" to some spiritual truth.[77]

---

73. Wainwright, "Jonathan Edwards and Hiddenness," 112.

74. Wainwright, *Reason and the Heart*, 7–53. This is chapter 1, entitled "Jonathan Edwards and the Heart."

75. Wainwright, "Jonathan Edwards and Hiddenness," 111–12.

76. Wainwright, *Reason and the Heart*, 148. See also Wainwright, "Theistic Proofs."

77. Kinghorn, "Spiritual Blindness, Self-Deception," 544; emphasis added. For further analysis on sin, nonbelief, and PDH, see also Kinghorn, *Decision of Faith*, 89–161; "Why Doesn't God."

Like Wainwright, Kinghorn notes that one's actions can contribute to one's belief (or nonbelief) in God.

In sum, what I have called type-3 objections attack premise (3) of Schellenberg's 1993 argument from reasonable nonbelief; I examined two variations, both of which maintain that inculpable (or reasonable) nonbelief does not obtain. From the examples provided above, I take it that the former (e.g., from Henry and Lehe) merely provides a defeater for premise (3), whereas the latter, perhaps from a more theologically robust perspective (e.g., from Talbot, Wainwright, and Kinghorn), attempt to *explain* nonbelief, though the two types are very similar.[78] Chapter 6 shows how a proponent of Reformed epistemology could reject premise (3).

2.2.3 Literature Review Part 1 Conclusion

Having presented notable theistic objections to premises (2) and (3), part 1's literature review will now be closed; given my findings, there are three ways in which my defense is applicable or relevant to the current analytic-philosophical debate on PDH. I discuss these here, coalescing them with part 2's conclusion in §2.4 below.

First, one chief purpose of this project, as mentioned, is to answer my research question ("Why, if God exists, is his existence not more obvious?") by using Plantinga's Reformed epistemic A/C models as a defense against PDH. Now, Reformed epistemology has been applied to various other comparable philosophical or theological problems, such as the problem of religious diversity,[79] but it has not, as far as I know, been applied explicitly to PDH.[80] (Although there are, as discussed above, at least some implicit Reformed epistemic "seeds" from the work of Talbot, Henry, and perhaps Wainwright.[81]) Further, neither of the two primary edited volumes on PDH contains specific Reformed epistemic analysis.[82] So, I do think that the

---

78. There are other ways of reviewing the literature that does not fall into the aforementioned categories and so deserve their own grouping; see the bibliographies in Schellenberg, "Divine Hiddenness," 517–18; Taylor and Murray, "Hiddenness." See also King, *Obstacles to Divine Revelation*, 154–74.

79. See Clark, "Pluralism and Proper Function."

80. As mentioned in my first chapter, the only *explicit* work on PDH and Reformed epistemology of which I am aware is Taber and McNabb, "Problem of Divine Hiddenness."

81. *DHHR* does contain a section called "The Calvinian Response" (74–82) that briefly mentions Plantinga on John Calvin but focuses mostly on Mark Talbot's work.

82. Howard-Snyder and Moser, *Divine Hiddenness*; Green and Stump, *Hidden Divinity*. The former volume does include an essay by Nicholas Wolterstorff, a leading

scholarly literature could benefit from my Plantingean Reformed epistemic defense.

Second, let me say with a bit more specificity how my Plantingean Reformed epistemic approach is relevant to PDH in light of the previously examined type-2 and type-3 objectors. Recall, then, that type-2 objectors insist that God is, to at least some measure, *hidden*,[83] in which case the objector then explains why a hidden God may permit instances of inculpable, or reasonable, nonbelief (e.g., free will/coercion response, filial response, etc.). Perhaps many type-2 objectors would agree with theologian and physicist John Polkinghorne when he writes, "If there is a God he is a hidden God. He does not make himself known unambiguously in acts of transparent significance."[84]

So, where type-2 objectors challenge the second premise by arguing that God is hidden, after which he or she provides possible reasons *why*, Reformed epistemology in general, as I see it, need not take this argumentative tactic. For "the central claim of Reformed epistemology," argues Dewey J. Hoitenga Jr., "is the immediacy of our knowledge of God."[85] Wolterstorff similarly writes that Reformed epistemology "consists of the double thesis that many people hold many of their beliefs about God basically (that is, immediately, not on the basis of other beliefs), and that often they are *entitled* thus to hold them."[86] It is further

> a theory of religious knowledge that holds that religious beliefs can be (and in appropriate circumstances are, in fact) *properly*

Reformed epistemologist, but the article itself is not explicitly Reformed epistemic ("Silence of the God"). For my review of the latter work, see Taber, "Review of *Hidden Divinity*."

83. Paul Moser (who identifies as a type-2 objector) writes, "The relevant available evidence [for God] is, it seems, less than obvious to all reflective people, or at least it doesn't make God's existence obvious to all such people. We might thus say that God's existence is at best *elusive, subtle, or incognito*" (*Elusive God*, ix; emphasis added). Robert McKim writes that his work "depends on the assumption that the world is religiously ambiguous" (*Religious Ambiguity*, 21). "To say that the world is religiously ambiguous," he adds, "is to say that it is open to being read in various ways, both religious and secular, by intelligent, honest people" (25). See also Meister, "Evil and the Hiddenness," 138; Garcia, "St. John of the Cross."

84. John Polkinghorne, *One World*, quoted in Henry, "Does Reasonable Nonbelief Exist?," 89n6.

85. Hoitenga, *Faith and Reason*, ix.

86. Wolterstorff, "Reformed Tradition," 205; emphasis in original. See also Wolterstorff, "Herman Bavinck."

basic beliefs that do not need to be supported by other beliefs one accepts.[87]

Plantinga himself, as good a Reformed epistemologist as any, explains that its "central claim is that belief in God (so thought of) can be 'properly basic.'"[88] Reformed epistemology can also argue, as Plantinga notes (by way of John Calvin and the Reformed tradition), that perhaps it is the case that God has "implanted in us all an innate tendency, or nisus, or disposition to believe in him"[89]—something like a *sensus divinitatis* that, when functioning properly (the way that God designed it to function), delivers basic, properly basic, and warranted theistic belief, warrant being that ingredient enough of which turns mere true belief into *knowledge*.

My claim is not that one can merely call on or summon Reformed epistemology to rebut premise (2). Nor is it to claim that Reformed epistemology is in fact true, but that if it is true then the Reformed epistemologist is not forced to sort out why a hidden God allows reasonable nonbelief; perhaps this is because the Reformed epistemologist may have reasons for thinking that if there is a God then he is not hidden in the sense for which most type-2 objectors suggest that he is. My chapter 3 aims to demonstrate how this could be the case, by utilizing Plantinga's Reformed epistemology, particularly his hypothetical A/C model, which shows how bare theism can be properly basic and how it may have warrant; it is a model that explains our natural knowledge of God. This, I think, has the advantage of showing where more work in the present PDH literature can be done, since there are few (if any) examples in the literature where such a Reformed epistemic approach is provided; such also will allow me to take the *first* step toward arguing for my thesis, which, roughly stated, is a defense—an epistemically possible "story" (to use Van Inwagen's term)—for why if there is a God his existence is not more obvious. I begin to take up this task in chapter 3 with Plantinga's A/C model and will say more about it below in §2.4.

Third, as mentioned, far less attention has been given in response to premise (3) and, in my appraisal of the literature, one reason for not doing so is that to challenge reasonable nonbelief is often *inflammatory* and *provocative*. Noted above were the bold theses of Talbot, Wainwright, Lehe, Henry, and Kinghorn, some of whose rebuttals included biblical/theological

---

87. Peterson, *Philosophy of Religion*, 647; emphasis in original. So a basic belief is a believed proposition without its basis on other beliefs (e.g., the belief that one plus two equals three, or I am seated at my desk, or there is a pain in my right knee; see Hoitenga, *Faith and Reason*, 177), and a properly basic belief is one that is suitable or appropriate for a person to accept in a basic way.

88. A. Plantinga, "Reformed Epistemology" (2010), 674.

89. A. Plantinga, "Reason and Belief," 65.

themes like self-deception, human defectiveness, the effects and consequences of sin, and so forth, all of which are difficult waters to navigate. I will not provide a rebuttal to premise (3) here, but I do think that the Reformed epistemologist who seeks to offer a defense for why God's existence is not obvious can use, and can build upon, the already-established argumentation from type-3 objectors, some of which is intrinsic in Reformed epistemology itself, particularly its construal of sin's effects. For Reformed epistemology articulates not only the immediacy of our knowledge of God (as Hoitenga puts it), but it also generally places a sturdy emphasis on humanity's fallenness and sin, and how the latter can confuse and warp the former; I surfaced earlier both Wolterstorff's and Plantinga's comments on sin's consequences, where Plantinga explains, for example, that many of us find belief in God difficult or absurd because of sin's effects, and where Wolterstorff argues that "one of the characteristic effects of sin is that we do resist [belief in God]."

Thus, given premise (3)'s lack of attention, I shall build upon the foundation that many type-3 objectors have already laid but also supplement their argumentation with more explicit theological substance by further analyzing, through a Plantingean Reformed epistemological defense for PDH, just *how* sin and its effects relates to PDH; I think Plantingean Reformed epistemology has the tools to carry out this chore. To do this, I apply to PDH the *extended* A/C model, engineered by Plantinga, to demonstrate how explicitly Christian belief may have warrant, especially the model's construal of sin's consequences; the model shows how we can have knowledge of God in our *postlapsarian* context. I take up this task in chapter 4 with Plantinga's extended A/C model and will say more about it below in §2.4.

In sum, I have not presented Plantingean Reformed epistemology as a rebuttal to Schellenberg's premises (2) and (3) in his 1993 argument; that is because, as explained in chapter 1, with Plantinga's help, I said that I seek not to rebut an argument from divine hiddenness—although, as shown above, there have been some helpful theistic rebuttals to what is perhaps the most important hiddenness argument in the literature—but rather aim to understand PDH from a Christian perspective: *How should Christians think about PDH?* I have used Schellenberg's premises (2) and (3) in order to show how my Plantingean Reformed epistemic thesis—which aims to provide a distinctly Christian defense for the hiddenness problem, thereby answering my research question—is relevant to, and how it can be included in, the current PDH debate. Part 2 of the literature review is continued below.

2.3 LITERATURE REVIEW PART 2: THE PROBLEMS OF EVIL AND DIVINE HIDDENNESS: SIMILARITY, DISSIMILARITY, AND THE RELEVANCE OF MY ARGUMENT

POE, put roughly, is said to exemplify a conflict between the claim that God exists, on the one hand, and the fact that evil exists, on the other. PDH, put roughly, is said to exemplify a conflict between the claim that God exists, on the one hand, and that God's existence is not clear, on the other. Many philosophers and theologians—perhaps most—suggest that the two problems enjoy a tight relationship. As a way to continue my literature review, this section analyzes the relationship between POE and PDH. First, I spell out *similarity* between POE and PDH; second, I spell out *dissimilarity* between the two. I will not provide reasons to *reject* the presented *similarity* but do, however, provide reasons to *accept* what I perceive to be the *dissimilarity* between POE and PDH. My claim is that my Reformed epistemic defense has the resources to address some of the perceived dissimilarity. I conclude this section, like part 1, by showing how my defense is applicable and relevant to current scholarship, after which (in §2.4) both literature reviews will be combined.

2.3.1 Similarity between the Problems of Evil and Divine Hiddenness

In what follows, I list several reasons for thinking there to be similarity between POE and PDH.[90]

First, it seems that POE and PDH can be understood in a similar way such that both pose a threat, or a problem, for *theism*. For one could argue that evil and the "hiddenness of God" are just what one would expect to find on, say, naturalism but that, given theism, these phenomena are just what they are: challenges or *problems*. As John Greco writes of both problems, "How is *God's existence* compatible with the thing at issue?"[91]

Second, in conjunction with the first provided reason, both POE and PDH can be understood as bad states of affairs, the former being rather self-evident, whereas for the latter, a theist, argues Schellenberg, "may keenly feel the value of what (she takes to be) an existing relationship with God

---

90. Though I disagree with some of his conclusions, variations of my reasons can be found in Schellenberg, "Divine Hiddenness," 512–13; "Hiddenness Problem."

91. Greco, "No-Fault Atheism," 111; emphasis added. For further analysis of POE and PDH, see 110–16.

and may therefore be inclined to view anything contributing to its absence, such as nonbelief [putatively caused by divine hiddenness], as *a bad thing*."[92]

Third, PDH can be thought of as *part* of POE, or POE as *part* of PDH. Consider first the former, how PDH might be thought of as part of POE. In his 1993 argument, Schellenberg claims that "the problem of reasonable nonbelief, as I develop it, must be viewed as a special instance of the empirical problem of evil."[93] Chad Meister, for example, explains that divine hiddenness is "one aspect of the problem of evil,"[94] whereas William Wainwright describes divine hiddenness as a "form of the problem of evil . . . aggravated by evil's pervasiveness."[95] Richard Swinburne writes that the hiddenness of God "is a variant on the normal argument from evil against the existence of God,"[96] noting elsewhere that "some human ignorance of God may be a moral evil."[97] Jeremy Evans asks his readers to "recall that divine hiddenness is a *subspecies* of the problem of evil."[98] C. Stephen Evans and Zachary Manis write, "One further *facet* of the problem of evil . . . focuses on the apparent fact that God's existence is not clearly manifest"[99] (i.e., PDH). Thomas Morris writes:

> The problem of the hiddenness of God can be viewed as *a limited version of* the problem of evil: What could possibly justify a good God's allowing us to be afflicted with so great an evil as the deprivation of any clear awareness of his presence, a deprivation bemoaned by both the psalmist and the saint?[100]

Similarly, Paul Moser explains that "God often seems hidden from some people at such times . . . and this fact of hiddenness emerges as a cognitive variation of the problem of evil."[101] T. J. Mawson writes that "this argument

---

92. Schellenberg, "Divine Hiddenness," 513; emphasis added.

93. *DHHR* 9. "It is interesting to note at this juncture that the problem posed for theology by the argument I develop may also be construed as a special instance of the problem of evil" (6). "Hence I seem to be in a position to claim that the problem of reasonable nonbelief is a problem of evil" (7).

94. Meister, "Evil and the Hiddenness," 138.

95. Wainwright, "Jonathan Edwards and Hiddenness," 107.

96. Swinburne, *Existence of God*, 267.

97. Swinburne, *Providence and the Problem*, 203.

98. J. Evans, *Problem of Evil*, 67; emphasis added.

99. C. S. Evans and Manis, *Philosophy of Religion*, 180; emphasis added.

100. T. Morris, *Making Sense*, 89; emphasis added. See also T. Morris, "Hidden God."

101. Moser, *Evidence for God*, 261. Moser writes, "It is doubtful that *divine hiddenness in particular or evil in general* will yield a successful defeater to this book's volitional theism" (263; emphasis added). However, Moser notes that we need not say

[divine hiddenness] may be correctly thought of as a version of the Problem of Evil."[102] Further, Daniel Howard-Snyder and Moser, in a descriptive essay, propose that PDH may be a *subset* of the traditional problem of suffering and evil,[103] just as Jonathan Kvanvig explains that, whatever divine hiddenness is, it is merely a special component *of* POE, in which case adding divine hiddenness *to* the traditional problem of evil does not tip the scales in favor of atheism.[104] Commenting on Eleonore Stump's work on suffering and evil (*Wandering in Darkness*), Evan Fales writes, "Divine hiddenness is problematic because it seems to represent one *type* of gratuitous evil."[105] So, in short, many contemporary philosophers take PDH to be a part of the greater POE.

Consider now the latter: POE as part of PDH. For instance, "The entire problem of evil," explains Robert McKim, "may be thought of *as a part of* the problem of the hiddenness of God, since the presence of evil in the world is a fact that makes for the hiddenness of God."[106] Morris, noted above, explains on the one hand that PDH can be taken to be a part of POE, arguing further that "on the other hand . . . the problem of evil can be seen *as a subcategory* of the problem of the hiddenness of God."[107] William Rowe seems to propose that POE inevitably *leads* to PDH; for God as a loving parent, if he exists, would want to be present alongside his suffering children, particularly if those same children could not understand the reasons he could have for allowing such suffering.[108] Finally, James Keller writes:

> The two problems are so closely related that either *can be construed as a part of the other*. Because some human suffering arises from a failure to have faith in God—or so theists usually allege—and from lack of knowledge of God's will, the hiddenness of God is part of the problem of evil; that is, if God is as many theists have claimed, we might find it inexplicable that God remains hidden, since that hiddenness causes suffering. . . . In this way, the evil in the world contributes to the hiddenness of God.[109]

---

that *all* cases of hiddenness are subsumable to the problem of evil. He maintains that God could have good purposes for hiding from some persons at some times, which may *not* arise from a situation of evil and/or suffering (email to author, May 14, 2014).

102. Mawson, "Praying to Stop," 175. See also Mawson, *Belief in God*, 198–217.
103. Howard-Snyder and Moser, "Introduction," 6–8.
104. Kvanvig, "Divine Hiddenness," 159–60.
105. Fales, "Journeying in Perplexity," 89; emphasis added.
106. McKim, "Hiddenness of God," 141; emphasis added.
107. T. Morris, *Making Sense*, 89; emphasis added.
108. W. Rowe, "Evidential Argument," 276, 285n35.
109. Keller, "Hiddenness of God," 14; emphasis added.

Fourth, from a Christian theistic perspective, it can be said that there is similarity between PDH and the so-called *soteriological* POE. The soteriological POE, at least from a Christian standpoint, is the problem that God has provided salvation for humanity but that there are some persons who never hear or accept the gospel of Jesus Christ, and so are lost. For if God's "salvific path" by way of the gospel of Jesus Christ were more obvious or more evident, as one might postulate, then more persons could respond to the gospel and be saved, but *that* there are some who go unsaved could be considered evil.[110]

Fifth, from a Christian theistic perspective, Scripture is full of places that prima facie appear to tie the two phenomena closely together. "Why do you hide your face?" the psalmist writes, "Why do you forget our affliction and oppression?" (Ps 44:24). "Why, O Lord, do you stand far away? Why do you hide yourself in times of trouble?" (10:1). And just a few passages later: "How long, O Lord? . . . How long will you hide your face from me?" (13:1). The author of Job confesses, "Why do you hide your face and count me as your enemy?" (Job 14:24; cf. Is 45:15).

Sixth, POE and PDH, in their generic form, can both lead to *arguments*, either logical (deductive) or evidential (inductive), against God's existence.[111] The argument from evil has a distinguished history, and I explored Schellenberg's 1993 hiddenness argument in part 1. In this case, like the very first line of similarity offered above, both POE and PDH, when they take argument form, can be said to count as *evidence* against, and not just generic problems for, theism.

Seventh, defenses and theodicies can be applied to either or to both POE and PDH. A defense is a *possible* "story" explaining the consistency of God's existence and evil (or divine hiddenness), whereas a theodicy is an *actual* "story" explaining the consistency of God's existence and evil (or divine hiddenness).[112]

Eighth, skeptical theism can be applied to either or to both POE and PDH. Skeptical theism is a response to the evidential POE, particularly with respect to gratuitous suffering, whereby the skeptical theist expresses

---

110. While the soteriological POE is widely discussed, I do not know of any instances in the literature where PDH is *specifically* linked to the soteriological POE (or vice versa). For discussion of the soteriological POE, see, for example, Hunt, "Middle Knowledge"; Basinger, "Divine Omniscience."

111. This specific point was in http://faculty.wwu.edu/howardd/HiddennessofGod.pdf (accessed May 7, 2014), but the link has since been discontinued.

112. This was discussed in chapter 1; see further Van Inwagen, "What Is the Problem," 30–31. The term "story" is Van Inwagen's.

skepticism about one's ability to determine if encountered evils truly are gratuitous.[113] Recently, skeptical theism has been used for PDH.[114]

Ninth, POE and PDH can both have *existential* repercussions. POE, as expressed above, can take both logical and evidential forms; but it is also customary to speak of the *existential* POE. Perhaps the same can be said with respect to PDH. One may find oneself, for instance, internally afflicted and troubled having experienced evil or suffering, just as one may feel abandoned or forsaken, having prayed to God for help only to receive silence or no answer. POE and PDH, however they are to be understood, both seem to share these themes. Yujin Nagasawa, in a recent essay, develops what he calls "'the problem of divine absence,' which is a combination of the most intense form of the problem of divine hiddenness and the most intense form of the problem of evil."[115]

In close, I have surveyed several reasons for thinking there to be much similarity between the two problems; noted also were putative theological (i.e., soteriological) and scriptural similarities. I do not provide reasons to reject the similarity, but will now attempt to give reasons to accept *dissimilarity* between POE and PDH.

2.3.2 Dissimilarity between Evil and Divine Hiddenness

My claim in this section is that, while clearly there *is* similarity between these two phenomena, there are motivations for seeing some dissimilarity; I explore philosophical as well as theological and biblical reasons to support my claim, saying in conclusion that my project on PDH has the resources to address some of the presented dissimilarity.

First, it appears that, for POE, there is something *present*, such as the existence of evil, or pain, or suffering. For PDH, however, there is something *absent*, such as the reality of God, or a shortage of religious experience, and so forth. Perhaps the reverse is true: for POE, it can be said that there is something *absent*, particularly for those who hold that evil is the privation of good, whereas for PDH, there is something *present*, such as nonbelief (which presumably would not arise if God were more obvious).

Second, PDH can be construed as a purely epistemological problem, perhaps in a way that POE cannot. According to Van Inwagen, POE is

---

113. See Bergmann, "Skeptical Theism."

114. McBrayer and Swenson, "Scepticism"; see also Dougherty and McBrayer, *Skeptical Theism*; Greco, "No-Fault Atheism," 115–16, for further examination of skeptical theism applicable to PDH.

115. Nagasawa, "Silence, Evil," 246.

roughly the problem of "bad things,"[116] of how to find meaning in a world where everything is touched by evil. But Van Inwagen asks us to imagine a secular utopia, a world with "alabaster cities, undimmed by human tears," where there is no pain or "premature death," no "violence, accident, or disease." Presumably, there would be no jealousy, adultery, or murder; can such a place, a possible world, be imagined? "Could someone in this world," he notes, "perhaps one of its atheists, raise the problem of divine hiddenness?"[117] It appears so, and I think that this point helps to show a dissimilarity between POE and PDH; Van Inwagen writes that "in a world that lacks any real suffering, the problem of the hiddenness of God is a purely *epistemological* problem, or a cluster of epistemological problems" (i.e., in which case POE is not).[118] Consider also Howard-Snyder's remarks:

> Inculpable nonbelief [as putatively caused by divine hiddenness] is supposed to be evidence against the existence of God *independent* of evil and suffering. To see how this can be, imagine a society in a world much like our own but in which there is no evil or suffering. While no argument from evil could arise in such a society, some of its citizens might maintain that there is a God while others maintain that there is not since there are inculpable nonbelievers.[119]

In these comments, Howard-Snyder, like Van Inwagen, has similar motivations for thinking there to be dissimilarity between POE and PDH. (Notably, Schellenberg since his 1993 argument has come to change his mind on the relationship between POE and PDH. "Another less than serious attempt to deal with the hiddenness problem," he writes, "involves sweeping it under the rug of the problem of evil" so that "the so-called problem of hiddenness may be safely ignored."[120])

---

116. Van Inwagen, *Problem of Evil*, 4. This brief exposition of Van Inwagen is helped by Van Inwagen, "What Is the Problem" (where the former expounds upon the latter); "Problem of Evil."

117. Van Inwagen, "What Is the Problem," 24–26. Van Inwagen is briefly alluding to Bates, "America the Beautiful," st. 4: "Thine alabaster cities gleam, / Undimmed by human tears."

118. Van Inwagen, *Problem of Evil*, 142; emphasis added. "The problem of evil and the problem of hiddenness are, therefore, not identical" (137).

119. From http://faculty.wwu.edu/howardd/HiddennessofGod.pdf (accessed May 7, 2014; now discontinued); emphasis added. See also Howard-Snyder, "Argument from Divine Hiddenness"; Howard-Snyder and Green, "Hiddenness of God."

120. Schellenberg, *Wisdom to Doubt*, 207; see also his *Hiddenness Argument*, 28–31, for discussion of PDH and POE.

Third, for PDH, it may be out of character for God to be less "hidden," as Michael Rea notes.[121] If so, then this may be motivation for seeing dissimilarity between POE and PDH, in which case God's perceived absence need not be taken as an evil, as some might claim. It being out of character for God to be less hidden is comparable to a Kierkegaardian examination of PDH, analyzed in chapter 1, which may argue that God does not make himself more obvious because that would not be God as *God really is*.[122] It is simply not how he behaves. But to take this reasoning a step further, a Christian theist could argue that it would be unfit for God, according to much of the Christian tradition, to make himself "less" hidden given the general revelation (in the created order) that he *has already provided*. The historical theologian Thomas Oden argues, for example:

> There is a substantive consensus of classic Christian commentary [from thinkers such as Athanasius, Basil, Gregory of Nazianzus and John Chrysostom in the east, and Ambrose, Jerome, Augustine, and Gregory the Great in the west] on Rom 1:18ff that confirms with Paul that all humanity is offered some true, even if limited, knowledge of God by contemplating the majesty and goodness of God in the whole of creation.[123]

Thus, from a Christian perspective, to demand that God give more revelation of himself than what he has already given may be comparable to asking the millionaire—who freely gave me a million dollars—for an additional million, as if the first million was insufficient; in this scenario, what exactly is the problem? Could it be a failure to appreciate or to acknowledge the first million? And, if so, then a failure to appreciate or to acknowledge something—either God or money—seems to me dissimilar from the problem of evil.[124]

Fourth, PDH can be taken as a problem that is "more characteristic of *humans* than of God" (I explain this phrase below). The same can be said, I suppose, with POE, but I will try to show in what follows that there is something distinctive about this from the perspective of divine hiddenness.

---

121. Rea, "Divine Hiddenness, Divine Silence," esp. 271—although Rea has explained that he takes POE and PDH to be *separate* problems (not just dissimilar problems; email to author, Aug. 12, 2014). "*Next to* the problem of evil," Rea writes, "the most important objection to belief in God is the problem of divine hiddenness" ("Narrative, Liturgy, and Hiddenness," 76n1; emphasis added). See also Rea, "Hiddenness and Transcendence"; *Evil and the Hiddenness*, 1–3.

122. To follow C. S. Evans, "Can God Be Hidden."

123. Oden, "Without Excuse," 68; *Classic Christianity*, 18. See also Demarest, *General Revelation*.

124. For a comparable line of argumentation, see O'Connell, "Divine Hiddenness."

To illustrate, hear the honest words of the agnostic philosopher Paul Draper on divine hiddenness:

> I must confess that at times the ambiguity of the evidence [for God] seems to me to be just a little too neat, a little too perfect. It seems almost contrived, as if the beans aren't being drawn randomly. But if this is so, then who *is* drawing the beans? Is it me? Am I manufacturing an apparent ambiguity *for myself*, either by refusing to recognize clear differences in the strength of different pieces of evidence or by refusing to take seriously supernaturalistic alternatives to theism? . . . Is it the result *of subconsciously rejecting God*, thereby *making me unable to see* that the evidence favoring theism is much stronger than the evidence favoring naturalism? Or do I sit on the fence because I am horrified by the possibility that the suffering of innocents has no purpose and no compensation, and so I refuse to recognize what seems so perfectly obvious to so many of my fellow philosophers, that belief in God is just silly superstition or, at best, understandable self-deception. I hope and even believe that my assessment of the evidence is the result of an open mind *rather than a closed or tender heart*. But if this is so, then is the ambiguity of the evidence just an unfortunate coincidence? Or is it designed, not by me, but by a God whose policy is, "Don't find me, I'll call you . . . when the time is right"? *I don't know the answer to these questions.* So for now I will sit on the fence, lost perhaps but still looking, leaning perhaps but not leaping, listening I hope, but not yet hearing.[125]

In this passage, Draper closes his essay, having reflected on various historic debates in philosophy of religion (e.g., natural theological arguments, the problem of evil, etc.), ultimately remaining agnostic about God given the current state of the evidence. These matters aside, however, Draper makes some important observations about divine hiddenness. For he mentions what I take to be self-deception ("subconsciously rejecting God"), the status of one's heart or "will" ("a closed or tender heart"), and so forth. His remarks about divine hiddenness do not "feel" like the problem of evil. Indeed, his comments are reminiscent of some of the historical contributions exposited in chapter 1 (specifically Pascal and perhaps Kierkegaard and Campbell).

Similarly, the agnostic philosopher Anthony Kenny asks us to suppose that the stars magically aligned to spell out the sentence "The end of the world is at hand":

---

125. Draper, "Seeking but Not Believing," 211; emphasis added.

This would, no doubt, provide reason both for believing that God existed (who else would be powerful enough to control the stars?) and that the end of the world was at hand.

He notes, however, that such evidence "would not necessarily be overwhelming. An atheist would, if he thought that was what he saw, no doubt wish to explore other avenues of inquiry before falling on his knees."[126] Note the importance of his comments. For while Kenny does suggest that this incident would provide at least some justification to believe in God, the reasons therein may not necessarily be overwhelming. Commenting here on Kenny, Timothy Paul Erdel explains, "Determined skeptics might not be persuaded regardless of the type or amount of evidence [for God's existence]. . . . Anthony Kenny seems very close to boasting of his own impermeable resistance to any evidence, saying that, *even if* God spoke by skywriting messages, there would be grounds for honest skepticism."[127] Consider also philosopher Thomas Nagel's well-known remarks:

> I want atheism to be true and am made uneasy by the fact that some of the most intelligent and well-informed people I know are religious believers. It isn't just that I don't believe in God and, naturally, hope that I'm right in my belief. It's that I hope there is no God! I don't want there to be a God; *I don't want the universe to be like that.*[128]

Neither Kenny nor Nagel's comments sound like POE. Commenting on this specific passage from Nagel, Paul Moser in a recent essay on divine hiddenness writes that

> Perhaps hiddenness is ultimately *more characteristic of humans than of God.* . . . Perhaps Nagel is motivated by a desire for moral independence of God. If so, it would be natural for him to suppose that God raises an intolerable problem of moral authority for humans.[129]

If Moser is correct that PDH is more characteristic of humans than of God, then this fosters reasons to think, despite considerable similarity, that POE and PDH are dissimilar.

Fifth, from a scriptural perspective, PDH (unlike POE) may involve the human inability to perceive God's presence, there being overlap between

---

126. Kenny, *Faith and Reason*, 73–74, as referenced in Erdel, "Divine Disclosures and Supernatural Signs," 3n7.

127. Erdel, "Divine Disclosures and Supernatural Signs," 3n7; emphasis added.

128. Nagel, *Last Word*, 130; emphasis added.

129. Moser, "Divine Hiddenness and Self-Sacrifice," 87; emphasis added.

this reason and the previously discussed one. Now, mentioned above were Old Testament (OT) passages that can be taken to touch on PDH (e.g., Ps 10:1), since certainly the "hiddenness of God" is a rich theme in the OT.[130] Joel Burnett, in his eminent work *Where Is God? Divine Absence in the Hebrew Bible*, notes that throughout the Hebrew Bible, humans "reflect a concern for divine absence," asking the "basic question of divine absence, 'Where is God?'"[131] Burnett does suggest, however, that the very first question posed in Scripture is from God himself: "Where are *you*?" (Gen 3:9), which "reflects a breach in the divine-human relationship that is universal in scope."[132] It is as if God, immediately after the fall (cf. Gen 3:1–7), searches out an elusive humanity who no longer seeks nor needs him. Here is Moser on Gen 3:9 with respect to PDH:

> The person who truly desires to overcome divine hiddenness should seek to experience and to cooperate with the self-sacrificial love on offer [i.e., through God the Son]. In failing to do so, one may exhibit a misplaced desire for divine hiddenness, perhaps in the interest of deadly human autonomy, self-sufficiency, or some other kind of waywardness from God. For the sake of honesty in inquiry, one should sincerely entertain the prospect of the priority of a question from God to oneself: "Where are you?" (Gen. 3:9).

Moser goes on to write that "God's question, 'Where are you?' can reveal in a human an oppositional attitude toward God."[133] (Further, the hiddenness theme in the Prophets, Major and Minor, is intimately tied to God's judgment, just as God's hiddenness, as portrayed in various psalms, is closely related to human sin.[134])

Burnett places much emphasis on God's absence from his people in the OT. However, with much praise for Burnett's seminal work, OT scholar Hubert Keener writes that Burnett

> does not tend to distinguish between *perceived divine absence* and *ontological divine absence*. Such a distinction will be vital for

---

130. See, for instance, Balentine, *Hidden God*; Hamilton, "Divine Presence"; Gellman, "Hidden God of Jews."

131. Burnett, *Where Is God?*, 175–76.

132. Burnett, *Where Is God?*, 81.

133. Moser, "Divine Hiddenness and Self-Sacrifice," 87.

134. See Terrien, *Elusive Presence*. Terrien writes: "The prophets interpreted Yahweh's absence from history as the sign of his presence in judgment" (265). Concerning sin in the psalms: "When a guilty man asks for forgiveness and rehabilitation, he begs at the same time for the renewal of [God's] presence" (323).

moving beyond description to contemporary theology. Perhaps the problem humans face is not so much the absence of God as the inability to perceive the presence of God.[135]

The point is not to critique Burnett (I leave these OT debates to OT experts); the point to be made here is how Keener *phrases* his critique of Burnett: ontological divine absence as distinguished from the inability to perceive God's presence. This distinction is helpful to understand PDH (for my project), particularly against the backdrop of analytic philosophy of religion, since perhaps one problem that humanity faces, in the OT as well as today, is not necessarily God's absence but is rather, as Keener insists, the inability to perceive his presence.

But is *this*—human inability to perceive God's presence—similar to POE? Such is not obviously so. For it may be that this inability, by some persons some of the time, is a failure not on God's part, as mentioned above, but on mankind's. From a Christian perspective, with the help of Moser (again), if there is a God then humans themselves can be guilty of "cognitive idolatry."

> [Cognitive idolatry] stems from the human desire to be, or at least to appoint, the ultimate authority for our lives, as if we were entitled to this. We thereby isolate ourselves from important *available evidence* of God, blinding ourselves from the supreme reality and authority over us dependent cognitive creatures. We thereby suppress the truth about God's reality.[136]

Such is what St. Paul appears to argue in Rom 1:18–25. In sum, I presented several reasons for thinking there to be dissimilarity between POE and PDH, but have not claimed that my comparison resolves the complex interplay between the two phenomena.

2.3.3 Literature Review Part 2 Conclusion

Let me now close part 2's literature review. In much of the philosophical and theological literature, both POE and PDH are said to be similar, and rightly so. My claim is that my Plantingean Reformed epistemic defense for PDH has the resources to address some of the perceived dissimilarity. I explain

---

135. H. Keener, "Review of *Where Is God?*," 377; emphasis added.

136. Moser, "Cognitive Idolatry," 137; emphasis in original. For a critique of Moser, see Cervantez and Coffman, "Hiddenness, Evidence, and Idolatry"; Fales, "Journeying in Perplexity."

myself in what follows, coalescing my explanation below (in §2.4) with part 1's above conclusion.

First, as a way to distinguish PDH from POE, it was described above that a Christian theist could argue that it would be unfit for God, according to much of the Christian tradition, to make himself "less" hidden given the general revelation—natural theistic knowledge—that he has *already* provided. Now, pointing to the doctrine of general revelation in the context of divine hiddenness does not solve the problem; it raises more questions that need explicated. But I do think that Plantinga's generic A/C model—designed to show how bare theism may have warrant—can help make sense of general revelation with respect to PDH; Plantinga in the model follows both Aquinas and Calvin in saying that there is natural theistic knowledge, God having revealed himself universally, arguing along with Calvin (as mentioned in part 1's literature review) that all persons have a *sensus divinitatis*, an innate faculty, that delivers theistic knowledge. I apply the A/C model to PDH in my third chapter.

Second, as a way to distinguish PDH from POE, it was described above that PDH may be more characteristic of humans than of God, *and* that PDH may involve the human inability to perceive God's presence. In the Christian tradition, these sorts of themes involve an analysis of sin and its effects. Pointing to sin and its effects does not solve the problem either; it raises more questions that need analyzing. But my contention is that Plantingean Reformed epistemology—which, as discussed in chapter 1 and above, is largely absent in the contemporary PDH literature—has the available tools to carry out such an analysis. For example, as discussed in part 1's conclusion, Plantinga's extended A/C model, which aims to demonstrate how Christian belief in its postlapsarian context may have warrant, examines sin's *noetic* consequences—sin's effects on the mind, which can negatively influence our theistic knowledge (arguing also on the extended model that sin has adverse *affective* consequences). And since my thesis aims to give a specifically Christian defense for PDH, then analyzing sin's effects on our knowledge of God, particularly in the context of PDH, seems imperative.[137]

Along these lines, Christians who analyze PDH should also consider how *Christ* saves us from sin—how the effects of grace not only put us right with God, but additionally how they restore and rejuvenate our natural theistic knowledge. (Paul Moser has made comparable arguments, having thus tried to reform how PDH can be appraised from a Christian perspective.[138]) Plantinga's extended model also examines these biblical and

---

137. As far as I am aware, not much literature exists on this specific point, one exception being Azadegan, "Divine Hiddenness."

138. See Moser, *Elusive God*; *Evidence for God*; as well as *Philosophia Christi's*

theological themes, themes such as atoning work of Christ, how the Holy Spirit instigates faith, the inspiration of Scripture, and the like. These doctrinal loci in the extended model can be brought to bear on the hiddenness problem. I say more about this below.

2.4 CONCLUSION: PART 1 AND PART 2'S LITERATURE REVIEWS COMBINED

The purpose of this section—having demonstrated my Plantingean Reformed epistemic defense's relevance to current PDH scholarship—is to *combine* the conclusions of part 1 and part 2's literature reviews, spelling out how I will exposit my argumentation in chapters 3–5. As discussed, I have chosen my project to be an exercise in Christian philosophy and theology, opting to provide a defense (as opposed to a theodicy) for PDH. My defense attempts to engage not only philosophical and epistemological concepts but also biblical and theological themes pertinent to PDH, concepts and themes surfaced in parts 1 and 2 above.

Now, some philosophers, even theistic ones, may have reservations with engaging theology and revelation in the context of PDH, even from an epistemological perspective. As William Abraham explains, in some philosophy circles (even theistic ones), "theology itself is secondary and treated as subservient; theology's central claims are seen as guilty *until* proven innocent."[139] "Philosophers," declares Abraham (rhetorically), "are very nervous about this kind of behavior. There is, we might say, a natural aversion to the concept of divine revelation."[140] For such is said to be "subjective and arbitrary" as well as a "pious laborsaving device that stops us *thinking for ourselves* and makes us slaves of authority."[141] Schellenberg appears to have this concern, writing with respect to PDH that

> theology starts off by accepting that God exists and so has to make God fit the world; in a way, that is its job. But our job as *philosophers*, faced with questions of God's existence, is to fight free from the distractions of local and historical contingency, to let the voice of authority grow dim in our ears, and *to think for*

"Symposium on Paul Moser's Religious Epistemology," where he contributed two essays relevant to PDH: "Gethsemane Epistemology"; "Natural Theology."

139. Abraham, *Crossing the Threshold*, 9; emphasis added.
140. Abraham, *Crossing the Threshold*, 83.
141. Abraham, *Crossing the Threshold*, 83; emphasis added.

ourselves about what a God and a God-created world would be like.[142]

But by stamping out revelation, and by allowing the voice of authority to grow dim in our ears, we do not give God a fair hearing.[143] "Philosophers," insists Abraham elsewhere, "who set up their own standards as to how God should be revealed run the risk not just of mistaking their standards but of cognitive idolatry."[144]

Heeding Abraham's counsel, then, the philosophically sensitive but theologically germane defense that I would like to give concerning PDH will come in three parts.[145] These parts were disclosed in the previous chapter by way of introduction (and briefly in both literature reviews), but let me describe them again in anticipation of subsequent chapters.

Part 1, my chapter 3, will explain Plantinga's hypothetical A/C model for how bare theistic belief can have warrant (spelled out in *WCB*); that is, how we can have *knowledge* of God. Embedded in the model are important theological concepts such as general revelation, what Calvin calls the *sensus divinitatis*, and so on, themes mentioned in part 1 and part 2's literature reviews that will be applied to PDH.

The second part of my defense—my chapter 4—uses the *extended* A/C model developed by Plantinga to demonstrate how full-blown Christian theism (and not just bare theism) might be warranted; I use particularly the model's construal of sin's noetic and affective effects, and how these effects in turn negatively influence our knowledge of and love for God. This part of my defense applies sin's effects on our knowledge of God to PDH. The third part of my defense—my chapter 5—also uses the extended A/C model for warranted Christian belief; it especially applies to PDH the portion of the model that describes the divine remedy proposed by God for human sin, demonstrating how we can have knowledge of God in our postlapsarian environment, through the atoning work of Jesus Christ, the inspiration of

---

142. Schellenberg, *Wisdom to Doubt*, 197; emphasis added.

143. See also Abraham, "Offense of Divine Revelation."

144. Abraham, "Existence of God," 31; emphasis added. See also Abraham and Aquino, *Epistemology of Theology*; Abraham, "Epistemology of Jesus."

145. Hoitenga explains, with respect to Reformed epistemology, that "no other subject perhaps brings out so clearly the intrinsic connection between *theology* and *philosophy*, as well as the need to question the sharp lines that so often have been drawn between natural and revealed theology" (*Faith and Reason*, xv; emphasis added). For a helpful methodological essay on how analytic-philosophical issues can be informed by theological matters, and vice versa, see Abraham, "Systematic Theology as Analytic Theology."

Scripture, what Aquinas and the Reformed tradition call the internal testimony of the Holy Spirit, and so on.

So, the A/C and extended A/C models, taken together, can be used as a defense for PDH, satisfying my defense desiderata, which state that I will (i*) develop a specifically Christian account describing why, if God exists, his existence is not more obvious; and (ii) show that this description is true for all we know. One way to show that the models are true for all we know is to answer objections; thus, each chapter considers various objections to my argumentation. Last, the models can ultimately answer my research question, from which my thesis was stated: *Plantinga's A/C models for how Christian belief may have warrant can be utilized as a defense to explain why, if God exists, his existence is not more obvious.* I now turn to chapter 3 to begin fleshing out the first part of my defense.

3.

The Problem of Divine Hiddenness and the Aquinas/Calvin Model

3.1 INTRODUCTION

CHAPTER 1 INTRODUCED THE problem of divine hiddenness (hereafter PDH). It was there that I defined the problem (*If God exists, then his existence would be more obvious*), which in turn led me to pose the research question that this project will attempt to answer (*Why, if God exists, is his existence not more obvious?*). Next, I followed Peter van Inwagen's counsel that theists who engage PDH can tell "stories"—taking the form of either a theodicy or a defense—spelling out reasons why if there is a God his existence is not more obvious. I chose the latter method, saying further that my defense, which aims not at mere logical but rather at *epistemic* possibility, intends to satisfy two desiderata; namely, that I will

(i*) Develop a specifically Christian account describing why, if God exists, his existence is not more obvious.

(ii) Show that this description is true for all we know.

Christians have available a Reformed epistemic story, drawing from Alvin Plantinga's A/C models, which can both answer the research question and can satisfy the two desiderata. This led me to formulate my thesis statement, in chapter 1, that *Plantinga's A/C models for how Christian belief may have warrant can be utilized as a defense to explain why, if God exists, his existence is not more obvious*. I then moved to chapter 2, a literature review, which explored PDH as it is examined in contemporary analytic philosophy of religion, showing how my defense is relevant to, and how it can be included in, the current debate. This positioned me, here in this chapter, to begin arguing explicitly for my defense.

Therefore, the broad purpose of this chapter is just to argue for the first portion of my thesis statement—forthcoming are the second and third portions in the two subsequent chapters—using Plantinga's epistemology. But Plantinga's epistemology is *extensive*; his *Warrant* trilogy alone—*Warrant: The Current Debate*; *Warrant and Proper Function*; *Warranted Christian Belief*—spans nearly a thousand pages. How can it be applied to PDH while ensuring a focused study? James Beilby explains that there are what he calls three *stages* or *periods* as well as three *layers* or *levels* to Plantinga's epistemology. The first stage or period includes Plantinga's seminal *God and Other Minds* (where he argues that belief in God is epistemically comparable to belief in other human minds). The second encompasses the basic seeds of Plantinga's Reformed epistemology, culminating in his influential essay "Reason and Belief in God." The *Warrant* trilogy mostly comprises the third stage.[1] In addition to these stages, Beilby also stipulates:

> It is possible to discern three important "layers" or "levels" to Plantinga's religious epistemology: (1) his "underlying" epistemology, (2) the *theological* implications of his account of the formation of faith, and (3) his methodological assumptions about the task of religious epistemology.[2]

To concentrate my argumentation, the aim in this chapter and in the ones that follow is to engage *stage* or *period* (3), the most mature stage of Plantinga's work, as well as *layer* or *level* (2), the theologically charged implications of his epistemology. But even more specifically, I concern myself, as expressed in my thesis statement above, with the A/C models found in *WCB*, the culmination of the *Warrant* trilogy.

So, in *WCB*, Plantinga presents in chapter 6 ("Warranted Belief in God") the hypothetical A/C model to explain how bare theistic belief may have *warrant*, the property enough of which converts mere true belief into knowledge (more on this later). Then, in chapters 7–8 of *WCB*, Plantinga extends the model—calling this the extended A/C model—to show how full-blooded, postlapsarian Christian belief may have warrant, drawing on theological themes such as the atoning work of Jesus Christ, the internal witness of the Holy Spirit, the inspiration and self-authenticating nature of Scripture, and so forth; the extended model also includes a lengthy treatise

---

1. Beilby, *Epistemology as Theology*, 34. In dividing Plantinga's epistemology into stages/periods, Beilby does not mean to imply that Plantinga has abandoned earlier stages/periods, just that Plantinga's epistemology has matured.

2. Beilby, *Epistemology as Theology*, 104; emphasis added.

on sin's noetic and affective consequences. Taken collectively, these models (so I think) form a coherent story (a defense), exemplifying possible reasons—answering my research question—for why if there is a God his existence is not more obvious. In this chapter, I engage various theological themes from *only WCB*'s bare A/C model—the first portion of my defense— and will apply them to divine hiddenness. Similarly, my two subsequent chapters on PDH explore *WCB*'s corresponding extended model.

The chapter outline is as follows: *explain, apply, respond*. First, I *explain* the A/C model, intentionally highlighting the model's theology;[3] still, the goal is to describe the model on Plantinga's own terms. Second, I *apply* the model to PDH. Third, I then *respond* to objections from the model when applied to PDH. If this chapter succeeds, then it will not only serve as the first of my three-part defense (fulfilling the desiderata), but it will also begin to answer my research question.

3.2 PLANTINGA'S AQUINAS/CALVIN MODEL EXPLAINED

3.2.1 Contextual Remarks

Alvin Plantinga has been at the forefront of Christian philosophy for several decades.[4] As a leading Reformed epistemologist, he has labored to provide an account describing how belief in God might be properly basic and warranted. In *Warrant: The Current Debate*, Plantinga explored the current epistemological scene on warrant, only to find the presented options there deficient. Then, in the same year (1993), *Warrant and Proper Function* was released; there he began to develop his own positive theory of warrant. Seven years later (2000), Plantinga published his magnum opus, *Warranted Christian Belief*. Fifteen years after *WCB*, *Knowledge and Christian Belief* (hereafter *KCB*), a popular and shorter version of *WCB*, was released. *WCB* begins by contrasting de facto and de jure objections; the former are objections to the truth of Christian belief (e.g., the argument from evil), whereas the latter, which depend upon the former, are objections to the justification

---

3. As James Beilby writes: "Many may be surprised at the overtly *theological* nature of much of this volume [i.e., *WCB*]" ("Plantinga's Model," 125; emphasis added).

4. For introductions to Plantinga's life and work, I am helped by A. Plantinga, "Self-Profile"; Mascord, *Alvin Plantinga*, 1–20; Baker, "Introduction"; Beilby, *Epistemology as Theology*, 5–32. Diller, *Theology's Epistemological Dilemma*, 94–127.

or to the rationality of Christian belief.[5] *WCB* is chiefly concerned with de jure objections.

In *WCB* part 1 ("Is There a Question?"), Plantinga asks if it is possible to refer to and discuss God or Christian belief. Having exposited and countered Immanuel Kant, Gordon Kaufman, and John Hick, Plantinga answers in the affirmative; it is, in fact, possible to do so.[6] Then, in part 2 ("What Is the Question?"), he investigates whether belief in God is epistemically deficient. Is it, in other words, unjustified or irrational (or even childish or insensible) to embrace Christian belief?

Let me briefly explore justification and rationality. *Justification*, following John Locke (and classical foundationalism), is concerned with deontology and evidence; a person has a relevant *duty*, to put it differently, to believe only those propositions for which she has *evidence*. Plantinga claims, however, that a person is justified to hold Christian belief in a properly basic (i.e., a non-derived or non-inferential) way, without evidence or argumentation, such that no epistemic duties or obligations are breached in so believing.[7] In this sense, Christian theistic belief can be properly basic with respect to *justification*.[8]

Rationality, for Plantinga, is tied to proper function, "the absence of dysfunction or pathology: you are rational if not subject to such pathology."[9] Theistic belief can be rational, he argues, thereby countering de jure complaints leveraged against it from, for example, Sigmund Freud, who posits that religious belief is illusory and wishful, and Karl Marx, who protests that religious belief arises from cognitive malfunction. Plantinga calls this the Freud/Marx complaint.[10] Like justification, theistic belief can be properly basic with respect to *rationality*. And rationality (conceived in terms of proper function) is included in Plantinga's construal of *warrant*, the property or quality enough of which distinguishes knowledge from mere true belief, since a person can have a true belief, Plantinga says, but still

---

5. *WCB* viii–xvi.

6. For critical analysis on *WCB*'s pt. 1, see Tapp, "Reference to Infinite Being." For my review of this volume, see Taber, "Review of *Plantinga*."

7. *WCB* 99–107; cf. also *KCB* 11–14.

8. As Andrew Moon rightly argues concerning Plantinga's epistemology, "Belief [in this case, theistic belief] is properly basic *with respect to some positive epistemic property* [such as justification, rationality, or warrant]" ("Recent Work," 881; emphasis in original).

9. *WCB* 110. Plantinga distinguishes between internal and external rationality; I discuss this distinction below and in the next chapter.

10. For Plantinga's treatment of Freud and Marx, see *WCB* 135–63.

not possess *knowledge*.¹¹ Thus, in addition to true belief, something else is needed: *warrant*. So, what of it? "A belief has warrant," writes Plantinga,

> for a person S only if that belief is produced in S by cognitive faculties functioning properly (subject to no dysfunction) in a cognitive environment that is appropriate for S's kind of cognitive faculties, according to a design plan that is successfully aimed at truth.¹²

Here are the fourfold warrant criteria and, like justification and rationality, theistic or Christian theistic belief can be properly basic with respect to *warrant*. First, there is *proper function*: that is, how one's cognitive equipment is *supposed* to work, which is intimately tied to the notion of a *design plan*, since (for instance) "there is a way in which a human organ or system works when it works properly, works as it supposed to work; and this way of working is given by its design or design plan."¹³ Second, the environmental condition for warrant must be met, whereby one's cognitive faculties work if they function in the environment for which they were designed (produced by God or by evolution); humans, for instance, are not designed to breathe in an underwater environment. Consider third *aimed at true belief*, which is to say that, for Plantinga, one's cognitive endowment must have the purpose of producing *true* beliefs and not, for instance, mere wish fulfillment (contra the Freud/Marx complaint mentioned earlier). The final warrant condition is *successfully aimed at true belief*: that is, the design plan must be good and "one such that there is a high probability that a belief produced according to that plan will be true (or nearly true)."¹⁴ Plantinga includes this latter condition because a design plan, even if aimed at truth, can still produce "glitches" or "ludicrously false beliefs," thus lacking warrant. For example, one's cognitive equipment working according to its design plan

---

11. Plantinga gives an example: an optimistic person wholeheartedly *believes* that it will be bright and sunny for tomorrow's hiking trip, despite the forecast's prediction of rain, snow, and sleet. Yet even if the forecast turns out to be *incorrect*—and the optimistic person correct—the optimistic person, according to Plantinga, has a *true belief* about the weather but not necessarily *knowledge*; she was just "lucky" (*KCB* 25–26). Such reasoning also attempts to safeguards against (Edmund) Gettier-type problems that have challenged the traditional analysis of knowledge summed up as justified true belief, on which see A. Plantinga, *Warrant and Proper Function*, 31–33.

12. *KCB* 28.

13. *KCB* 27. Kenny Boyce writes that Plantinga "maintains that the relevant notion of proper function presupposes that of a *design plan*—something that specifies the manner in which a thing is *supposed to function* in various circumstances" ("Proper Functionalism," 1.b., para. 1; emphasis added).

14. *KCB* 28; see further 26–28. See also *WCB* 153–63; Beilby, "Plantinga's Model," 127–28.

aimed at truth may still "constantly confuse horses and hearses, forming the odd beliefs that cowboys in the old west rode hearses and that corpses are usually transported in horses."[15] Now, is theistic and Christian theistic belief warranted? Can it, in other words, satisfy the warrant conditions?

In part 3 of *WCB* ("Warranted Christian Belief"), Plantinga builds two models, informed by his Reformed theological heritage, in order to explain how theistic and Christian theistic belief *could* or *may* satisfy the warrant conditions: the so-called A/C and extended A/C models.[16] Finally, in part 4 of *WCB* ("Defeaters?"), he addresses objections, or defeaters, to his offered models (objections or alleged defeaters from historical biblical criticism, postmodernity, religious pluralism, and the problem of evil), where a *defeater* can roughly be defined as a reason (or reasons) for giving up a belief that one holds.[17] I concern myself in this chapter (and in chapters 4–5) with part 3 of *WCB*, beginning with the A/C model, the purpose of which is then to apply the model to PDH.

3.2.2 The Aquinas/Calvin Model: Exposition and Explanation

What is it to give a model? "To give a model," Plantinga explains of both A/C and extended A/C models, "is to exhibit a possible state of affairs in which that proposition is true, thus showing how it *could* be true."[18] *If* Christian theistic belief is true, he notes, then it likely does have warrant.[19] There are four further specifics about the A/C-type models. First, they are not just logically but are *epistemically* possible, "consistent with what we know, where 'what we know' is what all (or most) of the participants in the [epistemological] discussion agree on."[20] Second, there are no cogent or success-

15. *KCB* 28.

16. I emphasize the words *could* and *may* because as Kevin Diller cautions: "An oft-made mistake in Plantinga interpretation is to assume that he is building a traditional-style deductive argument to the ultimate conclusion that Christian belief has warrant.... It should be clear, however, that Plantinga is not arguing that Christian belief has warrant *on the basis of his theory of warrant*. It is quite the opposite" (*Theology's Epistemological Dilemma*, 124–25; emphasis added). For as I will say below, the models are possible states of affairs. "Plantinga," says Diller, "argues that *if* Christian belief is true, then something like his Christian model of how Christian belief might have warrant is correct" (125; emphasis in original). See also *WCB* 351.

17. "Defeaters . . . are reasons for giving up a belief *B* you hold" (*KCB* 90). "Acquiring a defeater for a belief," writes Plantinga, "puts you in a position in which you can't rationally continue to hold the belief" (*WCB* 359; see also 359–73).

18. *KCB* 31; emphasis added.

19. *WCB* 188.

20. *WCB* 168.

ful objections to the models (as mentioned, Plantinga answers objections/defeaters to the models in *WCB* pt. 4). Third, the models are believed to be true, but Plantinga himself does not claim to *show* or to *demonstrate* that the models are true. Fourth, there may be a range of models—apart from the A/C-type models—for how theistic belief can have warrant.

Now, on the bare or generic A/C model, both Aquinas and Calvin, as Plantinga interprets them, concur that all persons have natural knowledge of God.[21] For "to know in a general and confused way," writes Aquinas, "that God exists is implanted in us by nature."[22] Similarly, "there is within every human mind," says Calvin,

> and indeed by natural instinct, an awareness of divinity. This we take to be beyond controversy. To prevent anyone from taking refuge in the pretense of ignorance, God himself has implanted in all men a certain understanding of divine majesty.... Therefore, since from the beginning of the world there has been no region, no city, in short, no household, that could do without religion, there lies in this a tacit confession of a sense of deity inscribed in the hearts of all.[23]

This sense of deity, notes Plantinga, is what Calvin called a *sensus divinitatis* (hereafter SD), a cognitive faculty that produces in us theistic belief. Awareness of God by way of the SD is both natural and widespread, and it cannot be destroyed. The SD, however, does require maturation, since from birth, humans have the *capacity* for this innate knowledge of God; but while it takes time to develop, it is nonetheless present in every human being. Calvin writes:

> Lest anyone, then, be excluded from access to happiness, he [God] not only sowed in men's minds that seed of religion of which we have spoken, but revealed himself and daily discloses himself in the whole workmanship of the universe. As a consequence, men cannot open their eyes without being compelled to see him.... But upon his individual works he has engraved unmistakable marks of his glory... wherever you cast your eyes, there is no spot in the universe wherein you cannot discern at least some sparks of his glory.[24]

---

21. I take for granted, for the sake of argumentation, Plantinga's account and interpretation of both Aquinas and Calvin; I do, however, answer some objections to his interpretation of Calvin below.

22. Thomas Aquinas, *Summa Theologiae* I, q.2, a.1, ad, as quoted in *WCB* 170.

23. John Calvin, *Institutes of the Christian Religion*, 1.3.1, as quoted in *WCB* 171.

24. John Calvin, *Institutes of the Christian Religion*, 1.5.1, as quoted in *WCB* 174.

So, God has given revelation of himself in "men's minds" but also in the "workmanship of the universe." Further, the SD is (as Plantinga puts it) "triggered or occasioned by a wide variety of circumstances, including in particular some of the glories of nature." For instance:

> the marvelous, impressive beauty of the night sky; the timeless crash and roar of the surf that resonates deep within us; the majestic grandeur of the mountains . . . the ancient, brooding presence of the Australian outback; the thunder of a great waterfall. But it isn't only grandeur and majesty that counts; he [Calvin] would say the same for the subtle play of sunlight on a field in spring, or the dainty, articulate beauty of a tiny flower, or aspen leaves shimmering and dancing in the breeze.[25]

The natural, created order, says Plantinga, is "telling" of God, thereby speaking to his very existence, and the SD, a belief-forming faculty, filters these situations or events mentioned above and in turn produces in a person theistic belief. "The central feature of this [A/C] model," Plantinga writes,

> is the stipulation that God has created us human beings with a belief-producing process or source of belief, the *sensus divinitatis*; this source works under various conditions to produce beliefs about God, including of course, beliefs that immediately entail his existence.[26]

Last, on the model, "knowledge requires proper function, and knowledge of God requires proper function of the *sensus divinitatis*."[27] When it operates correctly, the way that it is designed by God to operate, in its appropriate environment aimed successfully at truth, the SD produces *knowledge* of God: warranted theistic belief.

There are six further distinctive characteristics of the A/C model; I summarize these items (as they are given in WCB),[28] underscoring the implicit theology. First, the innate theistic belief produced by the SD is *basic*, not believed on the basis of other beliefs, perhaps resembling "perception, memory, and *a priori* belief."[29] Take perception: one does not stand at the summit of Pike's Peak or Mt. Everest, for example, only to conclude or to *infer* that there must be a Creator; indeed, grand or even seemingly miniscule events, argues Plantinga, do not serve as the basis for an argument for God's existence.

25. WCB 174.
26. WCB 199; emphasis added.
27. WCB 240.
28. WCB 175–86.
29. WCB 175.

> It is rather that, upon the perception of the night sky or the mountain vista or the tiny flower, these beliefs just arise within us. They are *occasioned* by the circumstances; they are not conclusions from them.[30]

Hence, these *circumstances*, or conditions, can spontaneously trigger the SD, such that one may simply find oneself believing in God in a *basic* way, not taken on the basis of other beliefs. Thus "God," writes Plantinga elsewhere, may have "so created us that we have a tendency or disposition to see his hand in the world about us."[31]

Second, the deliverances of the SD, theistic belief, can be properly basic with respect to *justification* (recall the above discussion on justification). A person is justified—within her epistemic rights—to hold theistic belief in a properly basic manner, even if she cannot muster any propositional evidence or argumentation for her position, in which case no intellectual duties or obligations are infringed.[32] For as Plantinga asks concerning theistic belief on this point: "How could someone sensibly claim that you [the theist, holding theistic belief] were being irresponsible . . . with respect to some epistemic duty?"[33]

Third, the deliverances of the SD can be properly basic with respect to *warrant* (as well as with respect to *rationality*, since rationality as proper function is included in the warrant conditions). When functioning properly—in accordance with its design plan, in a congenial epistemic environment aimed successfully at truth—the SD does, in fact, produce beliefs about God that are non-inferential. "On this [A/C] model," notes Plantinga,

> our cognitive faculties have been designed and created by God; the design plan, therefore, is a design in the literal and paradigmatic sense. It is a blueprint or plan for our ways of functioning, and it has been developed and instituted by a conscious, intelligent agent. The purpose of the *sensus divinitatis* is to enable us to have true beliefs about God; when it does function properly, it ordinarily *does* produce true beliefs about God. These beliefs therefore meet the conditions for warrant.[34]

Fourth, such theistic knowledge is (again) *natural*, part of humanity's *original* epistemic/cognitive equipment, when we were created by God, prior

---

30. WCB 175; emphasis in original.
31. A. Plantinga, "Is Belief in God Properly Basic?," 137.
32. See further A. Plantinga, "Reason and Belief"; "Is Belief in God Rational?"; "On Reformed Epistemology."
33. WCB 178.
34. WCB 179; emphasis in original.

to sin's entrance into the world.³⁵ Now, due to human fallenness (the "fall" being an event on which Plantinga does not take a precise historical stance),³⁶ the SD has been damaged, but not obliterated; as a result, we currently find ourselves in an *unnatural* epistemic condition, tainted by sin. Perhaps this is why James Beilby explains that the A/C model "describes a *prelapsarian* epistemic situation."³⁷ While Plantinga himself never uses the term, he does appear to suggest that the model is epistemically prelapsarian, but then, somewhat awkwardly and inconsistently, does at times refer to sin in the model (I discuss this more below and answer an objection to this later).

Fifth, Plantinga proposes that knowledge of God can come by way of either perception (e.g., a palpable sense of the presence of God) or by religious experience (e.g., through sensuous imagery), but that it is not important to the model, however, to explain *how* the SD could account for perception or religious experience.³⁸ The model, in other words, need not take a stance on these issues.

The sixth and final (main) feature of the A/C model is that human natural knowledge of God, genuine as it is, has been weakened, damaged, and impaired by sin (here is another instance whereby Plantinga discusses sin in the context of the model). Indeed, "prior to faith and regeneration," writes Plantinga, the SD "is both narrowed in scope and partially suppressed."³⁹ Now, the Freud/Marx complaint, vocalized above, suggests that belief in God is merely illusory or is simply wishful thinking, arising (perhaps) from cognitive malfunction; the believer in God may even be *insane*. But on Plantinga's model, however, God has revealed himself both in the created order and in our minds, and it therefore "really is the *unbeliever* who displays epistemic malfunction; failing to believe in God is a result of some kind of dysfunction of the *sensus divinitatis*."⁴⁰

> Failure to believe [in God] can be due to a sort of blindness or deafness, to improper function of the *sensus divinitatis*. On the present model, such failure to believe is irrational, and such withholdings lack the analogue of warrant.⁴¹

35. *WCB* 180.
36. See *WCB* 207.
37. Beilby, *Epistemology as Theology*, 181; emphasis added. See also Beilby, "Plantinga's Model," 129.
38. *WCB* 183-84. As Plantinga writes elsewhere: "The idea is that the *Sensus Divinitatis* is a faculty analogous, in some ways, to sense perception" (A. Plantinga and Tooley, *Knowledge of God*, 7).
39. *WCB* 184.
40. *WCB* 184; emphasis in original.
41. *WCB* 186.

Plantinga explains further that, if theistic belief is false (namely, if there is no God), then it is probably not warranted; theistic belief may then simply be the result of wish fulfillment, merely the product of blind evolutionary forces. In this case, belief in God would probably be *unwarranted* since, if there is no God, then it is thus unlikely that such belief is produced by properly functioning faculties, in an appropriate epistemic environment, aimed successfully at the production of true belief.

However, if theistic belief *is* true, then belief in God is probably warranted and it can, therefore, meet the warrant conditions. Additionally, it is not implausible to think, Plantinga suggests, that if there is a God, then he would intend for humans, made in his image, to be aware of his presence, or to know some things about him, or to form belief in him *naturally*. "And if *that* is so," Plantinga clarifies,

> then the natural thing to think is that the cognitive processes that *do* produce belief in God are aimed by their designer at producing that belief. But then the belief in question will be produced by cognitive faculties functioning properly according to a design plan successfully aimed at truth: it will therefore have warrant.[42]

But here Plantinga's de jure/de facto distinction is pertinent. For to show that belief in God is irrational or unjustified or unwarranted (the de jure objection), the nonbeliever will have to attack the *truth* of theism (by way of a de facto objection, such as the argument from evil).[43] For, as Plantinga claims, there are no de jure objections that are independent of de facto ones.

So, take the Freud/Marx complaint; suppose it is true that such need to believe in a higher power is a matter of mere wish fulfillment, and that religion is, in fact, the opium of the people—lacking warrant. It is not enough, Plantinga argues, to suggest that theistic belief is a matter of wish fulfillment, since de jure objections depend upon de facto ones; Freud and Marx—and their cohorts—will have to attack the *truth* of theism. As Plantinga writes elsewhere, "To argue that Christian or theist belief lacks warrant, one would first have to argue that such belief *isn't* true,"[44] the A/C model—again—describing a possible way that theistic belief could have warrant if true.

Now, what the A/C model suggests is that even if theistic belief does arise from wish fulfillment, then this need not imply that theistic belief has *no* warrant. "Perhaps human beings have been created by God," as mentioned above but stressed here again, and thus have

---

42. *WCB* 189; emphasis added.
43. *WCB* 193. See also ix–x.
44. A. Plantinga, "Ad Wiertz," 247; emphasis added.

a deep need to believe in his presence and goodness and love. Perhaps God designed us that way in order that we come to believe in him and be aware of his presence. Perhaps this is how God has arranged for us to come to know him. If so, then the particular bit of the cognitive design plan governing the formation of theistic belief is indeed aimed at true belief, even if the belief in question arises from wish-fulfillment.[45]

Hence, wish fulfillment on the A/C model is unproblematic. The converse of the Freud/Marx complaint is that, while *unbelievers* see theistic belief lacking in warrant,

> a believer will see the shoe as on the other foot. According to St. Paul [Rom 1:18–21], it is *unbelief* that is a result of dysfunction, brokenness, failure to function properly, or impedance of rational faculties. Unbelief, he says, is a result of sin; it originates in an effort, as Romans 1 puts it, to "suppress the truth in unrighteousness."[46]

In sum, I have attempted to provide an explanation and exposition of Plantinga's A/C model, which is intended to demonstrate how theistic belief, if true, can be properly basic and can have warrant.

3.3 THE AQUINAS/CALVIN MODEL APPLIED TO THE HIDDENNESS PROBLEM

This section applies the A/C model to PDH. But first a brief preliminary remark. Recall that my project attempts to give a three-part defense against PDH that aims to satisfy the defense desiderata ([i*] and [ii]). As discussed in chapter 1, Plantinga's models comport well with these desiderata, thus ultimately providing an answer to the research question. With reference to (i*), the A/C and extended A/C models, taken together, form a specifically Christian account that can be used to explain why God's existence is not more obvious. The bare or generic A/C model comprises the first part of my three-part defense; the extended model is used in chapters 4 and 5 containing parts 2 and 3 respectively. With reference to (ii), as said in my exposition above, Plantinga claims of his models that they are "consistent with what we know."[47] Dietrich Schönecker writes of the A/C model that "to say that the model is epistemically possible is to say that 'nothing we know commits us

---

45. *WCB* 197.
46. *WCB* 198; emphasis in original.
47. *WCB* 169.

to its falsehood."[48] One way to argue that nothing we know commits us to its falsehood is to respond to objections, just as Plantinga answers objections to his models in part 4 of *WCB*. I also will answer objections below to what the A/C model can do both to answer my research question and to support my defense (§3.4).

So, what precisely does it do to answer my research question and to support my defense? What do I claim of the A/C model concerning PDH? When the bare A/C model—including its epistemological account of proper basicality, justification, rationality, and warrant—is applied to PDH, there are motivations for thinking that God's existence is not hidden from humanity. What follows are five specific applications.[49]

Application 1: On the A/C model, God is not hidden from humanity, and theistic belief is basic. The model specifies that there is the *internal* or innate SD, a cognitive faculty or a natural human tendency or a disposition that enables us to form beliefs about God. It is, in other words, a sense of the divine, an awareness of God, universally present in all persons. But the model also describes God's witness of himself in the *external* creation, including revelation *extravagant* ("the blazing glory of the heavens," the "starry heavens above," "the glories of nature," the "impressive beauty of the night sky," "the brooding presence of the Australian outback") as well as revelation more *subtle* ("sunlight on a field in spring," the "dainty . . . beauty of a tiny flower," or "aspen leaves shimmering and dancing in the breeze").[50] For "there is no spot in the universe," as Plantinga quotes Calvin, "wherein you cannot discern at least some sparks of his glory."[51]

Further, according to Plantinga, the internal SD is stimulated or triggered by these external circumstances—the external circumstances wherein God's existence is clearly revealed—which fosters in us basic theistic belief. Nicholas Wolterstorff, writing of Herman Bavinck's theology, explains how this could go:

> What *activates* this innate disposition to theistic belief? Corresponding to the disposition is the fact that *nature* carries signs and indicators of its maker. . . . It is these signs of divinity in nature, these revelations, both those that are "exterior" and

---

48. Schönecker, "Deliverances," 23; cf. *WCB* xii.

49. Though these are my own applications of the A/C model to PDH, I have been helped on some of these points by James Beilby in email correspondence (Sept. 12, 2013), as well as by Alvin Plantinga in personal conversation (Sept. 26, 2014).

50. *WCB* 173-74.

51. *WCB* 174.

those that are "interior to us humans" . . . , that *activate* in us our innate disposition to form beliefs about God immediately.[52]

Thus, the "Reformed epistemologist," notes Plantinga, "may concur with Calvin in holding that God has implanted in us a natural tendency to see his hand in the world around us."[53] If this is right then, on the model, God is not hidden from humanity, and when the SD is triggered or prompted in various situations or conditions then theistic belief can be *basic*, or non-inferential, accepted not on the basis of other beliefs. A person does not behold the external grandeur or beauty of the created order where God has plainly or obviously revealed himself and therefore conclude, by way of an argument or by evidence, that there is a God. Rather, these beliefs (produced by the SD)

> are *occasioned* by the circumstances; they are not conclusions from them. The heavens declare the glory of God and the skies above proclaim the work of his hands [Ps 19]: but not by way of serving as premises for an argument.[54]

From this application, it may just seem clear or obvious or compelling to a person that there is a God and that he is not hidden, perhaps captured in the words of J. L. Schellenberg (when he was a theist):

> The world never had any difficulty inspiring wonder in me. But as a boy and as a teenager and right into early adulthood, I felt a sense of wonder filtered through belief in God. It was the majesty and glory of God I heard in the keening winter wind, and saw in sunlight spreading across waves of prairie grass after a thunderstorm.[55]

Application 2: On the A/C model, God is not hidden from humanity, and theistic belief is properly basic with respect to justification. A basic belief is non-inferential, and it is properly basic if it is believed in the basic way and (concerning justification) one is justified in so believing. I argue here that, on the model, God is not hidden from us, having clearly revealed himself in the external created order, such that when the internal SD is spontaneously activated or triggered or occasioned, then we will form theistic belief in a

---

52. Wolterstorff, "Herman Bavinck," 139; emphasis added. Wolterstorff quotes Bavinck, *God and Creation*, 72.

53. A. Plantinga, "Is Belief in God Properly Basic?," 141.

54. *WCB* 175; emphasis in original. As Plantinga notes elsewhere, "This sort of belief formation [in God] is not a result of movement from one set of beliefs (premises) to another (conclusion), but from a set of circumstances (being appeared to a certain way, for example) to a belief" (*Where Conflict Really Lies*, 244).

55. Schellenberg, "Why Am I Nonbeliever," 28.

properly basic way with respect to justification, in which case a person is a responsible theistic believer and is within her epistemic rights (thus violating no duties or obligations) in believing. For as Plantinga writes regarding justification, it just may seem "clear or obvious (perhaps even overwhelmingly so) that there is such a person as God."[56] He is not hidden. Herman Bavinck argues that there

> is not an atom of the universe in which his everlasting power and deity are not clearly seen. Both from within and from without, God's witness speaks to us. God does not leave himself without witness, in heart or conscience, in life or lot. The witness of God is so powerful. . . . All humans and peoples have heard something of the voice of the Lord.[57]

Perhaps you have in fact "heard something of the voice of the Lord." Indeed, it may be (as Plantinga says) that, on a

> beautiful spring morning (the birds singing, heaven and earth alight and alive with glory, the air fresh and cool, the treetops gleaming in the sun), a spontaneous hymn of thanks to the Lord—thanks for your circumstances and your very existence—may arise in your soul.[58]

If theistic belief is formed in this way, God's existence appearing clear and evident to you, then you are justified and are a responsible theistic believer.[59]

Application 3: On the A/C model, God is not hidden from humanity, and theistic belief is properly basic with respect to internal rationality. Plantinga conceives of rationality in terms of proper function, differentiating further between internal and external rationality.[60] Dieter Schönecker says, "The basic idea of internal rationality . . . is that one is not insane on one's own standards."[61] More simply, Plantinga writes that internal rationality is one's "'seemings'—for example, the seeming-to-be-true of various propositions."[62] My application here stipulates that when beholding the starry heavens or gazing upon the grandeur of a mountain or seeing a beautiful flower, you may form theistic belief and it may just seem obvious or true or compelling, by your own standards, that there is a God (he does not appear to be hiding

---

56. *WCB* 178; emphasis added.
57. Bavinck, *God and Creation*, 90.
58. *WCB* 174.
59. *WCB* 178; cf. also *WCB* 83–86.
60. *WCB* chapter 4 (see also 203–4; 255–56).
61. Schönecker, "Deliverances," 26; emphasis in original.
62. A. Plantinga, "Ad Schönecker," 238.

from you), in which case you would be internally rational in believing. Perhaps Jonathan Edwards (from his sermon on Ps 89) captures what by your own standards seems to be true concerning the clarity of God's existence, namely, that the

> beauty of trees, plants, and flowers, with which God has bespangled the face of the earth is delightsome, . . . the beauty of the moon and stars, is wonderful, the beauty of highest heavens, is transcendent, [and] the excellency of angels and the saints in light is very glorious.[63]

It may just be, regarding internal rationality, that, for you, the "very light of nature," as the Westminster Larger Catechism puts it, "declare[s] plainly that there is a God,"[64] or similarly, as the Belgic Confession explains, that God's existence revealed in creation is before your eyes "as a most elegant book."[65]

Application 4: On the A/C model, God is not hidden from humanity, and theistic belief is properly basic with respect to external rationality and warrant. "A belief is externally rational," Plantinga argues,

> if it is produced by cognitive faculties that are functioning properly and successfully aimed at truth (i.e., aimed at the production of true belief)—as opposed, for example, to being the product of wish-fulfillment or cognitive malfunction.[66]

External rationality is stronger than internal rationality and is included in the warrant conditions, particularly the proper function and the alethic criteria. Thus, the main concern is if theistic belief has *warrant*. Now, in order to explicate this particular application, I will purposefully follow Beilby, discussed earlier, who argues that the bare A/C model is *prelapsarian* (although recognizing that Plantinga somewhat confusingly does discuss sin in the model; I discuss this matter in the objection section below). So, a belief has warrant if it is produced by properly functioning faculties (according to a design plan) in a congenial environment aimed successfully at truth.

The argument to be made here is that, on the prelapsarian A/C model, the warrant conditions are always satisfied, and God is not hidden. The SD is functioning properly, and it is stimulated or occasioned or activated by the external created order to produce in us theistic belief; there is nothing—sin, for instance—to inhibit or constrain its function. Moreover, take

---

63. As quoted in D. Butler, "God's Visible Glory," 13.
64. Q. 2 in Van Dixhoorn, *Creeds, Confessions & Catechisms*, 337.
65. Art. 2 in Van Dixhoorn, *Creeds, Confessions & Catechisms*, 79. See also Van den Brink, "Most Elegant Book."
66. *WCB* 204; emphasis added.

the *design plan*, which is closely tied to proper function; the design plan is the way in which a thing should or is supposed to work. On the A/C model, the SD just has been designed by God, with a blueprint plan for how it ought to function:

> Like the rest of our organs and systems, our cognitive faculties can work well or ill; they can malfunction or function properly. They too work in a certain way when they are functioning properly—and work in a certain way to accomplish their purpose.[67]

The SD—constantly and consistently—does in fact accomplish its purpose of delivering *true* theistic belief. Thus, the *alethic* conditions for warrant are, to put it differently, persistently met, which is to say that they are aimed successfully at truth, and not, for instance, at mere wish fulfillment (or sheer survival or self-esteem).[68] So, then, in a world without sin these particular warrant conditions are always satisfied (and by implication we also are always externally rational).

But what about the *environmental* criterion? How is it satisfied? On Plantinga's epistemology, our cognitive endowment is meant to function in a certain sort of environment, not (for instance) on top of Mt. Everest or underwater or on the moon. Plantinga writes that under various

> circumstances, we develop or form theistic beliefs—or, rather, these beliefs are formed in us; in the typical case we don't consciously choose to have those beliefs. Instead, we find ourselves with them, just as we find ourselves with perceptual and memory beliefs.[69]

My argument concerning divine hiddenness is that, in a prelapsarian context, the environmental condition is constantly met; we are in fact in an appropriate or congenial epistemic environment, the one in which God has intended for us to be.[70] Our internal SD is always and everywhere occasioned or triggered by the external created order such that God's existence and presence are as clear and obvious as they can be, both in a qualitative sense and in a quantitative one (chapter 1 discussed the qualitative/

---

67. *KCB* 27.
68. *KCB* 36.
69. *WCB* 172–73.
70. Beilby writes that in a prelapsarian world the environmental condition is met (*Epistemology as Theology*, 210). Plantinga also distinguishes between what he calls a maxi- and a mini-environment, a distinction that I discuss in more detail in chapters 4–5.

quantitative distinction). Perhaps this is what Plantinga has in mind when he quotes Paul in Rom 1 that "what can be known about God is *plain*."[71]

Thus the SD is properly functioning (in step with its design plan) in a congenial epistemic environment, aimed successfully at truth, and theistic belief therefore is *warranted*. And since warrant is just what converts mere true belief into knowledge, then all persons can be said to *know* God. God is not hidden from us. Such a claim, I take it, is a fairly meager one. For as James Anderson writes of the A/C model, "on the assumption that theism is true, it is entirely natural to suppose that God has equipped us with cognitive faculties [i.e., SD] designed to furnish us with true beliefs about God; in which case, our beliefs about God . . . will normally be warranted."[72] Similarly, as Oliver Wiertz stipulates of the model:

> If the Christian God exists, it is very likely that there is a *sensus divinitatis* or some similar capacity which is reliably directed toward truth and functions properly. In other words, if the Christian God exists, then it is very likely that as a product of the *sensus divinitatis*, theistic-Christian beliefs have warrant.[73]

Now, last, warrant is an ingredient *enough of which* converts mere true belief into knowledge. Warrant, as Plantinga explains, comes in *degrees* of strength; the degree of warrant is contingent upon the strength of belief. "When my faculties are functioning properly," Plantinga writes in *Warrant and Proper Function*, "a belief has warrant to the degree that I find myself inclined to accept it; and this . . . will be the degree to which I *do* accept it."[74] As Wiertz writes on this point, "If all warrant conditions are fulfilled, then the degree of warrant for a belief depends upon the strength of that belief."[75] Diller clarifies this concept:

> Depending on the suitability of environment and cognitive function oriented toward and functioning according to the designed connection between belief formation and truth—if everything is properly oriented and functioning—the full degree of warrant will, without attenuation or intensification, be reflected in and finally established by the proper proportionate

---

71. WCB 171n5; emphasis in original.

72. J. Anderson, *Paradox in Christian Theology*, 176. Roughly half of Anderson's work applies Plantinga's construal of warranted Christian belief to the notion of paradox in theology. See also J. Anderson, "If Knowledge Then God."

73. Wiertz, "Is Plantinga's A/C Model," 86.

74. A. Plantinga, *Warrant and Proper Function*, 9; see also WCB 156, 456–57.

75. Wiertz, "Is Plantinga's A/C Model," 84.

strength of belief. If that degree of warrant is high enough, then the belief qualifies as knowledge.[76]

My further argumentation here is that, on the prelapsarian A/C model, one's degree of warrant, which depends on the strength of one's belief, is at full throttle. All persons everywhere, it can be said in my defense, believe in and know God, there being no warrant impedance or obstruction or prohibition.[77] God's existence (again) would be clear and obvious in both qualitative and quantitative senses; he is not hidden.[78] Plantinga writes of the SD that "if the beliefs produced are *strong enough*, then they constitute knowledge."[79] In a world without sin, the beliefs produced by SD are always strong enough. Perhaps on the model, belief in God, given by the SD, is comparable to having a *constant* and *uninterrupted* stream of belief in the existence of the past or in other minds, or perhaps it is like nonstop "self-knowledge, memorial knowledge, perceptual knowledge, testimonial knowledge, *a priori* knowledge, inductive knowledge."[80] To use an illustration, the flow (or strength) of warrant, on the bare A/C model, is like water rushing full speed—constantly and continually and persistently—*from* a garden hose *to* a plant; the stream is steady and stable. Thus all persons *believe* in God (and love him) and, having a high degree of warrant, all persons *know* God (and are attracted to his ways), perhaps finding themselves saying, as Jonathan Edwards puts it, that

> there is no one thing whatsoever more plain and manifest, and more demonstrable, than the being of God. It is manifest in ourselves, in our own bodies and souls, and in every thing about us wherever we turn our eye, whether to heaven, or to the earth, the air, or the seas.[81]

---

76. Diller, *Theology's Epistemological Dilemma*, 118. For fuller discussion, see 115–18.

77. If a person acquires a defeater or encounters an objection to their belief in God, then this can impede or obstruct one's "flow" of warrant, but on this particular application such would not be the case in a world without sin.

78. It could be argued from the A/C model that one's own *belief* in God is warranted (or has some other epistemic status: justification or rationality) even though God's *existence* is not obvious. In response, two comments are in order. First, Plantinga writes in the A/C model, following Paul in Rom 1:18–20, that what can be known about God is *plain*, stating also that the SD "works under various conditions to produce beliefs about God, including, of course, *beliefs* that immediately entail his *existence*" (*WCB* 199; emphasis added). Second, if we take the A/C model, following Beilby, to be prelapsarian, then it can be argued that, in a world before the fall, theistic belief would be warranted and God's existence would be obvious.

79. *WCB* 179; emphasis added.

80. J. Anderson, *Paradox in Christian Theology*, 171.

81. Edwards, "Man's Natural Blindness," 2:252.

Application 5: On the A/C model God is not hidden from humanity; there is a natural knowledge of God. The model stipulates, as Calvin and Aquinas indicate (according to Plantinga), that there is *natural* knowledge of God. While Plantinga never uses such terminology, this squares well with what some in the Christian tradition have taken to be the doctrine of *general revelation*, traces of which can be found, for instance, in the model's discussion (again) of the innate SD, its appeal to the external majesty of creation, its use of the *locus classicus* text Rom 1:18-21 (as well as Ps 19), and so forth. As Diller writes concerning general revelation within the model:

> From the perspective of Christian theology these two models [the A/C and extended A/C models] represent the classical . . . division between *general* and *special* revelation—the Book of Nature and the Book of Scripture.[82]

Further, Anderson writes, "The Reformed tradition also affirms a limited knowledge of God through *general revelation*—a form of revelation taken up . . . in Plantinga's defence of the *sensus divinitatis*."[83] Roughly stated, this is the doctrine, to follow historian Thomas Oden and the classical Christian consensus he presents (from, for instance, Origen, Ambrose, John Chrysostom, Basil, Augustine, Gregory of Nazianzus, and more), which teaches that God has revealed himself universally, in the natural order, to *all* persons, but that this revelation, however, is not salvific.[84] I add via the A/C model the SD to this definition.[85] If there is a natural knowledge of God—through general revelation—then God is not hidden, as discussed within the context of the A/C model. Moreover, that the doctrine of general revelation is found in the model comports well with both Scripture and Christian tradition, which are commendable qualities for my argumentation since my intent is to prescribe a defense for PDH that is specifically Christian. How, more precisely, does general revelation—the external created order and the internal SD—support my argumentation, from the model, that God is not hidden?

---

82. Diller, *Theology's Epistemological Dilemma*, 129n1; emphasis added (cf. also 141–42).

83. J. Anderson, *Paradox in Christian Theology*, 193n104; emphasis added. For others who take there to be general revelation in Plantinga's epistemology, see O. Anderson, *Reason and Worldviews*.

84. Oden, *Classic Christianity*, 17–18. See also Oden, "Without Excuse." See also Demarest, *General Revelation*; R. Plantinga et al., *Introduction to Christian Theology*, 53–54; O. Anderson, *Benjamin B. Warfield*.

85. As Rik Peels puts it: "I take 'general revelation' to be *both* what John Calvin called the *sensus divinitatis* and the way God reveals Himself to humankind in nature" ("Divine Foreknowledge," 171n3; emphasis added).

And how does my argumentation square with Scripture and tradition? Let me briefly answer in what follows.

Consider two biblical texts, Ps 19 and Rom 1, that Plantinga himself offers in the A/C model.[86] First, there is Ps 19:1–4:

> 1 The heavens declare the glory of God, and the sky above proclaims his handiwork. 2 Day to day pours out speech, and night to night reveals knowledge. 3 There is no speech, nor are there words, whose voice is not heard. 4 Their voice goes out through all the earth, and their words to the end of the world.

The words "declare" (מספרים) and "proclaims" (מגיד) are participles (Piel and Hiphil, respectively), whereby both suggest that the heavens demonstrate the *ongoing and constant display* of God. For wherever they can be seen, so too can the glory of God be known.[87]

Of this verse, Calvin explained that "there is nothing so obscure or despised, even in the most confined corners of the earth, wherein there is not some mark of God's might and wisdom to be seen."[88] Perhaps this is why the psalmist can claim that God's work is demonstrated "day to day" and "night to night."[89] The word "knowledge" in 19:2 can be translated as "knowledge about a subject."[90] The heavens do not literally speak, but their personified words carry throughout all creation.[91] Of these verses, Diodore of Tarsus writes:

> The voices of visible of creation . . . *are equally clear to everyone*, both Greeks and barbarians, giving everyone the one

---

86. See *WCB* 167, 171, 175 ("The heavens declare the glory of God" [Ps 19:1]), 198.

87. Perhaps Gregory of Nazianzus, commenting on the beauty of creation, captures the thrust of this passage: "For everyone who sees a beautifully made lute and considers the skill with which it has been fitted together and arranged, or who hears its melody, would think of none but the lutemaker or the luteplayer, and would recur to him in mind, though he might not know him by sight. And thus to us also is manifested that which made and moves and preserves all created things, even though he is not comprehended by the mind" ("On Theology, Theological Oration," as cited in Blaising and Hardin, *Psalms 1–50*, 69).

88. John Calvin, *Commentary on the Psalms*, as quoted in Waltke et al., *Psalms as Christian Worship*, 347; see also Selderhuis, *Calvin's Theology of Psalms*, 70–72.

89. Compare this with Ps 74:16: "Yours is the day, yours also the night; you have established the heavenly lights and the sun." Ps 97:6: "The heavens proclaim his righteousness, and *all the peoples see his glory*."

90. See "דעת," in *HALOT* 229.

91. Clifford, *Psalms 1–72*, 112–13. See also O. Anderson, *Clarity of God's Existence*, 1–20.

message, that they were made by someone and do not exist of themselves.[92]

Further, Robert Letham explains that creation reveals God:

> Eastern Christianity is particularly identified with the use of icons. These are not intended to be worshipped. They are teaching devices, windows through which to perceive greater realities that lie beyond. . . . Reformed theology believes in icons too! However, it regards the Eastern view as far too restrictive. For the Reformed, *the whole of creation is an icon.* All around us, *the natural world cries out with a loud roar,* or quietly and soothingly breathes a gentle whisper, to the effect that "the hand that made us is divine." . . . These are the clothes that God wears to display his glory. The clothes are not the person, nor is the world God, but as the clothes adorn the person, *so the world testifies with a powerful and beautiful voice to its triune Creator.*[93]

It seems that Ps 19, given in the A/C model by Plantinga, sits well with the model's claim that God has revealed himself clearly in the external natural world, the "book of nature" as it is sometimes called. But Plantinga's model also stipulates that all persons have an innate SD; consider Rom 1:18-21 (a text used in the model twice by my count).[94]

> 18 For the wrath of God is revealed from heaven against all ungodliness and unrighteousness of men, who by their unrighteousness suppress the truth. 19 For what can be known about God is plain to them, because God has shown it to them. 20 For his invisible attributes, namely, his eternal power and divine nature, have been clearly perceived, ever since the creation of the world, in the things that have been made. So they are without excuse. 21 For although they knew God, they did not honor him as God or give thanks to him, but they became futile in their thinking, and their foolish hearts were darkened.

As Douglas Moo notes of this passage, particularly in v. 19, God has given humanity an SD.[95] Nicholas Wolterstorff, in his discussion of SD, captures one main emphasis from this scriptural text:

---

92. Diodore of Tarsus, *Commentary on Psalms 1-51*, as cited in Blaising and Hardin, *Psalms 1-50*, 151; emphasis added.
93. Letham, *Holy Trinity*, 437-38; emphasis in original.
94. WCB 171, 198.
95. Moo, *Epistle to the Romans*, 123. Moo writes, "The emphasis on 'mind' in v. 19 strongly implies that the inner reason contributes to this knowledge (*sensus divinitatis*)" (123).

> Calvin's thought . . .—which he bases in part on Romans 1—is that God has planted in every human being a disposition to believe in the existence of a divine creator [i.e., the SD], and that this disposition is triggered, or activated, by our awareness of the richly complex design of the cosmos and of ourselves. It was not Calvin's thought that we *inferred* the existence of a divine Creator from perceptual knowledge of the existence of design. . . . It was rather his thought that the awareness of the design immediately causes the belief—just as having certain sensations immediately convinces us that we are in the presence of another human person.[96]

Thus these two biblical passages, Ps 19 and Rom 1, as well as various voices from the Christian tradition support the model in that there is general revelation or natural knowledge of God, which in turn supports my argument that on the model God is not hidden.[97]

3.3.1 The Aquinas/Calvin Model Applied to the Hiddenness Problem: Concluding Remarks

Let me draw together some conclusions regarding the previous argumentation. I have attempted to offer a specifically Christian defense for PDH, which comes in three parts. In this chapter, Plantinga's A/C model for how bare theism can have warrant has been used as the *first part* of my defense; the second and third parts are forthcoming in chapters 4–5. Five lines of application were provided. In short, the A/C model, as I see it, describes a state of affairs ultimately giving Christian theists a way to think that God is not hidden, that we can have warranted belief in him: *knowledge*.

Let me now offer a brief word about my argumentation's place against the backdrop of PDH as it is conceived in contemporary analytic philosophy

---

96. Wolterstorff, "Is Reason Enough?," 145; emphasis in original.

97. Other biblical passages could be included. Bruce Demarest, for example, in his seminal study on general revelation suggests "that human beings know more or less the following about God from the light of universal general revelation": "God exists (Ps. 19:1; Rom. 1:19), God is uncreated (Acts 17:24), God is Creator (Acts 14:15), God is Sustainer (Acts 14:16; 17:25), God is universal Lord (Acts 17:24), God is self-sufficient (Acts 17:25), God is transcendent (Acts 17:24), God is immanent (Acts 17:26–27), God is eternal (Ps. 93:2), God is great (Ps. 8:3–4), God is majestic (Ps. 29:4), God is powerful (Ps. 29:4; Rom. 1:20), God is wise (Ps. 104:24), God is good (Acts 14:17), God is righteous (Rom. 1:32), God has a sovereign will (Acts 17:26), God has standards of right and wrong (Rom. 2:15), God should be worshipped (Acts 14:15; 17:23), Man should perform the good (Rom. 2:15), God will judge evil (Rom. 2:15–16)" (*General Revelation*, 242–43).

and theology. *Nonbelievers* who analyze PDH of course think that God is "hidden" because he is not there; PDH prompts some, such as J. L. Schellenberg, to take the fact that God's existence is not more apparent to be "a reason to suppose that it is not a fact at all."[98] But as it was shown in chapter 2, most *believers* in the current PDH debate appear to think that if there is a God, then he is hidden,[99] and then justification for why God may behave in such a concealed fashion is offered (e.g., free will/coercion response, etc.). Discussing how the title of *DHHR* came about, Schellenberg explains in a more recent work that

> there's the fact that what I described in the [1993] argument's premises would indeed amount quite literally to the hiddenness of God *if God existed*—which of course my theistic critics believed to be the case. In their view, God really was hiding or hidden from us, and they were trying to explain why.[100]

But I think that if God exists, spelled out on the model, then he is not hidden; his existence is clear, and we can *know* him. This is the first portion of my defense, and I believe that it, so far, meets my defense desiderata (i*) and (ii). For instance, (i*) specifies that I will provide a specifically Christian account explaining why God's existence is not more obvious, and while it may be a bit puzzling to see how my argument that God is not hidden satisfies this particular defense desideratum, this point will become clearer in parts 2 and 3 of my defense. Still, it seems that what I have claimed with the A/C model here about the clarity of God's existence sits well with Scripture as well as with historic Christian doctrine,[101] which is important for a distinctly Christian defense against any problem.

Now, (ii) requires that my account be true for all we know, thus corresponding to what Plantinga claims of *his* models, although he does, in the last five chapters of *WCB*, consider and rebut objections (or defeaters). The next two parts of my defense, correlating to the extended A/C model, must

---

98. Schellenberg, *Hiddenness Argument*, vii.

99. Theist Robert McKim writes, "I assume that God is to a considerable extent hidden from all human beings and that this is an enduring feature of human life" ("Hiddenness of God," 143). "Those who believe in God . . ." writes theist Chad Meister, "carry the burden of providing a reasonable account of why God's existence is not readily evident and readily available" ("Evil and the Hiddenness," 138). Paul Moser: "The relevant available evidence [for God] is, it seems, less than obvious to all reflective people, or at least it doesn't make God's existence obvious to all such people. We might thus say that God's existence is at best elusive, subtle, or incognito" (*Elusive God*, ix).

100. Schellenberg, *Hiddenness Argument*, 16; emphasis in original.

101. See also Bray, *We Believe*, 7–11; Talbot, "Is It Natural," esp. 156–57.

wait until the two subsequent chapters; but before taking up those tasks, it is now time to consider objections to my *own* use of Plantinga's A/C model.

3.4 OBJECTIONS CONSIDERED

To argue that God is not hidden immediately raises a few eyebrows, so the purpose of this section is to respond to several objections to my use of the A/C model. Having responded to these objections, I then turn to the second part of my defense in chapter 4.

Objection 1: Plantinga's models do not prove much. As explained, Plantinga says of his hypothetical A/C model that if it is *true*, then theistic belief has *warrant*.[102] Call this TW (TW = if the model is true, then theistic belief has warrant). I have applied the model to PDH, saying that the model gives Christian theists a way to think about PDH: indeed, on the model God is not hidden. Now, in a new essay, Dieter Schönecker criticizes Plantinga with respect to TW, saying that TW amounts to very little; the models (both A/C and extended A/C), in other words, *do not prove much*. In fact, Schönecker's comments on TW are linked to PDH; I quote him here and then defend my use of the A/C model concerning PDH. Schönecker writes with respect to TW that

> there is reason to believe that Plantinga has only claimed something *fairly meager* and even something that is quite obvious: If God, as Christians typically understand him, exists, then our belief that He does exist is what He wants us to think about Him and so our belief that God exists is true.[103]

Schönecker says that Plantinga finds all this "natural," essential for how God has created us. He goes on: "If God is a loving God, and if he creates us in his image, then why should He do so in a way that we would have *no* knowledge of Him? Why would he (entirely) *hide* himself?"[104] Schönecker here seems to be arguing that, on Plantingean Reformed epistemology, God would not do so; he would not leave us with just *no* knowledge of himself, and he would *not* hide himself. Now, Schönecker suggests that this is all "fairly meager," and on my conception of the A/C model, he is right. For if there is a God, as Plantinga says, then he surely would have created us to believe in him naturally (i.e., as Schönecker says, "Our belief that He does

---

102. See *WCB* xii.
103. Schönecker, "Deliverances," 18; emphasis added.
104. Schönecker, "Deliverances," 18; emphasis on "no" in original, emphasis on "hide" in original.

exist is what He wants us to think about Him"); he does not hide himself, as I have argued, and that seems straightforward. But Schönecker goes on:

> And yet, God's possible *hiddenness* is a serious and much discussed topic; so I think it is surprising that Plantinga says little (in WCB) about the possibility of God hiding himself. Given that TW is obviously a very important result of WCB (to some even the main or only result), this is quite disappointing.... This objection is all the more relevant given that TW is introduced with regard to theism in general, not with regard to Christian belief; so even if the God of Christianity cannot be understood as a (completely) hidden God [i.e., on the specifically Christian *extended* A/C model], another God (a God from a Non-Christian perspective) [i.e., spelled out on the bare A/C model] could possibly have reasons not to reveal himself so TW wouldn't be "natural."[105]

In brief, Schönecker appears to be saying—setting aside specifically Christian belief, as conceived on the *extended* A/C model—that TW would not in fact be "natural," as one might think, since another God, as spelled out on the bare A/C model, may have reasons *not* to reveal himself, thus remaining hidden; TW would not be natural.

But his complaint that Plantinga says little in *WCB* about God being hidden—i.e., "it is surprising that Plantinga says little (in WCB) about the possibility of God hiding himself"—is not very forceful, for even though the A/C model is not concerned with divine hiddenness per se, Plantinga would have *no* reason to say that God *is* in fact hidden since, on the A/C model, he is not: "There is no spot in the universe," as Plantinga quotes Calvin, "wherein you cannot discern at least some sparks of his glory."[106] Schönecker himself appears to recognize this on the model, that Plantinga would have no reason to say that God is hidden, writing in a footnote: "However, the God relevant in these subsections [in Plantinga's exposition of the A/C model] is *already* described as a 'person who has created us in his image ... who loves us' (WCB, 188), etc."—that is, who would not hide from us.[107] Indeed, this means that although it is possible that the A/C model—a bare, generic theistic model—could be used to describe "another God" from a "Non-Christian perspective" (as Schönecker says) such is not, however, likely.[108] For, as I interpret Plantinga, it is the very *same* God in

---

105. Schönecker, "Deliverances," 18–19; emphasis added.
106. *WCB* 174.
107. Schönecker, "Deliverances," 19n39; emphasis added.
108. Schönecker, "Deliverances," 19.

view, contra Schönecker, on *both* A/C and extended A/C models. Thus, the God being described on the A/C model is the Christian God (the model is, after all, named after Thomas Aquinas and John Calvin, and it does include a few quotes from the Bible), in which case Plantinga is depicting a God who would not hide himself (i.e., God *would* "want us to think about him," as Schönecker notes), he having naturally created us to have warranted true belief in him. So, again, Schönecker's comments on PDH—specifically when he says that God "could possibly have reasons not to reveal himself so TW wouldn't be 'natural'"—are not forceful.

Now, a word on TW in general. Plantinga says of his models that if they are true, then theistic belief is warranted. Many philosophers and theologians have been critical of TW over the years because Plantinga gives no attempt in *WCB* to show that the models are in fact *true*, thereby making his project in *WCB* substandard, not proving much.[109] Diller recounts these complaints from philosophers such as Richard Swinburne, Richard Fumerton, and others.[110] This complaint resurfaces yet again in a few essays from Schönecker's edited volume (*Plantinga's "Warranted Christian Belief": Critical Essays with a Reply by Alvin Plantinga*), including the essay from Schönecker himself mentioned just above. Plantinga ends *WCB* asking, "But *is* it true [Christian belief, spelled out on the models]?," ultimately arguing that it is beyond philosophy's competence to say if it is in fact true, since philosophy's job, he thinks, is to clear away objections and obstacles to Christianity.[111] In a response essay to Schönecker, Plantinga clarifies:

> Why didn't I go on to argue for the *truth* of Christian belief [in *WCB*]? Well, in the context of a discussion involving both believers and unbelievers, such an argument should have premises accepted by the majority of the parties to the discussion, i.e., by unbelievers as well as believers and the fact is that I don't know of any sufficiently strong arguments of that sort for the truth of Christian belief. Of course I do believe the Christian faith; indeed, I'd say, *know* that it is true. . . . But this knowledge is a matter of faith. And as far as I can see, there are no purely

---

109. Plantinga says, "To show that these models are true . . . would also be to show that theism and Christianity are true; and I don't know how to do something one could sensibly call 'showing' that either of these *is* true. . . . Very little of what we believe can be 'demonstrated' or 'shown'" (*WCB* 170; emphasis in original). See my explanation of the A/C model above.

110. Diller, *Theology's Epistemological Dilemma*, 132.

111. *WCB* 499.

philosophical arguments sufficiently strong to undergird serious Christian belief.[112]

By way of clarification, this is how I conceive of my project with respect to Plantinga's models: I think the models are true but do not argue *for* their truth. My research question in this project on PDH is *Why, if God exists, is his existence not more obvious?*, and I have opted to give a defense (and not a theodicy) against the hiddenness problem, using Plantinga's models to answer the research question. So, it does not seem incumbent to argue for the models' truth (although I do think that the models' deliverances are true), just that they can be used as a defense for PDH, ultimately meeting my defense desiderata (i*) and (ii). And I have utilized the A/C model to argue that God is not hidden; although such a claim is fairly meager (since, as Schönecker says, if there is a God, then he would in fact create us to know him, and would not be hidden), it actually proves *much*. Schönecker's comments have afforded me the opportunity to respond to this objection as well as to clarify my own position.

Objection 2: The "it's-all-obvious" school. I have used the A/C model to argue that God is not hidden. Saying that God is not hidden, however, may be alarming even to those with theistic convictions. Robert McKim, for instance, writes:

> Some people seem to find the existence of God entirely *obvious*. Some people, including some philosophers and theologians, say things like this. "How can anyone wonder whether or not God exists? Look at the trees, the birds, the flowers, see how Spring comes every year . . ." And so on.[113]

McKim vocalizes the same concern elsewhere, explaining that

> some theists . . . assert that God is not hidden at all, and that on the contrary the facts about God are *obvious* and that people who do not recognize these *obvious* facts are blinded by sin, or for some other reason lack the ability to recognize these obvious facts. . . . And it would be obvious to others too if they were not blinded by sin or some other defect.[114]

Those who hold this position are part of what McKim calls the "it's-all-obvious" school, of whom he specifically lists Alvin Plantinga. ("Alvin Plantinga,"

---

112. A. Plantinga, "Ad Schönecker," 240; emphasis in original.
113. McKim, "Hiddenness of God," 143; emphasis added.
114. McKim, *Religious Ambiguity*, 9; emphasis added.

writes McKim, "is a representative of the it's-all-obvious school."[115]) As I read him, McKim would likely object to my use of Plantinga's model, labeling it part of the "it's-all-obvious" school, a stance that may be, as McKim appears to imply, a bit flat-footed, simplistic, and naive.

In response and as mentioned above, my project is a defense against PDH from a Christian philosophical and theological perspective; it is one where faith seeks to understand (although as Paul Helm says the understanding gained must never come at the expense of *the* faith itself),[116] in which case it does seem that Christians who examine PDH should use the biblical terminology (given in the A/C model itself), particularly the words that the psalmist writes, "The heavens declare the glory of God and the skies proclaim the work of his hands" (Ps 19:1), or Paul's comments penned in Romans that God's attributes and divine nature "have been *clearly perceived*" (Rom 1:20); Plantinga says that here Paul "seems to be speaking of *all* of us human beings; what can be known about God is *plain*, he says."[117] Romans 1:19–21 also appears to support the existence of something like an SD, as Wolterstorff above explained. This is all consistent with what both Aquinas (that to know God in a general way is implanted in us by nature) and Calvin (that there is within humanity an awareness of the divine) say concerning our knowledge of God, at least insofar as Plantinga uses their positions in the A/C model; this seems to be what both Scripture and important theologians note about the clarity of God's existence, so I do not find my position to be simplistic or naïve (as McKim's comments appear to imply).[118]

Objection 3: The A/C model does not apply to our current epistemic situation. Consider this objection here an extension of the "it's-all-obvious" school objection directly above. Now, in my application of the A/C model to PDH, it has been argued that God's existence is clear and obvious, and that humanity enjoys warranted theistic belief. It was also stated in one of my applications, following James Beilby, that the A/C model is prelapsarian. But herein lie two problems. First, is it technically correct to conceive of the A/C model as *prelapsarian*? Calling it prelapsarian (a term Plantinga never

---

115. McKim, *Religious Ambiguity*, 255n6.

116. See his contribution in Beilby and Eddy, *Divine Foreknowledge*, 164.

117. WCB 171n5; emphasis in original.

118. Consider also Plantinga's own comments: "The fact is that the vast majority of the world's people do believe in God, or something like God. So it's not that God is hidden in the sense that nobody knows about him or believes in him; all kinds of people do—I suppose, as I say, the vast majority of the world's people. God isn't as plain to us as other people, let's say, or as trees and houses or material objects. But why think that he would have to be? . . . He might have a good reason for being relatively hidden, hidden to the degree that he is, which, as I'm suggesting, *isn't all that great*" ("Alvin Plantinga," 0:44).

uses) seems to imply that the bare A/C model has a lot of *continuity* with the postlapsarian extended A/C model (also a term that Plantinga does not use but which is implied in *WCB*: the extended model, he says, "*adds* that we human beings have *fallen into sin*";[119] the existence of sin "throws a monkey wrench *into the A/C model*").[120] Diller writes:

> As the name implies, the extended A/C model bears a relation to the A/C model, though it is *clearly a different model altogether*. It is correct to view Plantinga's proposal not as one model with two parts but as two discrete models, the second having an impact on the first.[121]

So, Diller seems to stress *discontinuity* between the two models, and Plantinga (I think) is unclear at times on the precise relationship between the two. But whether continuity or discontinuity, however, my use of the A/C model to argue that God is not hidden still remains intact. Yet if Diller is right to stress discontinuity, then I may be wrong to call the A/C model *prelapsarian*. Nonetheless, despite Plantinga's ambiguity at times (and despite the fact that he does talk about sin in the A/C model, albeit briefly),[122] I think it is right to call the A/C model largely prelapsarian (and that perhaps Diller slightly overstates his case); I follow Beilby: "The A/C Model describes what might be called bare theistic belief. It also describes a prelapsarian epistemic condition. To account for our postlapsarian context, Plantinga develops the Extended A/C Model."[123] (In a more recent essay, Thomas Provenzola also refers to the A/C model as prelapsarian.[124])

But, second, even if it is correct to call the A/C model prelapsarian, perhaps another problem is lurking. For suppose my interlocutor (the one proposing, say, the "It's-all-obvious" school objection earlier) offers a counter to my above response; assume for argument's sake she agrees, on the hypothetical A/C model, that God's existence is clear and obvious, the *sensus divinitatis* being triggered regularly by the created order, thereby delivering properly basic and constant warranted theistic belief. Indeed, on the state of affairs described by the model, the interlocutor *concurs* that God's existence would be obvious in such an epistemic situation but then, on greater reflection, gently reminds me that the A/C model does not, in fact, describe

---

119. *WCB* 205; emphasis added.
120. *WCB* 499; emphasis added.
121. Diller, *Theology's Epistemological Dilemma*, 138.
122. *WCB* 180, 184, 198.
123. Beilby, *Epistemology as Theology*, 181.
124. Provenzola, "Epistemic Eucatastrophe."

humanity's *current* epistemic situation.¹²⁵ For we *currently* find ourselves, she goes on, in a so-called *post*lapsarian context, and not in a *pre*lapsarian one (spelled out by the bare model), in which case it is wrongheaded, irrelevant, and extraneous to answer a research question that asks why God is not more obvious by explaining that, on the model, God's existence just *is* obvious. It is mistaken, so the objection might go, to respond to a research question that conceives of the phrase "more obvious" in qualitative and quantitative senses (as chapter 1 explains) with a categorical answer ("God's existence *is* obvious"). Does this—perhaps the proponent of the "it's-all-obvious" school objection may suggest—undermine our use of the A/C model itself? Does the fact that the A/C model does not represent humanity's *current* epistemic situation spoil the previously made argumentation about PDH that God is not hidden and that we can know him?

No. For this project, as an exercise in Christian philosophy and theology, aims to analyze PDH in light of the main, skeletal Christian narrative: creation, fall, and redemption (that God has created us to know him, that we have fallen into sin, but that God has done something about sin through the redemption offered by Jesus Christ; this will become clearer in pts. 2 and 3 of the defense, chapters 4 and 5 respectively). It seems that Plantinga's A/C and extended A/C models also share this narrative.¹²⁶ On the A/C model, God has created us to know him, and (as I have argued) he is not hidden from us. It is correct to argue, on the state of affairs described by the A/C model, that God's existence is obvious in a categorical sense. For instance, Plantinga says that what can be known about God is *plain*, alluding to Rom 1; with respect to justification, he explains that it may seem to a person "clear or obvious (perhaps overwhelmingly so) that there is such a person as God."¹²⁷ Indeed, that God's existence is obvious—categorically stated—is all the more forceful if we follow Beilby in that the model is prelapsarian (Plantinga says, "Were there no sin [so I think] God's presence and properties would be utterly obvious to all of us, perhaps what is probably the case in heaven").¹²⁸ But we did note, particularly in applications 3 and 4 above,

---

125. I owe this point to James Beilby via email correspondence (c. late 2013).

126. Dewey J. Hoitenga Jr. writes with respect to knowledge of God conceived by Calvin (but which also applies, I think, to Plantinga's models): "First, what in our knowledge of God is owing to our nature, that is, to our being the kind of being God created us to be? Second, what are the effects of the fall on that natural knowledge of God? Finally, what are the effects of grace and redemption on that fallen natural knowledge of God?" (*Faith and Reason*, 150).

127. *WCB* 178.

128. Email to author, Mar. 5, 2014.

that, in addition to the categorical sense, the A/C model can also be used to address both qualitative and quantitative senses of "more obvious."

Nonetheless, even though the A/C model does not characterize humanity's present epistemic context (thus giving rise to the research question), it still does not follow that God himself is hidden from the human race, which is important to establish on an explicitly Christian conception of PDH, and which (to recall Schönecker's earlier comments) is really only a fairly meager claim, in that surely God, if he exists, would not create humanity only to hide from us, leaving us with no knowledge of himself.[129] Nor should the fact that the model is not our current epistemic situation prevent us from building the first part of our three-part defense story via the A/C model; parts 2 and 3 will be considered in chapters 4–5 (those chapters will also show how the research question is answered from qualitative and quantitative perspectives).

Objection 4: Scripture does not teach an SD. A major part of my argumentation concerns the SD, a cognitive mechanism that, when functioning appropriately, delivers properly basic and warranted theistic belief. Although the model (and its conception of the SD) is hypothetical, still there are objections to the SD from *believers* that need to be taken seriously; here I treat a scriptural objection to the SD.

Though responding to Reformed epistemology as expressed by Kelly James Clark (and not Plantinga), William Lane Craig, himself a believer, writes, "I am very skeptical that any *sensus divinitatis* exists," immediately thereafter stating, "I know of no scriptural warrant for such a *sensus divinitatis.*"[130] Then, in the context of critiquing Plantinga's epistemology, J. P. Moreland and Craig note, "When we turn to Scripture, neither do we find there any such suggestion of a special faculty . . . designed to produce belief in God."[131] This is, of course, an intramural debate between Christians about what Scripture is said to teach, and my response will thus reflect such attitude.

---

129. See also McNabb, who I take to be making the same point, when he writes of Plantinga's epistemology, "If God exists and if He has constituted the human cognitive system in such a way that when it is properly functioning belief in Him would come about *naturally* [then] it would appear that one could be warranted in believing that God exists" ("Warranted Religion," 478; emphasis added).

130. Craig, "Classical Apologist's Response," 285. Craig is responding to Clark's essay, "Reformed Epistemology Apologetics," in the same volume. And, though he does not give a reason, Daniel Howard-Snyder also appears skeptical of the SD in http://faculty.wwu.edu/howardd/HiddennessofGod.pdf (accessed May 7, 2014; now discontinued).

131. Moreland and Craig, *Philosophical Foundations*, 168.

Now, Plantinga (who claims to follow Calvin) quotes Rom 1:18-21 to undergird his construal of the SD, the implication of which is that he is at least attempting to align his epistemological argumentation with Scripture itself.[132] And, as it was shown above in my own biblical exposition, a good case can in fact be made, from Rom 1:18-21, that there is such a thing as the SD; I think that Wolterstorff (quoted earlier) captures one of Paul's main points.

Further, there is a rich tradition in Protestant theology, from Luther to the Reformed Scholastics and beyond, of interpreting Rom 1:18-21 to teach a universal knowledge of God,[133] which many have taken to entail an SD, or something comparable.[134] So, it appears that Plantinga's explanation of the SD is not in any way groundless, as Craig, and Moreland and Craig, appear to suggest. Ironically, neither Craig nor Moreland and Craig, in their critique(s), offer any exegetical attempts to clear up what the apostle Paul *may have meant* over against alleged faulty interpretations (from Plantinga, for example) of Rom 1:18-21. I simply agree to disagree with Craig and Moreland and Craig on this score; I think that Scripture is suggestive of an SD, or something like it. This also serves to respond to other Christians—say, Barth—who likely would *not* take Paul in Rom 1:18-21 to be instructing that all persons have an SD; although as Diller's important study has now shown, despite their disagreement on theological issues like the SD (including other matters relevant to general revelation), Barth's theology and Plantinga's philosophy in general are certainly not at *odds* with one another.[135]

Objection 5: Plantinga is incorrect about the SD's content and function. The following objectors agree with Plantinga that there is such a thing as the SD, but disagree with him on its precise function and content. "Plantinga's references to the SD," writes K. Scott Oliphint, "shy away from a description of it as *knowledge*." He explains that the A/C model's construal of the SD as a "faculty" or a "disposition" or an "innate tendency" is more like

> a view to knowledge *rather than knowledge itself*. It seems, however, that in Paul's mind [in Rom 1] the SD is more a deliverance itself than a device, more content than capacity, more *sensus* than set (of dispositions).[136]

---

132. WCB 171.

133. Sudduth, *Reformed Objection*, 9-40, 57-75.

134. Comparable to the SD is what Hugh of St. Victor called the *oculus contemplationis*, on which see Abraham, *Crossing the Threshold*, 69-72, 75-77.

135. See Diller's comments on Barth and Plantinga on the SD (*Theology's Epistemological Dilemma*, 216-22).

136. Oliphint, *Reasons for Faith*, 135; emphasis added.

As Oliphint explains elsewhere, the SD (contra Plantinga) "is *more* than merely a capacity" and that it "is, in fact, 'notitia.'"[137] Like Oliphint, Michael Sudduth suggests that Plantinga has revised the Reformed tradition's portrayal of humanity's natural knowledge of God,[138] writing that the A/C model presents the SD as merely, or only, a "faculty or mechanism utilised to produce theistic belief," rather than, as Calvin and the tradition have held, a "knowledge of God itself." He writes further that

> Plantinga thus loses the Reformed distinction between the *implanted* and *acquired* knowledge of God. Two distinct sources of theistic belief become two different elements involved in a single process of belief formation and knowledge.[139]

It is true that the model does describe the SD to give acquired, or an innate "capacity for,"[140] knowledge of God—which, though universally present in all persons, requires a little maturity.[141] Plantinga, in response to Sudduth, explains that he doubts that Calvin himself ever intended to bifurcate implanted and acquired knowledge of God (in the *Institutes*, book 1, chapters 3 and 5, respectively) but that it is his guess that Calvin "would have answered more or less along the lines of my [A/C] model."[142] Similarly, Georg Plasger, in a newer essay ("Does Calvin Teach a *Sensus Divinitatis*? Reflections on Alvin Plantinga's Interpretation of Calvin"), argues that Plantinga significantly misunderstands Calvin on SD, to which Plantinga responds that though his model is certainly inspired by Calvin, "it's my model, not Calvin's."[143]

However, lest we fall headfirst into the deep ocean of Calvin and the Reformed tradition's rendering of the SD, it needs to be asked how this all ties

---

137. Oliphint, "Review Essay," 163–64; emphasis in original. See also Jeffreys, "How Reformed Is Reformed Epistemology?" For Plantinga's comments on Jeffreys, see *WCB* 204n7.

138. Sudduth, "Plantinga's Revision," 83. Again, Sudduth gives a thorough account of what he takes to be the tradition's portrayal of natural knowledge of God (*Reformed Objection*).

139. Sudduth, "Plantinga's Revision," 84; emphasis added.

140. *WCB* 173.

141. Diller summarizes why Plantinga does not employ the SD to give implanted knowledge: "In Plantinga's view, knowledge and belief are inextricably linked. It is impossible that one could ever know something without believing it. Aquinas and Calvin employ the term *knowledge* without honed epistemological constraints, such that innate knowledge cannot be present without belief" (*Theology's Epistemological Dilemma*, 141).

142. A. Plantinga, "Reply," 134.

143. A. Plantinga, "Ad Plasger," 257.

to PDH; Diller may provide some assistance. For in recounting this debate on the knowledge of God between Plantinga and his critics, he writes:

> While Plantinga's A/C model may somewhat obscure a distinction in Calvin [i.e., the acquired/implanted distinction], there is no impact to the thrust of Calvin on *general revelation*, affirming an indispensable, though merely indirect, role for experience in the operation of a divinely designed, innate capacity.[144]

Thus, for our purposes, it is not too important to take a hard and fast stand on Plantinga on Calvin on Paul, particularly since the chief end of the A/C model is neither Calvin nor biblical exegesis—though I do think that the model sits well with both Calvin and the Bible (Rom 1:18–21)—but is instead aimed at providing an epistemic possibility for how belief in God can have warrant. James Anderson supports my point:

> Some reviewers have questioned whether Calvin conceived of the *sensus divinitatis* as a faculty or disposition toward true belief in God or as the resultant knowledge of God itself.... These criticisms are probably justified. However, this is partly a matter of terminology and partly a matter of tweaking the model. Plantinga's main contention—that theistic belief can easily meet the conditions of warrant—*is substantially unaffected*.[145]

Therefore, the claim that all persons have an internal SD—an innate "disposition or set of dispositions to form theistic beliefs in various circumstances, in response to the sorts of conditions or stimuli that trigger" this "sense of divinity"[146]—does the necessary "work" that we need it to do in a defense for thinking that God is not hidden: "It details a cognitive faculty that is part of God's design for human beings that, when functioning properly under certain conditions, produces warranted belief in the existence of God."[147]

Objection 6: An SD probably does not exist. It has been argued on the A/C model that God is not hidden, and to ford my case I have drawn heavily on Plantinga's conception of the SD, a cognitive faculty that delivers warranted belief in God. And, although the model conceives of the SD as

---

144. Diller, *Theology's Epistemological Dilemma*, 142–43; emphasis added. "At least on this point," explains Diller, "Sudduth's charge that Plantinga has revised the Reformed tradition on the natural knowledge of God fails to convince" (143n62). Though Diller does not comment on Oliphint, a helpful commentary on Plantinga, Sudduth, Calvin, and the SD can be found (140–42).

145. J. Anderson, *Paradox in Christian Theology*, 75n62; emphasis added.

146. WCB 173.

147. Diller, *Theology's Epistemological Dilemma*, 139.

hypothetical, still a major de facto objection lurks: a *sensus divinitatis* probably does not exist. Answering this objection will help me transition to the next chapter. Anderson, himself a believer, captures this objection's thrust, writing that despite

> the many virtues of Plantinga's A/C model, its logical cogency and the support it enjoys from certain streams of the Christian tradition, one objection immediately presents itself. How does all this square with the phenomenon of widespread disagreement about God and even outright unbelief? *Is this not compelling evidence against the existence of a sensus divinitatis* (or at least, against its proper function or successful design)?[148]

In the PDH literature, this has become known as the argument from the demographics of nonbelief.[149] For example, Stephen Maitzen, himself a nonbeliever, has recently argued that theistic belief is unevenly distributed worldwide. He gives contemporary data from Saudi Arabia and Thailand; Saudi Arabia, he explains, is

> at least 95 percent Muslim and therefore at least 95 percent theistic, while the populace of Thailand is 95 percent Buddhist and therefore at most 5 percent theistic. . . . If those data are even roughly accurate, the distribution of theistic belief is at least highly uneven between those two countries, and they are hardly unique in this respect.[150]

God, Maitzen thinks, would not tolerate such unevenness; besides, are these facts not something that "social scientists say they can explain entirely in terms of *culture*?"[151] Furthermore, this lopsided distribution is

> a phenomenon for which naturalistic explanations seem more promising. The "demographics of theism" not only confound theistic explanations of non-belief in God; they also cast doubt on the existence of a *sensus divinitatis, the awareness of God that theologians in the Reformed tradition* claim is innate in all normal human beings.[152]

So, for Maitzen, the SD probably does not exist, as conceived in the Reformed tradition, because of uneven theistic distribution worldwide, and naturalistic

---

148. J. Anderson, *Paradox in Christian Theology*, 176; emphasis added.
149. See Howard-Snyder and Green, "Hiddenness of God."
150. Maitzen, "Divine Hiddenness and Demographics," 179–80.
151. Maitzen, "Divine Hiddenness and Demographics," 187; emphasis added.
152. Maitzen, "Divine Hiddenness and Demographics," 177; emphasis added.

explanations can account for such "patchiness." Now, philosopher Evan Fales has a similar critique; in his review of Plantinga's *WCB*, Fales asks if there is any "independent evidence, presumably of an empirical sort,"[153] for the existence of the SD. (Anita Renusch, too, contra Plantinga: "There is no empirical evidence for the existence of a *sensus divinitatis*."[154]) Fales notes that there is good evidence, for instance, for one's sensory faculties (including memory and reason); but can anything comparable be given, he asks,

> on behalf of the SD and HS [Holy Spirit]? Plantinga certainly invites such an inquiry, when he cites Calvin's own argument for the SD. Calvin appeals to the alleged fact that "there is no nation so barbarous, no people so savage, that they have not a deep seated conviction that there is a God." In Calvin's day, the ignorance reflected in this claim was perhaps excusable. But today, such a view would indicate decided unawareness of the *data provided by ethnography*. Indeed, in view of the *diversity of religious beliefs*, including traditions that do not worship gods, one would think that this counts *against* Calvin's conclusion.[155]

Fales then adds:

> So far as I know, no competent investigation of the sort required to confirm the existence of a[n] SD *has* been done; and, short of some much more detailed specification of the alleged structures and processes, it is hard to see how it *could* be done. Perhaps there are no such structures; perhaps these "faculties" consist in ways God directly stimulates through our thoughts. Absent a physical substratum, there may be no independently detectable evidence to be had. But if so, then so much the worse for the epistemic status of the claim that there are such faculties.[156]

Thus, the presented arguments against the SD include the uneven distribution of theistic belief (i.e., from Maitzen), assorted ethnography, religious diversity (as well as nontheistic religions), and the lack of confirming empirical evidence (i.e., from Fales), rebuttals that show that the SD, as construed on the hypothetical A/C model, likely or probably does not exist. Call these collective complaints the "Maitzen/Fales complaint." I offer two responses.

First, suppose the Maitzen/Fales complaint succeeds, proving unlikely the existence of an SD. What would follow (recognizing, of course, that the

---

153. Fales, "Review of *Warranted Christian Belief*," 360.
154. Renusch, "Thank God," 159.
155. Fales, "Review of *Warranted Christian Belief*," 360; emphasis added.
156. Fales, "Review of *Warranted Christian Belief*," 361; emphasis added.

model is a hypothetical account for how theistic belief may have warrant)? Perhaps the model can be reengineered to describe how theistic belief can arise immediately (in a properly basic way) and have warrant *without* the SD; or perhaps God just infuses knowledge into human beings without an SD; or perhaps one could build something like natural theology into the model[157] so that theistic belief no longer arises immediately but rather *inferentially*, though still guaranteeing warrant.[158] The model could undergo these aforementioned remedies such that according to it God is *still* clearly revealed. For it can still be true, for instance, that the heavens tell the glory of God (Ps 19) even if no such SD, an innate cognitive faculty, exists.

Second, the A/C model is, as mentioned, only epistemically possible, and thus Plantinga's depiction of the SD is not an attempt, as Diller explains, "to prove the *factual existence* of a divinely inspired faculty . . . but to indicate precedence in the Christian theological tradition for the possibility of noetic equipment to yield properly basic belief in God."[159] So it is not Plantinga's intent to offer up any empirical evidence for the faculty itself.[160] But as I understand them, Maitzen and Fales appear to read the data—the data, for instance, from lopsided distribution of theistic belief, assorted ethnography, extreme religious diversity (including nontheistic religions), etc.—and then, consequently, interpret the relevant data to imply that, very probably, there is no SD; secular or naturalistic theories, they suggest, can do the heavy lifting in order to explain why.

But philosophers tell us that data *underdetermine* theories, "in that for any body of empirical data," as Del Ratzsch puts it, "no matter how large or complete, there are always in principle unlimitedly many theoretical interpretations consistent with those data."[161] Since this is true, can the theist not look at the same data presented by Maitzen and Fales and then, in so doing, offer a different explanation wholly consistent with the data, but only to conclude that, very probably, there *is* an SD (or something like it)? That seems fair enough.[162] But then a problem immediately surfaces: Plantinga's

157. See his comments in WCB 176, for how natural theology might be used in the context of the model. Plantinga elsewhere has offered two dozen (or so) theistic arguments in an appendix ("Two Dozen"). See also Walls and Dougherty, *Two Dozen*.

158. On this point, see further Sudduth, "Reformed Epistemology."

159. Diller, *Theology's Epistemological Dilemma*, 135n29; emphasis added.

160. Fales, in his assessment of *WCB*, recognizes this; Maitzen is concerned with the SD only as it broadly construed and not as it is presented in *WCB*.

161. Ratzsch, "Humanness in Their Hearts," 218.

162. For example, Max Baker-Hytch critiques Maitzen's argument, offering a theistic explanation of the so-called uneven distribution of belief and nonbelief, saying that this distribution is in fact about as probable on theism as it is on naturalism ("Mutual Epistemic Dependence"). For a Molinistic response to Maitzen, see Marsh, "Do the Demographics."

generic A/C model is *not* an explanatory hypothesis or theory for any sort of data; it is only an account of how theistic belief can or might be properly basic and warranted.[163] Can the proponent of the A/C model offer any type of reply or rejoinder or defense?

Though complete justice can hardly be done to this topic, there is some research from the ever-growing field of the cognitive science of religion (hereafter CSR) that may assist the advocate of the A/C model in responding to the Maitzen/Fales complaint against the SD. For instance, Kelly James Clark and Justin Barrett suggest that, despite differences,

> Reformed epistemology and cognitive science of religion have remarkably converged on belief in God. Reformed epistemology holds that belief in God is basic—that is, belief in God is a natural, non-inferential belief that is immediately produced by a cognitive faculty. Cognitive science of religion also holds that belief in gods is (often) non-reflectively and instinctively produced—that is, non-inferentially and automatically produced by a cognitive faculty or system.[164]

The authors then go on to flesh out how some of the findings of CSR may be compatible with Plantinga's presentation of the SD. In a recent article, Jeroen de Ridder and Mathanja Berger, defending the A/C model and the SD against recent attacks, propose that "some CSR findings offer *positive empirical support* for Plantinga's model."[165]

Grant the assumption, then, that CSR is at least amiable to the basic argumentation of the model (that there may be, for example, a natural cognitive faculty that produces non-inferential belief in God or gods, etc.); on such an assumption, I believe that this serves to answer both Fales's concern above that "no competent investigation" has been done "to confirm the existence of a[n] SD" (and that "it is hard to see how it *could* be done"), as well as

---

163. Plantinga writes that his models "show how it is clearly possible that theistic and Christian belief can have warrant, but not by way of being hypotheses that nicely explain a certain range of data" (*KCB* 83).

164. Clark and Barrett, "Reformed Epistemology," 174.

165. De Ridder and Berger, "Shipwrecked or Holding Water?," 57; emphasis added. In this article, the authors critique Herman Philipse's criticisms of Plantinga's religious epistemology in Philipse, *God in Age of Science*, 31–64. In those chapters, Philipse raises similar objections to those that Maitzen and Fales present against the SD (e.g., religious diversity, the lack of empirical evidence for the SD, secular explanations of religious belief, etc.). De Ridder and Berger, in defense of Plantinga (and in response to Philipse), appeal to current research in the cognitive science of religion—research that they believe at least lends support to the A/C model.

Maitzen's earlier doubts that the SD does not exist as construed by Reformed theologians and epistemologists. As Clark and Barrett note, CSR and Reformed epistemology both concede that belief in God is *natural*—that it "is produced by our primal and instinctive dispositions to believe in various circumstances."[166] Thus, CSR comports with the main thrust of the model.

Let me now sketch a brief reply to some of the remaining charges against the SD. Maitzen, interpreting the data from uneven theistic distribution, argues that there likely is no SD; he also explains that it merely changes the subject to construe theistic belief to something broader like "generic belief in the supernatural," since divine hiddenness is "a problem for theism in particular, not for supernaturalism in general." But is this true? Is divine hiddenness a problem for only the former and not the latter? And should this cause concern for the theist who believes there to be an SD, or something like it? Such is not clear; interestingly, as Maitzen himself admits, "belief in the supernatural *is more widespread and more evenly distributed* than belief in God."[167] (Moreover, Helen De Cruz says that although it does not privilege belief in God spelled out in the Abrahamic religions, still "CSR holds that belief in supernatural beings is *natural*."[168]) But this sits well with what Clark and Barrett argue, since perhaps the SD, what they call the "god-faculty," is only meant

> to make humans aware, in the most ordinary of circumstances, of the sacred dimension of reality rather than *clearly defined* Judeo-Christian conceptions of God; on this view, God might be willing to concede *culturally specific differences* in order to produce, by and large, true belief in a divine being. So, while the god-faculty alone (in ordinary circumstances unprompted by God) may be unreliable in securing belief in Yahweh and Yahweh alone, it may be reliable in producing belief in a divinity. . . . Indeed, such surface impurities and unclarities might include elves and fairies.[169]

Widespread and *evenly distributed* supernaturalism in general—and not full-blooded theistic belief in particular—is not, however, at odds with the claim

---

166. Clark and Barrett, "Reformed Epistemology," 188. See also Talbot, "Is It Natural." Moreover, J. L. Schellenberg writes that the "nascent field of study known as cognitive science of religion (CSR) has already provided striking evidence of the powerful hold that *agential* religious ideas—ideas of personal gods or of a personal God—might be expected to have on our minds, given our contemporary evolutionary heritage" ("Divine Hiddenness and Human Philosophy," 14).

167. Maitzen, "Divine Hiddenness and Demographics," 179; emphasis added.

168. De Cruz, "Divine Hiddenness," 57; emphasis added.

169. Clark and Barrett, "Reformed Epistemology," 187; emphasis added.

that there is an SD. It may just be, as Clark and Barrett argue, that "the god-faculty alone (without any special supernatural prompting) could produce reliable core beliefs in a morally provident superknower despite apparent *surface and culturally specific dissimilarities*."[170] So, Maitzen's attempt to construe divine hiddenness as a problem for only theistic belief, and not generic supernaturalism, does not prove there to be no SD. This same reasoning can be applied to Fales's raised doubts against the SD from religious diversity and assorted ethnography. In sum, all that has been offered is a minimalistic *defensive* strategy to fend off objections that there probably is no SD.

But there is an *offensive* strategy to be employed as well. To employ such strategy, consider what follows. Though CSR may lend support to the A/C model's presentation of the SD, why then, if all persons possess such a faculty, did God not merely "hardwire" into us full-blown mature theistic belief? Unfortunately, prescribing a comprehensive answer to this difficulty, which (again) stems from the Maitzen/Fales complaint, falls outside the scope of this chapter. Nonetheless, an *indirect* response can be offered by asking how this question relates *directly* to the SD and divine hiddenness. For if God has given all persons an SD, as the model suggests, then what is to be made (for example) of Richard Fumerton's remarks? "The God whom Plantinga believes in," he explains,

> is omnipotent and *wants* us to know that He exists. Since he wants us to know that He exists He wants us to believe that He exists. But one can't help but wonder why such a being doesn't make His existence a bit more obvious to those who, for whatever reason, are having trouble making up their minds. If God exists and wanted me to believe in Him, He could convince me of His existence within the next few minutes. An appropriately flashy entrance with a spectacular miracle or two would do the job in short order.[171]

"So why," Fumerton goes on, "is He deliberately making it more difficult for some people to believe than it would otherwise be?"[172] Offensively, I offer a direct response here to the relationship between the SD and PDH, illustratively expressed in Fumerton's remarks, which may serve to indirectly answer the inquiries raised just above regarding the lack of "hardwired" theistic belief (where pertinent to the SD).

170. Clark and Barrett, "Reformed Epistemology," 187; emphasis added. For a perspective different than Clark and Barrett's, see Green, "Cognitive Science."

171. Fumerton, "Plantinga, Warrant," 349; emphasis in original.

172. Fumerton, "Plantinga, Warrant," 349; Fumerton is not commenting *specifically* on the SD and divine hiddenness, but his comments still capture my needed point.

So, as I read them, Fumerton's remarks, in some form, ask why God is not doing *more* than he is doing to reveal himself. But as I have already argued, the A/C model as a defense against PDH gives support to the claim that God is (and has been) doing quite a bit on his part to make himself known; he is not hiding from us. If this is true, then Christian theists can understand challenges to the SD from divine hiddenness differently than do nonbelievers. For recall that in Plantinga's epistemology there is the warrant criteria. Take the proper functional and environmental criteria. When functioning properly, the SD (designed by God to produce belief in God) will, in fact, produce true beliefs about God, the result of which is knowledge; to my thinking, the SD everywhere and always produces warranted theistic belief. Further, the SD has been designed for its appropriate environment. This is compatible with Christian theology. However, as Christian theology goes, humanity is not functioning properly and its environment is tainted. There is the problem of sin (as the model does briefly analyze) having crept into the human race, which both alienates and makes us enemies of God (Col 1:21, Rom 5:10). And not only has the SD, the very faculty that CSR tells us may exist, been blemished and obscured, but even the created order (our environment) longs to be redeemed (Rom 8:20-23).

Thus, to answer the *indirect* inquiries more specifically: perhaps it is the case (as Barrett writes) that "a perfectly adequate concept of God" is part of humanity's "biological heritage" but that, *due to sin and its effects*, this has been horribly distorted.[173] To my thinking, where there should be specific theistic belief (with correct content), from our properly functioning endowment (according to a design plan), in an appropriate epistemic environment aimed successfully at truth, sin can divert the SD's original hardwired theistic belief (instead) toward mere generic belief in the supernatural. Indeed, due to sin, as Barrett writes, "Continued [human] rebellion *further* undermines accurate belief."[174]

This leads up to a brief *direct* response regarding the SD and the hiddenness of God. Comparable to the Freud/Marx complaint, the A/C model can take the hiddenness theme, when it is presented as an objection to theism, and "stand it on its head." It is unbelief itself, notes Plantinga, that "originates in an effort, as Rom 1 puts it, to 'suppress the truth [about God] in unrighteousness.'"[175] Thus, on the A/C model, it can be said that any false beliefs about God may (as Diller explains) "arise from an error stemming

---

173. Barrett, "Cognitive Science," 97.

174. Barrett, "Cognitive Science," 98; emphasis added. See further Clark, "Pluralism and Proper Function"; Kim, *Reformed Epistemology*; McNabb, "Warranted Religion."

175. WCB 198.

from *cognitive malfunction* or a misleading *cognitive environment*."[176] I think that this is consistent with the Christian narrative: that we have fallen into sin, which thereby affects both our environment as well as our belief in God; and, as Marilyn McCord Adams suggests, we are unclean before God.[177] Now, positing the doctrine of sin with respect to PDH—an important doctrine in any distinctly Christian defense story—raises a further question that needs answering: What, precisely, *is* the relationship between sin and the hiddenness of God?

To account for sin's consequences, Plantinga *extends* the bare A/C model (calling it the extended A/C model) to consider Christian belief in its postlapsarian context. Thus, a detailed examination must wait until the subsequent chapter in order to explain the precise relationship between divine hiddenness and sin, where I will give the second part of my defense following the extended model.

3.5 CONCLUSION

Let us take stock. The general purpose of this project is to answer the research question by way of my thesis statement; the latter says that Plantinga's A/C models for how Christian belief may have warrant can be utilized as a defense to explain why if there is a God his existence is not more obvious. This particular chapter used the bare or generic A/C model to argue for the first portion of my three-part defense. I believe also that, so far, I am satisfying the two defense desiderata.

First, I briefly *explained* the generic A/C model, on Plantinga's own terms, purposively emphasizing its theology. Second, I *applied* the model to the problem of divine hiddenness, arguing on the possible state of affairs described by the model that God is not hidden (a point worth getting clear on as the first part of my defense). Christians who analyze divine hiddenness can be comfortable with such a claim since it comports well with both Scripture as well as with historic Christian doctrine. Third, I *responded* to multiple objections. The last objection rebutted argued that sin can distort humanity's knowledge of God; chapter 4, my defense's second part for PDH, will consider sin's effects, to which I now turn.

---

176. Diller, *Theology's Epistemological Dilemma*, 161; emphasis added. As Diller writes of Plantinga on the same page, "I am assuming that anything in our environments that would mislead us with respect to the proper deliverances of faith can be understood to be an environmental consequence of *sin*" (161n131; emphasis added).

177. Adams, "Sin as Uncleanness."

4.

The Problem of Divine Hiddenness and the Effects of Sin

4.1 INTRODUCTION

CHAPTER 1 INTRODUCED THE problem of divine hiddenness (hereafter PDH). Chapter 2 showed how my own work fits within and is relevant to contemporary PDH literature. The main research question that this project seeks to answer asks *Why, if God exists, is his existence not more obvious?*, and I have opted to give a defense as opposed to a theodicy against PDH, saying that my defense, which aims not at mere logical but rather at *epistemic* possibility, will satisfy two desiderata; namely, that I will:

(i*) Develop a specifically Christian account describing why, if God exists, his existence is not more obvious.

(ii) Show that this description is true for all we know.

Christians have available a three-part Reformed epistemic defense, drawing from Alvin Plantinga's A/C models, which can both answer the research question and satisfy the two desiderata.[1] This led me to formulate my thesis statement that *Plantinga's A/C models for how Christian belief may have warrant can be utilized as a defense to explain why, if God exists, his existence is not more obvious.*

Chapter 3 expressed the first part of my defense by way of the bare or generic A/C model. Put very roughly, I argued via the model that God is not

---

1. A more detailed explanation of the defense desiderata can be found in chapters 1 and 3.

hidden from humanity. For not only has God given all persons an internal *sensus divinitatis* but also has revealed himself generally in the external created order such that, when the internal *sensus divinitatis* is triggered or occasioned by the external created order, we can believe in God in a properly basic way, so that belief in God is justified, rational, and has warrant; and since warrant is an ingredient enough of which turns mere true belief into knowledge, then we can be said to *know* God. The A/C model was the first part of my defense. Yet I ended chapter 3's exposition and application of the A/C model to PDH by arguing, as Plantinga does, that sin has grave effects on human knowledge of God, but that it fell out of the scope of chapter 3 to demonstrate precisely *how* sin affects us.

Therefore, the purpose of this chapter is to answer the question *How more precisely does sin relate to our knowledge of God in general as well as to PDH in particular?* To respond, I follow the *initial statement* of Plantinga's extended A/C model, which is concerned not with the state of affairs described on the bare A/C model but rather applies to humanity in its postlapsarian context. For as Plantinga notes on the extended model, sin has had, and continues to have, drastic noetic *and* affective consequences (terms to be defined later). By appealing to these consequences, the second part of my three-part defense against PDH can be formulated. The chapter outline is as follows: First, I offer contextual remarks regarding the initial statement of the extended A/C model. Second, I explain on Plantinga's own terms the *noetic* effects of sin. Third, I explain on Plantinga's own terms the *affective* effects of sin. Fourth, having explained these effects, I then apply them to PDH. Fifth, I answer objections to the explanations and applications. Finally, concluding remarks will be made. If this chapter succeeds, then I will have provided the second part of my three-part defense, satisfying the mentioned desiderata, and will continue to answer the main research question.

4.2 THE EXTENDED AQUINAS/CALVIN MODEL'S INITIAL STATEMENT: CONTEXTUAL REMARKS

The purpose of this section is to set the *initial statement* of the extended A/C model in context, on Plantinga's own terms. Recall from the previous chapter that, in *WCB*, Plantinga builds a model—the A/C model—in order to demonstrate how bare theistic belief may have warrant. A belief has warrant

> for a person S only if that belief is produced in S by cognitive faculties functioning properly (subject to no dysfunction) in a cognitive environment that is appropriate for S's kind of

cognitive faculties, according to a design plan that is successfully aimed at truth.[2]

But Plantinga *extends* the A/C model—calling this the extended A/C model—in order to show how full-blown *Christian* belief in its postlapsarian context may have warrant. For on the extended model the human race has fallen into sin, which, as Plantinga writes, "throws a monkey wrench into the [generic] A/C model."[3] So, the extended model is for postlapsarian Christian belief; it includes theological themes such as faith, the atoning work of Jesus Christ, the inner witness of the Holy Spirit, the inspiration of the Bible, and so forth.

But *prior to* giving the full extended model in chapter 8 of *WCB*, Plantinga, somewhat peculiarly, provides an initial statement of the extended model in chapter 7. As part of the initial statement, he explains at length how sin affects our *cognitive* endowment (chapter 7's title: "Sin and Its Cognitive Consequences"), which corresponds to Plantinga's conception of the *sensus divinitatis*, a *cognitive* faculty designed to produce warranted theistic belief (fleshed out in *WCB* chapter 6—the bare A/C model). He calls this the extended model's "initial statement," but technically it is not the full account of the model (as Plantinga says in the full model itself, "I gave an *initial statement* of this extended model"[4]). So, *WCB* chapter 7 demonstrates how sin influences the mind, and in *WCB* chapter 8 Plantinga gives the full extended model. But also somewhat peculiarly Plantinga discusses in chapter 7 not only the cognitive but also the *affective* consequences of sin—how sin influences the human "will" or "heart" since theistic *affection*, like theistic belief, can also have warrant (more on this below). My aim is to analyze the cognitive *and* affective effects of sin for PDH. And although it is the initial statement, not the full extended A/C model per se, I still at times will refer to the model in my chapter here as the "extended A/C model."[5]

So what, then, of the extended model? The extended model aims "to show how it can be that Christians can be justified, rational . . . , and warranted in holding full-blooded Christian belief."[6] While he writes from a broadly Reformed perspective, by "Christian belief" Plantinga means the system of belief summarized in, say, the Apostles' or Nicene Creed, but he also states that not much depends on the use of the term "Christian," for he

2. *KCB* 28.
3. *WCB* 499.
4. *WCB* 241.
5. The full extended A/C model is the topic of my next chapter.
6. *WCB* 200. See chapter 3 for a thorough overview of these terms, although I do discuss them below.

rather is "inquiring into the *epistemological status* of those beliefs."⁷ Comparable to the bare model, Plantinga claims three things of the extended one. First, it is hypothetical, exemplifying a possible state of affairs for how Christian belief *could* or *may* have warrant. Second, *if* Christian belief is true, then it likely does have warrant, but no attempt is made to show *that* the extended model is, in fact, true. Third, the model is one way—"though not necessarily the only good way"—available to Christians in order "to think about the epistemological status of Christian belief."⁸ (For instance, as James Beilby explains, the A/C-type models could have been called the Wesley/Arminius models or the Kierkegaard/Barth models.⁹)

More specifically, the model goes like this: we humans have been created in God's image, having both *intellect* and *will*. "Like God," Plantinga says,

> We are the sort of beings who have beliefs and understanding: we have intellect. There is also will, however: we also resemble God in having affections (loves and hates), in forming aims and intentions, and in being able to act to accomplish these aims and intentions. Call this the *broad* image of God.¹⁰

Plantinga goes on:

> But human beings as originally created also display a *narrow* image: they had extensive and intimate knowledge of God, and *sound* affections, including gratitude for God's goodness. They loved and hated what was lovable and hateful; above all, they knew and loved God. Part of this image was the *sensus divinitatis* [in the bare A/C model].¹¹

So, humans have been made in God's image, and this includes both intellect and will. As Plantinga explains, "Intellect is the province of *belief*; will, the province of *affection*."¹² The *sensus divinitatis* just is a cognitive or noetic faculty of the intellect which, when functioning properly, produces in us warranted theistic belief: *knowledge*. While there is no comparable *sensus divinitatis* faculty for the "will," even so the "will" or the "heart" is meant to function correctly, thereby producing in us warranted affections: we are to love and to desire God.

---

7. *WCB* 202–3; emphasis added.

8. *WCB* 201; see also *WCB* 350, as well as my chapter 3 where I describe Plantinga's claims for his models in more detail.

9. Beilby, *Epistemology as Theology*, 179.

10. *WCB* 204; emphasis in original.

11. *WCB* 204.

12. *WCB* 309; emphasis added.

But one main difference between the bare A/C model and the extended model has "to do essentially with *sin*."[13] Indeed, because of sin, both intellect and will are damaged, thereby skewing our belief in, and affection for, the Creator. And, unable to free ourselves from the ravaging effects of sin, God gives us his plan of redemption, spelled out in Scripture. The plan is that God sent forth his Son, Jesus Christ, to die and to rise again, providing us also the Holy Spirit, whose main job is to heal and to seal our broken intellect and will, restoring the broken image, bringing us ultimately back to fellowship with God.[14] When this happens, then explicitly Christian belief can have warrant. This, in short, is the crux or, as Plantinga calls it, the "outline" of the extended model, and these latter themes—i.e., the giving of Scripture, the work of Christ, the witness of the Spirit, etc.—are fleshed out in the *full* extended model (*WCB* chapter 8); I treat them in much greater detail in my next chapter.

But before rushing ahead to the full extended model and the theology contained therein, Plantinga explains the *nature* and *consequences* of sin, detailing from his Reformed epistemic perspective just *how* entrenched in sin we humans really are. Indeed, "our fall into sin has had *cataclysmic* consequences, both affective and cognitive."[15] I believe that the consequences of sin, as Plantinga spells them out in the context of warrant, are vitally important for a Christian defense against PDH. So, in the next two section sections, I describe with more precision the cognitive (or noetic) and affective effects of sin, ultimately applying these effects specifically to PDH.

4.3 THE NOETIC EFFECTS OF SIN EXPLAINED

Paul Moser writes that Plantinga's exposition of sin and its effects in *WCB* is "alone worth the price of admission."[16] The purpose of this section is to explain briefly Plantinga's construal of sin's *noetic* effects spelled out on the extended A/C model. But first: What is sin? On the model, there is "the phenomenon of *sinning*: of doing what is wrong, what is contrary to God's will." Viewed from this perspective, this sort of sin "is something for which the sinner is *responsible*." He or she is "guilty and warrants blame."[17] Usually theologians refer to this as *actual* sin, and it is indeed culpable. But Plantinga argues that there is also *original sin*, the "condition of *being in* sin, a state in

13. *WCB* 201; emphasis in original.
14. *WCB* 204–6.
15. *KCB* 47; emphasis added.
16. Moser, "Man to Man," 369.
17. *WCB* 206.

which we human beings find ourselves from our very birth," and unlike actual sin it is not necessarily blameworthy (that is, "original sin is not necessarily *original guilt*").[18] It is the traditional Christian answer to say that Adam and Eve, our original parents, caused humanity's current state or condition of sin. But "whether this is indeed how it happened," Plantinga writes, "is a matter on which the model need not take a stand; what *is* part of the model is that in fact we are in the condition."[19] For "we human beings have indeed fallen from a pristine state into sin, a condition that involves both *intellect* and *will*."[20]

In what ways does sin wound the intellect? Reformed theologians have historically referred to this as the noetic effects of sin,[21] and on the extended model Plantinga retains such terminology, arguing that there are several ways in which sin affects humans cognitively. In general, the *sensus divinitatis* (hereafter SD), a noetic faculty designed to deliver warranted theistic belief, no longer functions properly, it "having been damaged and deformed" due to, or because of, the fall. But not only has it been damaged, sin may also induce "in us a *resistance* to the deliverances of the *sensus divinitatis*," so much so that "we don't *want* to pay attention to its deliverances."[22] Although there is, the extended model stipulates, a highly complicated relationship "between what is due to my own sin . . . and what is due to the noetic effects of sin that are beyond my control,"[23] still the SD has been (as Plantinga writes elsewhere) "wounded, corrupted, overlaid by sin."[24]

Moreover, sin's effects on the SD can foster in us false *beliefs* about God, the worst of which is not believing in or that there is a God (more on this later). Perhaps almost as harsh, however, is having false beliefs about his character, since sin, for instance, can prevent

> us from seeing that we are the creatures of a just and loving God who has created us in his own image. We may come, instead, to think that God is terrible and to be feared rather than a good and loving Father, or distant and far off, or indifferent to us and our welfare.[25]

---

18. *WCB* 207; emphasis added. For a contemporary account of original sin without original guilt, see O. Crisp, "On Original Sin"; see also Couenhoven, "What Sin Is."

19. *WCB* 207; cf. 171–72n7, 198n38. For a contemporary account conjoining Reformed epistemology and sin's noetic effects with current evolutionary theory, see De Cruz and De Smedt, "Reformed and Evolutionary Epistemology."

20. *WCB* 213; emphasis added.

21. See Moroney, *Noetic Effects of Sin*. See also Helseth, "Right Reason."

22. *WCB* 205; emphasis in original.

23. *WCB* 216.

24. A. Plantinga, "Ad Plasger," 255.

25. *WCB* 282.

As Plantinga explains in *KCB*, sin may mislead us to believe that God is a source of threat or resentment or worry or danger. We may even be prone to hate God, "but, confusingly, in some way also inclined to love and seek him."[26]

Further, sin's effects on the SD horribly impair human *knowledge* of God, this being the most solemn of its noetic consequences. For the "most important cognitive consequences of sin," writes Plantinga, "is *failure to know* God."[27] Sin may cause "blindness [to God]," "imperceptiveness, dullness, stupidity," whereby it prevents, as the model stipulates, "proper knowledge of God and his beauty, glory, and love."[28]

> The most serious noetic effects of sin have to do with our knowledge of God.... The *sensus divinitatis* ... has indeed been damaged. Our original knowledge of God and his glory is muffled and impaired; it has been replaced (by virtue of sin) by stupidity, dullness, blindness, inability to perceive God or to perceive him in his handiwork.[29]

Sin and its cognitive consequences twist and distort not only human knowledge of God but also knowledge of *ourselves*. The two are connected, as John Calvin once argued, for knowing God is closely linked to knowing ourselves. Thus, *failing* to know God means that

> we don't know the first thing (the most important thing) about ourselves, each other, and our world. That is because (from the point of view on the model) the most important truths about us and them is that we have been created by the Lord and utterly depend upon him for our continued existence.[30]

Not knowing God connotes failing to know "what we need, what is good for us, and how to attain it." Sin may so warp some of us such that we even fail to understand our very *own* sin: "Thus among the ravages of sin is my very failure to note those ravages."[31]

Sin's noetic effects can impair knowledge of ourselves as well as knowledge of *others*, particularly fostering within us a sense of pride. Plantinga writes that, on the model, sin

---

26. *KCB* 51.
27. *WCB* 217; emphasis added.
28. *WCB* 207.
29. *WCB* 217.
30. *WCB* 217.
31. *WCB* 216. St. Augustine: "So blind can people be that they glory even in their blindness!" (*Confessions*, 3.6.40).

affects my knowledge of others in many ways. Because of hatred or distaste for some group of human beings, I may think them inferior, or less worth than I myself and my more accomplished friends. Because of hostility and resentment, I may misestimate or entirely misunderstand someone else's attitude toward me, suspecting them of trying to do me in, when in fact there is nothing to the suggestion.... I may vastly overestimate my own attainments and accomplishments, consequently discounting the accomplishments of others.[32]

Similarly, a good deal of what we humans believe or know is *testimonial* in nature. What is believed or known is on the basis of what others tell us, including one's background beliefs, the transmission of knowledge, and so forth; on the extended A/C model, sin's noetic effects can negatively influence what is believed or known by testimony, particularly all things theistic:

Perhaps I am brought up to think there is no such person as God, that belief in God is a result of superstition, belonging to the infancy of the race.... Perhaps I am brought up to think of serious theistic belief as the universal obsessional neurosis of humanity and begin to look upon the rest of believing mankind with a sort of amused condescension. For these reasons or others, I ignore the promptings of the sense of divinity, a little ashamed, no doubt, to note its stirring within my heart.[33]

It could be that one's beliefs about theism are largely informed by the new atheists (Richard Dawkins and Christopher Hitchens, to name a couple), most of whom are notorious for blaming "everything short of bad weather and tooth decay on religion."[34] The point is that sin in general (and its noetic consequences in particular) has a "deep and obvious *social* side" to it:

We humans are deeply communal; we learn from parents, teachers, peers, and others, both by imitation and by precepts.... Because of our social nature, sin and its effects can be like a contagious that spreads from one to another, eventually corrupting an entire society or segment of it.[35]

In sum, following Plantinga, I have presented several ways on the extended A/C model that sin has had pervasive noetic effects.[36] But on the model, sin

32. *WCB* 213–14.
33. *WCB* 215–16.
34. *KCB* viii.
35. *KCB* 49; emphasis in original.
36. Plantinga describes at least two more ways in which sin has cognitive consequences;

also has insidious affective effects as well, the consequences of which I now turn to describe.

4.4 THE AFFECTIVE EFFECTS OF SIN EXPLAINED

The purpose of this section is to describe, on Plantinga's own terms, the affective effects of sin, spelled out as they are on the extended A/C model. Examining sin's affective effects is significant, as James Beilby writes of the extended model, since

> many contemporary religious epistemologies have—I believe, to their detriment—been articulated *in purely cognitive terms*. The affective, volitional aspect of faith has been ignored, or to the degree it has entered into the conversation, it has been relegated to the status of an ancillary issue.[37]

Now, warrant is that ingredient enough of which turns mere true belief into knowledge, our cognitive endowment—the intellect—having been designed by God to function properly (in a congenial environment aimed successfully at truth), thereby producing in us warranted true belief in God; our affective equipment—the human "will" or heart—works in a similar or analogous way. For instance, affections, like beliefs, can also be justified or unjustified, rational or irrational, there even being "an analogue of *warrant* for affections."[38] Recall the warrant conditions; although Plantinga says relatively little about this, the human heart or will is designed by God to function properly (in conjunction with a design plan), thereby producing the right or correct or appropriate affections for or toward God, in an

---

but since these two ways are not as relevant theologically to my argument I only briefly summarize them here. First, sin can foster a sort of Humean skepticism about the origin and reliability of our cognitive equipment specifically as well as knowledge generally. Plantinga interprets Hume to argue that we cannot, in fact, know the reliability of our cognitive equipment, a position that is circular and incoherent because one must distrust those faculties whose very reliability is in question. The point is that "agnosticism with respect to origins destroys knowledge" (*WCB* 227; cf. 218–27). Second, Plantinga seems to say that sin can nurture belief in naturalism, the view that there is no God, which runs on the "twin engines of evolution" (i.e., random genetic mutation and natural selection, but without any referent to God; cf. *WCB* 228); if this sort of naturalism is true, Plantinga argues, then human beliefs are aimed not at truth but at mere survival and are only adaptively advantageous, including the very belief in naturalism itself, thus serving as a defeater for *belief* in naturalism (*WCB* 227–40; cf. also 281–82). See also A. Plantinga, *Warrant and Proper Function*, 194–237; "Introduction"; *Where Conflict Really Lies*.

37. Beilby, "Plantinga's Model," 159; emphasis added.
38. *WCB* 310; emphasis in original.

appropriate environment, successfully aimed at truth. Under these conditions, we value, love, and desire God:

> Chief among these right affections is love of God—desire for God, desire to know him, to have a personal relationship with him, desire to achieve a certain kind of unity with him, as well as delight in him, relishing his beauty, greatness, holiness, and the like. There is also trust, approval, gratitude, intending to please, expecting good things, and much more.[39]

But on the extended A/C model, things are not the way they ought to be; sin stifles our heart, the seat of our affections. Plantinga's description of sin's affective consequences, as opposed to his construal of sin's noetic effects, is not quite as systematic; still, I trace out how sin influences the will, according to Plantinga, in as orderly a way as I can. So, what effects has sin had on the human heart? How has it darkened and bent our affections ("the strongest motivations of the human self")?[40] On the model, our affections have become severely disoriented and confounded, so much so that "our hearts now harbor deep and radical evil: we love ourselves above all, rather than God."[41] Sadly, we love and hate the wrong things:

> Instead of seeking first the kingdom of God, I am inclined to seek first my own personal glorification and aggrandizement, bending all my efforts toward making myself look good. Instead of loving God above all and my neighbor as myself, I am inclined to love myself above all and, indeed, to hate God and my neighbor.[42]

Sin can foster in the human heart a sort of self-directed pride against God:

> And God himself, the source of my very being, can also be a threat. In my prideful desire for autonomy and self-sufficiency I can come to resent the presence of someone upon whom I depend for my every breath and by comparison with whom I am small potatoes indeed. I can therefore come to hate him too.[43]

"I want to be autonomous," he writes, "beholden to no one."[44] Due to the contortion to one's will, one may see or believe what is right yet *prefer* what

---

39. WCB 293.
40. McDermott, *Seeing God*, 31.
41. WCB 205; emphasis added.
42. WCB 207.
43. KCB 50.
44. WCB 208.

is wrong; one may crave and seek, due to fallen affections, not virtue but vice. He writes:

> Our affections are disordered; they no longer work as in God's original design plan for human beings. There is a failure of proper function, an affective disorder, *a sort of madness of the will*. In this condition, we know (in some way and to some degree) what is to be loved (what is objectively lovable), but we nevertheless *perversely turn away* from what ought to be loved and instead love something else.[45]

Indeed, this may mimic how demons feel about God, when it is written, for instance, that they believe but *shudder* (Jas 2:19). For one disparity between believers and the demonic may be a matter of the religious affections, in that (according to Plantinga) "the former is inspired to gratitude and love, the latter to fear, hatred, and contempt [toward God]."[46] He adds:

> The devils also know of God's wonderful scheme for the salvation of human beings, but they find this scheme—with its mercy and suffering love—*offensive and unworthy*. No doubt they endorse Nietzsche's notion that Christian love . . . is weak, whining, resentful, servile, duplicitous, pusillanimous, tergiversatory, and in general unappealing.[47]

A person's affections can be bent such that he or she simply does not *want* to believe in God. (If the model is true on this point, then perhaps Thomas Nagel's comments constitute an expression of sin's affective consequences: "I hope there is no God! I don't *want* there to be a God; I don't *want* the universe to be like that."[48]) So, sin on the extended model radically alters one's affections for God; it is a madness and "malfunction of the will," perhaps "involving blindness, an inability *to see the glory and the beauty of the Lord*."[49] We may know or believe he is there, sustaining the world moment by moment with his mighty right hand, all while holding "him at arm's length, refusing to love him."[50] Plantinga, quoting the answer to question 5 of the Heidelberg Catechism, argues that, on the model, "I have a natural

---

45. WCB 208; emphasis added. See also 209.
46. WCB 293. Oliver Crisp writes of this passage: "But clearly the demons believe that there is a God without trusting in God. They have known God, have had experience of God, but have no faith in God" (*Deviant Calvinism*, 29n21).
47. WCB 291; emphasis added.
48. Nagel, *Last Word*, 130; emphasis added.
49. WCB 303; emphasis added.
50. WCB 302; see also KCB 48–52.

tendency to hate God and my neighbor."[51] Cited also is the prophet Jeremiah: "The heart is deceitful above all things and desperately wicked; who can understand it?" (17:9).[52] Thus, according to the extended A/C model, sin has fundamentally altered our affections.

4.5 THE NOETIC AND AFFECTIVE EFFECTS OF SIN APPLIED TO THE PROBLEM OF DIVINE HIDDENNESS

Having explained sin's noetic and affective effects on the extended A/C model, I now apply them to PDH, there being several applications in what follows. In short, Christian theists can appeal to both the noetic and affective effects of sin, described in the state of affairs given in the extended A/C model's initial statement, in order to explain why God's existence is not more obvious. I think that appealing to sin's consequences is important for a distinctly Christian defense of PDH, this being the second part of my three-part defense.

Application 1: Given its noetic effects, sin can impede proper function of the SD, preventing warranted theistic belief, thereby accounting for why God's existence is not more obvious quantitatively and qualitatively. Recall that I argued on the bare A/C model (chapter 3) that God has given all persons an SD, a cognitive faculty, which when triggered or occasioned or stimulated by certain circumstances—beholding the starry heavens, for instance—delivers warranted theistic belief. I also conjectured that, in our prelapsarian condition, our SD is always triggered by our circumstances such that all persons' properly basic theistic belief has a high degree of warrant, warrant being that degreed ingredient enough of which turns mere true belief into knowledge; indeed, all persons on the bare A/C model spontaneously believe in and know God, his existence being evident, clear, and obvious.

But on the extended A/C model, however, things have gone awry. As Plantinga explains, the SD, our noetic equipment, is in general overlaid and covered by sin such that it no longer functions properly according to its design plan. Moreover, the extended model stipulates that, since the SD is deformed, we may even have *false* beliefs about God, about his love, character, and so forth: we may think "that God is to be feared and mistrusted; we may see him as indifferent or even malignant."[53] The noetic effects of sin, I think, can account for why God is not obvious. For, as Plantinga argues, the most serious noetic effects have ultimately to do with our *knowledge* of God,

51. WCB 208n13.
52. WCB 199.
53. WCB 215.

writing that were "it not for sin and its effects, God's presence and glory would be as *obvious and uncontroversial* to us all as the presence of other minds, physical objects, and the past."[54] As he suggests elsewhere, were

> it not for the existence of sin in the world, human beings would believe in God to the same degree and with the same natural spontaneity that we believe in the existence of other persons, an external world, or the past.[55]

Plantinga writes in *Warrant in Contemporary Epistemology*, "Were it not for sin and the fall, we human beings would find the existence of God as obvious and uncontroversial as that of trees and horses."[56] It appears that Plantinga has both quantitative and qualitative aspects of "obvious" in mind.

So, my main research question asks why, if God exists, is his existence not more evident or more obvious and, in our postlapsarian condition on the extended model, an answer is provided: sin can impede proper function and thus warrant, and since warrant is a property that converts mere true belief into knowledge, then it can be said that sin inhibits theistic *knowledge* (justification and rationality are discussed below). Applied to the hiddenness problem sin's noetic effects can serve to answer the research question quantitatively and qualitatively.

Now, suppose for argument's sake that sin's noetic effects do in fact explain why God is not more obvious; this has explanatory power, but more questions are generated. For instance, many persons (i.e., from a quantitative perspective) in our postlapsarian condition find God's existence to be unobvious but still fairly clear (i.e., from a qualitative perspective); why is this? Similarly, many persons find God's existence to be unobvious but still sort of clear. Others find God's existence to be unobvious and anything but clear, thus claiming to have no awareness or belief or knowledge about God whatsoever; there are several other variations as well. What accounts for such diversity?[57] How are we to think about such a *continuum*?

Plantinga explains that warrant comes in degrees of strength, and that the degree of warrant is contingent upon the firmness of belief that a person has.[58] On the generic A/C model, I conjectured that God is not hidden from us since all persons, unhindered by sin, have warranted theistic belief to the maximal degree of strength and firmness. But on the extended A/C

---

54. *WCB* 214; emphasis added.
55. A. Plantinga, "Reason and Belief," 66.
56. A. Plantinga, "Respondeo," 336.
57. I set aside, for argument's sake, the problem of *religious* diversity.
58. See *WCB* 114, 156, 456–57.

model, however, particularly with respect to sin's cognitive consequences, Plantinga seems to say that there is an assortment or spectrum or range of the SD's proper function; he argues, on the one hand, for instance that

> according to the extended A/C model, we human beings typically have *at least some knowledge of God*, and some grasp of what is required of us; this is so even in the state of sin and apart from regeneration. The condition of sin involves *damage* to the *sensus divinitatis*, but not *obliteration*; it remains partially functional in most of us. We therefore typically have *some* grasp of God's presence and properties and demands, but this knowledge is covered over, impeded, and suppressed.[59]

Thus there is damage but *not* obliteration to the SD; on the other hand, sin may so negatively affect some of us, Plantinga notes, that "there is also the possibility of special damage or disease; perhaps in some people at some times, the *sensus divinitatis doesn't work at all.*"[60] Beilby describes this latter point, saying that in "circumstances where we would have naturally formed beliefs about God, *no theological beliefs are formed.*"[61] Thus there may be a spectrum of proper function.

So, it does seem that, on the extended model, sin affects everyone everywhere, thereby accounting for why God's existence appears less than obvious. But perhaps sin's noetic effects can also be *person relative*; perhaps the SD is damaged in some persons more and in some persons less. *The more involved in sin we are, the greater the damage*; Ebrahim Azadegan writes, for instance, that "if we continue to do sinful actions we gradually extinguish [the SD's] light."[62] James Anderson notes that, on the extended model,

> sin involves an element of "cognitive disease" that affects (to one degree or another) the operation of the *sensus divinitatis*. Consequently, *for any particular person* the faculty may produce true beliefs but with insufficient strength, or fail to produce those beliefs at all, or even produce some false beliefs.[63]

Now, consider Anderson's comment that some may "fail to produce those beliefs at all." This reasoning could serve to answer an inquiry raised by Daniel Howard-Snyder and Paul K. Moser. Recall that two biblical texts

---

59. *KCB* 51; emphasis added.
60. *WCB* 215; emphasis added.
61. Beilby, "Plantinga's Model," 130; emphasis added.
62. Azadegan, "Divine Hiddenness," 84.
63. J. Anderson, *Paradox in Christian Theology*, 176; emphasis added. See also J. Anderson, "If Knowledge Then God."

are given by Plantinga in the generic A/C model, Ps 19:1 and Rom 1:18–21, which I used to argue, in chapter 3, that God is not hidden from us. Howard-Snyder and Moser write that many people "might deny that God has failed to make Himself sufficiently known."[64] They add:

> "What do you mean God is hidden? Just look around you and at yourself. What more could you want?" This response might seek inspiration from some biblical sources. "The heavens are telling the glory of God" . . . (Psalm 19:1, NRSV). The apostle Paul remarks: "Ever since the creation of the world God's eternal power and divine nature, invisible though they are, have been understood and seen through the things that he has made" (Romans 1:20, NRSV). Aside from what the psalmist and Paul actually had in mind (itself a matter of ongoing debate), *if God is evident through creation, we need an explanation of why many normal people fail to believe that God exists.*[65]

The extended model can help make sense of this. First, on the model, there are no "normal people." Sin affects us all (as Rom 3:10 reads, "None is righteous, no, not one"). Second, it may be that many persons fail to believe *in* God but not, contra Howard-Snyder and Moser, *that* God exists; Plantinga writes:

> Perhaps in *unfallen* humanity . . . the *sensus divinitatis* is a disposition to believe *in* God (to love him, trust him, see his beauty and glory and loveliness), but in fallen humanity only a tendency to believe *that there is* such a person, just as (according to the book of James) the devils do.[66]

Or, third, it could be the case that some persons, because sin has so affected the proper function of their SD, fail even to believe *that* God exists. Thus, there may be a range of damage done by sin to the proper function of the SD, and this can be person relative.

Application 2: Given its affective effects, sin can impede proper function of the "will," preventing (the analogous property of) warranted affection for God, accounting also for why God's existence is not more obvious quantitatively and qualitatively. As mentioned above, the affections, like our beliefs, can enjoy an analogue of warrant. (Plantinga does not coin a comparable term concerning warrant for the affections, but I will just use the phrase "warranted affections" for simplicity.) So, in the same way that humans are

---

64. Howard-Snyder and Moser, "Introduction," 8.
65. Howard-Snyder and Moser, "Introduction," 8; emphasis added.
66. *WCB* 172n7; emphasis added.

originally meant to have natural knowledge of God, unobstructed by sin, so too on Plantingean Reformed epistemology we are (as Anderson states) "originally made . . . to share God's affections; to love what God loves and to hate what God hates."[67] The extended A/C model does not specify, but my conjecture is that, in our prelapsarian condition, all persons do in fact have warranted affections for God, thereby meeting the analogous warrant criteria; the source of affection—the heart—is functioning properly (according to its design plan), in a congenial environment, aimed successfully at truth. There is thus warranted affection for God; and, in this sense, God is not "hidden" from us.

Further, just as the degree of warrant depends on the degree of belief, there can also be (Plantinga argues) "degree of affection."[68] Perhaps in our prelapsarian context, all persons have maximal degree of affection; everyone loves, delights, and finds attractive God and his ways, our hearts—as John Wesley once said—always being "strangely warmed" toward God. We all find ourselves saying, with the psalmist, "My soul longs, yes, faints for the courts of the Lord. My heart and my flesh sing for joy to the living God" (Ps 84:2). Perhaps without sin's hindrance our "affective capacities or faculties are *functioning properly*," in which case we do in fact "love the Lord on perceiving his loveliness, glory, and beauty; no doubt such a person will find him delightful."[69] Intellect and will, belief and affection, are in perfect harmony. Comparable to our SD, our hearts are triggered or occasioned *spontaneously* by the external environment—perceiving a beautiful sunset or the starry heavens, for instance—which delivers warranted affection for God. Thus having natural and instinctive warranted affections, with a high degree of warrant, God's existence would just be obvious.

But on the extended A/C model our hearts have been tinged by sin; Ebrahim Azadegan writes:

> Our most important sin is that our hearts love ourselves, and do not tend sufficiently to love God and our neighbors. This self-centeredness, which seems to be the root of our sins, makes our heart ill.[70]

The affections concern the deepest motivations and yearnings of the human self, things like "love and hate, attraction and repulsion, desire and

---

67. J. Anderson, *Paradox in Christian Theology*, 177; emphasis added.
68. *WCB* 310.
69. *WCB* 303; emphasis in original.
70. Azadegan, "Divine Hiddenness," 89.

detestation,"[71] it being my contention that sin generally inclines us more toward the latter, and not the former, of these couplets. But sin's affective effects may also, however, constitute a *spectrum* of improper function; there is some person relativity, ranging from general antipathy to God,[72] to those like Christopher Hitchens, who thought that Christianity is dangerous,[73] to those like Thomas Nagel, who does not *want* God to exist; but there may also be those, like Paul Draper, who say that they are much more open to God's existence, "waiting—indeed *hoping*—to be pulled over to one side or the other."[74] If this is right, then sin's affective consequences can stunt warranted affection (or its analogous equivalent) for God and, much like the noetic effects of sin, this can also account for why God's existence is not more obvious.

Application 3: Sin's effects can adversely affect our environment as well as our faculties' successful orientation toward truth. A belief has warrant in Plantinga's epistemology if it satisfies the warrant conditions, and I have explained how sin negatively affects proper function. But what about the environmental condition as well as the alethic conditions? What is the relationship between sin and these criteria?

Take the environmental condition. As Plantinga argues, our faculties "will achieve their purpose only if functioning in an environment much like the one for which they were designed (by God or evolution)."[75] Humans, for instance, were not designed to breathe underwater or on top of Mt. Everest; the correct environment is needed. Now, Plantinga distinguishes between what he calls *maxi-* and *minienvironments*. The maxienvironment

> is more general and more global than a cognitive minienvironment. Our cognitive maxienvironment here on earth would include such macroscopic features as the presence and properties of light and air, the presence of visible objects, of other objects detectable by cognitive systems of our kind, of some objects not so detectable, of the regularities of nature, of the existence and general nature of other people, and so on. Our cognitive faculties are designed (by God or evolution) to function in *this* maxienvironment, or one like it. They are not designed for a

---

71. WCB 292.
72. For more on this theme, see McLean, "Antipathy to God."
73. See his movie (with Douglas Wilson) Doane, *Collision*.
74. Draper, "Seeking but Not Believing," 197; emphasis added.
75. KCB 27.

maxienvironment in which, for example, there is constant darkness, or where everything is in a state of constant flux.[76]

So, a maxienvironment is a global or general environment, whereas a minienvironment is a local or a specific one.[77] Plantinga gives an example:

> I am not aware that Paul's look-alike brother Peter is staying at his house; if I'm across the street, take a quick look, and form the belief that Paul is emerging from his house, I don't know that it's Paul, even if in fact it is (it could just as well have been Peter emerging); again, if Peter hadn't been in the neighborhood, I would have known.[78]

In this case, Plantinga argues that one's cognitive faculties "display a certain *lack of resolution*. I am unable, by a quick glance" to "distinguish Paul from Peter just by a quick look from across the street."[79] What motivates the distinction between maxi and minienvironments for Plantinga is that warrant "requires both an *appropriate* maxi-environment and a *favorable* mini-environment."[80]

While our *maxienvironment* (e.g., the regularities of nature, the presence of visible objects, etc.) may be favorable, the *minienvironment*—or minienvironments—may be inappropriate or *misleading* (undermining warrant). "What makes a cognitive mini-environment unfavorable," Beilby explains, "is, primarily, the existence of specific irregularities that are misleading."[81] In the Peter-and-Paul example above, the maxienvironment was appropriate, but the minienvironment was not:

> The maxienvironment is right, but the minienvironment isn't; in those minienvironments the cognitive faculties in question . . . can't be counted on to produce true beliefs. . . . So even if the maxienvironment is favorable and the other conditions of

---

76. WCB 158.

77. J. Anderson, *Paradox in Christian Theology*, 171.

78. WCB 157.

79. WCB 157–58; emphasis in original. He defines warranted Christian belief as that which distinguishes knowledge from true belief. In this volume, Plantinga examines warrant's role in theistic belief, tackling the questions of whether it is rational, reasonable, justifiable, and warranted to accept Christian belief and whether there is something epistemically unacceptable in doing so. He contends that Christian beliefs are warranted to the extent that they are formed by properly functioning cognitive faculties, thus, insofar as they are warranted, Christian beliefs are knowledge if they are true.

80. Beilby, *Epistemology as Theology*, 84; emphasis in original.

81. Beilby, *Epistemology as Theology*, 84.

warrant are met, a belief could still be true "just by accident," thus not constituting knowledge.[82]

Hear John Wingard's questions concerning sin and the environment, which has ramifications for PDH; he asks:

> What about the cognitive *environment*? Has sin altered the *environment* sufficiently to render it unsuitable for reliable formation and maintenance of true beliefs? It is hard to see how this could be. While sin has certainly brought about ill effects in certain areas of the cognitive environment (for example, smog in urban and industrial regions that significantly impedes our nighttime vision of the heavens), it seems unlikely that the effects are so pervasive as to leave the environment unsuitable for the generally reliable formation and sustenance of true beliefs.... Moreover, Scripture gives no indication that the cognitive environment has been altered so radically by our sin as to leave it unfriendly to the production of true beliefs.[83]

Here I both agree and disagree with Wingard. Now, as far as I am aware, Plantinga says little in *WCB explicitly* explaining how sin affects the environmental condition for warrant in general and even less about the maxi and minienvironment distinction in particular.[84] Still, a little "reading between the lines" leads me to think that one could argue that the maxienvironment is comparable to external general revelation (the book of nature): the starry heavens, a majestic waterfall, or a beautiful flower. These appropriate or congenial environmental conditions trigger or occasion or activate both intellect and will such that we believe in and have affection for God spontaneously or naturally (with a high degree of warrant). However, humanity presently finds itself in a postlapsarian condition, which affects our environment, but not so much the *maxienvironment*. The maxienvironment has remained largely unaffected by sin; the heavens are *still* there, telling of God's glory, and the skies above *continue* to proclaim the work of his hands (cf. Ps 19); as Herman Bavinck writes, sin "brings about no change in the fact of revelation *itself*."[85] Thus, with respect to the maxienvironment, I agree with Wingard.

So, as Beilby argues, the "design plan for the cognitive maxi-environment is congenial to the formation of warranted beliefs about God. Even

---

82. *WCB* 158; cf. also 161.
83. Wingard, "Sin and Skepticism," 257; emphasis added.
84. In the fuller extended A/C model, Plantinga does *very briefly* say how regeneration by the Holy Spirit affects the maxi- and mini-environments (*WCB* 257), which I discuss in the next chapter.
85. Bavinck, *Prolegomena*, 310; emphasis added.

so, there is no guarantee that the cognitive *mini-environments* in which [we find ourselves] will be similarly congenial."[86] Plantinga gives an example; perhaps my friend tells me

> that she has a pet named Maynard who is a cat but who loves cooked green beans; having never met this Maynard, I believe on the basis of my friend's testimony that Maynard is a cat. As it turns out, my friend is indulging (unbeknownst to me) her penchant for telling whimsical (and false) stories. Then my belief that Maynard is a cat has little by way of warrant: the epistemic minienvironment . . . isn't right, *being polluted by my friend's thus lying to me*, so that the environmental condition for warrant is not met.[87]

From a Christian perspective, it can be argued that our minienvironments have been radically altered by sin, and when we find ourselves in various unfavorable minienvironments, then God's existence can seem hidden or unapparent or unobvious to us (perhaps in some environments we do not even find ourselves believing there to be a God); so here I *disagree* with Wingard. Mentioned earlier was how sin, on the model, can affect our families, our peer or community groups, even corrupting an entire segment of society. Suppose I am raised by a family who reads (religiously and devoutly) literature by the new atheists; because of my minienvironment, I have a constant stream of testimonial input whereby over time I form the belief that belief in God is a delusion, or that religion is merely the opium of the people (it being a crock or a crutch for those trying to make it in this cruel and harsh world), or that God if he does exist is a mean bully, someone to be feared, despised, hated, ridiculed, and so forth. There should be warranted theistic belief, but due to sin there is not because the (mini)environmental condition is not met. God appears or seems unobvious or hidden to us.

This can serve to answer the question about the *alethic* conditions for warrant, since a belief, as Plantinga argues, must be produced by faculties successfully aimed at *truth*, our faculties having been designed by God to do so. But (so I argue) perhaps for some persons sin can cause their beliefs (and affections) not to be successfully aimed at truth but rather at, say, wish fulfillment: "Unbelief can also be seen as resulting from wish fulfillment—a result of the desire to live in a world without God, a world in which there is no one to whom I owe worship and obedience."[88] Perhaps various hostile minienviron-

---

86. Beilby, *Epistemology as Theology*, 208; emphasis in original.

87. WCB 480; emphasis added.

88. KCB 44. This is given in the context of the Freud/Marx complaint, explained in detail in chapter 3.

ments can cause me, as Paul says, to "*suppress the truth* in unrighteousness" (Rom 1:18), in which case God's existence is hidden from me.[89]

Application 4: *PDH may be more so a problem of sin's effects on the intellect, or it may be more so a problem of sin's effects on the will.* The application alludes to a long-standing debate concerning the priority of intellect or will in matters of sin and faith.[90] Specifically, Plantinga asks if sin is

> primarily a matter of *intellect*, of blindness, of failing to see or believe the right things, thus leading to wrong affection and wrong action? Or is it primarily a matter of the wrong *affections*, of loving and hating the wrong things?[91]

Plantinga explores the relationship between sin's noetic and affective consequences at some length in *WCB*, ultimately saying that he need not take a stand on these sorts of questions; he does not stipulate, in other words, if one faculty or the other is primary in sin (writing also that he takes no stance whether intellect or will is primary in *regeneration*).[92] I think comparable questions are worth asking, as part of my defense, where relevant to the hiddenness problem. Could it be more so because of sin's *noetic* effects, for instance, that God's existence is not more obvious, or is it more so because of sin's *affective* effects that God's existence is not more obvious?[93]

Now, Plantinga says on the extended A/C model that were it not for sin's *noetic* effects, then God's existence *would* be obvious and uncontroversial to us all;[94] the model therefore does specify that sin's effects on the mind, although perhaps person relative (as said above), can at least account for why God's existence is not more obvious. The model does not specify concerning sin's *affective* consequences, but it does not seem to be a stretch to say that sin's affective effects can also be person relative (as said earlier) and can thus account for why God's existence is not more obvious (I will make this assumption moving forward). But the aforementioned questions, however, ask if one faculty is *more* tainted by sin than the other, which in

---

89. See *WCB* 198.

90. As Richard Muller writes, "The terms [intellectualism and voluntarism] refer to the two faculties of the soul, intellect and will, and to the question of which has priority over the other: intellectualism indicates a priority of the intellect; voluntarism, a priority of the will" (*Unaccommodated Calvin*, 162).

91. *WCB* 295; emphasis added.

92. *WCB* 211–13; 295–303.

93. Here we have in mind the comparative sense of "more obvious" as discussed in chapter 1.

94. A. Plantinga says, "Were there no sin (so I think) God's presence and properties would be utterly obvious to all of us, perhaps like what is probably the case in heaven" (email to author, Mar. 5, 2014).

turn can influence how PDH is analyzed. I list a few possible ways to think about these questions below.

First, it could be the case that, in some persons, the ambiguity or non-obviousness of God's existence is more *affective* in nature than cognitive; from this perspective, PDH is more of a "problem of the heart." Suppose that I am a lifelong smoker and that you present me with a strong argument—the premises of which are supported by the best medical science—for the conclusion that my smoking habits ought to be abandoned. My *mind* may tell me that the premises and conclusion are true and that I indeed ought to abandon smoking, but my *heart* still has a greater *desire* to continue smoking; I therefore ignore the best medical science. Arguing that the heart is the seat of one's desires, William Wainwright explains that the

> key is a distinction between good rational arguments and the conditions necessary for their acceptance. I may have good arguments against smoking, for example, but my *desire* to smoke prevents me from appreciating its force. What is needed is not a better argument but a *reorientation of my desires*.[95]

On the extended A/C model, sin's affective consequences can cause us not to desire but rather to *detest* and to *despise* God, in which case the necessary conditions for accepting God, at least in some persons, may not be in place. So, suppose I am a nonbeliever and that a *believer* presents me with the best defended arguments for God's existence from contemporary natural theology—found in, say, *The Blackwell Companion to Natural Theology*.[96] Perhaps I see that the premises and the conclusions from all the arguments are true, or at least verisimilitudinous; I can still fail to see the arguments' *force*, remaining unmoved and unpersuaded, in which case there is nothing wrong with the arguments per se but rather with *me*. As Paul Moser writes in the context of PDH, "Even if an argument [e.g., from natural theology] concludes with a recommendation [for God's existence], an agent still must decide on the recommendation: to endorse it, to reject it, or to withhold judgement regarding it."[97] On this point, Wainwright notes elsewhere that since

> an argument's cogency and convincingness can depend on the state of one's heart, and the states of one's hearts vary, an

---

95. Wainwright, *Reason and the Heart*, 50; emphasis added.
96. Craig and Moreland, *Blackwell Companion*.
97. Moser, "Divine Hiddenness and Self-Sacrifice," 83.

argument which is cogent and convincing for one person may or may not be cogent or convincing for another.[98]

Thus there is person relativity, and perhaps someone who thinks that PDH is more affective than noetic in nature could argue this way; they could say, as James Peters writes from a Pascalian perspective, that until "we seek God *with our hearts* properly humbled, God remains, according to his own incalculable wisdom, hidden from our sight."[99] This is one possible way to answer the previously posed questions.[100]

A second possible way is to say (mutatis mutandis) that, in some persons, the ambiguity or nonobviousness of God's existence is more *cognitive* in nature than affective; from this perspective, PDH is more of a noetic problem. Someone who takes this angle could follow the thought of George Berkeley, who writes:

> It seems to be a general pretense of [nonbelievers], that they cannot see God. Could we but see him, say they, as we see a man, we should believe that he is, and believing obey his commands.[101]

Berkeley thinks that nonbelievers would believe if they could see God, but they cannot, so they will not believe. This is comparable to what one of Berkeley's characters, Alciphron the freethinker, says in response to Euphranor, Berkeley's mouthpiece, when it is asked of Alciphron what sort of proof for God's existence he expects. Alciphron says he just wants "the facts":

> For instance, should a man ask why I believe there is a king of Great Britain? I might answer, because I had seen him; or a king of Spain? because I had seen those who saw him. But as for the King of kings [i.e., God], I neither saw him myself, nor any one else that did ever see him. Surely if there be such a thing as God, it is very strange that he should leave himself without a witness; that men should still dispute his being; and that there should be no one evident, sensible, plain proof of it.[102]

---

98. Wainwright, "Theistic Proofs," 87. See also Van den Brink, "What Is Wrong," for discussion of person relativity of arguments from natural theology.

99. Peters, *Logic of the Heart*, 186; emphasis added. As Jonathan Edwards writes, "So inclined is the *heart* of man to blindness and delusion, that it is prone to even atheism itself!" ("Man's Natural Blindness," 2:252; emphasis added).

100. See further C. A. Evans, "Hardness of Heart"; Meadors, *Idolatry and the Hardening*; Downey, *Desperately Wicked*.

101. Berkeley, *Principles of Human Knowledge*, 88.

102. Berkeley, "Alciphron," 1:385. See also Berkeley, *Alciphron*.

But according to Berkeley, via Euphranor, the Author of nature "constantly speaks to the eyes of all mankind."[103] Indeed, "we need only open our eyes to see the sovereign lord of all things with a more full and clear view."[104] That God's existence is clear (from creation) is "the constant language of Scripture."[105] Now, although

> God conceal himself from the eyes of the *sensual* and *lazy*, who will not be at the least expense of thought; yet to an unbiased and attentive mind, nothing can be more plainly legible, than the intimate presence of an *all-wise spirit*, who fashions, regulates, and sustains the whole system of being.[106]

So, why do some persons not see the clarity of God's revelation? Although Berkeley never uses such terminology, he seems to argue that sin negatively affects the mind; some do not perceive God's existence due to "want of attention." For "what truth is there," he writes, "which shines so strongly on the mind, than by an aversion of thought, a willful shutting of the eyes, we may not escape seeing it?"[107] One could take Berkeley's analysis to be consistent with Plantinga's extended A/C model, where Plantinga explains (discussed above) that were it not for sin's cognitive consequences then God's existence would be clear and obvious. Paul Helm writes that, due to sin's noetic effects, the SD may operate "at different levels, or at least in different ways in different people,"[108] in which case (as discussed earlier) it could be that, relative to some persons, PDH is in fact more *cognitive*.[109]

Moreover, Christian theists should also grapple with another facet of the noetic effects of sin applicable to PDH, particularly Paul's comments in 2 Cor 4:4, where Paul argues that "the god of this world has *blinded the minds* of the unbelievers, to keep them from seeing the light of the gospel of the glory of Christ, who is the image of God." Presumably the "god" of which he writes is Satan, the devil,[110] and in Paul's theology there is a sense in which various cosmic forces can hinder one's spiritual sensitivity for God

---

103. Berkeley, "Alciphron," 1:392.

104. Berkeley, *Principles of Human Knowledge*, 80.

105. Berkeley, *Principles of Human Knowledge*, 89. In this context, he alludes to Jer 10:13, Amos 5:8, Ps 68.

106. Berkeley, *Principles of Human Knowledge*, 90; emphasis in original.

107. Berkeley, *Principles of Human Knowledge*, 91. I am helped by James S. Spiegel in conversation, as well as Spiegel, "Immaterialism as a Boon"; "Theological Orthodoxy." See also Farris et al., *Idealism and Christian Theology*.

108. Helm, "John Calvin, *Sensus Divinitatis*," 100.

109. See further Moroney, *Noetic Effects of Sin*.

110. See C. Keener, *1–2 Corinthians*, 173.

(Eph 6:12).¹¹¹ Satan and his minions can divert our mind's concentration from what is real, and that certainly includes God. As the Eastern Orthodox theologian Andrew Louth says, why think that we struggle with our "own [i.e., mere human] propensities"? There are things both *seen* and *unseen* which may distract one's attention from God, "a foe [Satan] that seeks to outwit us."¹¹² To follow St. Basil: "If the *mind* is misled by demons, it will worship idols or be turned aside toward some other form of impiety."¹¹³ This is another possible way to answer the previously posed questions.¹¹⁴

A final way is to argue, as Plantinga does, that neither intellect nor will is primary in sin,¹¹⁵ perhaps deducing from this suggestion that it is neither more so because of sin's noetic effects nor more so because of sin's affective effects that God's existence is not more obvious; it is both faculties, there being an obscure relationship between heart and mind. Moreover, a passage like Eph 4:17-18 could be taken to teach simultaneously both sin's noetic and affective effects, where Paul argues that the gentiles are "darkened in their *understanding*" (v. 17) due to "hardness of *heart*" (v. 18). A proponent of this option may argue that such thinking is more consistent with what (Reformed) Protestant Christians have taken to be the doctrine of total depravity, which (put roughly) means that because of sin humans are not as bad as they could be but rather that "*every part* of our being has been affected by [sin]."¹¹⁶ Such a proponent could follow Christopher W. Morgan, who writes that, in the Bible, sin is said to effect more than *just* intellect and will; human fallenness, as expressed in Rom 3:11-18, has the following *range* of effects:

- *Mind*: "No one understands." (v. 11)
- *Will*: "No one seeks for God." (v. 11)

---

111. Collins, *Second Corinthians*, 93.

112. Louth, *Introducing Eastern Orthodox Theology*, 49; emphasis added.

113. "Letter 233, to Bishop Amphilochius, Who Has Asked a Question," in Basil, *On the Human Condition*, 109; emphasis added.

114. Consider also how Paul's comments in 1 Cor 13:12 ("For now we see only a reflection as in a mirror; then we shall see face to face. Now I know in part; then I shall know fully, even as I am fully known") may be taken to relate to knowledge of God in our postlapsarian context, on which see Peels, "Sin and Human Cognition."

115. "There is a complicated many-sided, dialectical relationship between intellect and will here, one such that it isn't possible to say that either [intellect or will] is absolutely prior to the other with respect to falling into sin" (*WCB* 212).

116. Bray, "Sin in Historical Theology," 178; emphasis added. For my review of the volume in which Bray's chapter appears, see Taber and Armitage, "Review of *Fallen*."

- *Actions*: "All have turned aside.... No one does good, not even one." (v. 12)
- *Words*: "Their throat is an open grave; they use their tongues to deceive." (vv. 13–14)
- *Ways*: "Their feet are swift to shed blood; in their paths are ruin and misery." (vv. 15–17)
- *Attitude*: "There is no fear of God before their eyes." (v. 18)[117]

4.5.1 The Effects of Sin Applied to the Problem of Divine Hiddenness: Conclusion

In sum, I have applied the extended A/C model's construal of sin's noetic and affective effects *to* PDH; four applications in total were given. I think that these effects fleshed out on the model can be used to answer the main research question qualitatively and quantitatively (as well as this chapter's research question), aiming to satisfy the two defense desiderata. With respect to (i*), the bare A/C model of chapter 3 was first used to argue that God is not hidden from us, there being a natural knowledge of God, but then sin's consequences *on* our natural knowledge of God (as well as on our affections), explained on the extended A/C model, were considered in this chapter; I shall give the third and final part of my defense, which also makes use of the extended model, in chapter 5. Collectively, these models qualify as a specifically Christian account.

With respect to (ii), Plantinga claims of his A/C and extended A/C models that they are not just logically but epistemically possible; they are true for all we know[118]—that is, nothing we know commits us to their falsity—answering objections or defeaters to his hypothetical models in *WCB* part 4. Similarly, as mentioned above, I have not attempted to demonstrate or prove that the models *are* true—which is what Plantinga claims of the models, although he does *believe* them to be true—but that they can be used for a defense against PDH. The below objections are considered for my application of the extended model.

---

117. Morgan, "Sin in Biblical Story," 152.

118. Beilby further discusses this in *Epistemology as Theology*, 115, on which see my first chapter.

4.6 OBJECTIONS CONSIDERED

The purpose of this section is to consider objections to my use of sin's noetic and affective consequences detailed on Plantinga's extended A/C model.

Objection 1: To apply sin's effects to the problem of divine hiddenness is to apply a theological answer to a philosophical problem. According to the extended model, the human condition is pretty bleak, both intellect and will having been radically altered by sin. I find that these effects, analyzed by Plantinga, comport well with Scripture and with the history of Christian doctrine—admirable qualities for a distinctly Christian defense against PDH. But to talk about sin, as I said in previous chapters, is usually inflammatory; sin—as Beilby writes—is one of several "theological concepts that many in academia have relegated to a bygone era."[119] The doctrine of sin may even be a "source of potential embarrassment for Christian faith in the modern world."[120] So, it is provocative, extended model or not, to say that all persons are in a condition of sin that has both noetic and affective effects. Philosopher Evan Fales, in a review of *WCB*, writes that "it is discomforting to be told that one's life is mired in sin."[121] And Schellenberg argues, in the context of PDH, that

> the idea that everyone everywhere is corrupt and in a state of resistance toward God is thought even by many theologians to be problematic. In theological quarters the onset of ecumenism and pluralism has reduced such views to an unsavory "cultish" status.[122]

Hence, talk of sin can be distasteful. I have argued that sin's effects, spelled out on the extended model, can keep us from seeing the clarity of God's existence, thereby making use of such theological themes and concepts for PDH.

Thus not only is discourse about sin incendiary, but (as this objection states) some may even be concerned about my *methodology*. For it could be said that I have really only provided a *theological* answer to a *philosophical* problem, PDH being mostly analyzed by contemporary analytic philosophers of religion. Thomas Schärtl captures an *analogous* objection in his critique of Plantinga's *WCB*, writing that Plantinga "offers an interesting picture

---

119. Beilby, "Plantinga's Model," 125.
120. McFadyen, *Bound to Sin*, 4.
121. Fales, "Review of *Warranted Christian Belief*," 363.
122. Schellenberg, *Hiddenness Argument*, 34. Writing that the doctrine of sin "generates a lot of hostility," Hans Madueme and Michael Reeves explain that "the very grain and alignment of modern thought, where individual autonomy is so sacred, seems to run counter to it" ("Threads," 209).

of human capacities concerning the knowledge of God." Schärtl explains of Plantinga's epistemology that "human nature is equipped with a sense of the divine (*sensus divinitatis*), which allows the 'production' of basic propositions referring to God." He says that this is "good news" and that Christians are "entitled to say that, under certain circumstances, human beings can actually have 'knowledge of God.'" Schärtl, however, has reservations:

> But *isn't* this picture of human capacities too good to be true? And isn't the whole idea of a human nature equipped with a cognitive capacity that secures the "production" of reliably basic beliefs a rather *theological* answer to a *philosophical* problem [i.e., the problem of theistic knowledge]?[123]

Schärtl explains that "no atheist is going to buy" the claim "that there might be a *sensus divinitatis*,"[124] even complaining a little later in his essay that it is wrongheaded for Christians to appeal to revelation as "an additional source to gain knowledge," since this ultimately places Christians in a better epistemic position than non-Christians:

> I have to admit that this is an attractive position *theologically*; nevertheless, *philosophically* it is disastrous, because the appeal to revelation does no good in the philosophers' rulebooks.[125]

This sounds remarkably close to Schellenberg's comments given in the context of PDH, explored in my second chapter, when he states that

> *Theology* starts off by accepting that God exists and so has to make God fit the world; in a way, that is its job. But our job as *philosophers*, faced with questions of God's existence, is to fight free from the distractions of local and historical contingency, to let the voice of authority grow dim in our ears, and *to think for ourselves* about what a God and a God-created world would be like.[126]

Schärtl's remarks apply specifically to Plantinga's Reformed epistemology, whereas Schellenberg's apply specifically to PDH, both of which are relevant to my own project in general as well as to my application of sin's effects to PDH in particular: my defense really supplies a theological answer to a philosophical problem, and this (so the objection goes) is *methodologically* inept.

123. Schärtl, "Moderating Certainty," 115–16; emphasis in original.
124. Schärtl, "Moderating Certainty," 120.
125. Schärtl, "Moderating Certainty," 128; emphasis in original.
126. Schellenberg, *Wisdom to Doubt*, 197; emphasis added. See also Schellenberg, "Plantinga-Style Christian Philosophy."

Now, Plantinga responds to Schärtl, arguing that "Christian philosophers have a perfect right to start with the views they hold as Christians" and that Schärtl's comments about what atheists would or would not buy is "irrelevant," particularly since Plantinga's aim (in *WCB*)

> is not to persuade the atheist that Christian belief is rational or warranted; the aim instead is to propose a sensible way for the Christian, philosopher or not, to think about the epistemology of theistic and/or Christian belief. The success of this project does not depend upon convincing or gaining the approval of the atheist.[127]

There is a similar theme running through my defense. For, as stated in previous chapters, I have tried to provide a distinctly Christian defense against PDH, the goal of which is not *necessarily* to gain the nonbeliever's approval. Christians have a right to argue from their Christian beliefs; thus, from this perspective, Schärtl's distinction between theology and philosophy is inconsequential.[128]

The same reasoning, it seems to me, can also be applied to Schellenberg's comments. Christians, whether theologians or philosophers, are not called to let the voice of authority grow dim in their ears. Indeed, they are to take Christian revelation seriously, Plantinga's Reformed epistemology doing just that.[129] So, the objection states that a theological answer has been applied to a philosophical problem, a sort of methodological misstep, but for reasons already stated, I find the objection unpersuasive, in which case taking Christian revelation seriously seems to entail that sin and its effects must *also* be taken seriously, and this (I think) applies specifically to PDH. Moreover, Oxford's William Wood, discussing recent developments between philosophy and theology in general—and "analytic theology" in particular—remarks that

---

127. Plantinga, "Ad Schärtl," 251. Although Plantinga does also say in response to Schärtl that there is a second project in *WCB* whereby it would be inappropriate to start from the presupposition of Christian belief: for example, he tries to show that "there are no decent *de jure* objections to Christian belief that do not presuppose the falsehood of Christian belief" (251). See also *WCB* xiii, as well as my third chapter where I discuss this in more detail. For my review of this volume, see Taber, "Review of *Plantinga*."

128. See Kevin Diller's critique of Schärtl on Plantinga in Diller, "Review of *Plantinga*."

129. Although Rik Peels is correct to say that (Plantingean) "Reformed Epistemology doesn't assume that God *has in fact* revealed himself, but merely claims that there is no reason to think that beliefs about God aren't properly basic and that, if God exists, belief that God exists probably has sufficient warrant to count as knowledge" ("Review of *Theology's Epistemological Dilemma*," 424; emphasis added).

theologians should be prepared to give a theological account of [human] reason, and so must take seriously the *cognitive consequences of sin* and the Fall. Analytic philosophers [i.e., with interest in theological issues] certainly show a confidence in reason that, to many theologians, does not seem to sit well with a robust account of the *noetic effects of sin*.[130]

This defense, which is simultaneously philosophical and theological, has tried intently to consider Wood's comments. Finally, having quoted St. Paul in Rom 1:18–24, particularly his claim in 1:18 that sinners "suppress the truth" about God, Merold Westphal (himself a philosopher) asks, "What would it mean for contemporary Christian philosophers to make this Pauline notion that as sinners we 'suppress the truth' a primary theme in our epistemological reflection?"[131] I have in part tried to answer his question by applying sin's effects, as explained on the extended A/C model, to PDH.

Objection 2: Appealing to sin's noetic effects in the context of the hiddenness problem makes rational nonbelief only easier. I have argued, as the second part of my three-part defense, that sin's noetic and affective consequences (described on the extended A/C model) can explain why God's existence is not more obvious. Let me consider an objection specifically regarding sin's *noetic* effects from Justin McBrayer and Philip Swenson. Having quoted Plantinga's *WCB* (i.e., where Plantinga says "were it not for sin and its effects" then God would be obvious and uncontroversial to us all; see above), the authors argue that appealing to sin's noetic effects in order to analyze PDH is mistaken. McBrayer and Swenson ask their readers to assume that Schellenberg's construal of rationality, in *DHHR*, is correct; it states that

> s has a rational belief that p if and only if his evidence, inductive standards, and beliefs as to p's probability on the evidence have been, in his own view at the time, adequately investigated.[132]

They emphasize that your epistemic state is rational "just in case you have investigated the issue by your own lights and come to believe that your investigation is adequate to support the epistemic state of believing, withholding belief, etc."[133] According to the authors, this definition of rationality, defended by esteemed epistemologist Richard Foley, is the right one and ought to be assumed.

---

130. Wood, "Philosophical Theology," 596; emphasis added.
131. Westphal, "Taking St. Paul Seriously," 202.
132. *DHHR* 61, as quoted in McBrayer and Swenson, "Scepticism," 139.
133. McBrayer and Swenson, "Scepticism," 139.

Given this definition, McBrayer and Swenson ask: "Would the existence of sin show how non-belief in God is not rational?" No, they say, for even if sin's noetic effects do impede one's evidence or one's ability to see "the logical entailments of one's beliefs [i.e., about God]," then it is "quite plausible to think that there could still be a person who—in her own view of things at the time—would come to think that her evidence and inductive standards fail to support the belief that God exists."[134] What, then, is wrong with utilizing the sin response? The authors explain in more detail:

> The basic problem for [theists who use] the sin objection [to the problem of divine hiddenness] is this: having damaged cognitive faculties or reduced evidence makes it even easier to have rational non-belief! For example, it is not rational for us to fail to believe that sugar causes cavities. It is, however, rational for someone who lacks the appropriate evidence to fail to believe this. Similarly, it is rational for someone who has the appropriate evidence but who is literally unable to "see" the connection between sugar and cavities to fail to believe this. Rationality is person-relative, and as long as a person adequately investigates his evidence and finds that the evidence doesn't seem to support a belief, it is rational for him to be a nonbeliever. And so weakening the investigative tools of the mind [by way of sin] only makes the set of things that are not rational to believe larger.[135]

Let me sketch two responses. First, suppose that McBrayer and Swenson are right that an appeal to sin's *noetic* effects in the context of PDH is unsuccessful. On the extended A/C model, however, sin has dire noetic *and* affective effects, in which case my application of the model to PDH could be modified, having now considered McBrayer and Swenson's objection, to include only the *affective* consequences of sin (the authors, quoting the extended model, fail to say anything about how sin, according to Plantinga in *WCB*, damages the "will"). It could be that sin's consequences on the human heart alone are *still* enough to save my argumentation that sin can make God's existence unobvious. But that is a worst-case scenario.

Second, McBrayer and Swenson ask their readers to *assume* their definition of rationality; I am unconvinced, however, that this is the correct assumption. But in response, let me first try to meet McBrayer and Swenson "halfway." Recall on Plantingean epistemology, explained in chapter 3, that there are *justification, rationality,* and *warrant*. Take justification, which is conceived by Plantinga in terms of deontology and evidence; classical

---

134. McBrayer and Swenson, "Scepticism," 139–40.
135. McBrayer and Swenson, "Scepticism," 140.

foundationalism, from a Lockean perspective, stipulates that a person has a relevant duty or obligation to believe only those things—statements or propositions—for which she has evidence, including belief in God; but Plantinga claims, however, that a person is justified to believe in God in a properly basic way, without evidence or argumentation, the result of which no duties or obligations are breached in so doing.[136] As Plantinga asks, "How could someone sensibly claim that you [a theist, holding theistic belief] were being irresponsible . . . with respect to some epistemic duty?"[137]

My attempt to meet McBrayer and Swenson "halfway" with respect to sin's noetic effects is to say, on a Plantingean conception, that perhaps it is the case that a nonbeliever can be *justified* in their nonbelief; perhaps she (as Schellenberg says) "adequately investigated" evidence for or against God's existence and finds the evidence lacking; perhaps her "inductive standards" (Schellenberg's words) do not support the belief *for her* that there is a God; and so forth. Plantinga's question, with respect to justification, could be rephrased: "How could someone sensibly claim that the nonbeliever is being irresponsible with respect to some epistemic duty for her nonbelief in God?" Thus, it could be the case that sin's noetic effects do not preclude what may be called justified nonbelief.[138]

But what about rationality? Can a nonbeliever be *rational* in their nonbelief? Plantinga conceives of rationality in terms of proper function, distinguishing further between *internal* and *external* rationality;[139] the former (in short)

> requires . . . that you have done your best or anyway well enough with respect to the formation of the belief in question. You have considered how it fits in with your other beliefs, engaged in the requisite seeking for defeaters, considered the objections that you have encountered, compared notes with the right people, and so on.[140]

Explaining internal rationality, Dieter Schönecker says, "The basic idea of internal rationality, I take it, is that one is not insane *on one's own standards*."[141]

---

136. WCB 99–107; cf. also KCB 11–14.

137. WCB 178.

138. In this sense, nonbelief—say, atheistic belief—could be, on my account, properly basic *with respect to justification*. Rik Peels argues, however, that while nonbelief (i.e., atheism) could be basic it cannot be *properly* basic. He seems to argue that proper basicality includes something *stronger* than justification ("Can Atheism").

139. WCB 108–34.

140. WCB 255; see also 203.

141. Schönecker, "Deliverances," 26; emphasis in original.

Even more simply, Plantinga writes that internal rationality is one's "'seemings'—for example, the seeming-to-be-true of various propositions."[142] Perhaps a nonbeliever can be internally rational with respect to their nonbelief; it may just seem to a nonbeliever that there is no God, she having done her best to form theistic belief but could not; she has considered defeaters and objections from theists (or other believers) but still finds that, by her own standards, nonbelief just appears right or correct. Hence, perhaps the noetic effects of sin do not preclude internally rational nonbelief.

External rationality, however, is a bit different. "A belief is externally rational," Plantinga says,

> if it is produced by cognitive faculties that are *functioning properly* and *successfully aimed at truth* (i.e., aimed at the production of true belief)—as opposed, for example, to being the product of wish-fulfillment or cognitive malfunction.[143]

External rationality is stronger and is included in the warrant criteria, particularly the proper functional and alethic conditions. My argument here is that sin's noetic effects *do* compromise a nonbeliever's nonbelief with respect to external rationality. If the model is correct, then a nonbeliever is not functioning properly; their SD, because of sin's noetic consequences, is malfunctioning and is not aimed successfully at true belief (in God). Thus when McBrayer and Swenson ask "Would the existence of sin show how non-belief in God is not rational?," my response, particularly with respect to *external* rationality, is yes. And since external rationality is intimately tied to *warrant*, then it can be said that a nonbeliever's nonbelief does not have warrant.[144]

Objection 3: "*The 'flawed atheist' response to the hiddenness problem is unsupported by an adequate epistemology of religious belief, insofar as that response looks for the explanation of nonbelief only in the atheist.*"[145] This objection, raised by theistic philosopher John Greco, is important and relevant to my argumentation and can be addressed by my defense.

Let me begin with some context: having quoted Rom 1:20–21 as well as Plantinga's A/C model on sin, Greco writes:

> It is hard to deny that there is something *awkward* about explaining nonbelief in terms of some moral or intellectual flaw

---

142. A. Plantinga, "Ad Schönecker," 238.
143. *WCB* 204; emphasis added.
144. Plantinga writes, "Failure to believe [in God] can be due to a sort of blindness or deafness, to improper function of the *sensus divinitatis*. On the present model . . . such withholdings *lack the analogue of warrant*" (*WCB* 186; emphasis added).
145. Greco, "No-Fault Atheism," 125; emphasis added.

in the nonbeliever. Of course, there are ways to soften the blow. We can quickly add that we are all sinners. Or we can make a distinction between original and personal sin, or distinguish between culpable and non-culpable flaws. But even with these additions, it seems to me, the flawed atheist response remains *awkward*.[146]

Greco then explains that "the flawed atheist response is not required, or even supported, by good epistemology."[147] To argue his case (which I can only briefly summarize), he makes use of recent work in social epistemology, particularly knowledge by testimony, since much of what we believe—even religious belief—comes through testimony. For instance, testimonial exchange occurs in (1) interpersonal, (2) informal social, and (3) formal institutional modes. The first includes a relationship between a hearer and a speaker; the second involves more defined social roles, such as parents talking to their children about their religious faith; the third includes testimony from religious institutions, from (for example) preaching, ritual, and so forth.[148] He then applies these social epistemic themes to PDH.

Greco explains that one's *social location*—which is "determined by one's personal relationships and by one's membership, participation, and roles in a community, including a community's formal institutions"[149]—is epistemically important for the transmission of testimonial knowledge; indeed, one's social location, which constitutes one's epistemic position, largely affects—either positively or negatively—the successful transmission of testimonial knowledge. Greco then argues that there can be various obstacles to this transmission: obstacles from the hearer, the speaker, and/or the social environment. He uses religious examples:

> The problem [of transmission of knowledge] might lie in the personal character of the speaker (for example, a believer), who lacks moral virtue, or the motivation, or the practical talent, or the intellectual trust in the hearer. Second, the problem might lie in the informal community (for example, a family), which lacks the motivation or resources to adequately teach its children about their own religious tradition. Third, the problem might lie in the formal institution (for example, a church), which lacks

---

146. Greco, "No-Fault Atheism," 112; emphasis added.
147. Greco, "No-Fault Atheism," 112.
148. Greco, "No-Fault Atheism," 123.
149. Greco, "No-Fault Atheism," 123.

the moral integrity or practical competence to attract new members and keep old ones.[150]

Greco, in short, says that "explanations of nonbelief [i.e., in the context of PDH] might also be found in *believers* and in the social environment." He argues, with help from social epistemology, that theists *themselves* "might better understand how aspects of their personal relationships, communities, and institutions can undermine the transmission of religious knowledge and faith and thus promote nonbelief."[151] Hence, the flawed atheist response does not work insofar as it looks for the explanation of nonbelief only in the *atheist*. Let me respond to Greco.

First, having quoted Paul in Rom 1:20–21 and Plantinga's model on sin, Greco states twice that it is "awkward" to appeal to sin to explain nonbelief; it is not clear, however, what he means exactly by "awkward." Greco would likely object to my use of the extended model, arguing that it is awkward to point to sin's noetic and affective consequences in order to explain why God is not more obvious. But saying that something is awkward is not a good argument. Moreover, Greco, himself a Christian theist, does not offer any alternative exegetical explanation of Rom 1:20–21, even seeming to *disagree* with the passage.[152]

Second, as I read him, Greco seems to say that our social environments—interpersonal relations, informal communities, and formal institutions—are not *themselves* affected by sin. But that appears to me to be false. For instance, on the extended model, as said above, sin (argues Plantinga) has a deeply *social* side to it. Sin "can be like a contagion that spreads from one to another, eventually corrupting an entire society or segment of it."[153] (Perhaps this applies to our minienvironments.) Further, as William Wainwright argues:

> *Social* (and not personal) sin is often the primary cause of epistemic failure. As Plantinga points out, in order to function properly, it isn't enough that our epistemic faculties be in good working order. They must also be functioning in the epistemic environment for which they were designed. If our epistemic environment has been corrupted, then even healthy and mature

---

150. Greco, "No-Fault Atheism," 125; cf. 123–25.

151. Greco, "No-Fault Atheism," 125; emphasis added.

152. Although Greco does say, "I do not mean to argue, of course, that no atheist is correctly diagnosed by the 'flawed atheist' response. That would require insight into the deep psychology of particular nonbelievers, and I make no claim to competence there" ("No-Fault Atheism," 116).

153. *WCB* 207; emphasis in original.

> epistemic faculties can go astray, and immature ones can be warped. When that happens, epistemic blindness is more the fault of others than our own.[154]

Wainwright goes on: "Given that our political, economic, social, and familial structures have been marred by sin, it is not surprising that people are blind to the Good."[155]

Third, I can agree with Greco that believers (e.g., theists) can and likely *do* help to promote nonbelief; surely it is true that believers "undermine the transmission of religious knowledge and faith and thus promote nonbelief." Indeed, he is right that, for theists, it is useful "to turn our attention away from 'the speck in our brother's eye' and 'notice the log in our own.'"[156] But we should be careful not to turn our attention too far away, as I think Greco does, for as the extended model stipulates, all persons are in fact influenced by sin, and this does include nonbelievers (which is not to try to "soften the blow," as he says). Last, these comments, given by Evan Fales (himself a nonbeliever), are relevant to this objection expressed by Greco:

> I want to explore the possibility that God hides himself from many nonbelievers because their hearts aren't in a condition properly to receive Him. Perhaps, out of respect for each person and the aim of achieving salvific union, God bides His time, awaiting an opportune moment when self-revelation stands a realistic chance of reordering the affective and conative structures of the nonbeliever's character. Perhaps, bringing about such an opportune moment requires the nonbeliever's taking certain initial steps in recognition of God's character (if He exists). If so, it'll behoove nonbelievers to reflect upon what such steps might be.[157]

My fifth chapter aims to examine some of these surfaced themes.

Objection 4: Many believers *do not find God's existence obvious.* One could take my use of Plantinga's extended A/C model, granting for argument's sake that sin's noetic and affective consequences can account for why God's existence is not obvious—particularly to *nonbelievers*—but then surface a relevant objection: Why do many *believers* not find God's existence obvious? For instance, David Taylor and Michael Murray write, "Very few people will claim that God's existence is an obvious feature of reality. Not

---

154. Wainwright, "Jonathan Edwards and Hiddenness," 111–12; emphasis in original.
155. Wainwright, "Jonathan Edwards and Hiddenness," 112.
156. Greco, "No-Fault Atheism," 116.
157. Fales, "Journeying in Perplexity," 90.

only atheists and agnostics, but *theists* too generally acknowledge that God is, at least to some extent, hidden."[158]

Further, Michael Rea, having quoted Paul in Rom 1:18–21, asks, "Does it sound like St. Paul would agree with the claim that God is mostly hidden?" "No," he writes, saying further that Paul would likely disagree that there are reasonable nonbelievers, sin having had drastic effects; people can even be self-deceived, he says: "After all, atheists say that sort of thing about theists all the time." But then Rea goes on:

> Still, this is a hard doctrine, and it has some real problems as a general explanation of the phenomenon of divine hiddenness. Remember, even *believers* struggle with God's hiddenness. Many people seem to be utterly broken by divine silence in the midst of their own suffering or the suffering of others, or simply by the ongoing and unsatisfied longing for the presence of God. I've seen more than one friend break down in tears over this sort of thing.[159]

In response, two things. First, as discussed in my second chapter, many philosophers and theologians interpret various psalms (e.g., Ps 10) to argue that God often is hidden from his people—*believers*. But as explained from an Old Testament perspective on "divine hiddenness," a distinction can be drawn between *ontological* divine absence and *perceived* divine absence; the latter and not the former (as Hubert Keener argues) is likely what characterizes many of the psalmist's descriptions of "divine hiddenness."[160] Perhaps this, too, is what characterizes many contemporary believers' conception of divine hiddenness. I think that many philosophers and theologians who analyze PDH overlook this distinction.

Rea acknowledges, from Rom 1, that God is *not* hiding from us (one of the arguments I made on the bare A/C model in chapter 3), pointing to themes like sin and self-deception as possible explanations for why some do not believe in God. But he then goes on to say that this is problematic as a general explanation of God's hiddenness since even *believers* struggle with God's hiddenness. Rea then argues that saying that God is not hidden from us

> seems to me to be just a way of relocating the problem—sort of like pushing around a bulge under the carpet instead of stomping it out entirely. And it seems that the only sensible answer is:

---

158. Taylor and Murray, "Hiddenness," 368; emphasis added.
159. Rea, "Divine Hiddenness, Divine Silence," 270; emphasis added.
160. H. Keener, "Review of *Where Is God?*" See Burnett, *Where Is God?*

> God must have some very good reason [for being hidden]. . . .
> Maybe God does have a good reason for remaining hidden.[161]

But if God is not, in fact, hidden from us, then it seems that when *believers* encounter "divine hiddenness"—the "silence" of God, as Rea says—they are encountering *perceived* and not ontological divine absence. I think Rea would likely acknowledge this point, for he goes on to argue that his claim is that "divine silence might just be an expression of God's preferred mode of interaction, and that we need not experience his silence as *absence*."[162] Yet it seems confused on Rea's part to reason *from* the fact that believers sometimes struggle with God's presence or silence—having already stated that God is not hidden, as he interprets Paul to say in Rom 1—*to* the conclusion that God himself is hidden from us.

Second, I think that Plantinga's epistemology can help make sense of this. The generic A/C model, as I argued in chapter 3, stipulates that God is not hidden; the SD is functioning properly so that we believe in God naturally and spontaneously; we have warranted theistic belief (and affection). But sin has had noetic and affective effects, as expressed on the extended model, and this affects not only nonbelievers but also to some degree *believers*, thereby accounting for why God's existence is not obvious even to *them* (as I said in the application section). For instance, as Kevin Diller explains of the extended model with respect to believers: "Until a human knower [a believer] is *completely* renewed [e.g., by God the Holy Spirit], there will be varying interference in the deliverances of faith that will reduce warrant and weaken belief."[163] In the next chapter I explore this theme further.

Objection 5: *Even on the assumption that God is not hidden and that sin therefore makes God's existence appear hidden or unobvious, still, why does he not make himself more obvious than he is or provide us with more evidence than he does?* Kevin Kinghorn, assessing Schellenberg's 1993 argument (in DHHR), writes:

> Even if we grant that some sort of spiritual blindness is affecting the way in which a person assesses the evidence available

---

161. Rea, "Divine Hiddenness, Divine Silence," 270.

162. Rea, "Divine Hiddenness, Divine Silence," 273. See also Rea, "Narrative, Liturgy, and Hiddenness"; "Hiddenness and Transcendence." Rea gave the Gifford Lectures at the University of St. Andrews on divine hiddenness in 2017: "Though the Darkness Hide Thee: Seeking the Face of the Invisible God." These lectures were later published (*Hiddenness of God*).

163. Diller, *Theology's Epistemological Dilemma*, 150; emphasis added.

to her, . . . we will still want to know why God has not provided *more* positive evidence for her consideration.[164]

Similarly, Thomas V. Morris says:

> We need an account of God's hiddenness that offers a conception not just of what God is and what we are but, centrally, of what he is *doing*, or to put it another way, of why he is not doing any *more* than he is in fact doing [i.e., to reveal himself].[165]

As it was argued in chapter 3 (on the generic A/C model), God's revelation of himself in the external created order triggers or activates the SD (perhaps also the "will"), producing in us theistic knowledge (and affection). This is how God has designed us to function.

But sin does not change or alter God's external revelation, in which case the problem, as Kinghorn and Morris seem to indicate, is not (in my defense) that God needs to give *more* evidence for us to consider or that he needs to do *more* than he is in fact doing; rather, the problem is that *we* now find ourselves in a postlapsarian condition, as the extended model stipulates, whereby sin affects *our* own proper function (as well as the other warrant conditions). Since evidence or other inferential means are not needed to believe in (and to have affection for) God, then to ask why God does not give more evidence or other inferential means to believe in him is, to my thinking, beside the point (which is not to say that Kinghorn and Morris's questions are unimportant). So, Richard M. Gale writes that many

> atheists have used the hiddenness of God as the basis for an argument against his existence. There is, they say, a presumption of atheism so that *no news is bad news*. Numerous quotations can be given from the Bible to the effect that God's intention in creating men was so that they would come to know of his existence and worship, obey, and enter into a communal loving relation with him. Thus, if we do not have good evidence that God exists *because he has chosen to remain hidden*, this constitutes good evidence against his existence.[166]

Without trying to rebut Gale, but instead to comment on his complaints, my defense argues that God has not chosen to remain hidden from us—this is the good news—but that sin's noetic and affective consequences numb us to

---

164. Kinghorn, "Why Doesn't God," 190; emphasis in original.
165. T. Morris, *Making Sense*, 97; emphasis added.
166. Gale, "Evil and Alvin Plantinga," 68; emphasis added.

him, this being the bad news. What is needed, then, is the restoration of our damaged noetic and affective equipment.

Due to damaged faculties, it is not so much that the evidence is lacking; it is rather, as Paul Helm notes, that through "such misconceptions we misinterpret evidence, hide from evidence, are a prey to imagination, accept common opinion, and the like."[167] As Nicholas Wolterstorff explains, at least some nonbelief "is not so much insufficient awareness of the evidence, as it is *resistance* to the available evidence."[168] Paul Gooch writes of Rom 1:18–25, "We need to take more seriously Paul's claims in Rom 1 that human beings have not made proper use of their cognitive equipment."[169] As Plantinga writes elsewhere of our damaged affections:

> Without a change of heart *even a great deal of evidence* won't convince us human beings [of God's existence]. ("If they do not listen to Moses and the Prophets, they will not be convinced even if someone rises from the dead," Luke 16:31).[170]

And William Wainwright, analyzing PDH from the perspective of Jonathan Edwards, reasons that an Edwardsian could answer the "more evidence" question by saying that

> critics like [J. L.] Schellenberg consistently underestimate human corruption and sinfulness. Given our perversity, and tendency to idolatry, it is likely that even a fuller divine self-disclosure would be corrupted by us, and would thus not help us. What is needed isn't *more evidence* or a fuller revelation but a new heart to appreciate the evidence and revelation we have.[171]

This is one way to think about this issue. Another way is to say that although God has designed humanity to believe *non-inferentially* or basically, still, *inferential* theistic belief could be at least *part* of our post-fallen epistemic condition. Michael Sudduth captures how this might go:

> It may be that there is some basic theistic belief-producing faculty F (such as the *sensus divinitatis*) that malfunctions. As a result of F's malfunctioning, some other faculty or set of faculties is casually responsible for generating or sustaining theistic belief. In fact, given the Reformed doctrine of the noetic effects of sin it looks

---

167. Helm, "John Calvin, *Sensus Divinitatis*," 100.
168. Wolterstorff, "Is Reason Enough?," 145; emphasis in original.
169. Gooch, "Paul, Mind of Christ," 94.
170. A. Plantinga, "Internalism, Externalism," 382n5; emphasis added.
171. Wainwright, "Jonathan Edwards and Hiddenness," 104; emphasis added. See also Oliphint, "Jonathan Edwards on Apologetics."

like there is good reason within the Reformed theological tradition to suppose that our knowledge of God is compromised by sin. One of its consequences may be damage to the operation of the *sensus divinitatis*, requiring *partial* dependence on inferential reasoning for theistic beliefs, at least until such time as this mechanism is healed, perhaps by spiritual regeneration or faith. Even if the cognitive design plan specified an exclusively basic mode of theistic belief formation, the noetic effects of sin suggest that human beings are by-and-large in a less than optimal cognitive situation, especially with respect to theistic belief. Other modes of theistic belief formation become relevant. And as Plantinga has argued, if it turned out that the faculty of basic theistic belief formation were damaged, such that another faculty or set of faculties casually generated or sustained theistic belief, it is likely that God would have adopted these as *part* of the design plan. This implies that inferential reasoning can easily be construed as at least *part* of our post-lapsarian cognitive design plan.[172]

This partial inferential reasoning could include, for example, arguments for God's existence from natural theology; if this line of thought is pursued, then it could be the case that these arguments, contra the objection, *do* constitute adequate evidence such that God does not need to give us *more* evidence. I myself do not favor this route, but it is an option.[173]

Objection 6: Sin cannot explain everything *with respect to the problem of divine hiddenness*. In this chapter, on the extended model, much emphasis has been placed on how sin affects our knowledge of, but also affection for, God. But sin and its consequences, this objection states, have only limited explanatory power. Perhaps Michael Murray captures this objection when he writes that "while the Fall may play *some part* in explaining the hiddenness of God, the Judeo-Christian theist would be hard pressed to lay the *full explanation* for hiddenness there."[174]

In response, this seems to me to be fundamentally correct. My aim has been to answer the research question by providing a defense—what Peter

---

172. Sudduth, "Reformed Epistemology," 314; emphasis added.

173. Keith Mascord argues erroneously (I think) that Plantinga's models should not be taken as *non-inferential* but rather as *inferential*: "Plantinga argues that when people, 'upon beholding the starry heavens, or the splendid majesty of the mountains, or the intricate beauty of a tiny flower,' form the belief that God is the creator of these, they are not doing so because of the existence of an implicit argument, such as a version of the teleological argument. I think that Plantinga is simply wrong here. Some version of the teleological argument *is* in the background to the thinking of most people" (*Alvin Plantinga*, 130; emphasis in original).

174. Murray, "*Deus Absconditus*," 63; emphasis added.

van Inwagen calls a "story"—against PDH that satisfies two desiderata, the first of which stipulates that a specifically Christian account will be developed describing why God is not more obvious. The bare A/C model was used to argue that God is not hidden from us; there is a natural knowledge of God. This was the first part of my defense. Sin, however, has entered the world, spelled out on the extended A/C model, which damages our cognitive and affective equipment, thus making God's existence unobvious. This is the second part of my defense, my "story." But as Deane-Peter Baker points out, in Plantinga's epistemology, *that* humans find themselves in a sinful condition

> *is not the end of the story*, however, for according to this [extended] model, God has intervened, through the life and substitutionary death of his son Jesus Christ, to rectify the situation. One consequence of this intervention is that humans now have access to the good news of the gospel of Jesus Christ, contained in the Holy Scriptures.

God, Baker writes, "rectifies the *cognitive* damage done to the *sensus divinitatis* by sin," while also healing "the damage sin causes to the *will*."[175] Diller argues that, on the extended model, "due to noetic effects of sin, it is only by the gracious redemptive work of the Spirit that there is any hope for the gradual repair of the *sensus divinitatis*."[176] The same can be said with respect to the human will. Plantinga examines these themes as they relate to the extended A/C model—the "full panoply of Christian belief"—asking, "How can we think of these beliefs . . . as reasonable or rational, let alone warranted, let alone having warrant sufficient for knowledge?"[177]

So, this objection—captured by Murray's comments—is right that sin cannot explain *everything* with respect to PDH, especially if one desires to give a specifically Christian defense for the problem; it is therefore also necessary to analyze how God in Christ saves us from our sin, and how this applies to our theistic belief and affections in our postlapsarian condition. Still, investigating sin in the context of PDH is important, for in doing so we "magnify divine grace."[178] Sarah Coakley argues, from the perspective of St. John of the Cross, that

---

175. Baker, "Plantinga's Reformed Epistemology," 79; emphasis added.

176. Diller, *Theology's Epistemological Dilemma*, 147.

177. WCB 241.

178. McFarland, "Fall and Sin," 156. Owen Anderson says, "The Christian Gospel does not make sense apart from an understanding of *sin*" (*Clarity of God's Existence*, 1; emphasis added).

the "problem of divine hiddenness" will now transmute into an invitation to a *practised* epistemic transformation *in response to divine grace*, a practised ascetic detachment from anything *other than* God.[179]

4.7 CONCLUSION

Let us take stock. First, I offered contextual remarks on the initial stages of the extended A/C model. Second, I explained the model's conception of sin's *noetic* effects. Third, I explained the model's conception of sin's *affective* effects. Fourth, I then applied these effects to PDH; four applications were made. Fifth, objections were considered. The purpose of this chapter was to continue answering my research question as well as to give the second part of my three-part defense for the problem of divine hiddenness (satisfying the defense desiderata); I claimed that the noetic and affective effects of sin, conceived on the hypothetical extended A/C model, can be used as part of my defense in order to explain why God's existence is not more obvious. I now turn to chapter 5, with the fuller extended A/C model in hand, to consider the third and final part of my defense.

---

179. Coakley, "Divine Hiddenness or Dark Intimacy?," 236; emphasis on "practised" and "other than" in original, other emphasis added.

5.

The Problem of Divine Hiddenness and the Extended Aquinas/Calvin Model

5.1 INTRODUCTION

CHAPTER 1 INTRODUCED THE problem of divine hiddenness (PDH). Chapter 2 showed how my work fits within present-day PDH literature. The research question asks *Why, if God exists, is his existence not more obvious?*, and I have chosen to answer the question not by way of a theodicy but rather a defense, arguing more specifically that my defense intends to satisfy two desiderata, which state that I will:

(i*) Develop a specifically Christian account describing why, if God exists, his existence is not more obvious.

(ii) Show that this description is true for all we know.

My defense against PDH comes in three parts, drawing from Alvin Plantinga's A/C models; it can be used to answer the research question as well as to satisfy the defense desiderata. My thesis statement is that *Plantinga's A/C models for how Christian belief may have warrant can be utilized as a defense to explain why, if God exists, his existence is not more obvious.* Chapter 3, the first part of my defense, argued by way of the bare A/C model that God is not hidden from us and that humanity can have warranted theistic belief, whereas chapter 4, which followed the *initial stages* of Plantinga's extended A/C model, contended that sin has not only drastic *noetic* effects, thus disrupting human knowledge of God, but also grave *affective* consequences, thus impeding love and desire for God.

Chapter 4, part 2 of my defense, argued that sin's noetic and affective effects, spelled out on the model, can be used to explain why God's existence is not more obvious. The chapter ended, however, by claiming that God himself has done something *about* sin through his Son Jesus Christ, but that it fell out of chapter 4's scope to demonstrate *how* the ravages of sin can be healed and repaired. The current chapter follows the full-blown extended A/C model, the model Plantinga develops in order to argue that specifically Christian belief in its postlapsarian context can have warrant. The extended model stipulates that the salvation provided by Jesus Christ renews and restores our theistic knowledge as well as our theistic affections; it will be shown how this relates to PDH.

Like the previous two, this chapter unfolds in three parts. First, I *explain* the extended A/C model on Plantinga's own terms. Second, I *apply* the model to PDH. Third, I *consider* objections to my use of the model when applied to PDH; these objections stem from either current literature on Plantinga's Reformed epistemology or PDH, and considering them will allow me to defend as well as to clarify my argumentation. Finally, concluding remarks will be made. If the argumentation here is successful, then I will have answered my research question and will have completed the third and final part of my defense against PDH, thus satisfying the desiderata.

5.2 THE EXTENDED AQUINAS/CALVIN MODEL EXPLAINED

The purpose of this section is to explain, from *WCB*, the extended A/C model for how postlapsarian Christian belief can have positive epistemic status. Positive epistemic status comprises several things, as listed by Plantinga, when he asks: "How can we think of the full panoply of Christian belief in all its particularity as enjoying *justification*, *rationality* in both its internal and external varieties, and *warrant*?"[1] *Justification*, considered from a Lockean perspective, is concerned with one's rights and obligations; comparable to the generic A/C model, Plantinga argues in the extended model that Christian belief can be justified, Christians violating no rights or obligations in so believing. *Rationality* is conceived in terms of proper function; Plantinga further distinguishes between *internal* and *external* rationality. The former, in short, is the proper function of one's cognitive equipment "'downstream from experience,'"[2] a metaphor used to describe one's own

---

1. *WCB* 241; emphasis added.
2. *WCB* 110.

"'seemings'—for example, the seeming-to-be-true of various propositions."³ "A belief is *externally rational*," Plantinga says,

> if it is produced by cognitive faculties that are functioning properly and successfully aimed at truth (i.e., aimed at the production of true belief)—as opposed, for example, to being the product of wish-fulfillment or cognitive malfunction.⁴

The extended model stipulates that Christian belief can be both internally and externally rational, and since external rationality is included in the warrant conditions, Plantinga argues that Christian belief in its postlapsarian context can have warrant, the property enough of which makes the difference between true belief and knowledge. A belief has *warrant*, Plantinga explains, if it is produced by properly functioning cognitive faculties, in a congenial epistemic environment, and according to a design plan aimed successfully at truth. These are called the warrant conditions.⁵

Similar to the generic A/C model, discussed in my third and fourth chapters, Plantinga makes three claims with respect to the extended model. First, the model is a possible description of how Christian belief *can* or *may* have warrant. Second, Plantinga argues that *if* Christian belief is true—a point that he does not seek to demonstrate—then it probably or likely is warranted. Third, the model is *a* way for Christians "to think about the epistemological status of Christian belief,"⁶ although "other models fitting other traditions can easily be constructed."⁷ (For a more thorough overview of the preceding discussion, particularly Plantinga's distinction between de facto and de jure objections to Christianity, see my chapter 3.)

> On the extended A/C model, which is "broadly Reformed or Calvinistic," we human beings were created in the image of God: we were created both with appropriate affections and with knowledge of God and his greatness and glory. Because of the greatest calamity to befall the human race, however, we fell into sin, a ruinous condition from which we require rescue and redemption.⁸

Concerning its affective consequences, sin has damaged the proper function of our affections such that

---

3. A. Plantinga, "Ad Schönecker," 238.
4. *WCB* 204; emphasis added.
5. See *WCB* 153–56.
6. *WCB* 201.
7. *WCB* 242; cf. also 350.
8. *WCB* 243.

they no longer work as in God's original design plan for human beings. There is a failure of proper function, an affective disorder, a sort of madness of the will. In this condition we know . . . what is to be loved . . . , but we nevertheless perversely turn away from what ought to be loved and instead love something else. . . . We know that we should love God and neighbor, but we nonetheless prefer not to.[9]

Moreover, Plantinga follows Calvin in that God has given all persons a *sensus divinitatis* (hereafter SD), a cognitive or noetic faculty that, when functioning as God designed it to function, produces in us warranted theistic belief: *knowledge*. Sin negatively affects not only knowledge of ourselves but also knowledge of others, although the most serious consequences of sin's noetic effects concern our knowledge of God. For were

> it not for sin and its [noetic] effects, God's presence and glory would be as obvious and uncontroversial to us all as the presence of other minds, physical objects, and the past. . . . The *sensus divinitatis* can malfunction; as a result of sin, it has indeed been damaged.[10]

Further, sin can foster in us resistance to the SD's deliverances, nurturing disbelief and distrust in God, thus undermining warrant.[11] On the extended A/C model, however, God has done something about human sin through the atoning sacrifice and subsequent resurrection of Jesus Christ, the result being "the possibility of salvation from sin and renewed relationship with God."[12] Thus, the model, notes Plantinga, "will complete and deepen the previous account [i.e., the generic A/C model] . . . of our knowledge of God."[13]

God made humanity aware of his salvific plan, the extended model argues, through a "three-tiered cognitive process."[14] First, God gave us the Bible, the main and important contents of which are what Plantinga (using the language of Jonathan Edwards) calls the "great things of the gospel," "the stunning good news of the way of salvation God has graciously offered."[15] Scripture, moreover, is testimonial in nature, "a communication from God

---

9. *WCB* 208.
10. *WCB* 214.
11. A. Plantinga says that "such withholdings [with respect to theistic belief] *lack the analogue of warrant*" (*WCB* 186; emphasis added).
12. *WCB* 243.
13. *WCB* 242.
14. *WCB* 243.
15. *WCB* 243.

to humankind; Scripture is a word from the Lord."[16] It is like ordinary testimony but different in that "the principal testifier is *God*."[17] Second, it is the Holy Spirit who not only heals the effects of sin but also helps us to believe and to grasp the truth of the gospel, that "'in Christ, God was reconciling the world to himself, not counting men's sins against them' (2 Corinthians 5:19)."[18] Without the Holy Spirit, who inspired the human authors of Scripture, we will not come to see or to believe that the scriptural testimony is in fact from God. For it is the work of the Spirit who enables us "to believe and appropriate its contents."[19] The third and final part of the process is the production of *faith* in the believer by the Holy Spirit; Plantinga adopts Calvin's definition that faith is

> a firm and certain knowledge of God's benevolence towards us, founded upon the truth of the freely given promise in Christ, both revealed to our minds and sealed upon our hearts through the Holy Spirit.[20]

As Plantinga interprets Calvin, faith has both a cognitive and an affective component (he also alludes to question 21 of the Heidelberg Catechism, that faith "is not only a knowledge and conviction" but that it is "also a deep-rooted assurance").[21] Consider first the former. The Holy Spirit heals the noetic effects of sin, thus rejuvenating our knowledge of God. Faith, Plantinga writes, is a "belief-producing process,"[22] "a cognitive activity." It is, moreover, "a matter of believing ('knowledge,' Calvin says) something or other."[23] What is the propositional content of faith, this belief produced? The content is

> the whole magnificent scheme of salvation God has arranged.... It is... knowledge of the main lines of the Christian gospel. The content of the faith is just the central teachings of the gospel; it is contained at the intersection of the great Christian creeds.[24]

---

16. *WCB* 251.
17. *WCB* 252; emphasis added.
18. *WCB* 243-44.
19. *WCB* 252.
20. John Calvin, *Institutes of the Christian Religion*, 3.2.7, as cited in *WCB* 244.
21. *WCB* 247.
22. *WCB* 256.
23. *WCB* 247.
24. *WCB* 248. For a critique of Plantinga arguing that faith does *not* entail belief, see Howard-Snyder, "Does Faith Entail Belief?"

On the model, the Holy Spirit does in fact heal and repair the SD, our *natural* and *original* cognitive faculty designed to deliver non-inferential, or basic, theistic belief comparable to perceptual, memorial, or testimonial beliefs.[25] However, the Holy Spirit, while renewing our SD, testifies to a believer the great things of the gospel, the difference being that these beliefs given by the Spirit

> do not come to the Christian just by way of memory, perception, reason, testimony, the *sensus divinitatis*, or any other of the cognitive faculties with which we human beings were *originally created*; they come instead by way of the work of the Holy Spirit.... These beliefs don't come just by way of the normal operation of our *natural* faculties; they are a *supernatural gift*.[26]

"The immediate cause of [Christian] belief," Plantinga notes, "is not to be found just in [the believer's] natural epistemic equipment."[27] Rather, it is what the model, following Aquinas and Calvin, calls the internal instigation or testimony or invitation of the Holy Spirit, who works "in concord with God's teaching in Scripture,"[28] the beliefs from whom are not accepted on the argumentative or evidential basis of other beliefs; they are therefore *basic*.

How does this go? How, in other words, is it that the belief content of faith can be basic? Although there are many ways that this might go, Plantinga argues that it is through the reading or teaching or hearing either Scripture or the gospel preached or proclaimed; the teaching or proclamation merely seems or appears correct or right. One may even find oneself saying,

> "Yes, that's right, that's the truth of the matter; this is indeed the word of the Lord." I read, "God was in Christ, reconciling the world to himself"; I come to think: "Right; that's true; God really was in Christ, reconciling the world to himself." ... What one hears or reads seems clearly and obviously true and (at any rate in paradigm cases) seems also to be something the Lord is intending to teach.[29]

The model specifies that the faith that arises in the believer—who has encountered some reading or teaching—results in the conviction "that what one reads or hears is true and a teaching of the Lord."[30] Consequently, the

25. *WCB* 184.
26. *WCB* 245; emphasis added.
27. *WCB* 256.
28. *WCB* 284.
29. *WCB* 250.
30. *WCB* 251.

conviction or belief may arise immediately or spontaneously, or perhaps it comes about slowly, over time. Nonetheless, it is *basic*, a result of the internal working—or instigation or testimony or invitation—of the Holy Spirit himself. Faith "is belief in the great things of the gospel that results from the internal instigation of the Holy Spirit."[31] (More on basicality below.)

Now, this in short is the cognitive or noetic perspective of Plantinga's extended A/C model. Still, faith as knowledge is not *merely* cognitive in nature but it "also involves the *will*";[32] Plantinga treats the restoration of our fallen affections in both the extended and testimonial models.[33] He writes on the testimonial model that "there is also the fact that we are inclined to be resentful and dismissive toward the Lord and competitive and self-serving with respect to other people" but that the "gift of faith" cures the "madness of the *will*."[34] Faith as Calvin argues is "revealed to our minds" but it is also "sealed upon our *hearts*," and it is

> the Holy Spirit who is responsible for this sealing upon our hearts of that firm and certain knowledge of God's benevolence toward us; it is the Holy Spirit who is responsible for this renewal and redirection of affections.[35]

Plantinga, on the testimonial model, goes on:

> The Holy Spirit produces knowledge, in the believer; in sealing this knowledge to our hearts, however, it also produces the right affections. Chief among these right affections is love of God—desire for God, desire to know him, to have a personal relationship with him, desire to achieve a certain kind of unity with him, as well as delight in him, relishing his beauty, greatness, holiness,

---

31. *WCB* 252.

32. *WCB* 247; emphasis added.

33. A comment on what Plantinga calls the *testimonial model*, the main topic of *WCB* chapter 10: The testimonial model, in short, is Plantinga's attempt to explain how humanity's fallen theistic *affections*—the deepest inclinations of the human will—can be restored so as to have the analogue of warrant; theistic affections, in other words, can be formed by properly functioning faculties (i.e., the human heart or will), in a congenial environment, according to a design plan that is aimed successfully at truth. Although Plantinga (somewhat confusingly) does describe within the confines of the extended A/C model how our affective equipment is restored from sin, he mostly analyzes this theme in the tenth chapter of *WCB*. For simplicity's sake, however, I will at times describe and reference the testimonial model as I describe and reference the extended model. So, too, when I *apply* the extended model to PDH below.

34. *WCB* 302-3; emphasis added.

35. *WCB* 292; emphasis in original.

and the like. There is also trust, approval, gratitude, intending to please, expecting good things, and much more.[36]

Thus, faith is not merely belief; "in producing faith, the Holy Spirit does more than produce in us the belief that this or that proposition is indeed true."[37] The Christian does of course *believe* the great things of the gospel, but she also, with respect to the affections, "finds the whole scheme of salvation enormously attractive, delightful, moving, a source of amazed wonderment."[38]

Theistic affections can also be held or taken in the *basic* way, much like when our SD is stimulated or triggered by various occasions (e.g., beholding the starry heavens or hearing Scripture preached); Plantinga argues, on the testimonial model, that this could go many different ways, but that it

> could be that perception of the beauty and delightfulness of the great things of the gospel directly and without intermediary occasions the formation of the relevant belief. . . . It could be that the Holy Spirit enables the believer to perceive that beauty and delightfulness and also enables her to make the right affective response of delight, admiration, and love: and it is that affective response which is the immediate occasion of the belief in question. You see that great things of the gospel are glorious and beautiful; you find them winsome, delightful, and attractive.[39]

Additionally, on the testimonial model, sin renders inoperative human *love* of God, what Plantinga calls *eros*. Appropriate eros—far more serious than an "inclination to spend the afternoon organizing your stamp collection"— is a deep-seated "longing" or "yearning" or "desire" for God, something comparable to the "thirst" for God depicted by, say, the psalmist (Ps 84:2, 63:1, 27:4).[40] Though ultimately not sexual, perhaps such hunger for God is *analogous* to sexual desire, a craving for intimacy and nearness, a sought-after union equivalent to being homesick.[41] Plantinga seems to argue that

36. *WCB* 293.
37. *WCB* 293.
38. *WCB* 292.
39. *WCB* 305.
40. *WCB* 311–12; these scriptural verses are the ones provided by Plantinga. See also 315–18.
41. Although as Plantinga writes, contra Freud, "It is *sexual* desire and longing that is a sign of something deeper; it is a sign of this longing, yearning for God that we human beings achieve when we are graciously enabled to reach a certain level of the Christian life. It is love for God that is fundamental or basic, and sexual eros is that sign or symbol or pointer to something else and deeper" (*WCB* 316; emphasis in original). See also Azadegan, "Divine Love."

conversion to Christ brought about by the Holy Spirit can repair and restore to a person correct theistic *eros*: a "longing, desire, a desire for some kind of union" (e.g., for or with God).[42]

Let me close my explanation of the extended A/C model, some of which includes the testimonial model, by briefly describing here (but fleshing out in more detail below) the model's account of how faith in a believer produces positive epistemic status: justification, rationality, and warrant. First, "the Christian who has received this gift of faith will of course be *justified* . . . in believing as he does" since "there will be nothing contrary to epistemic duty in so believing."[43] Second, Christian belief can be rational, which is proper functional in nature, since for the believer in the great things of the gospel, "there need be no cognitive malfunction . . . ; all her cognitive faculties can be functioning properly."[44] Last, rationality (particularly in its external variety) is *included* in the warrant conditions, Plantinga arguing that Christian belief can have warrant, the ingredient enough of which makes the difference between mere true belief and knowledge. Indeed, "faith . . . *is* knowledge,"[45] the model stipulates; faith thus satisfies the warrant conditions.

How, more particularly, are the warrant criteria fulfilled? How are they satisfied? First, what the Christian believes by *faith*, as a consequence of the internal testimony of the Holy Spirit, is the result of properly functioning cognitive faculties; and since proper function entails what Plantinga calls the design plan, it can be said that our cognitive faculties are functioning in accordance with God's design. Second, the environmental condition for warrant is met, which includes both maxi and minienvironments. The former is global, whereas the latter is more local in nature and, even though we currently find ourselves in a *postlapsarian* context, still these environments (maxi and mini) are the ones "for which this process is designed."[46] Third, beliefs produced by faith—the great things of the gospel—are aimed at truth, "such that," fourth, "the process in question is *successfully* aimed at the production of true beliefs."[47] When these conditions are met, then Christian belief can be basic, taken not on the basis of other beliefs, but more particularly *properly* basic with respect to warrant (as well as justification and

---

42. KCB 74.
43. KCB 56; emphasis added.
44. KCB 56.
45. KCB 63; emphasis in original; cf. WCB 256.
46. WCB 257; emphasis in original. The maxi-/mini-environmental distinction is discussed at length in chapter 4 and also briefly below. See also WCB 158–61.
47. WCB 257.

rationality).⁴⁸ (As noted, theistic *affections*, like theistic belief, can also be justified, rational, and warranted, in an analogous sense, as explained in the testimonial model.⁴⁹)

Now, if Christianity is true, as Plantinga contends (but does not set out to demonstrate), then it probably has warrant in the way that the model specifies; Plantinga notes that both the model's epistemology and its theology are good ways to think about warranted Christian belief, for if it

> is true, then, indeed, there is such a person as God, who has created us in his image; we have fallen into sin and require salvation; and the means to such restoral and renewal have been provided in the incarnation, suffering, death, and resurrection of Jesus Christ, the second person of the trinity. Furthermore, the typical way of appropriating this restoral is by way of faith, which, of course, involves belief in these things—that is, belief in the great things of the gospel. If so, however, God would intend that we be able to be aware of these truths. And if *that* is so, the natural thing to think is that the cognitive processes that do indeed produce belief in the central elements of the Christian faith are aimed by their designer at producing that belief. But then these beliefs will have warrant.⁵⁰

Finally, two comments need to be made. First, as mentioned, Plantinga notes that, on the model, faith constitutes knowledge since the beliefs produced by faith can in fact meet the warrant conditions; but warrant is a property that comes in *degrees*:

> If the degree of warrant (which, given the satisfaction of the [warrant conditions], is determined by the firmness or strength of belief) is high enough, then the beliefs in question will constitute knowledge.⁵¹

Second, Christian belief may be subject to defeaters, where a defeater is a proposition or a belief that conflicts with *other* beliefs one may hold. Plantinga imagines someone saying, in response to his extended model, that what has been argued "so far is only that theistic and Christian belief (taken in the basic way) can have warrant, *absent defeaters*. But defeaters are not absent."⁵² Thus, undefeated defeaters for Christian belief—the argument

---

48. See *WCB* 259, 268, 357 (cf. also the bare A/C model in 177–78).
49. *WCB* 309.
50. *WCB* 285.
51. *WCB* 258; cf. 357.
52. *WCB* 358; emphasis in original.

from evil against God's existence, for instance—can make Christian belief "*irrational* and hence unwarranted."[53] In chapters 10-14 of *WCB*, Plantinga argues, however, that there are no successful defeaters to the truth of Christian belief.[54] In sum, I have explained the extended A/C model, including the testimonial model, for how Christian belief in its postlapsarian context can have warrant. Having the above explanation in hand, I now turn to apply the model to the problem of divine hiddenness below.

5.3 THE EXTENDED AQUINAS/CALVIN MODEL APPLIED TO THE PROBLEM OF DIVINE HIDDENNESS

"The theological richness of Plantinga's Extended A/C Model," writes James Beilby, "provides many avenues for discussion."[55] One of those avenues, I believe, is PDH, and the purpose of this section is to apply the extended model to PDH; several applications are given below.

Application 1: On the extended A/C model, the believer in Jesus Christ experiences salvation from sin and spiritual regeneration. This application, though more theological in nature, is necessary for my defense against PDH. Now, in concert with the extended model's initial stages, my fourth chapter argued that sin's consequences touch many different areas, thus having a range of effects. Sin, for instance, can warp our affections so that we love and relish and delight in the wrong things; it may foster in us false beliefs about ourselves and our neighbor, even distorting the image of God in us, although the most ruinous of sin's effects have to do with our love and knowledge of God himself.

But salvation puts right what is wrong, and *faith* in Jesus Christ, as the extended model stipulates,

> is the means or vehicle of salvation: "for it is by grace that you have been saved, through faith" (Eph 1:8). It is also that by which we are *justified* . . . as well as that by means of which we are *regenerated*, becoming new creatures in Christ. And it is also under the foundation and substance . . . of Christian hope.[56]

Sarah Coakley, as discussed in the previous chapter, says that PDH, from a Christian perspective, can "transmute" into a "*response to divine*

---

53. *KCB* 89; emphasis in original; cf. *WCB* 357-73.

54. "What I claim for this model is that there aren't any successful philosophical objections to it (and in chapter 10 [of *WCB*] I'll look into some objections)" (*WCB* 285).

55. Beilby, *Epistemology as Theology*, 184.

56. *WCB* 265; emphasis added.

grace."⁵⁷ Taking Coakley's comments, here I draw on the extended model with respect to PDH. For those who have faith (the model specifies) have the "possibility of salvation from sin and renewed relationship with God."⁵⁸ Plantinga's Reformed epistemology places much emphasis on regeneration or conversion,⁵⁹ whereby Plantinga explains that

> according to Jesus Christ himself, "unless a person is born again, he cannot see the kingdom of God" (John 3:3). And according to the apostle Paul . . . a Christian believer becomes a new creature in Christ. The believer enters a process whereby she is regenerated, transformed, made into a new and better person. . . . Sin damaged our nature; regeneration, the work of the Holy Spirit, is . . . a matter of setting right and repairing that damage.⁶⁰

Regeneration, or conversion, moreover "gives me a much clearer view of the heinousness of sin, and of the degree and extent to which I am myself enmeshed in it."⁶¹ Both the cognitive as well as the affective effects of sin are redirected: "Regeneration consists in curing the *will*, so that we at least begin to love and hate the right things; it also includes *cognitive* renewal, so that we come to perceive the beauty, holiness, and delightfulness of the Lord."⁶² Salvation also repairs and restores the image of God in us,⁶³ helping us also to love our neighbor as well as ourselves.

Why is this necessary, theologically or epistemically? Why bother with themes like regeneration or conversion in the context of PDH? "Why have any truck," Plantinga asks, "with special faculties or supernatural belief-producing processes like faith and the internal instigation of the Holy Spirit?"⁶⁴ The reason—which applies to PDH—is because we are sunk in sin, prone to hating both God and our neighbor (having even "a natural

---

57. Coakley, "Divine Hiddenness or Dark Intimacy?," 236; emphasis added.

58. *WCB* 242.

59. Plantinga does not seem to advocate a particular *ordo salutis*, often using terms like regeneration and conversion interchangeably; I too will use them interchangeably hereafter.

60. *WCB* 280. "'You must be born again' all right—your affections, aims, and intentions must be recalibrated, redirected, reversed—and that requires special divine help" (271).

61. *WCB* 281; cf. 282.

62. *WCB* 304; emphasis added. "Conversion and regeneration alters affection as well as belief" (292).

63. *WCB* 205.

64. *WCB* 268.

antipathy to the message of the gospel"[65]) and are in need of salvation through faith in Christ.

Evan Fales explains concerning PDH that it is possible that God waits until nonbelievers stand a chance "of reordering the affective and conative structures of the nonbeliever's character."[66] He writes:

> Perhaps, bringing about such an opportune moment requires the nonbeliever's taking certain initial steps in recognition of God's character (if He exists). If so, it'll behoove nonbelievers to reflect upon what such steps might be.[67]

The extended model points us in the right direction, faith in Jesus Christ being the first step that one needs to take to be reconciled to God, which not only renews and restores our *knowledge* of God but also renews and restores (or at least begins to renew and restore) the perceived clarity of God's existence.

Application 2: On the extended A/C model, Christian belief can be properly basic with respect to both justification and internal rationality, and God's existence (or the great things of the gospel) can at times seem clear or evident or obvious. Christian belief on the extended model can be properly basic with respect to justification, rationality (in its internal and external forms), and warrant.[68] So, take justification, conceived in terms of rights and obligations; on the model, a Christian believer can be justified in her belief. "The believer," Plantinga writes, "is justified in accepting these beliefs in the basic way."[69] Concerning justification, my own defense against PDH argues more specifically that for those who have faith—having been saved from their sin through faith in Christ—God's existence or the great things of the gospel brought about by the Holy Spirit may often seem clear or evident or obvious: "If your belief is a result of the inward instigation of the Holy Spirit," the model stipulates, then "it may seem obviously true," "especially if it seems to you . . . that the teaching in question comes from God himself."[70] The Christian, a recipient of the Spirit's internal testimony, may feel that her faith, a benefit of which is salvation from sin but also (in my application) the clarity of God's existence, is a gift from God himself.[71]

65. WCB 269.
66. Fales, "Journeying in Perplexity," 90.
67. Fales, "Journeying in Perplexity," 90.
68. See WCB 177–78; KCB 36–37.
69. WCB 259.
70. WCB 252–53; emphasis added.
71. WCB 269. On the one hand, Plantinga appears to say that human faith is *itself* a gift from God, arguing on the other hand that faith is something humans can exercise

But is this not haughty, a bit proud to think that the gift of faith is not something that all persons yet possess? No, for the Christian whose belief is properly basic with respect to justification is not arrogant: "The fact is," Plantinga says, "there isn't any arrogance involved as such in recognizing that God has given you something he hasn't (or hasn't yet) given everyone." The Christian need not be thought proud if she believes that her "faith is a gift from the Lord and note[s] that not everyone has as yet to receive this gift."[72] Now, perhaps a believer encounters epistemic disagreement or objections or defeaters concerning her Christian belief (an argument, say, from divine hiddenness, the conclusion of which states that God does not exist). But suppose the believer, after deliberation and consideration of objections or defeaters to her Christian belief, *still* finds herself believing in God or the great things of the gospel, that God was in Christ reconciling the world to himself, and that these things at times appear evident or obvious or clear. Is she now, Plantinga goes on, *unjustified*? No, for the

> one who has faith ... is (or may very well be) justified according to the model. And even apart from the model: how could you fail to be justified, within your epistemic rights, in believing what seems to you, after reflection and investigation [i.e., after having considered defeaters and objections], to be no more than the truth?[73]

Jeroen de Ridder and Mathanja Berger, in defense of the extended model, write:

> In fact, it seems to us that this is how things sometimes go in disagreements about basic ethical, political, and philosophical issues. You disagree with people who appear to be your epistemic peers; you might become convinced that they feel just as confident and secure about their conflicting belief as you do

---

freely: "It is part of much traditional Christian teaching to hold that a necessary condition of my receiving the gift of faith is my acquiescing, being willing to accept the gift, being prepared to receive it" (257). However, Plantinga says (in personal conversation with James Beilby), "I'm thinking of the Holy Spirit as giving us a chance to see something of the beauty and truth of the great things of the gospel but it is still possible to freely accept and freely reject. The work of creating faith in us is subsequent to such an acceptance. *But that's not part of the [extended] model*—that's just the way I do in fact think it works. The Holy Spirit does not, on my way of thinking, cause me to accept the invitation" (Beilby, "Plantinga's Model," 157; emphasis added). Keith D. Stanglin and Thomas H. McCall argue that there are "'Arminian' elements in [Plantinga's] philosophical theology"(*Jacob Arminius*, 197–98).

72. WCB 254. See also A. Plantinga, "Defense of Religious Exclusivism."

73. WCB 255; emphasis added.

about yours; and you might be unable to produce arguments that would get them to reconsider their belief. *Nonetheless, you cannot help believing that you are right.* You have thought the issue over carefully, trying to take in all the relevant facts and circumstances and in full awareness of the diversity of opinion that surrounds the issue. Still, you find yourself with a strong belief that things are as you judge them to be and, by implication, that those who disagree with you are wrong.[74]

This is proper basicality concerning justification, but what about *internal rationality*? As explained above, internal rationality on the model is proper functionalist in nature, the proper functioning of one's cognitive equipment "downstream from experience," what is understood to be one's own *seemings*. Dieter Schönecker says, "The basic idea of internal rationality . . . is that one is not insane *on one's own standards*."[75] Like justification, Christian belief can be properly basic with respect to internal rationality; it may just *seem* to a believer, by her own standards, to be true or correct or right. For, Plantinga writes,

> suppose my experience is of the sort that goes with the testimony of the Holy Spirit . . . , so that the great things of the gospel seem *powerfully plausible* and *compelling* to me: then (given that I have no undefeated defeaters for these propositions) there will be nothing dysfunctional or contrary to proper function in accepting the beliefs in question. Indeed, given those experiences, it would be dysfunctional *not* to form them.[76]

My application here for PDH suggests that, for the Christian believer who has experienced salvation from sin by Jesus Christ, God's existence or the great things of the gospel do, as Plantinga says, appear *powerfully plausible* and *compelling*; these things do at times seem clear and evident, plain and obvious.

Now, internal rationality on the model also specifies that you have "considered how [a certain belief] fits in with your other beliefs, engaged in the requisite seeking for defeaters, considered the objections that you have encountered, compared notes with the right people, and so on."[77] So, perhaps a Christian believer stumbles upon a hiddenness argument, the conclusion stating that there is no God. She does her best to reflect on the premises, considers (as Plantinga notes) how the conclusion fits with her

74. De Ridder and Berger, "Shipwrecked or Holding Water?," 48–49; emphasis added.
75. Schönecker, "Deliverances," 26; emphasis in original.
76. *WCB* 255; emphasis on "not" in original, other emphasis added.
77. *WCB* 255.

other beliefs, and so forth. Is the Christian, having now encountered a hiddenness argument (but who still finds God's existence or the great things of the gospel plausible and compelling), internally *irrational* concerning her Christian belief? Not necessarily, for perhaps Christian belief *still seems* right or correct to her; perhaps she "compares notes with right people," still thinking that, by her own standards (to use Schönecker's phrase), God's existence and Christian belief are compelling, and she remains, therefore, internally rational. From this perspective, God's existence or the great things of the gospel may at times seem clear or obvious.

Application 3: *On the extended A/C model, Christian belief can be properly basic with respect to external rationality and warrant, and God's existence (or the great things of the gospel) may at times seem clear or obvious.* On the extended A/C model, external rationality, like internal rationality, is proper functionalist in nature, but since external rationality is included in the warrant conditions, the main issue (Plantinga argues) is if Christian belief does in fact have warrant. So, "according to the model, what one believes by faith (the beliefs that constitute faith) meets these four [warrant] conditions."[78] Moreover, Christian belief can be properly basic (and hence immediately or spontaneously formed) with respect to warrant. Describing this in more detail, Kevin Diller writes:

> If Christian beliefs can be properly basic, then the "most satisfactory way to hold them will not be as the conclusions of an argument" [*WCB* 210]. When warrant is obtained by a divinely designed and intended doxastic experience whereby the truth of Christian propositions becomes *apparent* without inference from other propositions, there is an analogy to direct perception. The warrant for the belief is obtained by a process wherein the believer is enabled immediately to apprehend the truth of the belief.[79]

In what follows, I use the four warrant conditions as an outline saying in more detail—that is, in more detail than what my above *explanation* of the extended model gave—how Christian belief can have warrant, interjecting this particular application to PDH along the way.

---

78. *WCB* 256.
79. Diller, *Theology's Epistemological Dilemma*, 133; emphasis added.

5.3.1 Proper Function

In Plantinga's epistemology, proper function is required for warrant in general and for warranted Christian belief in particular. Concerning the latter, the cognitive and affective equipment of human persons without Christ and without the Holy Spirit's restorative work are not functioning properly, since sin has negative cognitive and affective effects. Grace saves us from sin, making us right with God, also restoring proper function. For when Christian beliefs

> are accepted by faith and result from the internal instigation of the Holy Spirit, they are produced by cognitive processes *working properly*; they are not produced by way of some cognitive malfunction. The whole process that produces these beliefs is specifically designed by God himself to produce this very effect.... When it does produce this effect, therefore, it is working properly; thus the beliefs in question satisfy the *first condition* of warrant.[80]

The implications for divine hiddenness—why God's existence is not more obvious—are important for my defense. For as the extended model says, sin can numb us to God, "whereby we are *blinded* to God, cannot *hear* his voice, do not *recognize* his beauty and glory, may even go so far as to *deny* that he exists." Conversion renews the SD, also providing "us a much *clearer view* of the beauty, splendor, loveliness, attractiveness, glory of God."[81] Diller explains, on the extended model, that the

> cognitive impact of sin has a distorting and attenuating effect on the doxastic experiences of faith, while at the same time the very presence of the Spirit drawing us to Christ begins to rehabilitate and restore *proper function*.[82]

Without proper function, humanity's knowledge of God is muffled and impaired, sin affecting our capacity to know and to perceive God. One benefit of regeneration brought about by the Holy Spirit is that the Spirit not only gives us "eyes to see" and "ears to hear," but he also (as mentioned earlier) makes us aware of our *very own sin*; C. Stephen Evans clarifies that this

> is the truth that lies behind the claim of Reformed epistemologists that we come to know the truth of the gospel not simply by acquiring evidence but through the internal testimony of the

---

80. *KCB* 63–64; emphasis added.
81. *WCB* 281; emphasis added.
82. Diller, *Theology's Epistemological Dilemma*, 150; emphasis added.

Holy Spirit. The Holy Spirit's work in our lives is not simply a matter of giving us a certain kind of evidence; it is also a matter of the Spirit transforming us into the kinds of beings who can see the evidence and interpret it properly. Part of the evidence that the person can now see will include things such as the following: *I now recognize that I am a sinful being and that this is the root of my problems. I can also see that the remedy offered by the gospel is precisely what is needed to remedy my condition.*[83]

My application further specifies that, without proper function brought about the Holy Spirit, God's existence may seem unobvious, obscure, or hazy. "This repair of our cognitive capacities," William Abraham—who does not share Plantinga's Reformed leanings—argues,

> is in turn made possible by the healing activity of the Holy Spirit, who searches and cleanses the soul of impurity and fear. Given the human alienation from God, given the ingenuity of human agents in finding ways to oppose the truth, there has to be effective divine grace that will open the eyes of the soul and enable us to see the truth.[84]

As Ian McFarland writes (applicable to proper function and thus to divine hiddenness), "I do not know myself as a sinner until that identity has been fundamentally altered by grace thanks to which my identity is no longer simply that of a sinner."[85]

5.3.2 Congenial Environment

Consider now the environmental condition for warrant. Both mini- and maxienvironmental criteria must be met (explored in greater detail in the previous chapter), whereby the latter

> is more general and more global than a cognitive minienvironment. Our cognitive maxienvironment here on earth would include such macroscopic features as the presence and properties of light and air, the presence of visible objects, of other objects detectable by cognitive systems of our kind, of some objects

---

83. C. S. Evans, *Why Christian Faith*, 114; emphasis added.
84. Abraham, *Crossing the Threshold*, 56. Abraham rejects the Reformed construal of the Spirit's internal witness, opting instead for his own Arminian-Wesleyan account; see, for instance, Abraham, *Canon and Criterion*, 154-55; "Epistemological Significance" (on which see *WCB* 242n3); "Philosophical Reflection."
85. McFarland, "Fall and Sin," 152.

not so detectable, of the regularities of nature, of the existence and general nature of other people, and so on. Our cognitive faculties are designed (by God or evolution) to function in *this* maxienvironment, or one like it. They are not designed for a maxienvironment in which, for example, there is constant darkness, or where everything is in a state of constant flux.[86]

The maxienvironment can contain multiple minienvironments, a minienvironment being more specific and local; one's maxienvironment may be appropriate, but some "minienvironments . . . are *misleading* for some exercises of cognitive faculties, even when those faculties are functioning properly and even when the maxienvironment is favorable,"[87] and one may have a true belief just by accident. If both mini and maxienvironmental conditions are not met, then a belief cannot have warrant. Indeed, particular minienvironments can be "misleading," as Plantinga explains elsewhere, whereby "our faculties (more exactly, specific uses of them) display a certain deplorable *lack of resolution*."[88] But on the extended model, Plantinga explains that (in our postlapsarian condition)

> the *maxienvironment* in which we find ourselves, including the cognitive contamination produced by sin, is precisely the cognitive environment for which this process is designed. The typical *minienvironment* is also favorable.[89]

Now, in chapter 4, I conjectured for the second part of my defense against PDH that the maxienvironment is *general revelation*, the "book of nature": the starry heavens, a majestic waterfall, a beautiful flower, and so forth. The SD, I argued, is designed to be triggered or activated in these various circumstances or environments, in which case we will form theistic belief. Unfortunately, humanity has fallen into sin. Sin, however, does not inhibit God from revealing himself generally to all persons: the heavens are *still* there, even in our postlapsarian condition, *continually* telling of God's glory (cf. Ps 19). Thus, the maxienvironment, so I said, remains the same; the problem, rather, lies not only in our cognitive endowment, but also in our *environment*. Various minienvironments in which we find ourselves—for instance, a certain pocket of society, one's immediate family, and so forth—can be corrupt and unfavorable, thus undermining our theistic knowledge but also the clarity of God's existence. For as Diller explains of

---

86. *WCB* 158.
87. *WCB* 158; emphasis in original.
88. A. Plantinga, "Respondeo," 316; emphasis in original.
89. *WCB* 257; emphasis added.

the extended model, Plantinga "acknowledges that human sin and alienation from God have had a serious impact on both proper function and our *cognitive environment*."[90]

Even though Plantinga does not write (in *WCB*) with specificity *how* the environmental condition for warranted Christian belief is met, a little "reading between the lines" can yield applications for PDH. So, how is the environmental condition met *for the purposes of the hiddenness problem*? How is it that can we have not only knowledge but also clarity of God's existence in our postlapsarian environment? My answer, in short, is that it is the Holy Spirit who creates (as Diller says) "faith-conducive environments,"[91] particularly both *Scripture* and the *church*.

First, take *Scripture*. God's existence or the great things of the gospel or that God was in Christ reconciling the world to himself can be obvious or clear to us when we read or hear Scripture preached or proclaimed or read, the Bible being an important part of the extended A/C model's three-part cognitive process; this comes about through the Holy Spirit. For as James Anderson explains (of the extended model), "The activity of the Holy Spirit might be thought of as bringing about a *congenial epistemic environment* for the formation of testimonial beliefs based on *Scripture*."[92] On my application, God has revealed himself *generally* but also *specifically*, in Scripture, and one can know God by reading or hearing his word. For "Christians," writes Stephen Fowl,

> are committed to the belief that the triune God has revealed a passionate desire to have fellowship with them, even in light of their manifest sin. *Scripture* is chief among God's providentially ordered gifts directed to bringing about reconciliation and fellowship despite human sin.[93]

Moreover, the Bible (as Plantinga puts it) is *perspicuous* or clear:[94]

> According to the model, Scripture is *perspicuous*: the main lines of its teaching—creating, sin, incarnation, atonement, resurrection, eternal life—can be understood and grasped and properly accepted by anyone of normal intelligence.[95]

90. Diller, *Theology's Epistemological Dilemma*, 282; emphasis added.
91. Diller, *Theology's Epistemological Dilemma*, 269.
92. J. Anderson, *Paradox in Christian Theology*, 187; emphasis in original.
93. Fowl, "Scripture," 351; emphasis added.
94. For an overview of this doctrine, see Muller, *Post-Reformation Reformed Dogmatics*, 2:115–17; Thompson, *Clear and Present Word*. See also McGrath, *Reformation Thought*, 97–100.
95. *WCB* 374; emphasis in original. Further: "By virtue of this process, an ordinary

Applied to PDH, the perspicuity of Scripture may be one reason why God does not rearrange the heavens—although they do in fact tell of his glory—so as to vindicate or exonerate his existence. In fact, God has *accommodated* himself, as Reformed theologians have argued, to our fallen condition in Scripture, the scriptural witness being fit and appropriate for our finite human capacities.[96] He has "stooped down" and has condescended himself to us in the Bible, and even if God *were* to write in the clouds in some heavenly language (something like "the end of the world is at hand"[97]), then we humans would likely be unable to comprehend it (perhaps we could comprehend it, but could we *act* on it?).[98] Instead,

> what we learn from Scripture gathers, focuses, and clarifies what we learn by way of the *sensus divinitatis*, enabling us to see God and his love, glory, beauty, and the like with much *higher resolution*. [Calvin] could have added that [Scripture] also gives us a clearer view of our world: we now see what is most important about all the furniture of heaven and earth—namely, that it has been created by God.[99]

Thus, special revelation, the Bible (the "book of Scripture"), can clarify general revelation, the "book of nature."[100] God has given the "spectacles" of Scripture, writes Oliver Crisp of John Calvin on sin's noetic effects, "in order for us to be able to 'read' this revelation in creation."[101]

Christian, one quite innocent of historical studies, the ancient languages, the intricacies of textual criticism, the depths of theology, and all the rest can nevertheless know that these things [the teachings of the gospel] are, indeed, true."

96. Although, as Oliver Crisp argues, the incarnation is "the supreme instance of divine accommodation" (*Deviant Calvinism*, 35). See also Battles, "God Was Accommodating Himself"; Helm, *John Calvin's Ideas*, 184–208.

97. Kenny, *Faith and Reason*, 73–74.

98. As Jonathan Edwards notes: "Would it not be rational to suppose, that [God's] speech would be exceeding different from men's speech, that he should speak *like a God*; that is, that there should be such an excellency and sublimity in his speech or word, such a stamp of wisdom, holiness, majesty, and other divine perfections, that the word of men, yea of the wisest of men, should appear mean and base in comparison to it?" ("Divine and Supernatural Light," in Edwards, *Sinners in the Hands*," 166; emphasis added).

99. WCB 281; emphasis added. As Dewey Hoitenga Jr. writes, "When Christians believe in God, then, they do so because their natural awareness of him is enlarged by the testimony and illumination of the Holy Spirit to accept what he reveals himself in *Scripture* and Incarnation" (*Faith and Reason*, 222; emphasis added).

100. For the distinction between general and special revelation in Plantinga's thought, see Diller, *Theology's Epistemological Dilemma*, 129n1.

101. O. Crisp, *Retrieving Doctrine*, 17.

Scripture on the model is (Plantinga writes) "divine testimony."[102] Thus, belief in the great things of the gospel, upon reading the Bible, can be formed in us immediately or spontaneously, comparable to self-evident truths, and not inferred or deduced from other beliefs.[103] When Scripture is proclaimed or preached or taught or read—*this proclamation or preaching or teaching or reading thus comprising a favorable minienvironment*—then God's existence can become obvious to us. Although perhaps for most people what becomes obvious under such conditions is not something quite as generic as "the existence of God" but (as I have said) rather something more specific, such as the great things of the gospel, or that God was in Christ, reconciling the world to himself. Still, as Plantinga writes, there is the "phenomenon of being convinced, coming to see, forming of a conviction. There is the reading or hearing, and then there is the belief or conviction that what one reads or hears is true and a teaching of the Lord."[104]

How, more particularly, does this work? What is the process?

> The process [Thomas Crisp notes] works something like this: one hears the gospel preached, evinces an openness to the leading of the Holy Spirit and thereupon has belief in the great things of the gospel produced in one by the Holy Spirit. Belief thus arrived at is, says Plantinga, perfectly reasonable, perfectly respectable from the epistemic point of view.[105]

102. *WCB* 251.
103. *WCB* 262.
104. *WCB* 251.
105. T. Crisp, "On Believing," 204. See also McCall, "On Understanding Scripture," in the same volume. See further *WCB* 269. In the extended A/C model, Plantinga says that the Holy Spirit is responsible for bringing about faith in the believer, which is "known by way of an extraordinary cognitive process or belief-producing mechanism." Indeed, when Christian beliefs are produced by the Holy Spirit, "they are produced by cognitive processes working properly" (*WCB* 256-57). Many object to Plantinga's construal of the instigation of the Holy Spirit as a process or mechanism; for instance, J. P. Moreland and William Lane Craig note:

> Plantinga's understanding of the instigation of the Holy Spirit as a belief-forming process analogous to a cognitive faculty is surely suspicious. It is as though there were a faculty outside myself which forms beliefs in me. But since this faculty or process is not mine, not being part of my cognitive equipment, then it cannot literally be true that "*I* have believed in God," which contradicts both Scripture and experience. Certainly, the belief is formed in me, but I am not the one who formed it, and, therefore, I have not truly believed. (*Philosophical Foundations*, 169)

James Anderson writes, "While it makes sense to speak of a *faculty* as 'functioning properly,' it is less clear that it makes equal sense to speak of a *process* as 'functioning

Nicholas Wolterstorff, writing of Herman Bavinck, explains that it is not the conclusion of an argument whereby one is convinced that Scripture is the word of God; nor is it that the Holy Spirit gives us "an additional revelation telling us that Scripture truly is revelation." It is rather the Holy Spirit who testifies to us that Scripture is God's word:

> How is this testimony to be understood? We find ourselves believing that Scripture is God's word. The Spirit brings about that belief on our part, and the Spirit's bringing about that belief is the testimony of the Spirit.[106]

Indeed, to quote Plantinga again, "What one hears or reads seems *clearly and obviously true* and ... seems also to be something the Lord is intending to teach."[107] As Plantinga explains elsewhere, "Upon reading the Bible, one may be impressed with a deep sense that God is speaking to him."[108] Thus, the reading or hearing of Scripture can comprise a favorable minienvironment whereby God's existence or the great things of gospel seems clear or obviously true.

Second, in addition to Scripture, the *church* also encompasses a favorable or congenial minienvironment. For example, Diller argues that "the *church* is used by God in the restoration of proper function and in the creation of suitable *environments* for growth in faith."[109] And Plantinga says, "Perhaps the believer knows by way of [the internal instigation of the Holy Spirit] that the Holy Spirit has guided and preserved the Christian *church*, making sure that its teachings on important matters are, in fact, true."[110] My application here suggests that when we gather in church to hear Scripture preached or taught, or to sing the great hymns of the faith, or to take

---

properly.'" Anderson goes on: "Unlike faculties, processes *as such* do not have functions. Plantinga appears to be aware of this, but he does nothing to address it" (*Paradox in Christian Theology*, 184–85; emphasis in original; Anderson alludes to *WCB* 257). Then, Anderson, defending Plantinga, suggests that there are a few ways to resolve this matter. One of those ways is to conceive of the testimony of the Holy Spirit as bringing about testimonial beliefs on the basis of Scripture, just as I have quoted Anderson as saying in the body above. Here I prefer to follow Anderson. Finally, Deane Peter-Baker also discusses similar concerns about the Holy Spirit in Plantinga's epistemology, proposing a couple of avenues of rectification ("Plantinga's Reformed Epistemology," 81, 88–89).

106. Wolterstorff, "Herman Bavinck," 142.

107. *WCB* 250; emphasis added.

108. A. Plantinga, "Is Belief in God Rationally Acceptable?," 45.

109. Diller, *Theology's Epistemological Dilemma*, 157; emphasis added. Diller clarifies, "Although the Christian community does not itself ground the connection between belief formation and the truth of what is being believed, it may still be critical to *suitable cognitive environment* and proper function" (158; emphasis added).

110. *WCB* 380; emphasis added.

the Lord's Supper (or the Eucharist), or to pray corporately, or to bring our tithes and offerings unto the Lord, then God the Holy Spirit can foster a hospitable environment whereby God's existence or the great things of gospel just seems gripping, compelling, clear, and obvious; God will not appear hidden to us.

5.3.3 Design Plan Aimed Successfully at Truth

In addition to proper function and a conducive environment, Plantingean Reformed epistemology also stipulates that a belief must be successfully aimed at truth, in step with its design plan, and not, for instance, at mere wish fulfillment. The process for warranted Christian belief, he writes, "is designed to produce *true beliefs*; and . . . the beliefs it produces—belief in the great things of the gospel—are in fact *true*."[111] As explained earlier, this could be the way that God has designed or intended for us to become aware of these truths, belief in his existence or the great things of the gospel, in which case we can in fact have warranted Christian belief; my application here states that, when these conditions are met, then God or the great things of the gospel can appear clear or evident to us.

Application 4: On the extended A/C model, our theistic affections can be properly basic with respect to justification, rationality, and warrant, and God's existence or the great things of the gospel can at times seem clear or obvious to us. Justification, rationality, and warrant have all been detailed above, so this application, mutatis mutandis, will be briefer.[112] First, affections (like beliefs) can be justified (discussed above). On my application, a Christian is within her rights, thus violating no duties, to have strong theistic affections, the Holy Spirit stirring in her heart what seems obviously true: love and trust and approval and gratitude for God. The same is true—second—with rationality, which is proper functionalist in nature; a Christian longs or yearns or desires God in a way that perhaps she did not before regeneration, God's existence or the great things of the gospel after regeneration thus being compelling or gripping or convincing.

What, finally, of warrant? How can affections have the analogue of warrant? Plantinga writes that affections, like beliefs, can be formed by properly functioning faculties—the heart or the "will"—in a favorable environment, maxi and mini, according to a design plan aimed successfully at truth. Briefly consider *proper function*; at regeneration, the Holy Spirit

---

111. *WCB* 257.
112. What follows is summarized and applied from *WCB* 310–11.

reorients our fallen affections. To illustrate further, consider someone who distrusts or disapproves of God; on this theme, Paul Moser writes that a

> highly educated atheist acquaintance of mine has a similar attitude of God. When asked how he would respond if after death he met God directly, he replied that he would immediately kill himself.[113]

John Henry Gordon, recounting one reason for leaving the Christian faith, notes that God just seemed to him to be "such a horrible incarnation of everything foul and false, such a *monstrous monster*."[114] Perhaps similar sentiment is implicit in the British Humanist Association's slogan, "There's Probably No God. Now Stop *Worrying* and Enjoy Your Life."[115] It is as if God is a source of irrational fear and terror and fright, just as one writer, claiming that God is "mysterious, ineffable, beyond our ken, hiding," explains that divine hiddenness is

> one major reason I don't believe in the bastard [God], and would refuse to believe even if I did find God convincing in other ways. I'd refuse on principle; I'd say: "All right then I'll go to hell," like Huck Finn.
>
> Because what business would God have hiding? What's that about? What kind of silly game is that? God is all-powerful and benevolent but at the same time it's hiding? Please. We wouldn't give that the time of day in any other context. Nobody would buy the idea of ideal, loving, concerned, involved parents who permanently hide from their children, so why buy it of a loving God?[116]

Hence, where there might be a posture of distrust and disapproval and suspicion and anger toward God, it is the Holy Spirit who, upon regeneration, can conversely foster in us (as Plantinga notes) "trust, approval," as well as "gratitude, intending to please, expecting good things, and much more."[117] She who has faith, Plantinga writes,

> not only believes the central claims of the Christian faith; she also (paradigmatically) *finds the whole scheme of salvation*

---

113. Moser, "Reorienting Religious Epistemology," 70.

114. Gordon, *Public Statement*, quoted in Larsen, *Crisis of Doubt*, 120; emphasis added. Larsen's work surveys several nineteenth-century English figures explaining why they left the Christian faith as well as why they returned.

115. Humanists UK, "Atheist Bus Campaign," para. 2; emphasis added.

116. Benson, "Deal-Breaker," 24–25.

117. *WCB* 293.

> *enormously attractive, delightful, moving, a source of amazed wonderment.* She is deeply grateful to the Lord for his great goodness and responds to his sacrificial love with love of her own.[118]

Thus the Holy Spirit brings about proper function, "a healing of the disorder of affection that afflicts us."[119] Plantinga writes, "No doubt one whose affective capacities or faculties are functioning properly will love the Lord on perceiving his loveliness, glory, and beauty; no doubt such a person will find him delightful."[120]

What about our *environment*? How is this condition met such that God's existence (or the great things of the gospel) can appear or seem clear or obvious? My answer here is similar to the earlier ones: Scripture and the church. Perhaps a person hears the word of God preached or taught, whereby she finds herself, immediately and spontaneously, yearning for and delighting in God; indeed, the preaching of the word of God, Heinrich Bullinger says, *is* the word of God: "Wherefore when this Word of God is now preached in the church by preachers lawfully called, we believe that the very Word of God is preached, and received of the faithful."[121] Thus, when Scripture is proclaimed for the corporate edification of the congregation, or when the great hymns of the faith are sung, or the Lord's Supper observed, a person may, to quote John Wesley, just find her heart "strangely warmed"; her affections come about in the basic way. Something similar, I suppose, can be true of our affections when we find ourselves in nature, perhaps (for instance) upon seeing a beautiful flower, hiking through the Grand Canyon, or jogging through Vondelpark in Amsterdam on a clear, sunny day; these environments occasion or activate love and longing for our Creator; his existence can seem to us clear. Moreover, the affections can arise from a design plan aimed successfully at truth, God having designed our affective equipment to aim at himself, and not, say, at mere wish fulfillment or irrational fear and distrust of God, and so on. Indeed, due to fallen affections, we need a "change of heart":

> This is provided by the internal instigation of the Holy Spirit . . . ; he both turns our affections in the right direction and *enables us to see* the truth of the great things of the gospel. The process whereby we come to believe these things, therefore, satisfies the

---

118. *WCB* 292; emphasis added.
119. *WCB* 311.
120. *WCB* 303.
121. "The Second Helvetic Confession (1566)," in Leith, *Creeds of the Churches*, 133.

conditions for warrant (and also the conditions for the affective analogue of warrant).[122]

Application 5: On the extended A/C model, God's existence or the great things of the gospel (stemming from warranted Christian belief or affections) can seem more obvious more frequently throughout one's sanctification. Traditionally, Protestants take sanctification, which comes after regeneration or conversion (and justification), to be one's progressive growth in holiness throughout one's Christian life (finished ultimately at glorification).[123] I have argued that God's existence can seem obvious and convincing to us at certain times, but this application further suggests that God's existence (or the great things of the gospel or that God was in Christ reconciling the world to himself) can appear obvious or convincing more frequently as one disassociates oneself from sin and lives in the power of the Holy Spirit. To explain this application further I will make two (extensive) comments.

First, my application concerning PDH here is informed by what Plantinga has argued elsewhere:

> Part of what the Christian thus learns is that divine grace *restores* the image of God in the believer; part of the effect of the work of the Holy Spirit is for the doleful effects of sin to be *increasingly mitigated*. (In particular, this restoration cures, repairs the damage to the *Sensus Divinitatis*; *it removes our blindness to the existence of God and thus enables us to see, once more, some of his glory and majestic beauty.*) As a Christian sees it, then, she is a person in whom the image of God has been partly restored, so that once more she resembles God with respect to the ability to form true beliefs and have knowledge.[124]

Plantinga says here that sin's effects are "increasingly mitigated." In *WCB*, asking if knowledge of the facts of evil provide a defeater for Christian belief, he argues for something similar—which, again, is relevant to PDH. Here Plantinga notes that

> none of us human beings enjoys that pristine condition of *complete rationality* [in our current postlapsarian condition]. The *sensus divinitatis* has been heavily damaged by sin. For many of us (much of the time, anyways) both God's existence and his goodness are a bit shadowy and evanescent, nowhere nearly

---

122. *WCB* 324; emphasis added.
123. In the Reformed tradition, see Muller, *Calvin and Reformed Tradition*.
124. Plantinga, "Respondeo," 337; emphasis on "restores" in original, other emphasis added.

as evident as the existence of other people or the trees in the backyard.[125]

Still, Plantinga explains that such reasoning, if pressed too far, would ignore a further and an important facet of Christian theology, namely, that

> the damage to the *sensus divinitatis* is in principle and *increasingly repaired* in the process of faith ... and regeneration. The person of faith may be once more such that, *at least on some occasions*, the presence of God *is* completely evident to her.[126]

Now, although he does not use such theological terminology, this language—"increasingly mitigated" and "increasingly repaired"—is consistent with the doctrine of *sanctification* (or at least a Protestant's construal thereof). On my application, the more one grows in Christ—that is, where one lives not according to the flesh but submits to the Holy Spirit (Rom 7:5–7)—the more the effects of sin are mitigated or repaired, in which case God's existence (or the great things of the gospel) can appear clearer over time; growth in holiness results in growth of the perceived clarity of God's existence. There are several ways this can go. Perhaps a Christian disassociates herself with *faulty* minienvironments, instead placing herself in *congenial* minienvironments, thus allowing the Holy Spirit to foster in her heart and mind the things of God. Such minienvironments may consist of beholding the starry heavens, reading the Bible, praying, going to church where Scripture is clearly exposited for corporate edification, singing the great hymns of the faith (John Newton's "Amazing Grace," for instance, where it reads, "I once was lost, but now am found, / Was blind, but now I see"[127]), partaking of the Lord's Supper (thus proclaiming Christ's death until he returns [1 Cor 11:26]), and so on.

Another way is to say that the mitigation of sin helps to *harmonize* intellect and will, which have been damaged by sin; the two faculties, at regeneration but perhaps also to a greater extent throughout one's life, become therefore more "appropriately attuned to each other."[128] "There is an intimate relation," explains Plantinga, "between revealing and sealing, knowledge and affection, intellect and will; they cooperate in a deep and complex and intimate way in the person of faith."[129] Knowing God more and more leads to intensified and amplified affections for God, which can in turn lead to

125. *WCB* 487; emphasis added.
126. *WCB* 487; emphasis added.
127. Newton, "Amazing Grace," st. 1.
128. *WCB* 303.
129. *WCB* 323.

intensified and amplified knowledge of God. The converse of this, I think, is also true: God's existence can seem hazy or foggy or unclear to us the more we *associate* ourselves with sin (in hostile minienvironments), gratifying the desires not of the Spirit but of the flesh (Gal 5:16–26).

Here is my second comment. According to Plantinga, warrant is a property that comes in *degrees*. "When my faculties are functioning properly," Plantinga writes, "a belief has warrant to the degree that I find myself inclined to accept it; and this ... will be the degree to which I *do* accept it."[130] Diller here elaborates:

> Depending on the suitability of environment and cognitive function oriented toward and functioning according to the designed connection between belief formation and truth—if everything is properly oriented and functioning—the full degree of warrant will, without attenuation or intensification, be reflected in and finally established by the proper proportionate strength of belief. If that degree of warrant is high enough, then the belief qualifies as knowledge.[131]

How does this relate more specifically to Christian belief(s)? Christian belief(s), writes Plantinga on the extended A/C model,

> will seem to the believer to be true: that is part of what it is for them to be *beliefs*. They will have the internal features of belief, of seeming to be true; and they can have this to *various degrees*.[132]

Now, I argued in my third chapter (in conjunction with the generic A/C model) that, in our prelapsarian condition, all persons have a high degree of theistic warrant accompanied by a firm strength of belief, and thus theistic *knowledge*, one implication being that God's existence in our prelapsarian world is clear and obvious, evident and plain. In chapter 4 it was suggested that sin can stifle and smother the degree of warrant (as well as our firmness of belief), thus making God's existence obscure and unobvious, hidden and blurred (in both chapters, we oscillated between quantitative and qualitative aspects of obviousness). My application here continues this train of thought. It acknowledges that Plantinga distinguishes between *typical* and *paradigmatic* believers:

> In *typical* cases, as opposed to *paradigmatic* cases, degree of belief will certainly be less than maximal. Furthermore, degree of belief,

---

130. A. Plantinga, *Warrant and Proper Function*, 9; see also WCB 156, 456–57.

131. Diller, *Theology's Epistemological Dilemma*, 118. For fuller discussion, see 115–18.

132. WCB 284; emphasis on "beliefs" in original, emphasis on "various degrees" added.

on the part of the person who has faith, typically varies from time to time, from circumstance to circumstance. So what can be said is that under certain circumstances what is believed by faith has enough warrant to constitute knowledge; these circumstances, I should guess, are probably not typical, although they are sometimes approached by some Christians part of the time.[133]

My argumentation in this chapter agrees with this (that degree of belief can vary relative to one's circumstances or environments), but adds that the more a Christian is sanctified—made holy, more like Christ—the more sin's effects are repaired or mitigated. The implication for PDH, in my defense, is that God's existence or the great things of gospel often becomes clearer (qualitatively) over time (although as the Westminster Confession of Faith states, it may be that our faith is often "different in degrees, weak or strong; may be often and many ways assailed, and weakened," given our imperfect sanctification in this life).[134] It moreover seems at *glorification*, the final step in the so-called *ordo salutis* (Rom 8:29–30), that one will know God, and will thus perceive the clarity of his existence, not in *part* but in *full* (1 Cor 13:12).[135] Faith will then be replaced by pure sight, the *visio Dei beatifica*. As Plantinga writes in the extended model, regeneration "heals the ravages of sin—embryonically *in this life*, and with ever greater fullness *in the next*."[136] In the new heavens and the new earth, the people of God "will see his face, and his name will be on their foreheads. And night will be no more. They will need no light or lamp or sun, for the Lord God will be their light, and they will reign forever and ever" (Rev 22:4–5).

5.3.4 The Extended Aquinas/Calvin Model Applied to PDH Conclusion

Let me now draw together some conclusions concerning my application of the extended A/C model to PDH. I think that the model's construal of warranted Christian belief can be used to answer my research question, serving also as the third and final part of my three-part defense for PDH; my defense aims to satisfy two desiderata.

How have these desiderata been satisfied? Take (i*); in chapter 3, the first part of my account, it was argued with the generic A/C model that God

---

133. *KCB* 67; emphasis added.
134. Art. 14.3 in Van Dixhoorn, *Creeds, Confessions, & Catechisms*, 206.
135. On this scriptural passage, see Peels, "Sin and Human Cognition."
136. *WCB* 280; emphasis added.

is not hidden from humanity, that we can have warranted belief in him. The second part of my account, which corresponds to the extended model's initial stages, demonstrated that we live in a fallen world, sin having both grave noetic and affective effects, thus undermining warrant as well as the clarity of God's existence. Here in this chapter I have argued with the full-blown extended A/C model that Christian belief, in its postlapsarian context, can have warrant, God having done something about sin through the life, death, and resurrection of Jesus Christ.

More particularly, what God has done includes the three-tiered process of Scripture, the internal instigation of the Holy Spirit, and faith. Placing one's faith in Christ for salvation not only puts one right with God but also restores and rejuvenates one's damaged noetic and affective equipment, thus renewing and rejuvenating one's *knowledge* of and love for one's Creator. One benefit of conversion, as I applied the extended model, is that it helps us to see (or at least helps us to begin to see) God with a much higher resolution. So, collectively these models qualify as a specifically Christian account; along the way, I have tried to show that much of the theology contained within the models comports well with Scripture and Christian tradition, both important items for a distinctly Christian defense. Sarah Coakley writes that, from a Christian perspective, PDH can transmute into a response to divine grace; I believe this to be true of the extended A/C model, particularly its claims about Jesus Christ, and that a proponent of the model can analyze the hiddenness problem by way of the great things of the gospel.

What about (ii)? How is this condition satisfied? Although he does not argue *for* their truth, Plantinga says that the A/C and extended A/C models are epistemically possible. De Ridder and Berger say that the extended model is

> epistemically possible, i.e., *consistent with what we know*. It thus offers Christians (and others) a way to conceive of the positive epistemic status of Christian beliefs. . . . Although [Plantinga] himself believes the model to be true, or at least close to the truth, he does not claim to *show* that it is true.[137]

Plantinga answers objections or defeaters to his hypothetical models in *WCB* part 4. Similarly, as mentioned above and discussed in previous chapters, I have not attempted to show or demonstrate that the models are true—even though I believe them to be true for all we know—but that they can be used

---

137. De Ridder and Berger, "Shipwrecked or Holding Water?," 44; emphasis added. Beilby further discusses this in *Epistemology as Theology*, 115, on which see my first chapter.

as a defense for PDH; one way to show that this description is true for all we know is to consider objections. The below objections are considered for my application of the extended A/C model.

5.4 OBJECTIONS CONSIDERED

Objection 1: Plantinga's argument for warranted Christian belief—and by extension my application of it to PDH—is circular. This objection is important, for if it is successful, then my application of Plantinga's models to PDH would be compromised. Now, Oliver Wiertz, in an essay entitled "Is Plantinga's A/C Model an Example of Ideologically Tainted Philosophy?," writes that ideologies "in the pejorative sense are closed systems in that the arguments they produce always presuppose what they are required to prove and thus are *circular*."[138] Wiertz asks if Plantinga's epistemology for warranted Christian belief is circular, distinguishing between covert circularity and epistemic circularity. The former occurs when "one of the premises of the argument [for *p*] assumes the truth of *p* without expressly stating it." The latter occurs

> when the reliability of a belief forming mechanism or doxastic practice is argued for in a way that presupposes the reliability of that very mechanism or practice, because it assumes or relies on beliefs whose positive epistemic status (in the sense of their probable production of true beliefs) depends upon the epistemic reliability of that belief forming mechanism.

Wiertz then defends Plantinga against either form of circularity, saying that "Plantinga does not argue from the (actual) truth of theism to its (actual) being warranted, but rather he argues that if theism is true, then theistic beliefs very likely have warrant."[139] Indeed, as Kevin Diller writes, "The source of warrant is not an argument given by Plantinga; *that would clearly be a circular argument*."[140] And, as I explained in earlier chapters, Plantinga is unconvinced that the truth of Christian theism can be shown or demonstrated,[141] but this claim does not stop him from showing how Christian theism can or may have warrant. Diller offers helpful comments on this point:

---

138. Wiertz, "Is Plantinga's A/C Model," 88; emphasis added.
139. Wiertz, "Is Plantinga's A/C Model," 88.
140. Diller, *Theology's Epistemological Dilemma*, 125; emphasis added.
141. WCB 170; see my chapter 3.

> The tactic Plantinga adopts . . . is to give a hypothetical account of how it could be that Christian belief might arise from cognitive processes operating in the right kind of environment according to a design plan successfully aimed at truth. The power of the hypothetical model Plantinga chooses is that, being itself a piece of Christian theology, it relies on the truth of Christian belief. What this secures for Plantinga is that if—independent of the argument—Christian belief is true, then it follows that Christian belief likely does have warrant either in the way described, or in some similar way. . . . *This is not a circular argument because the argument itself is not trying to provide the warrant for Christian belief.*[142]

My thesis statement is that Plantinga's hypothetical A/C models for how Christian belief may have warrant can be utilized as a defense to explain why, if God exists, his existence is not more obvious. Moreover, that the A/C models are *hypothetical* sits well with my defense, which, unlike a theodicy, is a *possible* account explaining why God's existence is not more obvious. Having exonerated Plantinga from the charge of circularity, I believe that this in turn removes any charge of circularity from my own project.

Objection 2: Knowledge does not require proper function. A main—if not *the* main—condition in the warrant criteria is that a belief, in order to count as knowledge, must be formed by properly functioning faculties. This objection states that proper function is not necessary for warrant or knowledge (an example is given below). If successful, then it could undermine my use of the model for the hiddenness problem; for instance, I have argued alongside the extended model that we have fallen into sin, which in turn has major cognitive and affective consequences for our knowledge of God and thus for perceiving the clarity of his existence. Regeneration or conversion, however, repairs (or at least begins to repair) the improper function of our equipment. But if proper function is *not* required for knowledge, then this could undercut my application of proper function to PDH.

I can hardly do justice to an objection of this enormity and complexity; not only has Plantinga written an entire volume dedicated to proper function, but there are also countless replies and objections to proper function from other epistemologists in general.[143] I will have to be selective; thus, I have chosen a counterexample to proper functionalism called the Swampman counterexample. This example originates from Donald Davidson, but it has been adapted by epistemologist Ernest Sosa so as to work

---

142. Diller, *Theology's Epistemological Dilemma*, 131.
143. See A. Plantinga, *Warrant and Proper Function*; see also several of the essays in Kvanvig, *Warrant in Contemporary Epistemology*, which criticize proper functionalism.

against proper functionalism. Kenny Boyce gives a succinct description of the Swampman example:

> In that scenario, Davidson is standing next to a swamp when lightning strikes a nearby dead tree, thereby obliterating Davidson. Simultaneously, by sheer accident, the lightning also causes the molecules of the tree to arrange themselves into a perfect duplicate of Davidson as he was at the time of his demise. The Davidson duplicate—this "Swampman"—leaves the swamp, acting and talking as if it were Davidson, having all the same intrinsic properties that Davidson would have had, had he left the swamp without having his unfortunate encounter. . . . Yet, not being the product of intentional design, and not having any evolutionary history, it would seem that Swampman has no design plan. And so we have what appears to be a counterexample to proper functionalism.[144]

As Sosa himself writes: "Indeed it even seems logically possible for the original Swampman to have warranted beliefs not long after creation if not right away."[145] Thus Swampman has knowledge, so the scenario goes, but lacks proper function, in which case proper functionalism is not required for knowledge. In what follows, I will briefly sketch a few replies, aiming to show that Swampman is not a successful counterexample to proper functionalism.

First, it is unclear that the Swampman example is in fact possible. For as Kenny Boyce and Alvin Plantinga write,

> It's not clear . . . that the Swampman scenario that Sosa envisions is (broadly) logically possible (is it possible for a person to be created just by accident in this way?). So it is at least not clear that we are offered a genuine counterexample to proper functionalism here.[146]

Second, *even if it were* possible that Swampman can come into being just by accident, then it may (to quote Boyce and Plantinga again) "also at least be conceivable that an entity acquires a *design plan* by accident."[147] The idea

---

144. Boyce, "Proper Functionalism," 1.c., para. 1.
145. See Sosa, "Proper Functionalism," 256. This quote is omitted from my quotation of Boyce above; Boyce is quoting from Sosa, "Proper Functionalism" (*Noûs*), 54, whereas I am quoting from the same article as it reappears in Kvanvig, *Warrant in Contemporary Epistemology*.
146. Boyce and Plantinga, "Proper Functionalism," 130.
147. Boyce and Plantinga, "Proper Functionalism," 130.

here is that, on Plantingean epistemology, proper functionalism entails a design plan, and thus Swampman *could* obtain one.

Third, it may be that Swampman's beliefs are not truth aimed but rather arise only accidentally. For example, Tyler McNabb argues that Swampman "lacks a particular way in which his faculties *should* function."[148] McNabb gives an illustration (which I have adapted for my purposes): suppose an alligator chases after Jimmy; if Jimmy's faculties are functioning properly, then he will form the belief *There's a gator chasing after me* and not the belief *There's a beautiful Swamplady chasing after me*. If the latter, then something has gone awry with Jimmy's cognitive equipment: "There is a malfunction in this situation," McNabb writes, "because this isn't the type of belief that the faculties should produce under these conditions."[149] Suppose, however, that Swampman forms the belief *There's a gator chasing me* and that it just so happens that there is, in fact, an alligator chasing after him. In this case, Swampman's beliefs happen to be, as McNabb writes, "a genuine case of cognitive luck." He elaborates:

> It just so happens that his cognitive system produces a belief in an alligator instead of a beautiful Swamplady friend or another sort of belief. It is not as if his faculties have been designed (whether it be by God, by evolution, or both) to produce this belief under the appropriate circumstances. Because there are no ways in which his cognitive system should produce any beliefs appropriately in this way, it would appear that any true belief that is produced would lack a tight connection to truth.[150]

Thus, Swampman's beliefs lack warrant.

Fourth, it seems to some, from this scenario, that Swampman's own cognitive faculties do in fact exhibit something *like* proper function. For instance, as Michael Bergmann argues, if Swampman is a molecule-by-molecule duplicate of Davidson, then presumably we could say that Swampman's heart and lungs are healthy, that they are functioning the way they are *supposed* to function:

> And if we can say that about his heart and lungs, we can say the same thing about his cognitive faculties. It's true that there is no literal designer or evolutionary origin. But because of the physical similarities (down to the DNA level), we are inclined to think of Swampman as being human. And that leads us to think

---

148. McNabb, "Warranted Religion," 478; emphasis added.
149. McNabb, "Warranted Religion," 480.
150. McNabb, "Warranted Religion," 480. See also McNabb and Baldwin, "Reformed Epistemology."

that Swampman is supposed to function in the way humans are supposed to function.[151]

Fifth, the Swampman counterexample relies on the false intuition that if an ordinary human forms her beliefs in the same way that Swampman forms his, then the beliefs of an ordinary human would in fact be warranted, which motivates us to infer that Swampman's beliefs are also warranted. Kenny Boyce and Andrew Moon call this the Central Intuition, which states that

> (CI) If a belief B is warranted for a subject S and another subject S* comes to hold B in the same way that S came to hold B in a relevantly similar environment to the one in which S came to hold B, then B is warranted for S*.[152]

But Boyce and Moon argue that CI is unclear:

> First, it mentions one creature coming to hold her belief "in the same way" that another creature does. But of course, whether we judge one creature to have come to hold her belief in the same way as another creature depends on how we individuate ways of belief formation. Second, CI refers to "relevantly similar environments" without specifying any criteria for relevant similarity.[153]

Sixth, and finally, it just seems to me, from a Christian theistic perspective, that something like proper functionalism makes the most sense with respect to knowledge (and affections). Christian Tapp writes that the *sensus divinitatis* "functions properly *only because of* divine grace and salvation (this constitutes the extended version of the A/C model)."[154] Thus, it just appears to me to be fundamentally right that proper functionalism comports well with biblical and theological themes like sin, grace, salvation, the instigation of the Holy Spirit, regeneration or conversion, believing the great things of the gospel, sanctification, and the like.[155] This response to the Swampman counterexample, as sketchy as it is, serves to defend my use of proper functionalism for PDH.[156]

---

151. Bergmann, *Justification without Awareness*, 148.
152. Boyce and Moon, "Defense of Proper Functionalism," 2988.
153. Boyce and Moon, "Defense of Proper Functionalism," 2990.
154. Tapp, "Reference to Infinite Being," 42; emphasis added.
155. But it is not my intention to say that Christian philosophers/theologians who do not hold to proper functionalism do not take these mentioned theological themes seriously.
156. For more on proper functionalism in general, see Moon, "Recent Work."

Objection 3: There are sincere seekers for God whose search is or has been unsuccessful. There are those who "seek long and hard for God, wishing to be related in love to God," explains J. L. Schellenberg, yet "though they *seek,*" he goes on, "they do not find."[157] Some "search for God with apparent sincerity," Friedrich Nietzsche writes, "but come away feeling unfulfilled and disillusioned."[158] How can this objection be analyzed in my defense against PDH? I try to show in what follows that my defense has the resources to address this objection.

Now, C. Stephen Evans, asking why some persons form belief in God and why others do not, writes that, from a Plantingean Reformed epistemological perspective, one could

> suggest that our natural tendency to believe in God has been "overlaid or suppressed by sin." The atheist may find this a cheap victory, since it smacks of *ad hominen.* Plantinga could at this point shrug and say that he is simply telling it like it is, and if the atheist does not agree, that is the atheist's problem. (I am not suggesting that this is in fact what Plantinga would do.) There are, however, some good reasons not to break off the conversation *so abruptly.*[159]

One reason not to break the conversation off so abruptly, Evans argues, is because

> some of the atheists who find this move [the appeal to sin in the context of sincere seekers] a little high-handed may not be hostile opponents, but *sincere seekers,* honestly looking for an account of the reasonableness of belief in God which they can accept.[160]

Evans then pursues a fuller Plantingean-Kierkegaardian explanation as to why some persons do, or do not, form theistic belief, a fuller account that may "provide the honest seeker with a *point of contact.*"[161] Similarly, Nicholas Wolterstorff argues that, due to sin's effects, some in the Reformed tradition object that "there is in fact no *point of contact,* no common ground,

---

157. Schellenberg, "Divine Hiddenness Justifies Atheism," 1:32–33; emphasis added.
158. Nietzsche, *Daybreak,* 89–90.
159. C. S. Evans, *Kierkegaard on Faith,* 178; emphasis added.
160. C. S. Evans, *Kierkegaard on Faith,* 178; emphasis added. Deane-Peter Baker interacts with Evans on Plantinga on the same point (Baker, *Tayloring Reformed Epistemology,* 98).
161. C. S. Evans, *Kierkegaard on Faith,* 178; emphasis added. See 169–205 for Evans's comparison of Plantinga and Kierkegaard.

between the believer and unbeliever,"[162] but I concur with both Wolterstorff and Evans that Christian theists should try to maximize common ground, when possible, between sincere seekers and themselves. I offer three ways with which my defense could provide the honest seeker with a point of contact.

Point of contact 1. First, it should be recognized, whenever possible, that the seeker's search for God, taken from his or her own personal testimony, is (or has been) sincere or authentic or genuine. Perhaps Paul's comments in his Areopagus speech, for instance, are applicable here that all persons "should *seek* God," and "feel their way toward him and find him" (Acts 17:27). Moreover, J. L. Schellenberg offers helpful starting criteria for the investigation of God:

> Has he shown himself to be honest, a lover of the truth? Does he resist his wants when his head tells him he ought not to give in to them? We may also have reason to believe that S desires to have a well-justified belief that G [God] or that not-G [not God]. If this is clearly so in some particular case, then (unless there is very strong evidence to the contrary) we may surely conclude that S is not self-deceived in arriving at a parity belief [i.e., theistic nonbelief].[163]

As Schellenberg goes on to say:

> Thus, if we have reason to believe that G, or that not-G, we have reason to believe not only that S is not self-deceived, but, more generally, that his investigation [for God] was a thorough one.[164]

My defense takes seriously Schellenberg's comments, particularly his claim that one's investigation or search for God is or has been a "thorough one." Next, philosopher Randal Rauser, himself a Christian, has recently argued (in a book endorsed by Schellenberg) that Christian theists can often be unfair toward atheists (and other nonbelievers) who claim to have sought but have not found God; Rauser suggests that Christians can, and should, take better care to love nonbelievers as their neighbors.[165] Further,

162. Wolterstorff, "Is Reason Enough?," 147; emphasis added.
163. *DHHR* 66.
164. *DHHR* 66.
165. Rauser, *Is the Atheist*. On the back cover, Schellenberg writes, "There are some whose way of following the first of the great commandments has, in the matter of nonbelief, meant violating the second. In this brief and lively but remarkably full and acute discussion, Rauser shows the way out of this problem. Impressively fair, and writing not perfunctorily but with feeling, he has found a way to express genuine neighborliness both to atheists like me and to Christians who struggle to reconcile love and loyalty."

as discussed in my previous chapter, with the help of epistemologist John Greco, believers (e.g., theists) can and likely do help to promote nonbelief (he argues his case from social epistemology). Greco is right that, for theists, it is useful "to turn our attention away from 'the speck in our brother's eye' and 'notice the log in our own.'"[166] Perhaps there are things that believers do—acting contrary, say, to the teachings of Jesus Christ—that undermine a seeker's search for God.

Point of contact 2. Second, I believe that a Christian perspective on the nature of sincere seekers should consider the nature of *consistency*. As William Wainwright explains, many nonbelievers *do* want to believe in God. Still, "appearances can be deceptive." For "the fact that many agnostics and atheists want to believe in God is *consistent* with their also *not* wanting to do so. For both can be true of the same person."[167] If the Plantingean-Reformed epistemological account of sin that I have expounded in chapter 4 is correct, then Christians, working as hard as they can to find common ground, even so have theological incentives for thinking that sin can render a seeker's sincere search for God ineffective, misleading, or incomplete. For example, William Wood notes that, from a Pascalian perspective, "the Fall has left us with a secret instinct that draws us *toward* God and truth, in addition to the secret instinct *that drives us away.*"[168] Nonetheless, Christians can offer the seeker the *remedy* from sin through faith in Jesus Christ, a gift (as Plantinga writes) "given to anyone who is willing to accept it."[169]

Point of contact 3. There are some strategies that the Christian could implement to assist the sincere seeker. "One good apologetic strategy," writes Kelly James Clark,

> is to encourage unbelievers to put themselves in situations where people are typically taken with belief in God: on a mountain, for example, or at the sea, where we see God's majesty and creative power. We are far more likely to encounter the Creator if we attend his creation.[170]

Placing oneself in a congenial epistemic environment can help foster belief; Jeremy Evans notes (in the context of PDH) that "God-seekers will place themselves in the best epistemic situation through which belief (or more

---

166. Greco, "No-Fault Atheism," 116.
167. Wainwright, "Jonathan Edwards and Hiddenness," 109; emphasis added.
168. Wood, *Blaise Pascal on Duplicity*, 210; emphasis added.
169. WCB 244.
170. Clark, "Reformed Epistemology Apologetics," 279.

appropriately, acceptance) can be cultivated."[171] In addition to Clark's comments, I think that seekers can be encouraged to read the *Bible*, which, as it has been argued above on the extended model, is perspicuous testimony from God, the very book inspired by the Holy Spirit that tells of the great things of the gospel; by reading Scripture, one can come to be saved.

Now, Dallas Willard writes:

> *God is not obvious*, not even in the Bible, which offers so many opportunities for man to go wrong—as history and contemporary events surely witness. This is an undeniable fact, which is absolutely consistent with the further idea that he can be found, and found in the Bible also. By seeking.... He reveals himself, and uniquely in the Bible, but in a way that allows him to be hidden to all but those who resolutely seek him ([Is] 30:20; Job 23:9–10).[172]

Willard's comments, though helpful, can be supplemented by saying, in step with the extended model, that the Holy Spirit is necessary for one to understand Scripture and thus to come to believe the great things of the gospel.[173] For, as C. Stephen Evans argues, it is possible, given the Bible's perspicuity, "to hold that the *honest seeker* who is guided by the Spirit of God can understand what he or she needs to understand in the Bible to be saved."[174] As Evans writes elsewhere of Scripture's perspicuity:

> The idea is not that everything in the Bible is clear but that the most important things are clear enough for the *honest seeker* to grasp; such a seeker must believe in Jesus as the one sent from God and try to follow Jesus. This claim about the clarity [or perspicuity] of Scripture is usually accompanied by a claim that the Spirit of the God who gave this revelation will also help guide the person who is seeking the truth.[175]

Someone could push back, claiming that to posit the guidance of the Holy Spirit in order for the sincere seeker to read Scripture and so be saved is ad hoc, a bit contrived. According to some, it just does not work this way.

---

171. J. Evans, *Problem of Evil*, 69.

172. Willard, "Bible, University, and God," 35; emphasis in original.

173. I say "in step with the extended model" because it seems that Plantinga also thinks that the Holy Spirit is needed to read the Bible: "Can't we discover for ourselves, *without any special divine aid or assistance*, that the Bible (the New Testament, say) is in fact 'from God' ... ?" (*WCB* 271; emphasis added).

174. C. S. Evans, "Tradition, Biblical Interpretation," 326; emphasis added. In this essay, Evans examines scriptural interpretation from the perspective of the *regula fidei* (the rule of faith) and from that of Plantinga's epistemology.

175. C. S. Evans, *Why Christian Faith*, 78; emphasis added.

For example, "while I do feel strongly inclined to form beliefs about God when I read theistic scriptures," explains Paul Draper on divine hiddenness,

> the beliefs are of the sort, "Surely *this* wasn't inspired by God"; so what Calvin calls the "secret testimony of the Spirit" is clearly a secret kept from me. In general, then, I simply do not have vivid experiences of the sort that directly cause people to believe in God. Seeing is believing, but if God is real then I suffer from religious blindness or at least blurred religious vision.[176]

A complete response to these challenging comments can hardly be offered, but I will provide a brief twofold reply in what follows, which I think comports well with the extended model (saying in the second part why appealing to the Holy Spirit is not ad hoc). First, for Christians who analyze PDH, Peter van Inwagen recommends

> serious and sustained reflection on the possible meaning of two texts: Luke 16:31 ("If they do not listen to Moses and the Prophets, neither will they be persuaded if someone should rise from the dead"), and John 20:29 ("Have you believed because you have seen me? Blessed are they who, in not seeing, believe.").[177]

Both passages are discussed in *WCB*.[178] Taking Van Inwagen's proposal, Luke 16:19–31 is a parable that depicts a conversation between Abraham and a rich man who suffers in Hades; the rich man argues that the resurrection of Lazarus, if given, would provide the necessary miraculous sign that would lead to the rich man's brothers' repentance. But Abraham argues that if they do not *now* listen to and heed Moses and the Prophets, then not even a dead man's resurrection would convince them. Where pertinent to my purposes, this story is about the *rejection* of Scripture. For "they will not convert," argues Luke Timothy Johnson of the rich man's brothers, "*on the basis of hearing the Scripture* (16:30). The final words of the parable seal their rejection: even if someone came back from the dead, they would not listen (16:31)."[179] This can apply to sincere seekers.[180] As Plantinga writes elsewhere of this passage from Luke:

176. Draper, "Seeking but Not Believing," 197; emphasis in original.

177. Van Inwagen, "What Is the Problem," 31–32.

178. For Luke 16:31, see *WCB* 270n52; for John 20:29, see *WCB* 254, 265.

179. Johnson, *Gospel of Luke*, 256; emphasis added. Johnson writes further, "The reader cannot miss the reference in 16:31 to the resurrection of Jesus, whom the leaders will reject yet another time when they refuse to hear the words of the apostles in the narrative of Acts" (256).

180. As Paul R. House writes of Luke 16:31: "One might also ask, 'What if God showed people more signs and wonders? What if he gave them more evidence of his

Without a change of heart even a great deal of evidence won't convince us human beings [of God's existence]. ("If they do not listen to Moses and the Prophets, they will not be convinced even if someone rises from the dead," Luke 16:31).[181]

Consider also John 20:29. This verse summarizes Jesus's interaction with Thomas, who refuses to believe in the risen Jesus unless he sees him. Thomas does eventually see Jesus; and seeing, he *believes*, after which Jesus asks about those who, unlike Thomas, believe without having witnessed firsthand Jesus's life and ministry. One commentator explains of this verse, "The reader [of John's Gospel] knows of 'those who did not see, and believed,' because the reader is, almost by definition, one of them. The beatitude is for the *reader's* benefit."[182] To say it differently, it is as if, to follow Richard Bauckham, the message of John's Gospel "mediates the testimony of those who have seen [Jesus] *to those who have not*."[183] It may be that a seeker refuses to accept the scriptural witness *now* (Luke 16:31), which *currently* mediates testimony of the risen Messiah (John 20:29).

Second, Michael Kruger, writing in the context of the canon of Scripture, asks why so many people reject the Bible. He argues that the *testimonium spiritus sancti internum* is needed not only to *recognize* the marks of divinity in Scripture but also to *receive* Scripture.

> The *testimonium* is not a private revelation of the Spirit or new information given to the believer—as if the list of canonical books were whispered in our ears—but it is a work of the Spirit that overcomes the noetic effects of sin and produces the belief that the Scriptures are the word of God. The reason some refuse to believe the Scriptures is not that there is any defect or lack of

---

existence and goodness? Would people still sin?' By Numbers 13–14, the people have seen amazing things. God has sent numerous startling plagues on Egypt. He has parted the Red Sea. He has fed and clothed them in a desert. One more miracle would hardly convince them. John's Gospel tells a similar tale. Some of the people who saw Jesus raise Lazarus from the dead believed in him (John 11:45), but not all who saw did. Some wanted Jesus stopped (vv. 46–53). . . . No wonder Jesus stated flatly that those who do not believe Moses and the prophets would not believe if one rose from the dead (Luke 16:31)" ("Sin in the Law," 62).

181. A. Plantinga, "Internalism, Externalism," 382n5.

182. Michaels, *Gospel of John*, 1019; emphasis added.

183. Bauckham, "Fourth Gospel as Testimony," 136; emphasis added. As D. A. Carson writes, "Blessed . . . are those who cannot share Thomas' experience of sight, but who, in part because they read of Thomas' experience, come to share Thomas' faith" (*Gospel According to John*, 660).

> evidence in the Scriptures . . . but that those without the Spirit do not accept the things from God (1 Cor 2:10–14).[184]

Or, to put it more simply, the internal witness of the Holy Spirit is (as Richard Muller says) "the inward work of the Spirit that testifies to faith concerning the *truth* of Scripture."[185]

Thus, I do not see it as ad hoc to argue that the Holy Spirit is needed to understand and to apply and to receive Scripture, even for sincere seekers. For Scripture is (as Kruger explains)

> received by those who have the Holy Spirit in them. When people's eyes are opened [from the noetic effects of sin], they are struck by the divine qualities of Scripture—its beauty, harmony, efficacy—and recognize and embrace Scripture for what it is, the word of God. They realize that the voice of Scripture is the voice of the Shepherd.[186]

Kevin Diller appears to support my point:

> Because of the darkening of our minds and cognitive environments that results from our alienation from God, we cannot, without divine assistance and repair, adequately grasp what God is saying through scripture. Our interpretive grids distort the message, our corrupt wills impose our own desires, and our fallen imaginations fail to reach the heights to which they are called.[187]

While affirming the necessity of the Spirit's internal witness, it does not seem inconsistent also to affirm, as Paul Moser says, that "humans will apprehend the Spirit's reality only if they are willing, in the words of Jesus, to have 'eyes to see and ears to hear' what God intends for humans."[188]

In addition to Scripture, a *second strategy* is to encourage seekers to attend church, to be a part of an ecclesial community, for as I have argued, the church can comprise a favorable environment.[189] Now, the extended

---

184. Kruger, *Canon Revisited*, 99–100; much of Kruger's argumentation on the inner witness of the Holy Spirit is helped by Plantinga's argumentation in *WCB*. See also Kruger, *Question of Canon*.

185. Muller, *Dictionary*, 297; emphasis added. See also Jones, "Spirit's Witness"; Sawyer, "Witness of the Spirit."

186. Kruger, *Canon Revisited*, 101.

187. Diller, *Theology's Epistemological Dilemma*, 290.

188. Moser, "Inner Witness of Spirit," page number unavailable. See also Geivett and Moser, *Testimony of the Spirit*.

189. I have heard, but cannot confirm, that someone once asked Plantinga in a

A/C model is often criticized for being overly *individualistic*, a charge that Plantinga seems to anticipate in *WCB* but does not flesh out.[190] For instance, James Anderson says:

> Among other concerns, Roman Catholic and Eastern Orthodox qualms about the private interpretation of Scripture do not sit comfortably with Plantinga's model of warranted beliefs formed in the basic way on reading the biblical text alone, *independent of any ecclesiastical teaching*.[191]

Beilby appears to echo this concern, saying that an "immediate red flag for many theologians regarding Plantinga's epistemology is the fact that he seemingly completely ignores the role of the religious community in his description of the formation of faith."[192] Beilby elsewhere asks that, aside from the SD and the work of the Holy Spirit, "what of importance is left for the Christian *community* to do?"[193] Moreover, "it is on this point," Kruger argues, "that Plantinga's contribution to the [epistemology of the] internal testimony of the Spirit could be improved."[194]

One way to improve it is to say that God has established a church here on earth (Matt 16:18), a pillar and buttress of truth (cf. 1 Tim 3:15), the body of Christ (Col 1:24), to be his witness to all the nations (cf. Matt 28:19; Acts 1:8), and *even to seekers*. The *visible* church proclaims the *invisible* God. And, although the Holy Spirit is needed to receive and to apply the great things of the gospel found in Scripture, such reception and application ought to be done in the context of the one, holy, catholic, and apostolic church.[195] For instance, "liturgical practices," explains Helen De Cruz,

> scripture reading, and religious art *situate* believers, including those who do not enjoy direct religious experiences, within a

---

post-lecture question and answer session how he could help his seeking, nonbelieving friend become a Christian; Plantinga answered, "Have you tried bringing your friend to *church*?"

190. *WCB* 244n8; see also *KCB* 54n13.
191. J. Anderson, *Paradox in Christian Theology*, 198; emphasis added.
192. Beilby, *Epistemology as Theology*, 184–85.
193. Beilby, "Plantinga's Model," 141; emphasis added.
194. Kruger, *Canon Revisited*, 103n48. Diller provides a summary of, and a defense against, this complaint leveraged at the extended model, appearing to say that there is room for theological development within the extended model (*Theology's Epistemological Dilemma*, 154–58).
195. As I interpret him, Cornelius van der Kooi, while not downplaying the importance of the Spirit's witness in the believer's life, argues that Reformed theology can come to a greater appreciation of the importance of the historic church (Van der Kooi, "Appeal to Inner Testimony").

rich, sensory, and affective environment in which they can acquire religious beliefs they would not easily acquire under other circumstances.[196]

Douglas Henry, in the context of PDH, writes:

> What has proven fruitful for developing a relationship with God is an interested and ongoing participation in the kerygmatic and didactic life of the Church. Knowing God comes through experiencing God, but in general, Christian experiences of God are mediated *through the Church* and the collective life of the people of God.[197]

The church is where the gospel is proclaimed, where Scripture is taught, and where the Holy Spirit is active; Plantinga explains that it is the church that announces "the gospel" as well as "supports, instructs, encourages, and edifies believers of all sorts and conditions."[198] Writing again of the Bible's perspicuity and sincere seekers, C. Stephen Evans argues:

> If God is going to give humans knowledge about himself through a revelation, it makes sense that he would also create a community to pass along that revelation and to help people understand it. *That community is, of course, the church.* The witness of the Spirit is normally exercised in and through the church. . . . So the answer to the question as to how the Bible should be interpreted is this: it should be interpreted as the *church* has generally understood it.[199]

This applies to sincere seekers. For as Diller writes, "If this is true, then *the church* is used by God in the restoration of proper function and in the creation of suitable environments for growth in faith."[200] In sum, I believe that I have shown that the extended model has the resources to address the objection from sincere seekers.

Objection 4: Many Christian believers most often do not find God's existence clear or obvious. This objection is especially forceful since Plantinga (as discussed above) usually describes a paradigmatic or idealistic—and not a typical or every day—conception of Christian faith. In order to reply to this objection, I follow a criticism of Plantinga offered by Beilby. Beilby writes

---

196. De Cruz, "Divine Hiddenness," 66; emphasis added. See also Rea, "Narrative, Liturgy, and Hiddenness."
197. Henry, "Does Reasonable Nonbelief Exist?," 85; emphasis added.
198. *KCB* 54n13.
199. C. S. Evans, *Why Christian Faith*, 78–79; emphasis added.
200. Diller, *Theology's Epistemological Dilemma*, 157; emphasis added.

that many Christians hold their beliefs about God with varying degrees of firmness, calling this the "variability of belief" problem (VB hereafter); VB is especially accentuated, says Beilby, since Plantinga follows Calvin in defining faith as a "*firm* and *certain* knowledge."[201] A few possible explanations for VB are offered by Beilby, one of which says that VB can be explained by arguing that sin's noetic effects still, in some sense, *remain* on the Christian believer:

> The reason believers experience doubt and sometime[s] question their beliefs is because the effects of sin on the mind are not wholly cured by the regenerating effects of the internal instigation of the Holy Spirit.[202]

Then, in a section called "The Noetic Effects of Sin and Plantinga's Environmental Condition," Beilby argues that VB *undermines* the environmental condition for warrant:

> And if Plantinga's environmental condition is not met, then we have reason to believe that the beliefs formed as described by the Extended A/C Model, even if they are true and even if they are held with a high degree of confidence, will not be warranted.[203]

Beilby then writes:

> A little "reading between the lines" leads one to believe that Plantinga would respond to this objection in the following way: If God designed the Extended A/C model for a world in which sin exists, [then] of course the design plan would be a good one—it would "fit" the situation for which it was designed, and therefore the environment would be favorable. . . . But suppose Plantinga is right: the design plan for the cognitive maxi-environment is congenial to the formation of warranted beliefs about God. Even so, there is no guarantee that the cognitive *mini-environment* in which many believers find themselves will be similarly congenial. The state of affairs described by VB is perhaps the strongest piece of evidence for the hostility of the epistemic mini-environment.[204]

I do believe that Beilby's criticism here is helpful and (in general) on target; he writes, however, that the model can be "augmented" to account for

---

201. *WCB* 256; emphasis added.
202. Beilby, *Epistemology as Theology*, 206.
203. Beilby, *Epistemology as Theology*, 208.
204. Beilby, *Epistemology as Theology*, 208.

VB: "If one allowed for a robust role for human freedom in the formation of beliefs about God," Beilby stipulates, then "such diversity is explainable."[205] That seems to me to be right; the model (so I think) can be augmented to account for human freedom. So, with respect to Beilby's complaint about the minienvironmental condition: perhaps it is the case that we humans *do* have significant control over our minienvironment(s), and this goes hand in hand with the application I made earlier about *sanctification*. For in sanctification, we are to *cooperate* with God to grow in holiness, to be made more and more like Christ; a benefit of one's progressive or increased sanctification is that God's existence or the great things of the gospel can appear clearer and more obvious (qualitatively speaking) over time. One way to cooperate with God in sanctification is for a believer to freely place herself in congenial minienvironments: by attending to God in creation or reading Scripture or praying or singing the great hymns of the faith in church. The converse of this also seems true: a believer has the freedom to put herself in hostile minienvironments, wherein the clarity of God's existence or the great things of the gospel are unclear and hazy.

Finally, as mentioned just above, Beilby criticizes Plantinga for giving an ideal or paradigmatic conception of Christian faith, and I believe there to be at least some merit in this criticism; still, as Diller asks:

> Does this [i.e., that Plantinga often gives an idealistic or paradigmatic conception of faith] undermine the model as an account of how typical Christian belief can have warrant? The fact is that for many Christians faith fluctuates and with it so does the degree of warrant for Christian belief, *exactly as Plantinga's model describes*.[206]

Thus, I believe that this comports well with my above application that sin's effects throughout one's Christian life can be (as Plantinga says) "increasingly mitigated" or "increasingly repaired."

Objection 5: Christians do not think in terms of hypothetical models. My thesis statement says that Plantinga's conditional or hypothetical A/C models can be used as a defense against PDH (see above). But here it is argued that ordinary Christians do not, in fact, think in terms of hypothetical models. Beilby captures this objection when he writes that

---

205. Beilby, *Epistemology as Theology*, 209.

206. Diller, *Theology's Epistemological Dilemma*, 150n94; emphasis added. Diller also argues that "until a human knower is completely renewed [from sin], there will be varying interference in the deliverances of faith that will reduce warrant and weaken belief" (150). Kelly James Clark also discusses Plantinga's construal of idealistic or paradigmatic faith ("Pluralism and Proper Function," esp. 176–81).

Most Christians do not think in the hypothetical terms in which the Extended A/C Model is couched; they are not interested in "a way" in which "a hypothetical Christian *might be* warranted in their beliefs about God." They want to know whether or not *they* are in fact rational, justified, or warranted in their beliefs.[207]

As Beilby argues elsewhere, Plantinga does not give "typical believers some reason to believe that the model applies *to them*."[208] The Dutch atheist Herman Philipse raises a comparable concern, writing that

> because of its *conditional nature*, Plantinga's positive tactic to the effect that Christian beliefs may be properly basic *if* God exists, turned out to work only for Christians who do not doubt at all whether God exists or, indeed, whether any Christian belief is true.[209]

Christians who do not doubt God or Christianity are what Philipse calls "unwavering and dogmatic believers." But Christians, he notes,

> who have such doubts, or those who want to proselytise and persuade non-believers that the Christian creed is true, will need the arguments of natural theology. Furthermore, unbelievers will not be impressed by Plantinga's positive tactic [in *WCB* concerning warrant]. Even if they admit that the Christian creed *might* be warranted as properly basic in Plantinga's sense *if* the creed were true, they will hold that very probably it is not true, and hence that probably humans neither have a *sensus divinitatis* nor are subject to an internal instigation of the Holy Spirit, so that the creed will not be warranted as properly basic.[210]

This objection, if successful, could undercut my defense against PDH. For perhaps someone could say that my defense, which makes use only of hypothetical or conditional models, does not take seriously (or seriously enough) the hiddenness problem.

---

207. Beilby, *Epistemology as Theology*, 135; emphasis in original. Richard Swinburne seems to raise a similar objection: "There is . . . a monumental issue which Plantinga does not discuss, and which a lot of people will consider needs discussing. This is whether Christian beliefs do have warrant (in Plantinga's sense). He has shown that they do, if they are true; *so we might hope for discussion of whether they are true*" ("Plantinga on Warrant," 208; emphasis added).

208. Beilby, "Plantinga's Model," 147; emphasis added.

209. Philipse, *God in Age of Science*, 43; emphasis on "if" in original, emphasis on "conditional nature" added.

210. Philipse, *God in Age of Science*, 43; emphasis on "if" in original, emphasis on "might" added.

Now, my response, which is helped by Jeroen de Ridder and Mathanja Berger, will focus more specifically on Philipse's concerns, but can also be applied to Beilby's (raised above). So, De Ridder and Berger, defending Plantinga against Philipse, explain that it is Plantinga's intention to provide Christian theists with a way in which their Christian belief can or may have warrant, if in fact God exists or if Christianity is true, "thereby refuting the frequently voiced complaint that theistic belief is intellectually unacceptable regardless of whether it is true." (See chapter 3 for my exposition of the de facto/de jure distinction.) De Ridder and Berger go on:

> Perhaps Philipse deems the truth of theistic belief a more important issue; perhaps he wishes that Plantinga would have done more to argue for it. That's fine; *but this does not even so much as slyly* [slightly?] *suggest that there is a problem with the A/C model.*[211]

This is what I also think, that while it is permissible to wish that Plantinga do more to argue for his model's truth, this reasoning should not be used to argue that there is a *problem* with the model from an epistemic perspective. Moreover, as De Ridder and Berger go on to explain (contra Philipse):

> Various claims in the periphery of the model contain suggestions—all of them rooted firmly in the Christian tradition—for how the *sensus divinitatis* might be triggered and how the Holy Spirit might reveal the "great truths of the gospel" to our minds. Surely, this is of use to wavering and unwavering Christians alike, as well as to agnostics and atheists.[212]

To use De Ridder and Berger's response to Philipse for my purposes: I have chosen to utilize Plantinga's hypothetical or conditional models for warranted Christian belief as a defense, and not a theodicy, for PDH. Someone could argue that my argumentation is substandard or weak because I have not given an actual theodical Christian account for PDH. But the models, even though hypothetical, still provide Christians and others with a useful way—a defense—to analyze this important problem, drawing on resources (as De Ridder and Berger put it) that are rooted firmly in the Christian tradition.

---

211. De Ridder and Berger, "Shipwrecked or Holding Water?," 46; emphasis added.
212. De Ridder and Berger, "Shipwrecked or Holding Water?," 47.

5.5 CONCLUSION

Let us take stock. First, I explained Alvin Plantinga's extended A/C model (also describing what he calls the testimonial model) for how Christian belief in its postlapsarian context can have warrant. Second, I applied the extended model to the problem of divine hiddenness; several applications were made. Finally, I considered five objections to my use of the model. This completes my three-part defense, which has aimed to answer my research question on divine hiddenness from a distinctively Christian perspective. Along the way, I have tried to show how my defense satisfies what I call the defense desiderata. In the next and final chapter, I make concluding remarks.

6.

A Reformed-Epistemological Defense
Products, Problems, and Prospects

6.1 INTRODUCTION

CHAPTER 1 INTRODUCED THE problem of divine hiddenness (PDH). Chapter 2 reviewed contemporary PDH literature, showing how my work fits within and is relevant to current analysis on the problem. Chapters 3–5 used Alvin Plantinga's A/C models (the bare and extended models) whereby each specific chapter, drawing from the models, corresponded to one part of my three-part defense against PDH (more on this below). Call my Reformed epistemic defense against PDH the "Reformed epistemic defense," or RED for short. This sixth and final chapter ties up some loose ends, particularly by attempting to accomplish four things: first, to explain contributions and advantages RED has made regarding PDH in comparison with the existing body of literature; second, to respond to a few final potential concerns or worries about RED; third, to consider future work concerning PDH in light of RED; and fourth, to consider future work on other related issues in philosophy of religion in light of RED. Finally, concluding remarks will be given.

6.2 THIS STUDY'S ADVANTAGES OR CONTRIBUTIONS

In this section, several advantages or contributions will be listed. First, RED accomplished what it set out to do. The research question that asked *Why, if God exists, is his existence not more obvious?* has been answered, and the twofold defense desiderata have been satisfied. Both were considered in each part of my three-part defense as fleshed out in chapters 3–5. The first part alongside Plantinga's A/C model argued—perhaps somewhat surprisingly—that God's existence is not hidden and that humanity can have warranted theistic belief: *knowledge* of God. Part 2 was quick to emphasize, however, that we find ourselves in a fallen world, where sin touches everything, and that sin can undermine the clarity of God's existence as well as our knowledge of him. Part 3, using Plantinga's extended A/C model, explained how God through the "great things of the gospel" restores, or at least begins to restore, the effects of sin so that we can know and perceive God.

Second, as stated in chapter 1, there has been no explicit work on PDH from the perspective of Reformed epistemology, but this gap has now been filled by RED; this is significant given that the literature on PDH, according to J. L. Schellenberg, has seen the publication of more than sixty books or articles since 2010.[1] Andrew Moon has recently argued that Reformed epistemology, particularly *Plantingean* Reformed epistemology, is very much a viable and flourishing field.[2] It is to RED's advantage that it constructively connects two important areas of research that are largely unconnected.

Third, it was argued in chapter 1 that the vast majority of scholars who analyze PDH do so from an almost purely *philosophical* perspective. While not compromising philosophical rigor, RED did show how theology—drawing especially from the theology contained in Plantinga's models—can "speak into" a contemporary problem. This theology included themes such as our natural knowledge of God, sin's noetic effects, and the way in which (most importantly) God in Christ saves us from sin; with respect to the latter point, it is my expectation that RED is not *merely* a defense but, as a piece of constructive Christian thinking, that it ultimately is Christocentric, pointing to Christ. Many in the Reformed or (more specifically) the Calvinistic tradition are typically quick to point to *sin* to explain why God's existence is not more obvious, and rightly so. This seems to be what Schellenberg has in mind when he describes "the Calvinian response" to nonbelief, which "is apparently shared by Alvin Plantinga."[3] But Christians (Reformed or not) ought to be just as quick to point to God's grace in Jesus Christ that saves us from our sin, and how this in turn affects our thinking about PDH (a potential worry about this will be addressed below).

Fourth, it may appear to some that, in my defense against PDH, the "Reformed" in Reformed epistemology is fairly palpable, given that I have utilized various doctrines and themes that are commonplace among

---

1. Schellenberg, "Divine Hiddenness: Part 1," abstract.
2. Moon, "Recent Work."
3. *DHHR* 74; cf. 74–82.

Reformed Protestants:[4] the *sensus divinitatis*, sin's noetic effects, the perspicuity of Scripture, the internal witness of the Holy Spirit, and so on.[5] Still, RED has sought to be as ecumenical as possible, hopefully also providing Christians from other traditions with a way to analyze PDH from a Christian perspective (more on this below, in the section on future work).[6]

6.3 POTENTIAL CONCERNS OR WORRIES FOR THIS STUDY

In this section, I briefly discuss remaining potential concerns or worries that readers, believers or otherwise, may have about RED. First, it may be that some *believers* worry that RED does not start with the proper assumptions. I could imagine this concern coming from a Christian in the presuppositional apologetic tradition, perhaps from someone like K. Scott Oliphint, who has written of Plantinga with admiration but not without criticism.[7] Stated roughly, presuppositionalism, from an apologetic standpoint, assumes or presupposes the truth of Christianity as a basis for defending it.[8] Someone in this tradition could criticize Plantinga for attempting to show how Christian belief can satisfy the warrant conditions—that is, proper function, conducive environment, truth aimedness—which are technically *religiously neutral*, and which do not come, say, from Scripture itself (in this sense, Christian belief can have warrant *in much the same way* as knowing everyday mundane things, such as knowing there to be a tree in Vondelpark in Amsterdam). Someone could extend this criticism against RED, arguing that Christian discussions of PDH should *start* from Scripture, and not from religiously neutral criteria for knowledge.

---

4. Plantinga seems to lament the title "Reformed epistemology," saying that, despite its Reformed *theological* heritage, "the name is not meant to suggest that Roman Catholic theology or epistemology stands in need of Reformation" ("Reformed Epistemology" [1997], 383).

5. Recently, Gijsbert van den Brink and Johan Smits have argued that Reformed theology is not characterized by one or more unique doctrines of its own that are not shared by other Christian traditions, but by a particular set of concerns and emphases (or a particular "stance") within the wider catholic tradition (Van den Brink and Smits, "Reformed Stance").

6. Interestingly, Dewey J. Hoitenga Jr. argues that seeds of Plantinga's epistemology can be found in Plato, Augustine, Calvin (and others), saying that it "may be called Platonic—Augustinian—Reformed" (*Faith and Reason*, back cover).

7. Oliphint, "Review Essay"; "Plantinga on Warrant." Although as James Anderson has pointed out, one of presuppositionalism's most esteemed thinkers, Cornelius van Til, has quite a bit in common with Plantinga (J. Anderson, "If Knowledge Then God").

8. See, for instance, Frame, "Presuppositional Apologetics."

While I cannot give a full-scale rebuttal here, I do appreciate this worry, and in turn argue that Christians should always consider their epistemological assumptions or presuppositions, the place of Scripture in their studies, and so forth. But this complaint does not show that there is anything wrong with Plantinga's warrant criteria per se, or that there is anything wrong with the models themselves, or that Plantinga has said anything that contradicts Scripture. The objector would need to take up such a task. Perhaps it is also the case that Scripture does not advocate one type of apologetic methodology over another (assuming that it is even right to conceive of Reformed epistemology as an apologetic methodology or an apologetic "school").[9] Kelly James Clark writes that "there is simply not enough unambiguous evidence from Scripture to support [one apologetic methodology over another] as *the biblical view*."[10] Acts 17, for instance, appears to advocate at least two different approaches to defending Christianity. Acts 17:1–9 records Paul and Silas reasoning about the Christian faith to the Thessalonians, whereby they begin their reasoning "*from* the Scriptures" (17:2), proving *from* the Old Testament that Jesus is the Christ (cf. also 17:10–15); whereas Acts 17:22–33 records Paul at the Areopagus, in the context of a new audience, not starting *from* Scripture but reasoning *to* Scripture, or *to* scriptural truths about Christ. RED could be characterized more along the lines of the latter, which does not make it any less legitimate. Oliver Crisp says that theology

> should not be novel—or, at least, it should not be novel for the sake of novelty. To my mind . . . theology should be faithful to Scripture and take seriously the chorus of voices that constitute the Christian tradition.[11]

I think that this is true of Plantinga's Reformed epistemology in general and—as repeatedly emphasized in the previous chapters—to my application of it to PDH in particular.[12]

Second, it may be a concern for some, believers or not, that a defense against PDH is not enough, that it is subpar, too meager; is a defense really the best we can do? Recall in chapter 1 the distinction between a defense and a theodicy; both are accounts concerning some problem against theism, one of which is *possible* (a defense) and the other of which is taken to

---

9. Michael Sudduth argues that Reformed epistemology is an epistemology of religious belief, and is "not a distinct school of apologetics" ("Reformed Epistemology," 317).

10. Clark, "Reformed Epistemology Apologetics," 274; emphasis in original.

11. O. Crisp, *Divinity and Humanity*, xiii.

12. I have been helped on this point by Kees van Kralingen's unpublished paper, "Theological Responses to Alvin Plantinga's Aquinas/Calvin Model of Warranted Christian Belief."

be *actual* (a theodicy). RED is a defense, an account that is possible, which seeks to answer the research question.

Now, in response, it seems that this worry may ultimately come down to *one's own intuitions* about what can be shown or demonstrated. Plantinga is unconvinced, for instance, that the truth of Christian theism can be demonstrated or proven, although such thinking does not preclude him from attempting to give a description, by way of hypothetical models, for how Christian belief can or may have positive epistemic status: justification, rationality, and warrant. RED shares Plantinga's thinking, which is why it opts for a defense, and not a theodicy; the fact that Plantinga's models are hypothetical squares well with the fact that a defense is a possible account or explanation regarding PDH.[13] But it needs to be pointed out that giving a defense, even if not a theodicy, is still no small feat; one can be reminded of the enormous impact that Plantinga's free will *defense* against the problem of evil has had.[14] Moreover, RED has sought to satisfy two desiderata, which state that (i*) a specifically Christian account for why God is not more obvious should be given that is (ii) true for all we know (where "true for all we know" in the latter desideratum means something stronger than mere logical possibility but rather *epistemic* possibility). And in each chapter many objections stemming from many different angles and perspectives to my application of Plantinga's models were considered. All in all, given that academic progress is usually achieved incrementally rather than by great leaps, RED contributes in this way by extending our grasp of a problem.

Third, one facet of RED has been to argue that Christian theism in general and Plantinga's Reformed epistemology in particular *have the resources* to address PDH; but some may be concerned that "having the resources" to examine a problem could be anyone's game, including the atheist's or agnostic's, in which case the atheist or the agnostic could tell a much different story about PDH.

In response, it is true that atheists and agnostics can examine PDH, perhaps by giving an argument that states that, in light of "God's hiddenness," there just is no God or that his existence is unlikely; no doubt some of the best thinking on the problem comes from Schellenberg, himself a nonbeliever. But it also needs to be said, as it has been said in previous chapters (especially chapter 1), that Christians have a perfect right to analyze and to examine problems or questions from their own perspectives

---

13. Chapter 1 also explained in more detail reasons for giving a defense, and not a theodicy.

14. See A. Plantinga, *God, Freedom, and Evil*. Even if unconvinced of Plantinga's free will defense (FWD) surely one can acknowledge its impact as evidenced by the sheer amount of studies analyzing FWD.

or assumptions (the presuppositionalist would surely agree here). For as Plantinga argues concerning the problem of evil, there comes a point when Christians should, from a Christian perspective, *seek to understand* the evil that exists in this world.[15] There is of course a time and a place to consider arguments (with specific premises) from evil against God's existence from nonbelievers, but Christians do not *always* have to be on the defensive, apologetically speaking, attempting to counter arguments from nonbelievers. The same reasoning can be applied to PDH; there are Christians and other theists who attempt to rebut hiddenness arguments, with specific premises, against God's existence (as chapter 2 explains), but that has not been the primary burden of my project. Instead, I have tried to show how PDH could be understood and elucidated from a Christian perspective. Still, the atheist may want to see how RED may respond to the claim that divine hiddenness at least provides some evidence for atheism. Below, in the section devoted to future work in philosophy of religion, I show how the advocate of RED could reject a vital premise in an argument from divine hiddenness, as given by Schellenberg, the conclusion of which states that God does not exist.

Fourth, some *philosophers*, believers or not, may be concerned that my defense against PDH sounds or looks or feels too *theological*, especially since as a field of study PDH is normally examined by analytic philosophers. Though complete justice to his argument cannot be given here, I suspect that Schellenberg might raise such a worry, particularly in light of a recent (and excellent) paper of his entitled "Is Plantinga-Style Christian Philosophy Really Philosophy?" He argues there that Plantingean Reformed epistemology, what he calls Reformed Christian philosophy (RCP), is not in fact philosophy; rather, it is actually *theology*, and that "we should learn to call RCP *theology*, full stop."[16]

In response, it may be countered that this is a nonstarter since what matters is whether or not the developed defense is successful. Moreover, it is not always clear to me, at least from a Christian perspective, where one discipline ends and the other begins; as I see it, the line between philosophy and theology (if there is in fact a line) is hazy. If some worry that RED is too theological, then that is a worry that can be tolerated. Of course, one can just as easily imagine a theologian worrying that RED is too *philosophical*. But that, too, is tolerable. It was said in chapter 1 that my defense against

15. A. Plantinga, "Supralapsarianism," 4–5.
16. Schellenberg, "Plantinga-Style Christian Philosophy," 17–18. Schellenberg argues that Plantinga-style Christian philosophy does not meet what he calls the Communal Condition: "The Communal Condition: to be doing philosophy one must aim not just to solve certain fundamental problems, or contribute thereto, but to do so together with likeminded others in a shared enterprise leading to informed consensus" (5).

PDH seeks to be a distinctively *Christian* one, and of course I would be worried if either the philosopher or the theologian argued that RED came up short on that point.[17]

Now, suppose one pushes back on this point, arguing that, while the theological rigor of RED is admirable, the amount of theological components or assumptions built into RED make it more difficult to accept than, say, a philosophical defense against PDH that is theologically "thinner." Does RED, in other words, have excess (theological) "fat"? One way to respond is to argue that the detractor should try to spell out which parts she thinks are fatty and which parts are not. Another way to respond is to look back at the desiderata that this defense attempted to satisfy, the first desideratum stating that a distinctively Christian defense against PDH would be offered. Thus RED, in virtue of it being decidedly Christian, will necessarily have at least a few theological components to it (minimally, for example, it must talk about *Christ*), but so, too, will any other Christian defense; as discussed below (in the future work section) some Christians from other traditions may want to offer a Christian defense against PDH using the resources in their own tradition. Yet another way to respond is to say that if one is not concerned to give a specifically Christian theistic defense but rather just a *broadly theistic* one, then they could modify the desideratum to reflect such a stance.

6.4 FUTURE WORK ON THE PROBLEM OF DIVINE HIDDENNESS

This section briefly points to future research that could be conducted concerning PDH, which could come in light of RED. First, Plantinga's models, although rightly philosophical, contain many theological or doctrinal themes that have been used and applied to a problem that is hosted primarily by analytic philosophers of religion; perhaps there are *other* doctrines or theological loci that can be employed so as to investigate PDH. For instance, in chapter 5, I argued from Plantinga's extended model that various *hostile* environments in which we find ourselves—societal, peer, familial, etc.—can undermine the clarity of God's existence, but that, conversely, God's existence can be clear to us in certain *congenial* environments. One such congenial environment, drawn from the model, includes the reading or hearing (or preaching) of *Scripture*, and Scripture, as argued, is perspicuous and is accommodated to our finite capacities. Still, Plantinga says that it is the Holy Spirit who ultimately helps us to see what God is saying or teaching in

---

17. In chapter 4 (in the objections section) another form of the theology/philosophy worry is discussed.

Scripture, a theme that I applied (but only briefly) to PDH. Perhaps others could offer a more developed or nuanced account of Scripture, pneumatology, and how these relate to PDH.[18]

Second, RED may have important *methodological* ramifications. For example, there is a growing current tradition entitled analytic theology that intentionally fosters dialogue between analytic philosophers on the one hand and theologians (as well as biblical scholars) on the other. My defense against PDH may be characterized as analytic theology, and although there has been examination of PDH from the perspective of analytic theology,[19] there are those who specifically want to explore the relationship between analytic theology and traditional *systematic* theology.[20] Perhaps by taking this cue, more work from a systematic-theological perspective could be pursued on PDH. Similarly, there may be biblical scholars who, via analytic theology (or otherwise), could examine PDH with special reference to biblical passages in the Old Testament—Ps 10 or 13, for instance—that touch on the perceived absence of God (as chapter 2 discussed briefly).[21]

Third, RED as mentioned analyzes PDH by way of various doctrines from Plantinga's models, doctrines that of course are informed by Plantinga's Protestant Reformed theological heritage. Thus RED, though as ecumenical as possible, does admittedly have a Protestant Reformed "feel" (discussed above). Still, there are other Christian traditions, following in the same vein as RED, that could respond to PDH from their particular heritage (e.g., Roman Catholicism, Greek Orthodoxy, Pentecostalism, or Evangelicalism more broadly conceived). They could give a defense against PDH using doctrines or themes or emphases that have special weight in their tradition—a defense that is presumably more convincing than RED to members of their tradition who grapple with PDH (or a divine hiddenness argument against God's existence by, say, Schellenberg).[22] Comparably, non-Christian religions could analyze PDH from their perspective.[23]

18. See Paul K. Moser's work on this theme so far ("Inner Witness of Spirit"); see also Geivett and Moser, *Testimony of the Spirit*.

19. For instance, one of the leading voices in the analytic theology tradition is Michael Rea, who gave the 2017 Gifford Lectures on PDH: "Though the Darkness Hide Thee: Seeking the Face of the Invisible God." This was published the following year (*Hiddenness of God*).

20. See two articles that bear similar titles: Abraham, "Systematic Theology as Analytic Theology"; O. Crisp, "Analytic Theology as Systematic Theology."

21. See Balentine, *Hidden God*; Hamilton, "Divine Presence."

22. From a Thomistic/Catholic perspective, see Dumsday, "Thomistic Response"; Di Ceglie, "Christian Belief." For a discussion on PDH and Eastern Orthodoxy, see Trakakis, "Hidden Divinity."

23. For instance, see Gellman, "Hidden God of Jews."

Similarly—fourth—RED has used the religious epistemology of Plantinga, one of the great thinkers of our time, to engage PDH, but one can only wonder which other major thinkers there are, old and new, whose thought could be mined to engage PDH. Chapter 1 gave a historical overview, briefly describing PDH in the thought of Blaise Pascal, Joseph Butler, Søren Kierkegaard, David Hume, Alexander Campbell, and Friedrich Nietzsche. Others have analyzed the problem from the perspective of St. John of the Cross and Jonathan Edwards.[24] As I point out in my review of the latest and most important volume on PDH—edited by Adam Green and Eleonore Stump[25]—there are surely countless others who, like Plantinga, could be used to examine PDH.[26]

Fifth, nearly two decades ago, Daniel Howard-Snyder and Paul Moser opened their edited volume *Divine Hiddenness: New Essays* by saying that there is an existential aspect to PDH, and the book closed with an essay by Nicholas Wolterstorff, who examines what he calls the silence of God.[27] In this sense, it can be said that PDH, like the problem of evil, while having a logical and an evidential component, also has an existential or pastoral aspect to it. More work should be done on PDH from an existential or pastoral perspective (which is "widely recognized to be left relatively untouched by *conceptual* explanations"),[28] and RED may be of use to accomplish such a task.[29] For instance, in chapter 5, it was shown via the extended A/C model how RED could address the objection from sincere seekers, that there are those who claim to have honestly searched for God but who, due to "divine hiddenness," have come up short; future work may want to engage the notion of sincere seekers from an existential or pastoral angle.

6.5 FUTURE WORK ON OTHER ISSUES IN PHILOSOPHY OF RELIGION IN LIGHT OF RED

This section will explore how RED may contribute to, or have ramifications for, other areas of research or discussion specifically within philosophy of religion. Four areas of research or discussion will be examined.

24. Wainwright, "Jonathan Edwards and Hiddenness"; Coakley, "Divine Hiddenness or Dark Intimacy?"
25. Taber, "Review of *Hidden Divinity*."
26. Trickett and Taber, "Divine Hiddenness, Soteriological Problem."
27. Howard-Snyder and Moser, "Introduction," 1–3; Wolterstorff, "Silence of the God."
28. "Introduction," in Green and Stump, *Hidden Divinity*, 9; emphasis added.
29. For work on the existential problem, see DeWeese-Boyd, "Lyric Theodicy."

First, consider how RED may inform one's conception of the relationship between PDH and the problem of evil (POE). Recall that, in chapter 2, POE and PDH were compared and contrasted; several lines of similarity and several lines of dissimilarity were presented. RED may show, as it turns out, that POE and PDH are not just *dissimilar* but that they may be *different* problems altogether. For RED has argued that God is not hidden from humanity, that there is a natural knowledge of God, or general revelation, and that God has shown himself plainly in the things that are made (Rom 1:19–20). The human race has even been created by God to have warranted theistic belief, or knowledge; this was the fruit of the A/C model in chapter 3. Of course, to argue that God is not hidden is rather forthright, and it is a claim that needs to be substantiated, especially given a research question that asks why God's existence is not more obvious.

But RED just is in a position to substantiate such a claim by arguing that God's existence is not more obvious because *sin*, on Plantinga's extended model, has had grave noetic and affective consequences. Suppose that is true, that sin, on RED, hinders the clarity of God's existence. If RED is accurate about this point, then PDH starts to look and sound like a *different* problem than POE, which is not necessarily to deny similarities, or common ground, that the two problems may share (chapter 2 discussed this point at length). Given this, consider some brief objections, coupled with some brief replies, the objections and replies of which some in analytic philosophy of religion may want to utilize (in either agreement or disagreement with RED) toward future research on PDH.

Schellenberg's 1993 *DHHR* argued that PDH (or reasonable nonbelief) is a part of the larger POE,[30] but since that time he appears to have changed his mind, saying that PDH and POE are *separate* problems, such that the theist cannot sweep PDH "under the rug of the problem of evil" so that "the so-called problem of hiddenness may be safely ignored."[31] One disagreement with or objection to RED, given Schellenberg's comments, may be that, if they are two separate problems, then this seems to *multiply* problems against theism, POE counting as one problem and PDH counting as another, such that the theist must now defend herself on "two fronts." In other words, does RED, with its claim that PDH may be a different problem than POE altogether, make theism more vulnerable?

One response is just to deny (coupled with convincing reasons) that POE and PDH are in fact separate problems by in turn denying (against

---

30. *DHHR* 6–7, 9.

31. Schellenberg, *Wisdom to Doubt*, 207; see also his *Hiddenness Argument*, 28–31, for discussion of PDH and POE.

RED) the perceived dissimilarities, which in this case would be to deny that sin counts as a dissimilarity; in so doing, the two fronts decrease back to one, and theism is less vulnerable. Another response to the "two fronts" objection is to draw upon the *similarity* between POE and PDH, particularly the similarity that states that *defenses* (like theodicies) can be applied to either problem. Available defenses in the literature include, as discussed, a free will defense, an improper response defense, an epistemic distance defense, among others. This similarity in hand, it can then be argued that RED should be considered as yet *another* line of defense that theists can draw upon to defend themselves against PDH; thus, even if another problem is "gained," so too is *another* defense; "trade-offs and compromises," so to speak.[32]

Second, consider how RED may bear upon two other problems in philosophy of religion that, like POE, at least appear to parallel PDH: the problem of religious diversity (PRD) and the soteriological problem of evil (SPE). Let me briefly define both, saying along the way how one could use RED to inform each problem while also trying to shed light on other pertinent avenues of discussion. PRD is the problem that there are many competing religious claims about God, sin, salvation, and so on; it relates to PDH because, as one may be inclined to argue, if God were more obvious, then presumably there would not be so many varying descriptions of God from such diverse world religions.[33] This is relevant to RED because if God is not hidden from the human race, as RED has argued from a Christian standpoint, then it needs to be asked what this means for PRD. Of course, putting the question this way seems to set Christianity up, on RED, as the exclusively true religion. The advocate of RED could push back, once again, by arguing that sin inclines the human race toward other religions outside of Christianity, religions that are ultimately false.

But then saying *that* now seems to put us in the realm of what some call SPE; SPE, at least from a Christian standpoint, is the problem that God has provided salvation for humanity but that there are some persons who never hear or accept the gospel of Jesus Christ, and so are lost.[34] For if God's "salvific path" by way of the gospel of Jesus Christ were more obvious or more evident, as one may postulate, then more persons could respond to the gospel and be saved, but *that* there are some who go unsaved could be considered evil. RED could offer a response to SPE once again by pointing to sin, arguing that the unsaved are ultimately unsaved because of unrepentant

---

32. See further Taber, "Divine Hiddenness."

33. Robert McKim has written on the relationship between these two problems (*Religious Ambiguity*).

34. For discussion of SPE, see Peels, "Divine Foreknowledge."

sin. Or, perhaps a bit more modestly, the advocate of RED might respond by way of skeptical theism. Recently, skeptical theism has been applied to PDH,[35] and it could be applied to SPE via RED. Perhaps here the skeptical theist proposes that God has reasons, reasons *unknown* to us but *known* by him, for why there are persons who are not saved.

Stepping back, there appears to be rapport between PDH, PRD, and SPE. Suppose one is a religious exclusivist, like Plantinga,[36] holding that there is only one uniquely true religion (which in this case is Christianity); suppose it is asked of the exclusivist why, on her position, God's particular path for salvation is not better known, or more apparent or obvious, which could in turn ensure that large swaths of alternative religious adherents are not led down the wrong "salvific path" (the wrong "salvific path," according to the exclusivist, could be another religion outside of Christianity). What, precisely, is being asked of the exclusivist? Is it PDH, which asks why God is not more evident? Is it SPE, since the fact that some find themselves on the so-called wrong "salvific path" amounts to an evil of sorts? Is it PRD? It is not easy to say. One may inquire if PDH is the cause or the "culprit" (so to speak) of these other related problems. If it is, then RED could be used to see to what extent it elucidates PRD and SPE. One may also inquire, conversely, if these *other* problems are the cause, or at least contribute to, PDH. Last, suppose that one could determine the exact relationship between PDH and SPE; what implications could this have for the exact relationship between PDH and POE (since presumably SPE is a part of the larger POE)? What would this mean for RED?

Third, consider another area where future work in philosophy of religion could be conducted, which comes at the intersection of RED, PDH, and *sin's* effects in particular. This area asks that if RED is *so* keen to argue that sin undercuts our knowledge and thus the perceived clarity of God, then what ramifications could such a position have for the Reformed epistemologist confronted with an *argument* that contains premises against God's existence offered by, say, Schellenberg? Recall (from chapter 2 especially) Schellenberg's 1993 argument from divine hiddenness against God's existence:

1. If there is a God, he is perfectly loving.
2. If a perfectly loving God exists, reasonable nonbelief does not occur.
3. Reasonable nonbelief occurs.

---

35. McBrayer and Swenson, "Scepticism"; Greco, "No-Fault Atheism."
36. A. Plantinga, "Defense of Religious Exclusivism." For critical evaluation of Plantinga's exclusivism, see Renusch, "Thank God." Plantinga responds to Renusch in within that same essay (252–54).

4. No perfectly loving God exists.
5. There is no God.[37]

Presently, since his 1993 argument, Schellenberg examines nonbelief not in terms of "reasonable nonbelief" but in terms of what he calls "*nonresistant* nonbelief." A simplified Schellenbergian argument against God's existence from "nonresistant nonbelief" states:

1. If God exists, then God is perfectly loving, desiring loving relationship with all created persons.
2. If God is perfectly loving, then God would ensure that all persons can participate in relationship with God unless they have excluded themselves through some kind of resistance.
3. There are nonresistant nonbelievers.

Therefore, God does not exist.[38]

Premise (3) in both arguments appears to be the most relevant with respect to RED's analysis of sin. RED has not taken an explicit position on whether there are or are not reasonable nonbelievers or nonresistant nonbelievers. But RED's discussion of sin's noetic and affective effects may provide the Reformed epistemologist (or others who discuss sin in the context of PDH) with a way to examine, or perhaps even reject, premise (3) in both arguments. To give one brief example, one could argue (given RED) that nonbelievers are culpable for their nonbelief for refusing (or resisting) to place themselves in congenial epistemic environments whereby theistic belief can be fostered (such environments may include, as chapter 5 discussed, the reading of Scripture, going to church, praying, attending to God in creation, and the like). Chapter 2 discusses those in the literature who do reject premise (3) (i.e., premise [3] from the 1993 argument), and chapter 4 analyzes nonbelief from the extended A/C model examining whether nonbelief can be justified, rational, or warranted. Others in philosophy of religion may want to consider these issues with greater depth, especially given RED.

Fourth, RED may assist others in the philosophy of religion to further engage particular aspects of Plantingean *epistemology* relevant to PDH. While Plantinga is known for his work in many areas of philosophy, including philosophy of science and metaphysics, he is especially known for his epistemology, and although his epistemology is quite extensive (the *Warrant*

---

37. DHHR 83.

38. "Introduction," in Green and Stump, *Hidden Divinity and Religious Belief*, 1. For a more complex version of the argument, see Schellenberg, "Divine Hiddenness and Human Philosophy"; *Hiddenness Argument*.

trilogy alone spanning three volumes), there is one "subfield" within his epistemology that, as RED has argued, is uniquely pertinent to PDH: the *sensus divinitatis* (SD), an area of research that never seems to go away in the literature. Let me briefly point to potential areas of work concerning this issue in light of RED.

In chapter 3, I defended the SD against the objection that it probably does not exist. Now, suppose a Reformed epistemologist in the vein of Plantinga becomes convinced that there is no SD, perhaps due to Hans van Eyghen's (excellent) paper "There Is No *Sensus Divinitatis*." Could the Reformed epistemologist somehow "reengineer" Plantingean Reformed epistemology so that it functions properly without the SD? If so, how would this affect the Reformed epistemologist's conception of PDH? Would it undermine it?

Or perhaps a Reformed epistemologist becomes unconvinced of one of Reformed epistemology's main tenets—that theistic belief can be noninferential as well as justified, rational, and warranted without evidence—but still wishes to retain the notion of the SD in her work; Trent Dougherty and Blake McAllister have sought to retain the SD but are eager to reform the SD's conception such that it squares well with evidentialism (and *inferential* theistic belief).[39] One could analyze PDH given such a move. Comparably, one could build natural theology, (inferential) arguments for God's existence, into a Plantingean Reformed epistemology, and then examine PDH.[40]

Or perhaps a Reformed epistemologist becomes convinced that Plantinga's conception of the SD, although *inspired* by John Calvin, very much *misconstrues* Calvin's own conception of the SD (having read the work of Georg Plasger),[41] but feels loyal to what she believes is Calvin's conception of SD (being the good Calvinist she is); she could, to use a certain theological term, "retrieve"[42] what she takes to be Calvin's conception of the SD, replacing Plantinga's with Calvin's, and then in turn assess PDH.[43]

Or perhaps one is concerned to probe the intersection of Reformed epistemology (and its conception of the SD) with evolutionary theory so

---

39. McAllister and Dougherty, "Reforming Reformed Epistemology."

40. Plantinga has offered two dozen (or so) theistic arguments for God's existence in an appendix ("Two Dozen"). See also Walls and Dougherty, *Two Dozen*.

41. Plasger, "Does Calvin Teach." Plantinga responds to Plasger at the end of the volume ("Ad Plasger").

42. "Retrieval" in theological studies means to use the resources of the past so that one may in turn go forward, on which see (in the Reformed tradition) Allen, *Reformed Catholicity*.

43. In this case, one may wish to draw up on the work of Helm, "John Calvin, *Sensus Divinitatis*."

as to see how such work may affect our thinking about PDH; briefly, Helen De Cruz and Johan De Smedt argue that the coupling of Reformed epistemology and evolutionary theory (since both converge that theistic belief can be basic) requires that Reformed epistemology rework its conception of sin's noetic effects; someone motivated by their research could in turn examine PDH.[44] Along the same lines of De Cruz and De Smedt's work on evolutionary theory, there may be those who (given RED) want to analyze the conjunction of the SD, Reformed epistemology, and the *cognitive science of religion*, and then in turn apply these results to PDH.[45]

Here I close this study on the problem of divine hiddenness by quoting the eighteenth-century Anglican bishop and philosopher George Berkeley, who concludes his *Treatise Concerning the Principles of Human Knowledge* by saying that his work aims to inspire his "readers with a pious sense of the presence of God," hoping ultimately to encourage them to "embrace the salutary truths of the Gospel, which to know and to practice is the highest perfection of human nature."[46]

---

44. De Cruz and De Smedt, "Reformed and Evolutionary Epistemology."

45. De Cruz, "Divine Hiddenness"; Clark and Barrett, "Reformed Epistemology." Van Eyghen's paper would also be relevant to consider here with respect to cognitive science and the SD ("No *Sensus Divinitatis*").

46. Berkeley, *Principles of Human Knowledge*, 92.

Bibliography

Abraham, William J. *Canon and Criterion in Christian Theology: From the Fathers to Feminism.* Oxford: Clarendon, 1998.
———. *Crossing the Threshold of Divine Revelation.* Grand Rapids: Eerdmans, 2006.
———. "The Epistemological Significance of the Inner Witness of the Holy Spirit." *Faith and Philosophy* 7 (1990) 434–50.
———. "The Epistemology of Jesus: An Initial Investigation." In *Jesus and Philosophy: New Essays*, edited by Paul K. Moser, 149–68. Cambridge: Cambridge University Press, 2009.
———. "The Existence of God." In *The Oxford Handbook of Systematic Theology*, edited by John B. Webster et al., 19–34. Oxford Handbooks. Oxford: Oxford University Press, 2007.
———. "The Offense of Divine Revelation." *Harvard Theological Review* 95 (2002) 251–64.
———. "Philosophical Reflection on Revelation and Scripture." In *A Companion to Philosophy of Religion*, edited by Charles Taliaferro et al., 695–701. 2nd ed. Blackwell Companions to Philosophy 9. Malden, MA: Wiley-Blackwell, 2010.
———. "Systematic Theology as Analytic Theology." In *Analytic Theology: New Essays in the Philosophy of Theology*, edited by Oliver D. Crisp and Michael C. Rea, 54–69. Oxford: Oxford University Press, 2009.
Abraham, William J., and Frederick D. Aquino, eds. *The Oxford Handbook of the Epistemology of Theology.* Oxford Handbooks. Oxford: Oxford University Press, 2017.
Adams, Marilyn McCord. "Sin as Uncleanness." *Philosophical Perspectives* 5 (1991) 1–27.
Aijaz, Imran, and Markus Weidler. "Some Critical Reflections on the Hiddenness Argument." *International Journal for Philosophy of Religion* 61 (2007) 1–23.
Allen, Michael. *Reformed Catholicity: The Promise of Retrieval for Theology and Biblical Interpretation.* Grand Rapids: Baker Academic, 2015.
Anderson, James. "If Knowledge Then God: The Epistemological Theistic Arguments of Alvin Plantinga and Cornelius Van Til." *CTJ* 40 (2005) 49–75.
———. *Paradox in Christian Theology: An Analysis of Its Presence, Character, and Epistemic Status.* Paternoster Theological Monographs. Milton, UK: Paternoster, 2007.
Anderson, Owen. *Benjamin B. Warfield and Right Reason: The Clarity of General Revelation and Function of Apologetics.* Lanham, MD: University Press of America, 2005.
———. *The Clarity of God's Existence: The Ethics of Belief after the Enlightenment.* Eugene, OR: Wipf & Stock, 2008.

———. *Reason and Worldviews: Warfield, Kuyper, Van Til and Plantinga on the Clarity of General Revelation and Function of Apologetics*. Lanham, MD: University Press of America, 2008.

Anselm. "Proslogion." In *Anselm: Basic Writings*, edited and translated by Thomas Williams, 75–98. Hackett Classics. Indianapolis: Hackett, 2007.

———. *"Proslogion": With the Replies of Gaunilo and Anselm*. Translated by Thomas Williams. Indianapolis: Hackett, 1995.

———. *Saint Anselm: Basic Writings*. Translated by Sidney N. Deane. La Salle, IL: Open Court, 1974.

———. *St. Anselm: Basic Writings: "Proslogium," "Mologium," Gaunilo's "In Behalf of the Fool," "Cur Deus Homo."* Translated by Sidney N. Deane. LaSalle, IL: Open Court, 1974.

Augustine. *The Confessions*. Translated by Maria Boulding and Patricia Hampl. Vintage Spiritual Classics. New York: Vintage, 1999.

Azadegan, Ebrahim. "Divine Hiddenness and Human Sin: The Noetic Effect of Sin." *Journal of Reformed Theology* 7 (2013) 69–90.

———. "Divine Love and the Argument from Divine Hiddenness." *European Journal for Philosophy of Religion* 6 (2014) 101–16.

Babolin, Albino. "*Deus Absconditus*: Some Notes on the Bearing of the Hiddenness of God upon Butler's and Pascal's Criticism of Deism." In *Joseph Butler's Moral and Religious Thought: Tercentenary Essays*, edited by Christopher Cunliffe, 29–35. Oxford: Clarendon, 1992.

Baker, Deane-Peter. "Introduction: Alvin Plantinga, God's Philosopher." In *Alvin Plantinga*, edited by Deane-Peter Baker, 1–14. Contemporary Philosophy in Focus. Cambridge: Cambridge University Press, 2007.

———. "Plantinga's Reformed Epistemology: What's the Question?" *International Journal for Philosophy of Religion* 57 (2005) 77–103.

———. *Tayloring Reformed Epistemology: Charles Taylor, Alvin Plantinga, and the de Jure Challenge to Christian Belief*. London: SCM, 2007.

Baker-Hytch, Max. "Mutual Epistemic Dependence and the Demographic Divine Hiddenness Problem." *RelS* 52 (2016) 375–94.

Balentine, Samuel E. *The Hidden God: The Hiding of the Face of God in the Old Testament*. Oxford Theological Monographs. Oxford: Oxford University Press, 1983.

Barrett, Justin. "Cognitive Science, Religion, and Theology." In *The Believing Primate: Scientific, Philosophical, and Theological Reflections on the Origin of Religion*, edited by Jeffrey Schloss and Michael J. Murray, 76–99. Oxford: Oxford University Press, 2010.

Barth, Hans-Martin. *The Theology of Martin Luther: A Critical Assessment*. Translated by Linda M. Maloney. Minneapolis: Fortress, 2013.

Barth, Karl. *The Doctrine of God*. Edited by G. W. Bromiley and T. F. Torrance. Translated by T. H. L. Parker and J. L. M. Haire. Vol. 2.1 of *Church Dogmatics*. Edinburgh: T&T Clark, 1957.

Basil. *On the Human Condition*. Translated by Nonna Verna Harrison. Popular Patristics 30. Crestwood, NY: St. Vladimir's, 2005.

Basinger, David. "Divine Omniscience and the Soteriological Problem of Evil: Is the Type of Knowledge God Possesses Relevant?" *RelS* 28 (1992) 1–18.

Bates, Katharine Lee. "America the Beautiful." *Wikipedia*, edited July 19, 2024. https://en.wikipedia.org/wiki/America_the_Beautiful.

Battles, Ford L. "God Was Accommodating Himself to Human Capacity." *Int* 31 (1977) 19–38.
Bauckham, Richard. "The Fourth Gospel as the Testimony of the Beloved Disciple." In *The Gospel of John and Christian Theology*, edited by Richard Bauckham and Carl Mosser, 120–39. Grand Rapids: Eerdmans, 2008.
Bavinck, Herman. *God and Creation*. Edited by John Bolt. Translated by John Vriend. Vol. 2 of *Reformed Dogmatics*. 4 vols. Grand Rapids: Baker, 2003.
———. *Prolegomena*. Edited by John Bolt. Translated by John Vriend. Vol. 1 of *Reformed Dogmatics*. 4 vols. Grand Rapids: Baker Academic, 2003.
Beilby, James K. *Epistemology as Theology: An Evaluation of Alvin Plantinga's Religious Epistemology*. Aldershot, UK: Ashgate, 2005.
———. "Plantinga's Model of Warranted Christian Belief." In *Alvin Plantinga*, edited by Deane-Peter Baker, 125–65. Contemporary Philosophy in Focus. Cambridge: Cambridge University Press, 2007.
Beilby, James K., and Paul R. Eddy, eds. *Divine Foreknowledge: Four Views*. Downers Grove, IL: InterVarsity, 2001.
Benson, Ophelia. "A Deal-Breaker." In *50 Voices of Disbelief: Why We Are Atheists*, edited by Russell Blackford and Udo Schüklenk, 23–27. Chichester, UK: Wiley-Blackwell, 2009.
Bergmann, Michael. *Justification without Awareness: A Defense of Epistemic Externalism*. Oxford: Clarendon, 2006.
———. "Skeptical Theism and the Problem of Evil." In *The Oxford Handbook of Philosophical Theology*, edited by Thomas P. Flint and Michael Rea, 374–99. Oxford Handbooks. Oxford: Oxford University Press, 2009.
Berkeley, George. *Alciphron: In Focus*. Edited by David Berman. London: Routledge, 1993.
———. "Alciphron: Or the Minute Philosopher, in Seven Dialogues." In *The Works of George Berkeley*, edited by G. N. Wright, 1:293–528. London: Elibron Classics, 2005.
———. *A Treatise Concerning the Principles of Human Knowledge*. Edited by Kenneth P. Winkler. Hackett Classics. Indianapolis: Hackett, 1982.
Berkhof, Louis. *Systematic Theology*. Grand Rapids: Eerdmans, 1938.
Blaising, Craig A., and Carmen Hardin. *Psalms 1–50*. ACCS. Old Testament 7. Downers Grove, IL: InterVarsity, 2008.
Boyce, Kenneth. "Proper Functionalism." *Internet Encyclopedia of Philosophy*, n.d. https://iep.utm.edu/prop-fun.
Boyce, Kenneth, and Alvin Plantinga. "Proper Functionalism." In *The Continuum Companion to Epistemology*, edited by Andrew Cullison, 124–40. London: Continuum, 2012.
Boyce, Kenny, and Andrew Moon. "In Defense of Proper Functionalism: Cognitive Science Takes on Swampman." *Synthese* 193 (2016) 2987–3001.
Boyer, Steven D., and Christopher A. Hall. *The Mystery of God: Theology for Knowing the Unknowable*. Grand Rapids: Baker Academic, 2012.
Bray, Gerald L. "Sin in Historical Theology." In *Fallen: A Theology of Sin*, edited by Christopher W. Morgan and Robert A. Peterson, 163–85. Theology in Community. Wheaton, IL: Crossway, 2013.
———. *We Believe in One God*. Ancient Christian Doctrine 1. Downers Grove, IL: IVP Academic, 2009.

Brown, Hunter. "Incarnation and the Divine Hiddenness Debate." *HeyJ* 54 (2013) 252–60.

Burnett, Joel S. *Where Is God? Divine Absence in the Hebrew Bible*. Minneapolis: Fortress, 2010.

Butler, Diana. "God's Visible Glory: The Beauty of Nature in the Thought of John Calvin and Jonathan Edwards." *WTJ* 52 (1990) 13–26.

Butler, Joseph. *The Analogy of Religion: With a Selection from the Correspondence between Joseph Butler and Samuel Clarke*. Edited by David McNaughton. Oxford: Oxford University Press, 2021.

———. "Upon the Ignorance of Man." In *The Works of Bishop Butler*, edited by David E. White, 140–46. Rochester Studies in Philosophy. Rochester, NY: University of Rochester Press, 2006.

———. *The Works of Bishop Butler*. Edited by David E. White. Rochester Studies in Philosophy. Rochester, NY: University of Rochester Press, 2006.

Cahn, Steven M., ed. *Classics of Western Philosophy*. 6th ed. Indianapolis: Hackett, 2002.

Calvin, John. *Institutes of the Christian Religion*. Edited by John T. McNeill. Translated by Ford L. Battles. Philadelphia: Westminster, 1960.

Campbell, Alexander. "Letters to Humphrey Marshal, Esq.—No. I." *Millennial Harbinger* 1 (1830) 513–17.

Carson, D. A. *The Gospel According to John*. Pillar New Testament Commentary. Grand Rapids: Eerdmans, 1990.

Center for Philosophy of Religion. "Skeptical Theism." *Center for Philosophy of Religion*, n.d. https://philreligion.nd.edu/research-initiatives/the-problem-of-evil-in-modern-and-contemporary-thought/skeptical-theism.

Cervantez, Jeff, and E. J. Coffman. "Hiddenness, Evidence, and Idolatry." In *Evidence and Religious Belief*, edited by Kelly James Clark and Raymond J. VanArragon, 95–113. Oxford: Oxford University Press, 2011.

Cherok, Richard J. *Debating for God: Alexander Campbell's Challenge to Skepticism in Antebellum America*. Abilene: Abilene Christian University Press, 2008.

Chignell, Andrew. "Prolegomena to Any Future Non-Doxastic Religion." *RelS* 49 (2013) 195–207.

Clanton, J. Caleb. "Alexander Campbell on the Problem of Divine Hiddenness." *Stone-Campbell Journal* 15 (2012) 191–204.

———. "Alexander Campbell's Revealed-Idea Argument for the Existence of God." *Restoration Quarterly* 54 (2012) 105–24.

———. *The Philosophy of Religion of Alexander Campbell*. Knoxville: University of Tennessee Press, 2013.

Clark, Kelly J. "Pluralism and Proper Function." In *Alvin Plantinga*, edited by Deane-Peter Baker, 166–87. Contemporary Philosophy in Focus. Cambridge: Cambridge University Press, 2007.

———. "Reformed Epistemology Apologetics." In *Five Views on Apologetics*, edited by Steven B. Cowan, 265–84. Counterpoints. Grand Rapids: Zondervan, 2000.

Clark, Kelly J., and Justin L. Barrett. "Reformed Epistemology and the Cognitive Science of Religion." *Faith and Philosophy* 27 (2010) 174–89.

Clifford, Richard J. *Psalms 1–72*. AOTC. Nashville: Abingdon, 2002.

Coakley, Sarah. "Divine Hiddenness or Dark Intimacy? How John of the Cross Dissolves a Contemporary Philosophical Dilemma." In *Hidden Divinity and*

Religious Belief: New Perspectives, edited by Adam Green and Eleonore Stump, 229–45. Cambridge: Cambridge University Press, 2016.
Collins, Raymond F. *Second Corinthians*. Paideia. Grand Rapids: Baker Academic, 2013.
Cordry, Benjamin S. "Divine Hiddenness and Belief De Re." *RelS* 45 (2009) 1–19.
Couenhoven, Jesse. "What Sin Is: A Differential Analysis." *Modern Theology* 25 (2009) 563–87.
Craig, William Lane. "A Classical Apologist's Response." In *Five Views on Apologetics*, edited by Steven B. Cowan, 285–90. Counterpoints. Grand Rapids: Zondervan, 2000.
Craig, William Lane, and J. P. Moreland, eds. *The Blackwell Companion to Natural Theology*. Malden, MA: Wiley-Blackwell, 2009.
Crisp, Oliver D. "Analytic Theology as Systematic Theology." *Open Theology* 3 (2017) 156–66.
———. "Desiderata for Models of the Hypostatic Union." In *Christology, Ancient and Modern: Explorations in Constructive Dogmatics*, edited by Fred Sanders and Oliver D. Crisp, 19–41. Los Angeles Theology Conference Series. Grand Rapids: Zondervan Academic, 2013.
———. *Deviant Calvinism: Broadening Reformed Theology*. Minneapolis: Fortress, 2014.
———. *Divinity and Humanity: The Incarnation Reconsidered*. Current Issues in Theology. Cambridge: Cambridge University Press, 2007.
———. "On Original Sin." *International Journal of Systematic Theology* 17 (2015) 252–66.
———. *Retrieving Doctrine: Essays in Reformed Theology*. Downers Grove, IL: IVP Academic, 2010.
Crisp, Oliver D., and Michael C. Rea. *Analytic Theology: New Essays in the Philosophy of Theology*. Oxford: Oxford University Press, 2009.
Crisp, Oliver D., and Fred Sanders. "Introduction." In *Advancing Trinitarian Theology: Explorations in Constructive Dogmatics*, edited by Oliver D. Crisp and Fred Sanders, 13–20. Los Angeles Theology Conference Series. Grand Rapids: Zondervan Academic, 2014.
Crisp, Thomas M. "On Believing That the Scriptures Are Divinely Inspired." In *Analytic Theology: New Essays in the Philosophy of Theology*, edited by Oliver D. Crisp and Michael C. Rea, 187–213. Oxford: Oxford University Press, 2009.
Cuneo, Terence D. "Another Look at Divine Hiddenness." *RelS* 49 (2013) 151–64.
De Cruz, Helen. "Divine Hiddenness and the Cognitive Science of Religion." In *Hidden Divinity and Religious Belief: New Perspectives*, edited by Adam Green and Eleonore Stump, 53–68. Cambridge: Cambridge University Press, 2016.
De Cruz, Helen, and Johan De Smedt. "Reformed and Evolutionary Epistemology and the Noetic Effects of Sin." *International Journal for Philosophy of Religion* 74 (2013) 49–66.
Demarest, Bruce A. *General Revelation: Historical Views and Contemporary Issues*. Grand Rapids: Zondervan, 1982.
De Ridder, Jeroen, and Mathanja Berger. "Shipwrecked or Holding Water? In Defense of Alvin Plantinga's Warranted Christian Believer." *Philo* 16 (2013) 42–61.
DeWeese-Boyd, Ian. "Lyric Theodicy: Gerard Manley Hopkins and the Problem of Existential Hiddenness." In *Hidden Divinity and Religious Belief: New Perspectives*, edited by Adam Green and Eleonore Stump, 260–77. Cambridge: Cambridge University Press, 2016.

Di Ceglie, Roberto. "Christian Belief, Love for God, and Divine Hiddenness." *Philosophia Christi* 18 (2016) 179–94.

Dillenberger, John. *God Hidden and Revealed: The Interpretation of Luther's Deus Absconditus and Its Significance for Religious Thought*. Philadelphia: Muhlenberg, 1953.

Diller, Kevin. *Theology's Epistemological Dilemma: How Karl Barth and Alvin Plantinga Provide a Unified Response*. Downers Grove, IL: IVP Academic, 2014.

Diller, Kevin S. "Review of Plantinga's 'Warranted Christian Belief': Critical Essays with a Reply by Alvin Plantinga, edited by Dieter Schönecker." *Notre Dame Philosophical Review*, June 12, 2016. https://ndpr.nd.edu/reviews/plantingas-warranted-christian-belief-critical-essays-with-a-reply-by-alvin-plantinga.

Doane, Darren, dir. *Collision: Is Christianity Good for the World?* Jamul, CA: Level 4, 2009.

Dougherty, Trent, and Justin P. McBrayer. *Skeptical Theism: New Essays*. New York: Oxford University Press, 2014.

Downey, Patrick. *Desperately Wicked: Philosophy, Christianity and the Human Heart*. Downers Grove, IL: IVP Academic, 2009.

Drange, Theodore M. *Nonbelief and Evil: Two Arguments for the Nonexistence of God*. Amherst, NY: Prometheus, 1998.

———. "Nonbelief vs. Lack of Evidence: Two Atheological Arguments." *Philo* 1 (1998) 105–14.

Draper, Paul. "Seeking but Not Believing: Confessions of a Practicing Agnostic." In *Divine Hiddenness: New Essays*, edited by Daniel Howard-Snyder and Paul K. Moser, 197–214. Cambridge: Cambridge University Press, 2001.

Dumsday, Travis. "Divine Hiddenness as Deserved." *Faith and Philosophy* 31 (2014) 286–302.

———. "Divine Hiddenness as Divine Mercy." *RelS* 48 (2012) 183–98.

———. "Divine Hiddenness, Free-Will, and the Victims of Wrongdoing." *Faith and Philosophy* 27 (2010) 423–38.

———. "A Thomistic Response to the Problem of Divine Hiddenness." *American Catholic Philosophical Quarterly* 87 (2013) 365–77.

Eames, S. Morris. *The Philosophy of Alexander Campbell*. Bethany, WV: Bethany College Press, 1965.

Edwards, Jonathan. "Man's Natural Blindness in the Things of Religion." In *The Works of Jonathan Edwards*, edited by Edward Hickman, 2:247–56. Peabody, MA: Hendrickson, 2005.

———. *"Sinners in the Hands of an Angry God" and Other Puritan Sermons*. Edited by David Dutkanicz. Mineola, NY: Dover, 2005.

Erdel, Timothy P. "Divine Disclosures and Supernatural Signs: Could My Persistent Experience of God's Presence Help to Resolve My Neighbor's Problem of Divine Hiddenness?" Paper given at Evangelical Philosophical Society Conference, Baltimore, MD, November 2013.

Evans, Craig A. "Hardness of Heart." In *Dictionary of Jesus and the Gospels: A Compendium of Contemporary Biblical Scholarship*, edited by Joel B. Green et al., 298–99. IVP Bible Dictionary Series. Downers Grove, IL: InterVarsity, 1992.

Evans, C. Stephen. "Can God Be Hidden and Evident at the Same Time? Some Kierkegaardian Reflections." *Faith and Philosophy* 23 (2006) 241–53.

———. *Kierkegaard: An Introduction*. Cambridge: Cambridge University Press, 2009.

———. *Kierkegaard on Faith and the Self: Collected Essays*. Provost Series. Waco: Baylor University Press, 2006.

———. *Natural Signs and Knowledge of God: A New Look at Theistic Arguments*. Oxford: Oxford University Press, 2010.

———. "The Relevance of Historical Evidence for Christian Faith: A Critique of a Kierkegaardian View." *Faith and Philosophy* 7 (1990) 470–85.

———. "Tradition, Biblical Interpretation and Historical Truth." In *"Behind" the Text: History and Biblical Interpretation*, edited by Craig G. Bartholomew, 320–36. Scripture and Hermeneutics Series 4. Carlisle, UK: Paternoster, 2003.

———. *Why Christian Faith Still Makes Sense: A Response to Contemporary Challenges*. Acadia Studies in Bible and Theology. Grand Rapids: Baker Academic, 2015.

Evans, C. Stephen, and R. Zachary Manis. *Philosophy of Religion: Thinking about Faith*. 2nd ed. Contours of Christian Philosophy. Downers Grove, IL: IVP Academic, 2009.

Evans, Jeremy A. *The Problem of Evil: The Challenge to Essential Christian Beliefs*. B&H Studies in Christian Apologetics. Nashville: B&H Academic, 2013.

Fales, Evan. "Journeying in Perplexity." In *Hidden Divinity and Religious Belief: New Perspective*, edited by Adam Green and Eleonore Stump, 89–106. Cambridge: Cambridge University Press, 2016.

———. "Review of *Warranted Christian Belief*, by Alvin Plantinga." *Noûs* 37 (2003) 353–70.

Farris, Joshua R., et al., eds. *Idealism and Christian Theology*. Vol. 1 of *Idealism and Christianity*. New York: Bloomsbury Academic, 2016.

Ferreira, M. Jamie. "A Kierkegaardian View of Divine Hiddenness." In *Divine Hiddenness: New Essays*, edited by Daniel Howard-Snyder and Paul K. Moser, 164–80. Cambridge: Cambridge University Press, 2002.

Flew, Antony. "The Presumption of Atheism: Contemporary Perspectives on Religious Epistemology." In *Contemporary Perspectives on Religious Epistemology*, edited by R. Douglas Geivett and Brendan Sweetman, 19–32. New York: Oxford University Press, 1992.

Flew, Antony, and Roy A. Varghese. *There Is a God: How the World's Most Notorious Atheist Changed His Mind*. New York: HarperOne, 2007.

Fowl, Stephen E. "Scripture." In *The Oxford Handbook of Systematic Theology*, edited by John B. Webster et al., 345–61. Oxford Handbooks. Oxford: Oxford University Press, 2007.

Frame, John M. "Presuppositional Apologetics." In *Five Views on Apologetics*, edited by Steven B. Cowan, 207–30. Counterpoints. Grand Rapids: Zondervan, 2000.

Franks, W. Paul. "Original Sin and Broad Free-Will Defense." *Philosophia Christi* 14 (2012) 353–71.

Fumerton, Richard A. "Plantinga, Warrant, and Christian Belief." *Philosophia Christi* (2001) 341–51.

Gale, Richard M. "Evil and Alvin Plantinga." In *Alvin Plantinga*, edited by Deane-Peter Baker, 48–70. Cambridge: Cambridge University Press, 2007.

Garcia, Laura. "St. John of the Cross and the Necessity of Divine Hiddenness." In *Divine Hiddenness: New Essays*, edited by Daniel Howard-Snyder and Paul K. Moser, 83–97. Cambridge: Cambridge University Press, 2002.

Gaskin, J. C. A. "Hume on Religion." In *The Cambridge Companion to Hume*, edited by David Fate Norton, 313–44. Cambridge Companions to Philosophy. Cambridge: Cambridge University Press, 1993.

———. "Hume on Religion." In *The Cambridge Companion to Hume*, edited by David F. Norton and Jacqueline A. Taylor, 480–514. 2nd ed. Cambridge Companions to Philosophy. Cambridge: Cambridge University Press, 2008.

Geivett, R. Douglas, and Paul K. Moser, eds. *The Testimony of the Spirit: New Essays*. New York: Oxford University Press, 2017.

Gellman, Jerome I. "The Hidden God of the Jews: Hegel, Reb Nachman, and the Adequah." In *Hidden Divinity and Religious Belief: New Perspectives*, edited by Adam Green and Eleonore Stump, 175–91. Cambridge: Cambridge University Press, 2016.

Gemes, Ken, and John Richardson. "Introduction." In *The Oxford Handbook of Nietzsche*, edited by Ken Gemes and John Richardson, 1–18. Oxford Handbooks. Oxford: Oxford University Press, 2013.

Gerrish, Brian A. "To the Unknown God: Luther and Calvin on the Hiddenness of God." *JR* 53 (1973) 263–92.

Goetz, Stewart. "The Argument from Evil." In *The Blackwell Companion to Natural Theology*, edited by William Lane Craig and J. P. Moreland, 449–97. Malden, MA: Blackwell, 2009.

Gooch, Paul W. "Paul, the Mind of Christ, and Philosophy." In *Jesus and Philosophy: New Essays*, edited by Paul K. Moser, 84–105. Cambridge: Cambridge University Press, 2008.

Greco, John. "No-Fault Atheism." In *Hidden Divinity and Religious Belief: New Perspectives*, edited by Adam Green and Eleonore Stump, 109–25. Cambridge: Cambridge University Press, 2016.

Green, Adam. "Cognitive Science and the Natural Knowledge of God." *Monist* 96 (2013) 399–419.

Green, Adam, and Eleonore Stump, eds. *Hidden Divinity and Religious Belief: New Perspectives*. Cambridge: Cambridge University Press, 2016.

Groothuis, Douglas R. *On Pascal*. Wadsworth Philosophers Series. Belmont, CA: Wadsworth, 2003.

Habermas, Gary R., and Antony Flew. "My Pilgrimage from Atheism to Theism: A Discussion between Antony Flew and Gary Habermas." *Philosophia Christi* 6 (2004) 197–211.

Hamilton, James M. "Divine Presence." In *Dictionary of the Old Testament: Wisdom, Poetry & Writings; A Compendium of Contemporary Biblical Scholarship*, edited by Tremper Longman III and Peter Enns, 116–20. IVP Bible Dictionary Series. Downers Grove, IL: IVP Academic, 2008.

Hammond, Nicholas, ed. *The Cambridge Companion to Pascal*. Cambridge Companions to Philosophy. Cambridge: Cambridge University Press, 2003.

Helm, Paul. "John Calvin and the Hiddenness of God." In *Engaging the Doctrine of God: Contemporary Protestant Perspectives*, edited by Bruce L. McCormack, 67–82. Grand Rapids: Baker Academic, 2008.

———. "John Calvin, the '*Sensus Divinitatis*,' and the Noetic Effects of Sin." *International Journal for Philosophy of Religion* 43 (1998) 87–107.

———. *John Calvin's Ideas*. Oxford: Oxford University Press, 2004.

Helseth, Paul Kjoss. *"Right Reason" and the Princeton Mind: An Unorthodox Proposal.* Phillipsburg, NJ: P&R, 2010.
Henry, Douglas V. "Does Reasonable Nonbelief Exist?" *Faith and Philosophy* 18 (2001) 75–92.
———. "Reasonable Doubts about Reasonable Nonbelief." *Faith and Philosophy* 25 (2008) 276–89.
Hick, John. *Evil and the God of Love.* Rev. ed. London: Macmillan, 1977.
Hoitenga, Dewey J. *Faith and Reason from Plato to Plantinga: An Introduction to Reformed Epistemology.* Albany: State University of New York Press, 1991.
Holmes, Christopher R. J. "Disclosure without Reservation: Re-Evaluating Divine Hiddenness." *ZST* 48 (2006) 367–80.
Horton, Michael. *The Christian Faith: A Systematic Theology for Pilgrims on the Way.* Grand Rapids: Zondervan Academic, 2011.
House, Paul R. "Sin in the Law." In *Fallen: A Theology of Sin*, edited by Christopher W. Morgan and Robert A. Peterson, 39–63. Theology in Community. Wheaton, IL: Crossway, 2013.
Howard-Snyder, Daniel. "The Argument from Divine Hiddenness." *Canadian Journal of Philosophy* 26 (1996) 433–53.
———. "Divine Openness and Creaturely Nonresistant Nonbelief." In *Hidden Divinity and Religious Belief: New Perspectives*, edited by Adam Green and Eleonore Stump, 126–38. Cambridge: Cambridge University Press, 2016.
———. "Does Faith Entail Belief?" *Faith and Philosophy* 33 (2016) 142–62.
———. "Introduction." *RelS* 49 (2013) 141.
———. "Schellenberg on Propositional Faith." *RelS* 49 (2013) 181–94.
Howard-Snyder, Daniel, and Adam Green. "Hiddenness of God." *Stanford Encyclopedia of Philosophy*, Winter 2016. Edited by Edward N. Zalta. https://plato.stanford.edu/archives/win2016/entries/divine-hiddenness.
Howard-Snyder, Daniel, and Paul K. Moser, eds. *Divine Hiddenness: New Essays.* Cambridge: Cambridge University Press, 2002.
———. "Introduction: The Hiddenness of God." In *Divine Hiddenness: New Essays*, edited by Daniel Howard-Snyder and Paul K. Moser, 1–23. Cambridge: Cambridge University Press, 2002.
Humanists UK. "Atheist Bus Campaign." *Humanists UK*, n.d. https://humanists.uk/campaigns/successful-campaigns/atheist-bus-campaign.
Hume, David. *The Natural History of Religion.* Edited by H. E. Root. Library of Modern Religious Thought. Stanford: Stanford University Press, 1957.
Hunsinger, George. *How to Read Karl Barth: The Shape of His Theology.* New York: Oxford University Press, 1991.
Hunt, David P. "Middle Knowledge and the Soteriological Problem of Evil." *RelS* 27 (1991) 3–26.
Jeffreys, Derek S. "How Reformed Is Reformed Epistemology? Alvin Plantinga and Calvin's '*Sensus Divinitatis*.'" *RelS* 33 (1997) 419–31.
Johnson, Luke Timothy. *The Gospel of Luke.* Sacra Pagina. Collegeville, MN: Liturgical, 2006.
Jones, Barry. "The Spirit's Witness: A Historical and Theological Examination of the *Testimonium Spiritus Sancti Internum*." PhD diss., Wheaton College, 2008.
Keener, Craig S. *1–2 Corinthians.* New Cambridge Bible Commentary. Cambridge: Cambridge University Press, 2005.

Keener, Hubert J. "Review of *Where Is God? Divine Absence in the Hebrew Bible*, by Joel S. Burnett." *JETS* 54 (2011) 376–78.

Keller, James A. "The Hiddenness of God and the Problem of Evil." *International Journal for Philosophy of Religion* 37 (1995) 13–24.

Kenny, Anthony. *Faith and Reason*. Bampton Lectures in America 22. New York: Columbia University Press, 1983.

Kierkegaard, Søren. *Concluding Unscientific Postscript*. Edited by Walter Lowrie. Translated by David F. Swenson. Princeton, NJ: Princeton University Press, 1941.

———. *Provocations: Spiritual Writings*. Edited by Charles E. Moore. Maryknoll, NY: Orbis, 2003.

Kim, Joseph. *Reformed Epistemology and the Problem of Religious Diversity: Proper Function, Epistemic Disagreement, and Christian Exclusivism*. Eugene, OR: Pickwick, 2011.

King, Rolfe. *Obstacles to Divine Revelation: God and the Reorientation of Human Reason*. London: Continuum, 2008.

Kinghorn, Kevin P. *The Decision of Faith: Can Christian Beliefs Be Freely Chosen?* London: T&T Clark International, 2005.

———. "Spiritual Blindness, Self-Deception and Morally Culpable Nonbelief." *HeyJ* 48 (2007) 527–45.

———. "Why Doesn't God Make His Existence More Obvious?" *AsTJ* 57 (2002) 187–205.

Kinlaw, C. J. "Determinism and the Hiddenness of God in Calvin's Theology." *RelS* 24 (1988) 497–509.

Kline, Peter. "Absolute Action: Divine Hiddenness in Kierkegaard's Fear and Trembling." *Modern Theology* 28 (2012) 503–25.

Kruger, Michael J. *Canon Revisited: Establishing the Origins and Authority of the New Testament Books*. Wheaton, IL: Crossway, 2012.

———. *The Question of Canon: Challenging the Status Quo in the New Testament Debate*. Downers Grove, IL: IVP Academic, 2013.

Kuhn, Stephen T. "Is." In *The Cambridge Dictionary of Philosophy*, edited by Robert Audi, 444. 2nd ed. New York: Cambridge University Press, 1999.

Kvanvig, Jonathan L. "Divine Hiddenness: What Is the Problem?" In *Divine Hiddenness: New Essays*, edited by Daniel Howard-Snyder and Paul K. Moser, 149–63. Cambridge: Cambridge University Press, 2002.

———, ed. *Warrant in Contemporary Epistemology: Essays in Honor of Plantinga's Theory of Knowledge*. Studies in Epistemology and Cognitive Theory. Lanham, MD: Rowman & Littlefield, 1996.

Larsen, Timothy. *Crisis of Doubt: Honest Faith in Nineteenth-Century England*. Oxford: Oxford University Press, 2006.

Lee, Sloan. "David Hume's Theism in the Dialogues Concerning Natural Religion." Paper given at Dallas Socratic Society Conference, 2013.

Lehe, Robert T. "A Response to the Argument from the Reasonableness of Nonbelief." *Faith and Philosophy* 21 (2004) 159–74.

Leith, John H., ed. *Creeds of the Churches: A Reader in Christian Doctrine, from the Bible to the Present*. 3rd ed. Louisville: John Knox, 1982.

LePore, Ernest. "De Dicto." In *The Cambridge Dictionary of Philosophy*, edited by Robert Audi, 211. Cambridge: Cambridge University Press, 1999.

Letham, Robert. *The Holy Trinity: In Scripture, History, Theology, and Worship*. Phillipsburg, NJ: P&R, 2004.
Lewis, Gordon R. "Attributes of God." In *Evangelical Dictionary of Theology*, edited by Walter A. Elwell, 451–59. Baker Reference Library 1. Grand Rapids: Baker, 1984.
Louth, Andrew. *Introducing Eastern Orthodox Theology*. Downers Grove, IL: IVP Academic, 2013.
Loux, Michael J. *Metaphysics: A Contemporary Introduction*. Routledge Contemporary Introductions to Philosophy. New York: Routledge, 2002.
Lovering, Robert. "Divine Hiddenness and Inculpable Ignorance." *International Journal for Philosophy of Religion* 56 (2004) 89–107.
Luther, Martin. *On the Bondage of the Will*. In *Luther's Works*, edited by Philip P. Watson, 33:3–296. Philadelphia: Fortress, 1958.
Madueme, Hans, and Michael D. Reeves. "Threads in a Seamless Garment: Original Sin in Systematic Theology." In *Adam, the Fall, and Original Sin: Theological, Biblical, and Scientific Perspectives*, edited by Hans Madueme and Michael D. Reeves, 209–24. Grand Rapids: Baker Academic, 2014.
Maitzen, Stephen. "Divine Hiddenness and the Demographics of Theism." *RelS* 42 (2006) 177–91.
Marsh, Jason. "Do the Demographics of Theistic Belief Disconfirm Theism? A Reply to Maitzen." *RelS* 44 (2008) 465–71.
Mascord, Keith A. *Alvin Plantinga and Christian Apologetics*. Paternoster Theological Monographs. Waynesboro, GA: Paternoster, 2006.
Mawson, T. J. *Belief in God: An Introduction to the Philosophy of Religion*. Oxford: Clarendon, 2005.
———. "Praying to Stop Being an Atheist." *International Journal for Philosophy of Religion* 67 (2010) 173–86.
McAllister, Blake, and Trent Dougherty. "Reforming Reformed Epistemology: A New Take on the *Sensus Divinitatis*." *RelS* 55 (2019) 537–57.
McBrayer, Justin P., and Philip Swenson. "Scepticism about the Argument from Divine Hiddenness." *RelS* 48 (2012) 129–50.
McCall, Thomas. "On Understanding Scripture as the Word of God." In *Analytic Theology: New Essays in the Philosophy of Theology*, edited by Oliver D. Crisp and Michael C. Rea, 171–86. Oxford: Oxford University Press, 2009.
McCall, Thomas H. *An Invitation to Analytic Christian Theology*. Downers Grove, IL: IVP Academic, 2015.
McDermott, Gerald R. *Seeing God: Jonathan Edwards and Spiritual Discernment*. Vancouver, Canada: Regent College Press, 2000.
McFadyen, Alistair I. *Bound to Sin: Abuse, Holocaust, and the Christian Doctrine of Sin*. Cambridge Studies in Christian Doctrine 6. Cambridge: Cambridge University Press, 2000.
McFarland, Ian A. *The Divine Image: Envisioning the Invisible God*. Minneapolis: Fortress, 2005.
———. "The Fall and Sin." In *The Oxford Handbook of Systematic Theology*, edited by John B. Webster et al., 140–59. Oxford Handbooks. Oxford University Press, 2007.
McGrath, Alister E. *Luther's Theology of the Cross: Martin Luther's Theological Breakthrough*. Oxford: Blackwell, 1985.
———. *Reformation Thought: An Introduction*. 4th ed. Malden, MA: Wiley-Blackwell, 2012.

McKim, Robert. "The Hiddenness of God." *RelS* 26 (1990) 141–61.

———. *Religious Ambiguity and Religious Diversity*. New York: Oxford University Press, 2001.

McLean, G. R. "Antipathy to God." *Sophia* 54 (2015) 13–24.

McNabb, Tyler D. "Warranted Religion: Answering Objections to Alvin Plantinga's Epistemology." *RelS* 51 (2015) 477–95.

McNabb, Tyler D., and Erik D. Baldwin. "Reformed Epistemology and the Pandora's Box Objection: The Vaiśeṣika and Mormon Traditions." *Philosophia Christi* 18 (2016) 451–65.

Meadors, Edward P. *Idolatry and the Hardening of the Heart: A Study in Biblical Theology*. New York: T&T Clark, 2006.

Meister, Chad V. "Evil and the Hiddenness of God." In *God and Evil: The Case for God in a World Filled with Pain*, edited by Chad V. Meister and James K. Dew Jr., 138–51. Downers Grove, IL: IVP, 2013.

Michaels, J. Ramsey. *The Gospel of John*. NICNT. Grand Rapids: Eerdmans, 2010.

Migliore, Daniel L. *Faith Seeking Understanding: An Introduction to Christian Theology*. Grand Rapids: Eerdmans, 1991.

Mitchell, Basil. "Butler as a Christian Apologist." In *Joseph Butler's Moral and Religious Thought: Tercentenary Essays*, edited by Christopher Cunliffe, 97–116. Oxford: Clarendon, 1992.

Moo, Douglas J. *The Epistle to the Romans*. NICNT. Grand Rapids: Eerdmans, 1996.

Moon, Andrew. "Recent Work in Reformed Epistemology." *Philosophy Compass* 11 (2016) 879–91.

Moreland, J. P., and William Lane Craig. *Philosophical Foundations for a Christian Worldview*. Downers Grove, IL: IVP Academic, 2017.

Morgan, Christopher W. "Sin in the Biblical Story." In *Fallen: A Theology of Sin*, edited by Christopher W. Morgan and Robert A. Peterson, 131–62. Theology in Community. Wheaton, IL: Crossway, 2013.

Moroney, Stephen K. *The Noetic Effects of Sin: A Historical and Contemporary Exploration of How Sin Affects Our Thinking*. Lanham, MD: Lexington, 2000.

Morris, Thomas V. "The Hidden God." *Philosophical Topics* 16 (1988) 5–21.

———. *Making Sense of It All: Pascal and the Meaning of Life*. Grand Rapids: Eerdmans, 1992.

Morris, W. A. *Writings of Alexander Campbell: Selections Chiefly from the Millennial Harbinger*. Austin: Boeckmann, 1896.

Moser, Paul K. "Christianity and Miracles." In *Debating Christian Theism*, edited by J. P. Moreland et al., 287–97. Oxford: Oxford University Press, 2013.

———. "Cognitive Idolatry and Divine Hiding." In *Divine Hiddenness: New Essays*, edited by Daniel Howard-Snyder and Paul K. Moser, 120–48. Cambridge: Cambridge University Press, 2002.

———. "Confirmation Model." In *Four Views on Christianity and Philosophy*, edited by Stanley N. Gundry et al., 175–200. Counterpoints. Grand Rapids: Zondervan, 2016.

———. "Divine Hiddenness and Self-Sacrifice." In *Hidden Divinity and Religious Belief: New Perspectives*, edited by Adam Green and Eleonore Stump, 71–88. Cambridge: Cambridge University Press, 2016.

———. "Divine Hiddenness Does Not Justify Atheism." In *Contemporary Debates in Philosophy of Religion*, edited by Michael L. Peterson and Raymond J. VanArragon, 42–54. Contemporary Debates in Philosophy. Hoboken, NJ: Blackwell, 2004.

———. "Divine Hiding." *Philosophia Christi* 3 (2001) 91–107.

———. *The Elusive God: Reorienting Religious Epistemology*. New York: Cambridge University Press, 2008.

———. *The Evidence for God: Religious Knowledge Reexamined*. Cambridge: Cambridge University Press, 2010.

———. "Gethsemane Epistemology: Volitional and Evidential." *Philosophia Christi* 14 (2012) 263–74.

———. "A God Who Hides and Seeks: A Response to Davis and Deweese." *Philosophia Christi* 3 (2001) 119–25.

———. "The Inner Witness of the Spirit." In *The Oxford Handbook of the Epistemology of Theology*, edited by William J. Abraham and Frederick D. Aquino, 111–25. Oxford Handbooks. Oxford: Oxford University Press, 2017.

———. "Man to Man with Warranted Christian Belief and Alvin Plantinga." *Philosophia Christi* 3 (2001) 369–77.

———. "Natural Theology and the Evidence for God: Reply to Harold Netland, Charles Taliaferro, and Kate Waidler." *Philosophia Christi* 14 (2012) 305–11.

———. "Religious Epistemology Personified: God without Natural Theology." In *The Blackwell Companion to Science and Christianity*, edited by J. B. Stump and Alan G. Padgett, 151–61. Malden, MA: Wiley-Blackwell, 2012.

———. "Reorienting Religious Epistemology: Cognitive Grace, Filial Knowledge, and Gethsemane Struggle." In *For Faith and Clarity: Philosophical Contributions to Christian Theology*, edited by James K. Beilby, 65–81. Grand Rapids: Baker Academic, 2006.

———. "Reply to Schellenberg." In *Contemporary Debates in Philosophy of Religion*, edited by Michael L. Peterson and Raymond J. VanArragon, 56–58. Contemporary Debates in Philosophy. Hoboken, NJ: Blackwell, 2004.

———. *The Severity of God: Religion and Philosophy Reconceived*. Cambridge: Cambridge University Press, 2013.

———. *Why Isn't God More Obvious?* Atlanta: RZIM, 2000.

Muller, Richard A. *Calvin and the Reformed Tradition: On the Work of Christ and the Order of Salvation*. Grand Rapids: Baker Academic, 2012.

———. *Dictionary of Latin and Greek Theological Terms: Drawn Principally from Protestant Scholastic Theology*. 2nd ed. Grand Rapids: Baker Academic, 2017.

———. *Post-Reformation Reformed Dogmatics: The Rise and Development of Reformed Orthodoxy, ca. 1520 to ca. 1725*. 4 vols. Grand Rapids: Baker Academics, 2003.

———. *The Unaccommodated Calvin: Studies in the Foundation of a Theological Tradition*. Oxford Studies in Historical Theology. New York: Oxford University, 2000.

Murray, Michael J. "Coercion and the Hiddenness of God." *American Philosophical Quarterly* 30 (1993) 27–38.

———. "*Deus Absconditus*." In *Divine Hiddenness: New Essays*, edited by Daniel Howard-Snyder and Paul K. Moser, 62–82. Cambridge: Cambridge University Press, 2002.

———. "Heaven and Hell." In *Reason for the Hope Within*, edited by Michael J. Murray, 287–317. Grand Rapids: Eerdmans, 1999.

———. "Why Doesn't God Make His Existence More Obvious to Us?" In *Passionate Conviction: Contemporary Discourses on Christian Apologetics*, edited by Paul Copan and William Lane Craig, 38–50. Nashville: B&H Academic, 2007.

Murray, Michael J., and Michael C. Rea. "Anti-Theistic Arguments." In *An Introduction to the Philosophy of Religion*, 157–90. Cambridge Introductions to Philosophy. Cambridge: Cambridge University Press, 2008.

———. *An Introduction to the Philosophy of Religion*. Cambridge Introductions to Philosophy. Cambridge: Cambridge University Press, 2008.

Nagasawa, Yujin. "Silence, Evil, and Shusaku Endo." In *Hidden Divinity and Religious Belief: New Perspectives*, edited by Adam Green and Eleonore Stump, 246–59. Cambridge: Cambridge University Press, 2016.

Nagel, Thomas. *The Last Word*. New York: Oxford University Press, 1997.

Newton, John. "Amazing Grace." *Hymnary*, 1779. https://hymnary.org/text/amazing_grace_how_sweet_the_sound.

Nietzsche, Friedrich W. *The Antichrist*. Translated by Anthony M. Ludovici. Great Books in Philosophy. Amherst, NY: Prometheus, 2000.

———. *Daybreak: Thoughts on the Prejudices of Morality*. Translated by R. J. Hollingdale. Cambridge Texts in the History of Philosophy. New York: Cambridge University Press, 1982.

———. *The Gay Science*. Translated by Walter Kaufmann. New York: Vintage, 1974.

Noll, Mark A. "Foreword." In *Evangelicalism & the Stone-Campbell Movement*, edited by William R. Baker, 9–15. Downers Grove, IL: IVP Academic, 2002.

Norton, David F. "Hume, David." In *The Cambridge Dictionary of Philosophy*, edited by Robert Audi, 398–403. 2nd ed. Cambridge: Cambridge University Press, 1999.

Oberman, Heiko A. *Luther: Man between God and the Devil*. New Haven: Yale University Press, 1989.

O'Connell, Jake H. "Divine Hiddenness: Would More Miracles Solve the Problem?" *HeyJ* 54 (2013) 261–67.

O'Connor, David. *Hume on Religion*. Routledge Philosophy Guidebooks. London: Routledge, 2001.

Oden, Thomas C. *Classic Christianity: A Systematic Theology*. New York: HarperOne, 2009.

———. "Without Excuse: Classic Christian Exegesis of General Revelation." *JETS* 41 (1998) 55–68.

O'Leary-Hawthorn, John. "Arguments for Atheism." In *Reason for the Hope Within*, edited by Michael J. Murray, 116–34. Grand Rapids: Eerdmans, 1999.

Oliphint, K. Scott. "Jonathan Edwards on Apologetics: Reason and the Noetic Effects of Sin." In *The Legacy of Jonathan Edwards: American Religion and the Evangelical Tradition*, edited by D. G. Hart et al., 131–46. Wheaton, IL: Crossway, 2003.

———. "Plantinga on Warrant." *WTJ* 57 (1995) 415–35.

———. *Reasons for Faith: Philosophy in the Service of Theology*. Phillipsburg, NJ: P&R, 2006.

———. "Review Essay: Epistemology and Christian Belief." *WTJ* 63 (2001) 151–82.

Pascal, Blaise. *Christianity for Modern Pagans: Pascal's "Pensées" Edited, Outlined and Explained*. Edited by Peter Kreeft. San Francisco: Ignatius, 1993.

———. *Pensées*. Translated by A. J. Krailsheimer. Penguin Classics. Harmondsworth, UK: Penguin, 1966.

———. "*Pensées*" *and Other Writings*. Edited and translated by Honor Levi. Oxford World's Classics. Oxford: Oxford University Press, 2008.
Peels, Rik. "Can Atheism Be Properly Basic?" *Prosblogion*, March 21, 2015. http://prosblogion.ektopos.com/2015/03/21/can-atheism-be-properly-basic. Website discontinued.
———. "Divine Foreknowledge and Eternal Damnation: The Theory of Middle Knowledge as Solution to the Soteriological Problem of Evil." *ZST* 48 (2006) 168–83.
———. "Review of *Theology's Epistemological Dilemma: How Karl Barth and Alvin Plantinga Provide a Unified Response*, by Kevin Diller." *Journal of Analytic Theology* 4 (2016) 421–27.
———. "Sin and Human Cognition of God." *SJT* 64 (2011) 390–409.
Penelhum, Terence. *Butler*. Arguments of the Philosophers. London: Routledge & Kegan Paul, 1985.
———. "Butler and Human Ignorance." In *Joseph Butler's Moral and Religious Thought: Tercentenary Essays*, edited by Christopher Cunliffe, 117–40. Oxford: Clarendon, 1992.
———. *David Hume: An Introduction to His Philosophical System*. Purdue University Series in the History of Philosophy. West Lafayette, IN: Purdue University Press, 1992.
———. "Hume and Religion: Keith Yandell's Assessments." In *Philosophy and the Christian Worldview: Analysis, Assessment and Developments*, edited by David Werther and Mark D. Linville, 139–43. Bloomsbury Studies in Philosophy of Religion. New York: Continuum, 2012.
———. "Hume's Criticisms of Natural Theology." In *In Defense of Natural Theology: A Post-Humean Assessment*, edited by James F. Sennett and Douglas Groothuis, 21–41. Downers Grove, IL: IVP Academic, 2005.
———. *Themes in Hume: The Self, the Will, Religion*. Oxford: Clarendon, 2000.
Peters, James R. *The Logic of the Heart: Augustine, Pascal, and the Rationality of Faith*. Grand Rapids: Baker Academic, 2009.
Peterson, Michael L. *Philosophy of Religion: Selected Readings*. 3rd ed. New York: Oxford University Press, 1996.
Pettit, Peter A. "Christ Alone, the Hidden God, and Lutheran Exclusivism." *WW* 11 (1991) 190–98.
Philipse, Herman. *God in the Age of Science? A Critique of Religious Reason*. Oxford: Oxford University Press, 2012.
Plantinga, Alvin. "Ad Plasger." In *Plantinga's "Warranted Christian Belief": Critical Essays with a Reply by Alvin Plantinga*, edited by Dieter Schönecker, 254–57. Berlin: De Gruyter, 2015.
———. "Ad Schärtl." In *Plantinga's "Warranted Christian Belief": Critical Essays with a Reply by Alvin Plantinga*, edited by Dieter Schönecker, 249–52. Berlin: De Gruyter, 2015.
———. "Ad Schönecker." In *Plantinga's "Warranted Christian Belief": Critical Essays with a Reply by Alvin Plantinga*, edited by Dieter Schönecker, 236–40. Berlin: De Gruyter, 2015.
———. "Ad Wiertz." In *Plantinga's "Warranted Christian Belief": Critical Essays with a Reply by Alvin Plantinga*, edited by Dieter Schönecker, 245–49. Berlin: De Gruyter, 2015.

———. "Advice to Christian Philosophers." *Faith and Philosophy* 1 (1984) 253–71.
———. "Alvin Plantinga." *Closer to Truth*, n.d. https://closertotruth.com/video/plaal-002.
———. "A Christian Life Partly Lived." In *Philosophers Who Believe: The Spiritual Journeys of 11 Leading Thinkers*, edited by Kelly James Clark, 45–82. Downers Grove, IL: Intervarsity, 1994.
———. "A Defense of Religious Exclusivism." In *The Rationality of Belief and the Plurality of Faith: Essays in Honor of William P. Alston*, edited by Thomas D. Señor, 191–215. Ithaca, NY: Cornell University Press, 1995.
———. *God and Other Minds: A Study of the Rational Justification of Belief in God*. Contemporary Philosophy. Ithaca, NY: Cornell University Press, 1967.
———. *God, Freedom, and Evil*. Grand Rapids: Eerdmans, 1977.
———. "Internalism, Externalism, Defeaters and Arguments for Christian Belief." *Philosophia Christi* 3 (2001) 379–400.
———. "Introduction: The Evolutionary Argument against Naturalism." In *Naturalism Defeated? Essays on Plantinga's Evolutionary Argument against Naturalism*, edited by James Beilby, 1–14. Ithaca, NY: Cornell University Press, 2002.
———. "Is Belief in God Properly Basic?" In *Contemporary Perspectives on Religious Epistemology*, edited by R. Douglas Geivett and Brendan Sweetman, 133–41. New York: Oxford University Press, 1992.
———. "Is Belief in God Rational?" In *Rationality and Religious Belief*, edited by C. F. Delaney, 7–27. University of Notre Dame Studies in the Philosophy of Religion 1. Notre Dame, IN: University of Notre Dame Press, 1979.
———. "Is Belief in God Rationally Acceptable?" In *Philosophy of Religion: A Reader and Guide*, edited by William Lane Craig, 40–56. New Brunswick: Rutgers University Press, 2002.
———. "On Reformed Epistemology." *Reformed Journal* 32 (1982) 13–17.
———. "Reason and Belief in God." In *Faith and Rationality: Reason and Belief in God*, edited by Alvin Plantinga and Nicholas Wolterstorff, 16–93. Notre Dame, IN: University of Notre Dame Press, 1983.
———. "Reformed Epistemology." In *A Companion to Philosophy of Religion*, edited by Charles Taliaferro et al., 383–89. Blackwell Companions to Philosophy 9. Malden, MA: Wiley-Blackwell, 1997.
———. "Reformed Epistemology." In *A Companion to Philosophy of Religion*, edited by Charles Taliaferro et al., 674–80. 2nd ed. Blackwell Companions to Philosophy 9. Malden, MA: Wiley-Blackwell, 2010.
———. "Reply." *Analytic Philosophy* 43 (2002) 124–35.
———. "Respondeo." In *Warrant in Contemporary Epistemology: Essays in Honor of Plantinga's Theory of Knowledge*, edited by Jonathan L. Kvanvig, 307–78. Studies in Epistemology and Cognitive Theory. Lanham, MD: Rowman & Littlefield, 1996.
———. "Self-Profile." In *Alvin Plantinga*, edited by James E. Tomberlin and Peter Van Inwagen, 3–97. Profiles 5. Dordrecht: Reidel, 1985.
———. "Supralapsarianism, or 'O Felix Culpa.'" In *Christian Faith and the Problem of Evil*, edited by Peter van Inwagen, 1–25. Grand Rapids: Eerdmans, 2004.
———. "Two Dozen (or so) Theistic Arguments." In *Alvin Plantinga*, edited by Deane-Peter Baker, 203–27. Contemporary Philosophy in Focus. Cambridge: Cambridge University Press, 2007.
———. *Warrant and Proper Function*. Gifford Lectures. New York: Oxford University Press, 1993.

———. *Warrant: The Current Debate*. Gifford Lectures. New York: Oxford University Press, 1993.

———. *Where the Conflict Really Lies: Science, Religion, and Naturalism*. New York: Oxford University Press, 2011.

Plantinga, Alvin, and Michael Tooley. *Knowledge of God*. Great Debates in Philosophy. Malden, MA: Blackwell, 2008.

Plantinga, Alvin, and Nicholas Wolterstorff, eds. *Faith and Rationality: Reason and Belief in God*. Notre Dame, IN: University of Notre Dame Press, 1983.

Plantinga, Richard J., et al. *An Introduction to Christian Theology*. 2nd ed. Introduction to Religion. Cambridge: Cambridge University Press, 2023.

Plasger, Georg. "Does Calvin Teach a *Sensus Divinitatis*? Reflections on Alvin Plantinga's Interpretation of Calvin." In *Plantinga's "Warranted Christian Belief": Critical Essays with a Reply by Alvin Plantinga*, edited by Dieter Schönecker, 169–89. Berlin: De Gruyter, 2015.

Poston, Ted, and Trent Dougherty. "Divine Hiddenness and the Nature of Belief." *RelS* 43 (2007) 183–98.

Provenzola, Thomas A. "Epistemic Eucatastrophe: The Favorable Turn of the Evidence." In *Building on the Foundations of Evangelical Theology: Essays in Honor of John S. Feinberg*, edited by Gregg R. Allison and Stephen J. Wellum, 91–112. Wheaton, IL: Crossway, 2015.

Quash, Ben. "Revelation." In *The Oxford Handbook of Systematic Theology*, edited by John B. Webster et al., 325–44. Oxford Handbooks. Oxford: Oxford University Press, 2007.

Quinn, Philip L., and Charles Taliaferro, eds. *A Companion to Philosophy of Religion*. Blackwell Companions to Philosophy. Malden, MA: Blackwell, 1997.

Ratzsch, Delvin L. "Humanness in Their Hearts: Where Science and Religion Fuse." In *The Believing Primate: Scientific, Philosophical, and Theological Reflections on the Origin of Religion*, edited by Jeffrey Schloss and Michael J. Murray, 215–45. Oxford: Oxford University Press, 2010.

Rauser, Randal. *Is the Atheist My Neighbor? Rethinking Christian Attitudes toward Atheism*. Eugene, OR: Cascade, 2015.

Rea, Michael C. "Divine Hiddenness, Divine Silence." In *Philosophy of Religion: An Anthology*, edited by Louis P. Pojman and Michael C. Rea, 266–75. 6th ed. Boston: Cengage, 2012.

———. *Evil and the Hiddenness of God*. Stamford, CT: Cengage, 2015.

———. "Hiddenness and Transcendence." In *Hidden Divinity and Religious Belief: New Perspectives*, edited by Adam Green and Eleonore Stump, 210–25. Cambridge: Cambridge University Press, 2016.

———. *The Hiddenness of God*. Oxford: University Press, 2018.

———. "Narrative, Liturgy, and the Hiddenness of God." In *Metaphysics and God: Essays in Honor of Eleonore Stump*, edited by Kevin Timpe, 76–96. Routledge Studies in the Philosophy of Religion. New York: Routledge, 2009.

Reich, Lou. *Hume's Religious Naturalism*. Lanham, MD: University Press of America, 1998.

Renusch, Anita. "Thank God It's the Right Religion!—Plantinga on Religious Diversity." In *Plantinga's "Warranted Christian Belief": Critical Essays with a Reply by Alvin Plantinga*, edited by Dieter Schönecker, 147–68. Berlin: De Gruyter, 2015.

Rowe, Chip. "Richard Dawkins." *Playboy*, August 20, 2012. http://www.playboy.com/articles/playboy-interview-richard-dawkins.
Rowe, William. "The Evidential Argument from Evil: A Second Look." In *The Evidential Argument from Evil*, edited by Daniel Howard-Snyder, 262–85. Indiana Series in the Philosophy of Religion. Bloomington: Indiana University Press, 1996.
Sawyer, M. James. "The Witness of the Spirit in the Protestant Tradition." In *Who's Afraid of the Holy Spirit? An Investigation into the Ministry of the Spirit of God Today*, edited by Daniel B. Wallace and M. James Sawyer, 71–94. Dallas: Biblical Studies, 2005.
Schärtl, Thomas. "Moderating Certainty." In *Plantinga's "Warranted Christian Belief": Critical Essays with a Reply by Alvin Plantinga*, edited by Dieter Schönecker, 115–46. Berlin: De Gruyter, 2015.
Schellenberg, J. L. "'Breaking Down the Walls That Divide': Virtue and Warrant, Belief and Nonbelief." *Faith and Philosophy* 21 (2004) 195–213.
———. "Divine Hiddenness." In *A Companion to Philosophy of Religion*, edited by Charles Taliaferro et al., 509–18. 2nd ed. Blackwell Companions to Philosophy 9. Malden, MA: Wiley-Blackwell, 2010.
———. "Divine Hiddenness and Human Philosophy." In *Hidden Divinity and Religious Belief: New Perspectives*, edited by Adam Green and Eleonore Stump, 13–32. Cambridge: Cambridge University Press, 2016.
———. "Divine Hiddenness Justifies Atheism." In *Contemporary Debates in Philosophy of Religion*, edited by Michael L. Peterson and Raymond J. VanArragon, 30–41. Contemporary Debates in Philosophy. Hoboken, NJ: Wiley Blackwell, 2004.
———. "Divine Hiddenness: Part 1 (Recent Work on the Hiddenness Argument)." *Philosophy Compass* 12 (2017) e1–9.
———. *Evolutionary Religion*. Oxford: Oxford University Press, 2013.
———. *The Hiddenness Argument: Philosophy's New Challenge to Belief in God*. Oxford: Oxford University Press, 2017.
———. "The Hiddenness Argument Revisited (I)." *RelS* 41 (2005) 201–15.
———. "The Hiddenness Argument Revisited (II)." *RelS* 41 (2005) 287–303.
———. "The Hiddenness Problem and the Problem of Evil." *Faith and Philosophy* 27 (2010) 45–60.
———. "Is Plantinga-Style Christian Philosophy Really Philosophy?" *J. L. Schellenberg*, n.d. http://www.jlschellenberg.com/uploads/8/5/6/1/8561683/is_plantinga-style_christian_philosophy_really_philosophy.pdf.
———. "My Stance in Philosophy of Religion." *RelS* 49 (2013) 143–50.
———. "On Not Unnecessarily Darkening the Glass: A Reply to Poston and Dougherty." *RelS* 43 (2007) 199–204.
———. "On Reasonable Nonbelief and Perfect Love: Replies to Henry and Lehe." *Faith and Philosophy* 22 (2005) 331–42.
———. *Prolegomena to a Philosophy of Religion*. Ithaca, NY: Cornell University Press, 2005.
———. "Replies to My Colleagues." *RelS* 49 (2013) 257–85.
———. "Reply to Aijaz and Weidler on Hiddenness." *International Journal for Philosophy of Religion* 64 (2008) 135–40.
———. "Reply to Moser." *Contemporary Debates in Philosophy of Religion*, edited by Michael L. Peterson and Raymond J. VanArragon, 54–56. Contemporary Debates in Philosophy. Hoboken, NJ: Wiley Blackwell, 2004.

———. "Response to Howard-Snyder." *Canadian Journal of Philosophy* 26 (1996) 455–62.
———. "Response to Tucker on Hiddenness." *RelS* 44 (2008) 289–93.
———. "What the Hiddenness of God Reveals: A Collaborative Discussion." In *Divine Hiddenness: New Essays*, edited by Daniel Howard-Snyder and Paul K. Moser, 33–61. Cambridge: Cambridge University Press, 2002.
———. "Why Am I a Nonbeliever?—I Wonder . . ." In *50 Voices of Disbelief: Why We Are Atheists*, edited by Russell Blackford and Udo Schüklenk, 28–32. Malden, MA: Wiley-Blackwell, 2009.
———. *The Will to Imagine: A Justification of Skeptical Religion*. Ithaca, NY: Cornell University Press, 2009.
———. *The Wisdom to Doubt: A Justification of Religious Skepticism*. Ithaca, NY: Cornell University Press, 2007.
Schloss, Jeffrey, and Michael J. Murray, eds. *The Believing Primate: Scientific, Philosophical, and Theological Reflections on the Origin of Religion*. Oxford: Oxford University Press, 2010.
Schönecker, Dieter. "The Deliverances of Warranted Christian Belief." In *Plantinga's "Warranted Christian Belief": Critical Essays with a Reply by Alvin Plantinga*, edited by Dieter Schönecker, 1–40. Berlin: De Gruyter, 2015.
———, ed. *Plantinga's "Warranted Christian Belief": Critical Essays with a Reply by Alvin Plantinga*. Berlin: De Gruyter, 2015.
Selderhuis, Herman J. *Calvin's Theology of the Psalms*. Texts and Studies in Reformation and Post-Reformation Thought. Grand Rapids: Baker Academic, 2007.
Sessions, William L. *Reading Hume's Dialogues: A Veneration for True Religion*. Indiana Series in the Philosophy of Religion. Bloomington: Indiana University Press, 2002.
Shalkowski, Scott A. "Atheological Apologetics: Contemporary Perspectives on Religious Epistemology." In *Contemporary Perspectives on Religious Epistemology*, edited by R. Douglas Geivett and Brendan Sweetman, 58–73. New York: Oxford University Press, 1992.
Sosa, Ernest. "Proper Functionalism and Virtue Epistemology." *Noûs* 27 (1993) 51–65.
———. "Proper Functionalism and Virtue Epistemology." In *Warrant in Contemporary Epistemology: Essays in Honor of Plantinga's Theory of Knowledge*, edited by Jonathan L. Kvanvig, 253–70. Studies in Epistemology and Cognitive Theory. Lanham, MD: Rowman & Littlefield, 1996.
Spiegel, James S. "Immaterialism as a Boon to Faith: Berkeley and Christian Theology." In *Christian Theology and the Modern Philosophers*, edited by Greg Ganssle and Ben Arbour. Grand Rapids: Zondervan, forthcoming.
———. "The Theological Orthodoxy of Berkeley's Immaterialism." *Faith and Philosophy* 13 (1996) 216–35.
Stanglin, Keith D., and Thomas H. McCall. *Jacob Arminius: Theologian of Grace*. New York: Oxford University Press, 2013.
Stump, Eleonore. *Wandering in Darkness: Narrative and the Problem of Suffering*. Oxford: Clarendon, 2010.
Sudduth, Michael C. "Plantinga's Revision of the Reformed Tradition: Rethinking Our Natural Knowledge of God." *Philosophical Books* 43 (2002) 81–91.
———. "Reformed Epistemology and Christian Apologetics." *RelS* 39 (2003) 299–321.
———. *The Reformed Objection to Natural Theology*. Ashgate Philosophy of Religion Series. Farnham, UK: Ashgate, 2009.
Swinburne, Richard. *The Existence of God*. 2nd ed. Oxford: Clarendon, 2004.

———. "Plantinga on Warrant." *RelS* 37 (2001) 203–14.
———. *Providence and the Problem of Evil*. Oxford: Clarendon, 1998.
———. *Revelation: From Metaphor to Analogy*. 2nd ed. Oxford: Oxford University Press, 2007.
Taber, Tyler M. "Divine Hiddenness and the Problem of Evil." In *Evil and a Selection of Its Theological Problems*, edited by Benjamin H. Arbour and John R. Gilhooly, 14–30. Newcastle upon Tyne, UK: Cambridge Scholars, 2017.
———. "Review of *Hidden Divinity and Religious Belief: New Perspectives*, edited by Adam Green and Eleonore Stump." *European Journal for Philosophy of Religion* 9 (2017) 240–43.
———. "Review of *Plantinga's 'Warranted Christian Belief': Critical Essays with a Reply by Alvin Plantinga*, edited by Dieter Schönecker." *Journal of Reformed Theology* 10 (2016) 268–69.
Taber, Tyler M., and Sten-Erik Armitage. "Review of *Fallen: A Theology of Sin*, edited by Christopher W. Morgan and Robert A. Peterson." *BSac* (forthcoming).
Taber, Tyler M., and Tyler D. McNabb. "Is the Problem of Divine Hiddenness a Problem for the Reformed Epistemologist?" *HeyJ* 59 (2018) 783–93.
Talbot, Mark R. "Is It Natural to Believe in God?" *Faith and Philosophy* 6 (1989) 155–71.
Taliaferro, Charles. "Incorporeality." In *A Companion to Philosophy of Religion*, edited by Philip L. Quinn and Charles Taliaferro, 271–78. Blackwell Companions to Philosophy. Malden, MA: Wiley-Blackwell, 1997.
Tapp, Christian. "Reference to an Infinite Being." In *Plantinga's "Warranted Christian Belief": Critical Essays with a Reply by Alvin Plantinga*, edited by Dieter Schönecker, 41–64. Berlin: De Gruyter, 2015.
Taylor, David E., and Michael J. Murray. "Hiddenness." In *The Routledge Companion to Philosophy of Religion*, edited by Chad V. Meister and Paul Copan, 368–77. Routledge Philosophy Companions. London: Routledge, 2007.
Terrien, Samuel L. *The Elusive Presence: Toward a New Biblical Theology*. Religious Perspectives 26. San Francisco: Harper & Row, 1978.
Thompson, Mark D. *A Clear and Present Word: The Clarity of Scripture*. Edited by D. A. Carson. New Studies in Biblical Theology 21. Downers Grove, IL: IVP Academic, 2006.
Thune, Michael. "A Molinist-Style Response to Schellenberg." *Southwest Philosophy Review* 22 (2006) 33–41.
Tierno, Joel T. "On Defense as Opposed to Theodicy." *International Journal for Philosophy of Religion* 59 (2006) 167–74.
Tooley, Michael. "The Problem of Evil." *Stanford Encyclopedia of Philosophy*, Winter 2021. Edited by Edward N. Zalta. https://plato.stanford.edu/archives/win2021/entries/evil.
Trakakis, Nick. "An Epistemically Distant God? A Critique of John Hick's Response to the Problem of Divine Hiddenness." *HeyJ* 48 (2007) 214–26.
Trakakis, N. N. "The Hidden Divinity and What It Reveals." In *Hidden Divinity and Religious Belief: New Perspectives*, edited by Adam Green and Eleonore Stump, 192–209. Cambridge: Cambridge University Press, 2016.
Trickett, Gregory E., and Tyler M. Taber. "Divine Hiddenness, the Soteriological Problem of Evil, and Berkeleyan Idealism." In *Being Saved: Explorations in Human Salvation*, edited by Marc Cortez et al., 24–39. London: SCM, 2018.

Tucker, Chris. "Divine Hiddenness and the Value of Divine-Creature Relationships." *RelS* 44 (2008) 269–87.
Van den Brink, Gijsbert. "A Most Elegant Book: The Natural World in Article 2 of the Belgic Confession." *WTJ* 73 (2011) 273–91.
———. "What Is Wrong with Revelation? Herman Philipse on the Priority of Natural Theology." *Philo* 16 (2013) 24–41.
Van den Brink, Gijsbert, and Johan Smits. "The Reformed Stance: Distinctive Commitments and Concerns." *Journal of Reformed Theology* 9 (2015) 325–47.
Van der Kooi, Cornelis. "The Appeal to the Inner Testimony of the Spirit, Especially in H. Bavinck." *Journal of Reformed Theology* 2 (2008) 103–12.
Van Dixhoorn, Chad, ed. *Creeds, Confessions & Catechisms: A Reader's Guide*. Wheaton, IL: Crossway, 2022.
Van Eyghen, Hans. "There Is No *Sensus Divinitatis*." *Journal for the Study of Religion & Ideologies* 15 (2016) 24–40.
Van Inwagen, Peter. *The Problem of Evil*. Gifford Lectures. Oxford: Clarendon, 2006.
———. "The Problem of Evil, the Problem of Air, and the Problem of Silence." In *The Evidential Argument from Evil*, edited by Daniel Howard-Snyder, 151–74. Indiana Series in the Philosophy of Religion. Bloomington: Indiana University Press, 1996.
———. "What Is the Problem of the Hiddenness of God?" In *Divine Hiddenness: New Essays*, edited by Daniel Howard-Snyder and Paul K. Moser, 24–32. Cambridge: Cambridge University Press, 2002.
Van Kralingen, Kees. "Theological Responses to Alvin Plantinga's Aquinas/Calvin Model of Warranted Christian Belief: Its Relation to the Truth Question." Unpublished paper, presented at Free University of Amsterdam, June 2017.
Wainwright, William J. "Jonathan Edwards and the Hiddenness of God." In *Divine Hiddenness: New Essays*, edited by Daniel Howard-Snyder and Paul K. Moser, 98–119. Cambridge: Cambridge University Press, 2002.
———. *Reason and the Heart: A Prolegomenon to a Critique of Passional Reason*. Cornell Studies in the Philosophy of Religion. Ithaca, NY: Cornell University Press, 1995.
———. "Theistic Proofs, Person Relativity, and the Rationality of Religious Belief." In *Evidence and Religious Belief*, edited by Kelly James Clark and Raymond J. VanArragon, 77–94. Oxford: Oxford University Press, 2011.
———. "Theology and Mystery." In *The Oxford Handbook of Philosophical Theology*, edited by Thomas P. Flint and Michael C. Rea, 78–102. Oxford Handbooks. Oxford: Oxford University Press, 2009.
Walls, Jerry L., and Trent Dougherty, eds. *Two Dozen (or so) Arguments for God: The Plantinga Project*. New York: Oxford University Press, 2018.
Waltke, Bruce K., et al. *The Psalms as Christian Worship: A Historical Commentary*. Grand Rapids: Eerdmans, 2010.
Westphal, Merold. "Taking St. Paul Seriously: Sin as an Epistemological Category." In *Christian Philosophy*, edited by Thomas P. Flint, 200–226. Notre Dame Studies in the Philosophy of Religion 6. Notre Dame, IN: University of Notre Dame Press, 1990.
Wiebe, Mark. "Letters to a Skeptic: Alexander Campbell on Rationality, Religious Belief, and Evil." *Stone-Campbell Journal* 15 (2012) 15–33.
Wiertz, Oliver J. "Is Plantinga's A/C Model an Example of Ideologically Tainted Philosophy?" In *Plantinga's "Warranted Christian Belief": Critical Essays with a*

Reply by Alvin Plantinga, edited by Dieter Schönecker, 83–114. Berlin: De Gruyter, 2015.

Willard, Dallas. "The Bible, the University, and the God Who Hides." In *The Bible and the University*, edited by David Lyle Jeffrey and C. Stephen Evans, 17–39. Scripture and Hermeneutics Series 8. Grand Rapids: Zondervan, 2007.

Williams, Stephen N. *The Shadow of the Antichrist: Nietzsche's Critique of Christianity*. Grand Rapids: Baker Academic, 2006.

Wingard, John C., Jr. "Sin and Skepticism about the Trustworthiness of Our Cognitive Endowment." *Philosophia Christi* 6 (2004) 249–62.

Wolterstorff, Nicholas. "Herman Bavinck—Proto Reformed Epistemologist." *CTJ* 45 (2010) 133–46.

———. "Is Reason Enough?" In *Contemporary Perspectives on Religious Epistemology*, edited by R. Douglas Geivett and Brendan Sweetman, 142–49. New York: Oxford University Press, 1992.

———. "Reformed Tradition." In *A Companion to Philosophy of Religion*, edited by Charles Taliaferro et al., 204–9. 2nd ed. Blackwell Companions to Philosophy 9. Malden, MA: Wiley-Blackwell, 2010.

———. "The Silence of the God Who Speaks." In *Divine Hiddenness: New Essays*, edited by Daniel Howard-Snyder and Paul K. Moser, 215–28. Cambridge: Cambridge University Press, 2002.

Wood, William. *Blaise Pascal on Duplicity, Sin, and the Fall: The Secret Instinct*. Changing Paradigms in Historical and Systematic Theology. Oxford: Oxford University Press, 2013.

———. "Philosophical Theology in the Religious Studies Academy: Some Questions for Analytic Theologians." *JAAR* 81 (2013) 592–600.

Yoder, Timothy S. *Hume on God: Irony, Deism and Genuine Theism*. Continuum Studies in British Philosophy. London: Bloomsbury, 2008.

www.ingramcontent.com/pod-product-compliance
Lightning Source LLC
Chambersburg PA
CBHW022028240426
43667CB00042B/1362